CHARLIE LORAM first travelled to India in 1992 having graduated in geography from Newcastle University. Fascinated by the Himalaya and the self-reliant, compassionate people whose home it is, he returns almost every year. In addition to many months in Ladakh researching and updating this guide he has spent time studying the culture and environment of neighbouring Lahaul where he worked closely with local environmental organisations as co-ordinator of a research expedition. Charlie leads treks throughout the Himalaya and has also contributed to Trailblazer's *Trekking in the Annapurna Region*.

When not writing or travelling he teaches the Alexander Technique in Britain and escapes as often as he can to walk, climb and cycle in the island's wilder corners.

Trekking in Ladakh
First edition: 1996; this second edition 1999

Publisher
Trailblazer Publications
The Old Manse, Tower Rd, Hindhead, Surrey, GU26 6SU, UK
Fax (+44) 01428-607571
Email: info@trailblazer-guides.com
www.trailblazer-guides.com

British Library Cataloguing in Publication Data
A catalogue record for this book is available from the British Library

ISBN 1-873756-30-5

The quotation from *The Way of the White Clouds* by Lama Anagarika Govinda is
reproduced on p9 by permission of Rider. The quotation from *The Snow Leopard* by
Peter Matthiessen is reproduced on p44 by permission of The Harvill Press.
The quotation from *A Journey in Ladakh* by Andrew Harvey is reproduced on p118
by permission of Jonathan Cape Ltd and Aitken Stone & Wylie.
Quotations from *Getting Started in Ladakhi* by Rebecca Norman are reproduced by
permission of Melong Publications.
Many thanks to all the above for your help and kind permission.

Editor: Patricia Major
Associate editor and typesetter: Anna Jacomb-Hood
Layout: Bryn Thomas
Cartography and index: Jane Thomas

Every effort has been made by the author and publisher to ensure that the
information contained herein is as accurate and up to date as possible. However,
they are unable to accept responsibility for any inconvenience, loss or injury sus-
tained by anyone as a result of the advice and information given in this guide.

Front cover photograph: Phuktal Gompa (photo: © Charlie Loram)

Printed on chlorine-free paper from farmed forests by
Technographic Design & Print (☎ 01206-303323) Colchester, Essex, UK

TREKKING
IN
LADAKH
includes
LEH, MANALI & DELHI

CHARLIE LORAM

TRAILBLAZER PUBLICATIONS

For Tor

Acknowledgments

This book couldn't have been written without the help of many kind and generous people. First, I'd like to thank my wife Victoria – the best companion – who has contributed in so many ways; accompanying me into the mountains, writing the section on p78, supplying the photograph opposite p96, rearranging my rambling text into a more readable form and giving unwavering support from beginning to end.

I am greatly indebted to the people of Ladakh from whom I feel I will never stop learning. I'd also particularly like to thank several people who have provided detailed information which has made this guide all the more comprehensive through its two editions: Ben Stephenson (UK) for his knowledgeable advice on Zanskar and contributions to the text on p41 and p105; Elana Vollen (USA) and Holger Barra (Germany) for inspiring times together, much help in researching new trails and providing refreshing alternatives to life's problems, p50 and p77; Sunder N Namgail (Footprints Adventure, Fort Road, Leh) for never failing to get me to where I wanted to go, no matter how complicated the logistics and for continued expert advice on all matters trekking; David King and Emma James (UK) for putting me right on Stok Kangri; Marcel Schouten and Heleen Besselink (Netherlands) for details on cycling over the Himalaya, p101; Espen Skorstad (Norway) and Matthew Connor (Australia) for their notes on the route from Sumdah-Chenmo to Skiu; Tenzing Herman Van Den Bulck (Netherlands) for filling in information blanks to remote corners of Ladakh; Dot Fisher-Smith for feedback, corrections and introductions.

For patiently answering my questions and advising me on things Ladakhi I'd like to thank Stanzin Tonyot (ISEC), Sonam Wangchuk (SECMOL), T. Dorji (Lehling books), 'Soso' Sonam Dorje (Dzomsa), Helena Norberg-Hodge (ISEC), Mehboob Ali (Assistant Tourist Officer in Leh), Wangchok Shali (Explore Himalayas), Mohd Omar Nadvi (Imam, Jama Masjid in Leh), Tundup Namgyal (Tourist Officer in Padum). Thanks also to Narendra Kothiyal at the India Tourist Office, Delhi.

I am very grateful for the help I received in such varied capacities from so many, in particular Jan Stephenson (UK), Ann Wright (UK), Scot 'one T' Nichols (USA), Beth Robinson (USA), Eric Hollerbach (USA), Diana Glockner (Germany), Tim Hakin (UK), John and Jo Dunn (UK), Bruce Reid (UK), Mr Gyalson (Hotel Shaynam, Leh), Chris Beall (UK), Dave Stamboulis, David O'Brien (UK) and Carola Buhse (ISEC, UK).

Special thanks must go to all those at Trailblazer: Jane Thomas for drawing and updating the maps, Patricia Major and Anna Jacomb-Hood for editing the text and Bryn Thomas, without whom none of this would have happened.

A request

The author and publisher have tried to ensure that this guide is as accurate and up to date as possible. Nevertheless things change: prices rise, new hotels are built and trails are rerouted. If you notice any changes or omissions that should be included in the next edition of this book, please write to Charlie Loram at Trailblazer (address on p2). A free copy of the next edition will be sent to persons making a significant contribution.

Updated information will shortly be available on the Internet at
www.trailblazer-guides.com

SHRIVASTA, THE ENDLESS KNOT SYMBOL USED AT THE START OF EACH PART OF THIS BOOK, IS A BUDDHIST SIGN OF GOOD FORTUNE, REPRESENTING LONG LIFE AND INFINITE LOVE.

CONTENTS

INTRODUCTION

Sandwiched between the vast ranges of the Karakoram and the Himalaya in the far north of India, Ladakh is the highest, most remote and least populated region in the whole country. The name is derived from *Ladags* which means 'the land of high passes'. Its corrugated, arid landscape is often described as a mountain desert which does not do justice to the inherent beauty of its chaotic ridges, twisted and exposed geological strata, snow-shrouded peaks, dark gorges and wide valleys. The eye is relieved from this relentless desolation by the vibrant green oases of the villages, where the resourceful inhabitants make up for the almost non-existent rain by channelling glacial meltwater across miles of precipitous mountainside to irrigate their barley fields and willow groves. It is a land of climatic extremes: fiercely hot days are followed by freezing nights just as the brief summer is followed by a long ice-bound winter, which completely isolates much of the region from the rest of the world for seven to eight months every year.

Until recently, Western visitors to Ladakh were rare. Its inaccessibility and hostile landscape initially kept them away and then, just when Ladakh's communications were improving, the Indian government imposed a ban on foreign tourists because of Ladakh's strategic position near the borders with Pakistan and China. Since this ban was raised in the 1970s Ladakh has become a popular destination for aficionados of wild mountain scenery and those interested in a unique culture. As much of the region is accessible only on foot, trekking is the ideal way to explore this fascinating land.

At various times in the past, Ladakh has been politically part of western Tibet and this influence is still prominent today throughout most of the region. Indeed it is said that Ladakh is a more accurate representation of Tibet before the Chinese invasion than Tibet itself. The Ladakhi people are principally of Tibetan origin and Tibetan Buddhism is still practised here, as it has been for hundreds of years, alongside a significant population of Muslims. *Gompas*, or monasteries, overlook the valleys from their solitary positions on top of craggy hills and these religious institutions still play an active role in all Ladakhi life. Even deep in the mountains you are reminded that this is mainly a Buddhist culture as you walk past *mani* walls and *chortens* at the entrance of every village, or over high passes where tattered prayer flags flutter from the summit cairn.

Trekking in Ladakh is very different from hiking in the West as the trails are the lifeline between villages. It's not unusual to find yourself sharing the trail with a lama on his way to a remote gompa, or a shepherd making his way up to a high pasture and it is this close interaction with the local people that makes it such an enriching experience. However, unlike the busy tea-house trails in Nepal, where you can guarantee food and shelter every day, in Ladakh you need to be totally self-sufficient. Villages are often several days apart and these subsistence communities grow only enough food to feed themselves. The best way to carry your camping equipment and food is to trek with a local who will bring along one or two pack-horses and will be only too happy to act as your guide and companion. All the necessary arrangements can be made both cheaply and easily in Leh, the atmospheric capital of Ladakh.

A trek is a rejuvenating experience. Day by day, mile by mile, you become leaner and fitter, slowly peeling away the constraints of modern life. Time for once is on your side and you have the privileged opportunity to immerse yourself in 'the naked mountains and the blessed sunshine and the merry rosy people' (*The Himalayan Letters of Gypsy Davy and Lady Ba* by Robert and Katherine Barrett). The trekking industry is still young here and, at present, is free from rules and regulations. Each trekker must therefore accept his or her individual responsibility for ensuring that the magic of what the Barretts called these 'high quiet places' is never lost.

PART 1: PLANNING YOUR TREK

What is trekking?

Just as a white summer-cloud, in harmony with heaven and earth, freely floats in the blue sky from horizon to horizon, following the breath of the atmosphere – in the same way the pilgrim abandons himself to the breath of the greater life that wells up from the depth of his being and leads him beyond the farthest horizons to an aim which is already present within him, though yet hidden from his sight.
Lama Anagarika Govinda *The Way Of The White Clouds*

Trekking is the most natural way to travel through a mountain land – on foot and at human speed. As with all travel, it is at its best when it becomes a sort of pilgrimage, a challenging game played to enrich you physically, emotionally and occasionally spiritually. Of course, this kind of game can be played at home. Yet there are some places that lend a hand to the 'pilgrim'; places where it is easier to live simply and at a slower pace, where the landscape creates awe and demands respect, and where the way of life challenges your preconceptions and offers refreshing alternatives.

Travelling on foot with few luxuries but with all your basic needs is a liberating experience. This may be hard to appreciate on the first few days of a trek as you struggle with the physical pain of exercise, the discomfort of few possessions, and the mental torment of veering from intense happiness one moment to the depths of despair the next. Then suddenly you break through the barrier. Rising with the sun, walking all day and sleeping under the stars feels the most natural thing in the world. Your body thrives on its new-found energy while your mind, lulled by the rhythm of walking, is freed from its habits and rush. This is the intoxication of being truly alive.

Trekking offers wonderful opportunities for direct interaction with unique cultures and the natural world, while also providing precious moments to explore your own values and capabilities. If you walk through the Himalaya with an open mind, as well as awareness and sensitivity, you will have done everything to ensure a fascinating and rewarding trip. That fit, tanned figure may not last but the experiences gleaned from along the trail can change your whole life.

With a group or on your own?

Foreign travellers have been following Ladakh's mountain trails for centuries. For over a thousand years long rambling caravans of heavily-loaded pack animals accompanied the exotic traders from Central Asia, the Middle East and Tibet, as they made their way through the arid mountains before crossing over the Great Himalayan Range or the mighty Karakoram.

The first Westerner in this region was a Portuguese traveller, Diogo d'Almeida, who crossed the high passes in 1600. He was followed by a slow trickle of missionaries, merchants, explorers and adventurers ranging from an impoverished Transylvanian in the 1820s, Csoma de Koros, the self-styled pioneer of Tibetan studies, who wandered the remote trails dressed as a tramp, to the mildly eccentric Robert and Katherine Barrett, alias Gypsy Davy and Lady Ba, who trekked for a year in 1923-24 with a luxurious entourage of 'twenty or more ponies...eight menservants, a lot of coolies carrying loads from one village to the next, and always a village headman or two.' (*The Himalayan Letters of Gypsy Davy and Lady Ba*).

The trails fell quiet for a little over 25 years until 1974, when the previously imposed ban on foreign visitors was lifted. The popularity of trekking holidays has developed rapidly in the intervening decades but the basic approaches remain the same as those developed by the early pioneers. Today's trekker has several choices. You can experience the splendour of the mountains with the minimum of discomfort by joining a fully organised trek, complete with crew and a caravan of ponies; you can adopt a lightweight, sensitive and less costly approach (as advocated by the great explorer mountaineers, Eric Shipton and HW Tilman) by employing a local pony-man with a few pack animals; or you can trek completely independently, carrying everything you need on your back.

ORGANISING THE TREK YOURSELF

Backpacking

From the point of view of organising a trek, backpacking is simplest. This is the usual and preferred form of trekking in the West and one that is also common in Nepal, where the popular routes have a well-established system of inns, or tea houses in which you can sleep and eat. However, it doesn't adapt quite so easily to the mountains of Ladakh.

First, the villages in Ladakh are often far apart and it's rare to be able to find food or somewhere to sleep along the trail. On most treks, therefore, you need to be self-sufficient as regards food and shelter. Secondly, there's the problem of route finding. Trails are frequently hard to follow, and there are few locals from whom to ask the way. Thirdly, the mountains are larger than anything in the West. Not only will you be walking uphill for several days on end, but you'll be doing so at altitudes in excess of 3500m/11,480ft – hard enough without a 15+kg pack on your back.

There are, however, one or two shorter and lower level treks that can quite easily be backpacked but for the majority of routes this is an unnecessarily punishing way to walk. Despite this, there will be a few people for whom reading these sentences will only serve to whet their appetite for adventure. For those with a high level of fitness and experience, backpacking can be a very exciting way to explore the mountains. However, you should consider that for little extra cost and effort you could employ a pony-man who would enrich your experience even more and by giving him work you'd be helping the local economy.

Pack animals and pony-men

Keeping to the principles of low weight, low cost and low impact does not mean you have to forgo all comfort. Ladakh is ideally suited to independent individuals or small groups making their own arrangements with a pony-man on arrival. Ladakhis are caravan traders, not porters, so this is a traditional means of carrying your gear into the mountains. The pony-man will not only provide the ponies or donkeys to carry your luggage (£3-6/US$5-9 per animal per day) but will also act as your guide for no extra charge and possibly your cook as well. This is an excellent way to travel particularly if you keep the size of the group small.

A party of up to about four people, along with the pony-man and two or three ponies can walk together at the same speed, pitch camp in the smallest of spaces, alter the itinerary with ease and, perhaps more importantly, will be welcomed into villages and houses along the way. A friendship between you and your guide will develop as you practise your Ladakhi and he practises his English, which will certainly be better than your attempts at his language, while both of you learn more about each other's cultures. Understanding and appreciation of what you are seeing will be greatly increased, while a huge weight is taken off your back.

Organising such a minimal outfit is simple (see p165) and need take no more than two or three days. Leh is the best place to buy food and hire any camping equipment that you need, while pony-men can be organised either there or at the village at the start of your trek.

GUIDED TREKKING GROUPS

There is a certain amount of overlap between the approach mentioned above and guided trekking groups: the distinction is really in how much organisation you are prepared to do yourself.

Local trekking agencies

As the size of a group increases, or the level of service you require grows, it begins to make sense to employ the help of a local trekking agency in Leh. While you may well use an agency just to help you find a pony-man, their real skill lies in organising a complete trek from start to finish. For those for whom cost is not of major importance, or those who would rather let someone else worry about where and how to pitch the tent, how far to walk each day and what to have for dinner, a fully organised and guided trek is the answer.

Almost anything can be arranged from a simple but efficient trek with tents, food, ponies, guide and cook for as little as £13/US$20 per person per day, up to a luxury trek with excellent food, separate toilet, dining and kitchen tents plus a slick crew costing anything up to £55/$80 per person per day. The price becomes slightly lower per person the more people you have in the group.

This kind of organised group trek can easily be arranged when you arrive in Leh. It will take the agency between three and seven days to get everything together (the higher the level of service and the more complicated the itinerary, the longer everything takes), which gives you ample time to acclimatise and explore the local area.

If you are very short of time, require a very high level of service, or there are six or more of you (not to be recommended), it might be wiser to make preliminary arrangements before you reach India. Try contacting an Indian trekking agency from abroad via the state tourist office (see p92) but note that this can be a frustrating and time consuming business; allow at least two months. Alternatively, sign up with an adventure travel company from your own country.

Foreign trekking agencies

The growth of adventure travel companies in the West over the last decade has been phenomenal. All the companies listed on p14 offer treks in Ladakh, many choosing the most popular routes, while others make a point of taking you off the beaten track, or even up a mountain or two.

● **What you get for your money** A complete pre-planned trekking package is laid on so that there is almost nothing left for you to organise: international flights, high quality hotels, most meals, guided tours, transfers and transportation are all included. On the trek itself everything is provided, all you have to do is keep placing one foot in front of the other. The success of the trip depends on the quality of the leader and the local ground-handling agents. Most companies employ Western leaders to accompany the group for the whole of the trip, while leaving the day to day logistics of the trek in the hands of an experienced local guide. A few companies use local representatives throughout.

● **Pros and cons** Booking a trip with a trekking agency in your home country is a sensible choice for those who want to cram as much as possible into a limited amount of time and who enjoy being looked after. No time is wasted finding hotels, booking transport or getting a trekking crew together; someone else is being paid to worry about all that. Another benefit is that if you don't fancy the idea of travelling on your own, group treks are an excellent way to meet like-minded people.

However, not everyone finds it easy to travel with total strangers and rifts in the group are not uncommon. There can also be problems with sticking to such a fixed itinerary and always being with the group. There's little time to go off exploring on your own, to interact independently with the locals, to meet fellow trekkers or to take a rest day when you feel like it. Things can get more serious at high altitude, when in the interest of saving time, the group is forced to ascend rather more quickly than may be appropriate, causing unnecessary discomfort. This is without a doubt one of the most expensive ways to trek. While this style suits some, there are others who book with a commercial group because they don't realise that arranging a trekking holiday to Ladakh themselves is really very easy.

● **What to ask before making a booking** If you do decide to trek with a commercial company, there are a few questions you should ask before parting with your money. Some companies attract a certain type of clientele so it's worth finding out who your fellow trekkers will be and whether you think you'll get along with them. The top companies now give audiovisual shows so that you can meet other people interested in going on trips and get an idea of what trekking with that company is like.

Try to find out who will be leading your trip and what experience he or she has of leading groups, travelling in India and Ladakh, and of walking that particular route. A knowledgeable leader can teach you so much about a region. Ask for a detailed itinerary of your trek, how difficult it is and how big the group will be. Good indicators of the level of comfort that you can expect are the sort of food you will be eating and the standard of equipment that you will be using.

Perhaps most importantly, you should enquire about how comprehensive their medical kit is, whether the trek will be accompanied by anyone with medical training and what the policy is if someone falls ill, especially with Acute Mountain Sickness (AMS, commonly known as altitude sickness, see p272). Have they worked out emergency descent routes and will it be possible for someone to escort the AMS sufferer back to lower altitude if it's necessary?

❑ **On the trail with a trekking group**
If you've always thought that camping is best left to those with masochistic tendencies, then trekking with a commercial group will come as a luxurious surprise. You are woken up in your spacious tent and snug sleeping bag with a cup of steaming tea, which is soon followed by a bowl of hot water for washing. You then tuck into a sustaining breakfast while the crew strikes camp and loads up the ponies.

Carrying just a small day-pack containing a jacket, camera and water bottle, you set off gently. There's plenty of time to take photos, catch your breath or just enjoy the scenery. A simple packed lunch gives you an excuse to sit down and recuperate, while your crew rushes on ahead to set up camp before you arrive. The afternoon's walking is much shorter and you arrive at camp in time for tea and biscuits. With several hours of daylight left you can explore around the camp-site, relax in the sun or have a wash by a mountain stream. After a wonderful three-course dinner, miraculously prepared on a couple of kerosene stoves, most trekkers are only too happy to turn in early.

TREKKING AGENCIES

Trekking agencies in the UK

Most UK trekking agencies quote prices including return airfares from London, all accommodation in India, all transport and a fully guided and equipped trek. Prices range from about £1200 for a 16-day trip, to £2500 for 30 days away. Some companies also offer other adventurous activities in Ladakh, such as mountaineering, white-water rafting and mountain biking.

● **Abercrombie and Kent** (☎ 0171-730 9600, ☎ 0171-559 8777, 🖹 0171-730 9376, 🖳 info@abercrombiekent.co.uk), Sloane Square House, Holbein Place, London SW1W 8NS, arrange independent itineraries for trekking as well as for horse riding, mountain biking, rafting etc.

● **Beyond the Horizon** (☎ 01434-606383, 🖳 beyond.the.horizon@line one.net), 35 Dickson Drive, Hexham, Northumberland NE46 2RB; also offer mountaineering and rafting.

● **Classic Nepal** (☎ 01773-873497, 🖹 01773-590243, 🖳 www.himalay a.co.uk), 33 Metro Ave, Newton, Alfreton, Derbyshire, DE55 5UF.

● **Exodus** (☎ 0181-675 5550, 🖹 0181-673 0779, 🖳 www.exodustravel s.co.uk), 9 Weir Rd, London SW12 0LT, also offer mountaineering.

● **Explore Worldwide** (☎ 01252-760100, 🖹 01252-760001, 🖳 www.expl ore.co.uk), 1 Frederick St, Aldershot, Hampshire GU11 1LQ.

● **High Places** (☎ 0114-275 7500, 🖹 0114-275 3870, 🖳 www.highpl aces.co.uk), Globe Centre, Penistone Rd, Sheffield S6 3AE; also organise mountaineering holidays.

● **Himalayan Kingdoms** (☎ 0117-923 7163, 🖹 0117-974 4993, 🖳 www.himalayankingdoms.com), 20 The Mall, Clifton, Bristol BS8 4DR.

● **HKE Jagged Globe** (☎ 0114-276 3322, 🖹 0114-276 3344, 🖳 www.hke xpeds.demon.co.uk), 45 Mowbray St, Sheffield S8 8EN; also offer mountaineering and private guiding.

● **KE Adventure Travel** (☎ 017687-73966, 🖹 017687-74693, 🖳 keadvent ure@enterprise.net), 32 Lake Rd, Keswick, Cumbria CA12 5DQ, also offer mountaineering and mountain-biking.

● **OTT Expeditions** (☎ 0114-258 8508, 🖹 0114-255 1603, 🖳 www.ottexp editions.co.uk), South West Centre, Suite 5b, Troutbeck Rd, Sheffield S7 2QA. Mountaineering only.

● **Roama Travel** (☎ 01258-860298, 🖹 01258-861382, 🖳 roama@city2 000.net), Shroton, Blandford Forum, Dorset DT11 8QW, specialise in organ-ising individual itineraries.

● **Terra Firma** (☎/🖹 0181-943 3065, 🖳 www.users.globalnet.co.uk/~ter rafir), 63 Holmesdale Rd, Teddington, Middlesex TW11 9LJ; also offer mountaineering.

● **Wilderness Adventure** (☎/🖹 01296-624225, 🖳 WildAdv@compu serve.com, www.wildernessadventure.co.uk), 15 Moor Park, Wendover, Aylesbury, Bucks HP22 6AX, arrange independent itineraries for trekking, mountaineering, rafting and cycling holidays.

- **World Expeditions** (☎ 0800 0744 135, 🖳 enquiries@worldexpeditio ns.co.uk, www.worldexpeditions.com.au), 4 Northfields Prospect, Putney Bridge Rd, London SW18 1PE; also offer mountain-biking.
- **Worldwide Journeys and Expeditions** (☎ 0171-381 8638, 🖹 0171-381 0836, 🖳 www.wwj.co.uk), 8 Comeragh Rd, London W14 9HP; also offer mountaineering.

Trekking agencies in Continental Europe

- **Belgium Divantoura** (☎ 03-233 1916, 🖳 antwerpen@divantoura.com), St Jacobsmarkt 5, 2000 Antwerpen; (☎ 09-223 0069), Bagatten- straat 176, B-9000 Gent. **Joker Tourism** (☎ 02-426 0003, 🖹 02-426 0360, 🖳 info@joker.be, www.joker.be) Avenue Verdilaan 23-25, 1083 Brussels. **Boundless Adventures** (☎ 02-426 40 30, 🖹 02-426 03 60), Verdilaan 25, 1083 Brussels.
- **Denmark Inter-Travel** (☎ 33 15 00 77), Frederiksholms Kanal 2, DK-1220 Kobenhavn K. **Topas Globetrotterklub** (☎ 86 89 36 22, 🖹 86 89 36 88, 🖳 info@topas.dk), Bakkelyvej 2, 8680 Ry.
- **Germany DAV Summit Club** (☎ 089-64 24 00) Am Perlacher Forst 186, 81545 München. **Explorer Fernreisen** (☎ 0211-99 49 02, 🖹 0211-37 70 79), Huttenstrasse 17, 40215 Dusseldorf. **SHR Reisen** (☎ 0761-210 078) Kaiser Joseph Strasse 263, D-7800 Freiburg.
- **Ireland Maxwells Travel** (☎ 01-677 9479, 🖹 01-679 3948), D'Olier Chambers, 1 Hawkins St, Dublin 2. Agents for Explore (UK). **Collette Pearson Travel** (☎ 01-677 1029, 🖹 01-677 1390), 64 South William St, Dublin 2. Agents for Exodus (UK).
- **Italy Agiata SRL** (☎ 02-86 12 30, 🖹 02-86 90 617), Corso Di Porta Romana 6, 20122 Milano.
- **Netherlands Nepal Reizen Snow Leopard** (☎ 070-388 28 67, 🖳 www.snowleopard.nl) Calandplein 3, 2521 AB Den Haag; Stok Kangri climbs and treks across Zanskar. **Himalaya Trekking** (☎ 0521-551 301, 🖳 www.himtrek.nl) Ten Have 13, 7983 KD Wapse. **Nederlandse Klim en Bergsport Vereniging** (☎ 030-233 40 80) Oudkerkhof 13, 3512 GH Utrecht. **SNP** (☎ 024-360 52 22, 🖳 www.snp.nl) Groesbeekseweg 181, 6523 NR Nijmegen. **Adventure World** (☎ 023-5382 954, 🖳 atc@euronet.nl), Muiderslotweg 112, 2026 AS, Haarlem. **NBBS** (☎ 071-22 1414) Schipholweg 101, PO Box 360, 2300 AJ Leiden. **De Wandelwaaier** (☎ 020-622 6990, 🖳 www.wandelwaaier.nl) Singel 3951, 1012 WN, Amsterdam.
- **Spain Banoa (Bilbao)** (☎ 94-424 00 11, 🖹 423 20 39, 🖳 banoabio@correo.net) C/Ledesma, 10-bis, 2°, 48001 Bilbao. **Banoa (Barcelona)** (☎ 93-318 96 00, 🖹 318 00 37, 🖳 banoabcn@correo.net) Ronda de Sant Pere, 11, àtic 3a, 08010 Barcelona.
- **Switzerland Suntrek Tours** (☎ 01-387 78 78, fax 01-387 78 00, 🖳 info@suntrek.ch), Bellerivestr 11, PO Box 8034, Zurich, **Exodus GSA Switzerland** (☎ 064-22 76 63, 🖹 064-23 10 84), Rain 35, PO Box 2226, 5001 Aarau.

Trekking agencies in the USA

North American trekking agencies quote land-cost only. Sample costs are US$2400 for a 21-day trip and US$3400 for 32 days.

• **Adventure Centre** (☎ 800-227-8747, 🖻 415-654-4200), 1311 63rd St, Suite 200, Emeryville, CA 94608. Agents for Explore (UK).

• **Journeys** (☎ 734-665-4407 ☎ 800-255-8735, 🖻 734-665-2945, 💻 www.journeys-intl.com), 107 Aprill Dr, Suite 3, Ann Arbor, MI 48103.

• **Snow Lion Expeditions** (☎ 800-525-TREK, ☎ 801-355-6555, 🖻 801-355 6566, 💻 www.snowlion.com), Oquirrh Place, 350 South 400 East, Suite G2, Salt Lake City, UT 84111. Trekking and mountaineering.

• **Wilderness Travel** (☎ 510-548-0420, ☎ 800-368-2794), 801 Allston Way, Berkeley, CA 94710.

Trekking agencies in Canada

• **Adventure Centre** (☎ 416-922-7584), 17 Hayden St, Toronto, Ontario M4Y 2P2. Agents for Explore (UK).

• **Canadian Himalayan Expeditions Ltd** (☎ 416-360-4300, ☎ 800-563-8735, 🖻 416-360-7796, 💻 treks@chetravel.com, www.chetravel.com), 2 Toronto St, Suite 302, Toronto, Ontario, M5C 2B6.

• **GAP Adventures** (☎ 416-922-8899, 🖻 416-922-0822), 264 Dupont St, Toronto, Ontario M5R 1V7.

• **Trek Holidays** (☎ 800-661-7265), agents for Explore (UK), have offices in **Calgary** (☎ 403-283-6115), 336 14th St NW, Calgary, Alberta T2N 1Z7, and **Edmonton** (☎ 403-439-0024).

Trekking agencies in Australia

• **Adventure World**, agents for Explore (UK): **Adelaide** (☎ 08-8231 6844), 7th Floor, 45 King William St, Adelaide SA 5000; **Brisbane** (☎ 07-3229 0599), 3rd Floor, 333 Adelaide St, Brisbane Qld 4000; **Melbourne** (☎ 03-9670 0125), 3rd Floor, 343 Little Collins St, Melbourne Vic 3000; **Perth** (☎ 09-9221 2300), 2nd Floor, 8 Victoria Ave, Perth WA 6000; and **Sydney** (☎ 02-9956 7766), 73 Walker St, North Sydney NSW 2059.

• **Exodus** (☎ 02-9251 5430, 🖻 02-9251 5432), Suite 5, Level 5, 1 York St, Sydney NSW 2000. Agents for Exodus (UK).

• **World Expeditions** (☎ 02-9264 3366, 💻 enquiries@worldexpeditions.com.au), 3rd Floor, 441 Kent St, Sydney NSW 2000.

Trekking agencies in New Zealand

• **Adventure World** (☎ 09-524 5118, 🖻 09-520 6629), 101 Great South Rd, Remuera, PO Box 74008, DX 69501, Auckland, are agents for Explore and Exodus (UK).

• **Himalaya Trekking** (☎ 06-868 8595, 💻 treks@clear.net.nz, www.trailblazer-guides.com/trek-nepal/), 54a Darwin Rd, Gisborne, organise individual itineraries.

• **Suntravel** (☎ 09-525 3074, 🖻 09-525 3065), PO Box 12-424, 407 Great South Rd, Penrose, Auckland. Trekking, mountain biking and rafting. **Venturetreks**, agents for World Expeditions (above), are a division of Suntravel.

Getting to India

VISAS

Unless you are from either Nepal or Bhutan you won't get into India without a visa. **Tourist visas** are available for six months' duration only and are valid from the date of issue, not from the date of entry into India. These visas are difficult to extend. Get your visa from the Indian embassy or consulate in your home country (see p269) if at all possible since it's usually cheaper and more straightforward this way. UK passport holders applying at an Indian embassy outside the UK, for example, may be asked for a letter of recommendation from the British embassy.

Taking your passport in person is by far the quickest method. In the UK your visa will be processed the same day but if you apply by post it can take up to three months. The cost depends on your nationality. The British currently pay £19 for a six-month tourist visa. US citizens pay double this. Three photos are required.

On the visa application form you are asked how many entries into India you are going to make. It costs no more to request a multiple-entry visa and this gives you the option of crossing over into Pakistan or Nepal. Very occasionally, travellers who specify that they are going to Ladakh are given a visa stamped with a 10-day restricted area pass for Ladakh. Since most of Ladakh ceased to be a restricted area years ago this occurs only because a few embassy bureaucrats remain ignorant of changes to visa regulations. While most people encounter no problems by specifying Ladakh, it might be wiser to write down a typical tourist itinerary, such as Delhi, Jaipur, Agra, Varanasi. This has no effect on where you are allowed to go once you are in India.

❏ **Getting to Ladakh from Delhi**
See p95 for details of how to get to Ladakh from Delhi. It's easy to make travel arrangements once you've arrived in India, but for those on a very tight schedule, who are planning to fly into or out of Leh, it is possible to book Indian Airlines domestic flights from your home country through the same travel agent with whom you booked your international flight (although not every travel agent will do this for you). If all the flights seem to be fully booked, don't panic – it's usually easier to get a seat once you've arrived in India.

An alternative is to use an agent with offices in India who can arrange to have your Indian Airlines tickets waiting for you on arrival. In the UK, Indus Tours and Travel Ltd (☎ 0181-426 0069, 🖷 0181-863 0255, Premier House, 2 Gayton Rd, Harrow, Middlesex, HA1 2XU) has been recommended. American Express card holders can book Indian Airlines flights through the AMEX office in Delhi.

BY AIR

Although there are numerous carriers to Delhi, the nearest international airport to Ladakh, you should book early. For the best deals check the travel pages of newspapers and magazines and phone as many travel agents as you can – a few hours' research can save you a lot of money. Although it's occasionally worth contacting the airlines themselves for special offers, the best deals will usually be through an agent. When you find an attractive price, check the restrictions on the ticket, the flight route and timings. You may find it's worth paying a little extra for a more convenient flight or for the security of using a more reputable travel agency. Some airlines increase their prices for flights to Delhi in July, August and December. Many offer discounts to students and people under 26.

From the UK

Prices of return flights start from £310 for an off-season flight with an Eastern European or Central Asian airline (with dubious safety standards and lengthy stop-overs in inhospitable airports), or from about £500 for a high season direct flight with a well-respected carrier. Search for bargains in London's listings magazines such as *Time Out*, or check the travel pages of the Sunday papers. Recommended travel agents include:
● **Campus Travel** who have many offices throughout the country and accept telephone bookings on ☎ 0171-730 8111 (**London**); ☎ 0161-273 1721 (**Manchester**); and ☎ 0131-668 3303 (**Edinburgh**).
● **Quest Worldwide** (☎ 0181-547 3322), Quebec House, 10 Richmond Rd, Kingston, Surrey KT2 5HL.
● **STA Travel** have many branches in Britain and can be contacted for telephone sales on ☎ 0171-361 6262 (**London**); ☎ 0161-834 0668 (**Manchester**); ☎ 0117-929 4399 (**Bristol**): ☎ 01223-366966 (**Cambridge**); ☎ 01865-792800 (**Oxford**).
● **Trailfinders** have offices in **London** (☎ 0171-938 3366, 42-50 Earls Court Rd, W8 6FT), **Birmingham** (☎ 0121-236 1234, 22-24 The Priory, Queensway, B4 6BS), **Bristol** (☎ 0117-929 9000, 48 Corn St, BS1 1HQ), **Glasgow** (☎ 0141-353 2224, 254-284 Sauchiehall St, G2 3EH), **Manchester** (☎ 0161-839 6969, 58 Deansgate, M3 2FF) and **Newcastle-upon-Tyne** (☎ 0191-261 2345, 7-9 Ridley Place, NE1 8JQ).

From USA and Canada

Flights from the west coast cost from around US$1400 return and are slightly cheaper from the east coast. The independent travel specialists, **STA Travel**, have offices throughout the USA and can usually offer some very competitive prices. Contact the New York branch (☎ 1-800-836-4115), 10 Downing St, NY 10014, for details of other offices. Try **Travel Cuts** in Canada (☎ 416-979-2406, 187 College St, Toronto, Ontario M5T 1P7).

From Australasia

Return flights start from around A$1300 from Australia and NZ$1800 from

New Zealand. **Trailfinders** have offices in **Sydney** (☎ 02-9247 7666, 8 Spring St, Sydney, NSW), **Cairns** (☎ 07-4041 1199, Hides Corner, Lake St, Cairns, Queensland) and **Brisbane** (☎ 07-3229 0887, 91 Elizabeth St, Brisbane, Queensland). **STA Travel** have several offices in both countries. Contact the following offices for further details: **Australia** (☎ 02-9212 1255, 855 George St, Ultimo, Sydney NSW); **New Zealand** (☎ 09-309 0458, 10 High St, Auckland).

OVERLAND

The classic overland route to India from the UK is much harder than it was in the '60s, but plenty of travellers are still undertaking this fascinating journey. The most popular route goes through Hungary, Romania, Bulgaria, Turkey, Iran and Pakistan. It's quite possible to organise independently, using public transport or your own vehicle. For complete information on all the possible routes into Asia see *Asia Overland* by Mark Elliott and Wil Klass (Trailblazer).

There are also several specialist overland companies in the UK who will transport you in their well-equipped trucks: **Dragoman** (☎ 01728-861133); **Encounter Overland** (☎ 0171-370 6845); **Exodus** (see UK trekking agencies above); **Top Deck Travel** (☎ 0171-370 4555).

Budgeting

COSTS IN TOWNS

India is one of the cheapest countries in which to travel. A basic double room with communal bathroom in Delhi, which is one of the most expensive places in India, will cost you about £3/US$5 a night, whereas in Manali and Leh you will get far nicer double rooms with a common bath from £1.50/US$2.50. Very comfortable rooms with attached bathroom and running hot water in an up-market hotel will cost you about £8-15/US$13-24 a night.

Expect to pay from around £1.50/US$2.50 for a good evening meal and about £1/US$1.60 for a bottle of beer. Restaurant prices in Leh and Manali are pretty uniform but in Delhi you can pay far more than this for a meal in a top restaurant.

If your budget is tight it's quite possible to find a room for under £1/US$1.60 and to eat an evening meal for less than £0.60/US$1. Many people who have brought their own trekking stoves find that cooking their own meals makes an interesting change and is a good way to keep the costs down; some wonderful organic vegetables can be bought in the bazaars.

INDEPENDENT TREKKING COSTS

If you're organising the trek totally independently and have all your own equipment, the main costs will be pack animals and food. Each trekker should expect to pay £3-6/US$5-9 per day for pack animals and a pony-man, and about £2-3/US$3-5 a day for food and fuel. A fully organised trek, arranged in Leh, costs from about £13/US$20 per person per day.

There is very rarely anything to buy on the trail apart from the occasional packet of biscuits or bar of chocolate. Expect to pay camping charges of about £0.40/US$0.60 per tent each night when near a village.

YOUR OVERALL BUDGET

Budget travellers should reckon on spending £50-90/US$80-150 a week, which will cover food and accommodation, local travel, sightseeing, trekking and pocket money for chocolate, paperbacks, a few cheap souvenirs and the odd phone call home.

Travel from Delhi to Ladakh and back again will cost about £50/US$80 if you go by bus, £130/US$210 by plane, or £90/US$145 if you take the bus one way and fly the other.

Once you've calculated how much you will need for the trip, bring a little more in case you get ill and require a doctor and a quick flight back to Delhi, or if you get tempted into going rafting on the Indus, or buy a 'very good price' Kashmiri rug!

When to go and for how long

Ladakh is surrounded by a ring of high mountains and snow-covered passes which, before the airport was built at Leh, effectively cut it off from the rest of the world for seven or eight months every year. Although the modern visitor can now fly into Leh at any time of the year, trekking is restricted to the five months when the region is free from the grip of winter. The great advantage of Ladakh as a trekking destination is that rainfall is rare. This makes it one of the only Himalayan regions in which it is possible and pleasurable to trek from late June to mid-September, when most other areas are suffering from the constant deluge of the monsoon.

SEASONS

Ladakh's four seasons are not as even in length as those of Europe and North America, the year being dominated by the long, cold winter which is separated from the short but hot summer by a brief spring and autumn. In many ways, spring and autumn are little more than the end and the beginning of winter and can hardly justify being called separate seasons.

June, July and August

The trekking season begins in about the middle of June. This is a good time to come as there won't be many visitors, but you may have to fly in to Leh as the roads may not have opened and some passes may prove difficult to trek across if there is still a lot of snow around.

Ladakh is at its busiest from the beginning of July to the end of August. This coincides with the opening of the Manali to Leh road, linking Himachal Pradesh to Ladakh, which is guaranteed by the government to be kept open from the first week of July until 15 September.

The weather is good for trekking, with hot days and refreshingly cool nights, although at lower altitudes it can sometimes be too hot to trek in the middle of the day. A decade or so ago you could almost guarantee a completely dry summer but recent changes in the weather patterns of the Himalaya (thought by some to be the result of global warming) mean that a few days' rain is now a distinct possibility – come prepared. One drawback at this time of year is the number of visitors. The classic treks may be busy and popular guest-houses in Leh fill up quickly.

September and October

September is one of the best months to come trekking, as the number of people both on the trails and in Leh begins to tail off towards the end of August. If you come at the beginning of the month your stay will coincide with the Ladakh Festival (see p73). The temperatures are pleasantly warm during the

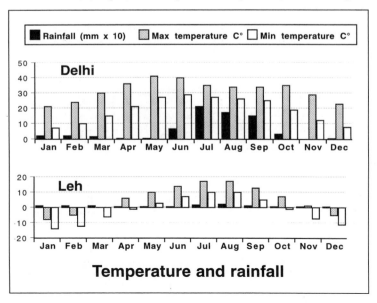

Temperature and rainfall

day, without being too hot, but you should come prepared for cold nights, particularly when you're in the mountains. Many of the tea houses in the mountains will have closed and disappeared from the beginning of September and some tourist businesses in Leh shut down come mid-September. This can be seen as a benefit as the locals have much more time for you and it is easier to get a sense of the real Ladakh without the commercial pressures of the tourist season.

The Manali to Leh road is guaranteed to be open until 15 September and often remains open for much longer. Some years it can remain open throughout October but you should be prepared to consider flying if the winter snows come early. It's usually possible to trek right up until the end of October, although you will need to be suitably equipped for freezing temperatures after the sun has gone down.

November to March
At the beginning of November the lasting snows of winter begin to fall and the streams freeze over for five months. The coldest months are January and February when temperatures fall as low as -40°C transforming the Zanskar River into a frozen trade route known as the Chadur (see p40). By March this savage cold has gone. For very experienced and well-prepared winter mountaineers and ski tourers the winter can provide some exciting possibilities. Read Guy Sheridan's account of the first winter journey from Kargil to Manali, through Zanskar and Lahaul, in *Tales of a Cross Country Skier*.

April and May
It is still quite cold during these months and snowfall is not uncommon at the beginning of April, but by now the ground in the valleys has begun to thaw and activity has resumed in the villages. Trekking is feasible on low-altitude routes, such as from Likir to Temisgam and for those with winter walking experience some higher routes could be attempted. The snow still lies deep on the passes, but with an early start you should be able to cross most on the firm crust of the frozen snow. But if you leave it too late, you'll be sinking up to your chest. The roads into Ladakh will still be closed, so flying in and out is the only practical option.

HOW LONG DO YOU NEED?

Despite its remoteness, Ladakh can be reached remarkably quickly from the West, and it's quite possible to fit an exciting and rewarding trekking holiday into three weeks. A typical itinerary might be: **Day 1**: fly to Delhi; **Day 2**: fly to Leh; **Days 3 to 5**: acclimatising, organising your trek and sightseeing; **Days 6 to 14**: trekking; **Day 15**: in Leh; **Day 16**: fly to Delhi; **Days 17 to 20**: sightseeing; **Day 21**: fly home.

If you are on a tight schedule and have to be back home by a certain date, you should be aware that buses and planes to and from the region occasionally get cancelled or delayed by the weather. You must allow yourself a few days' leeway to get back to Delhi from Leh.

A schedule that works well for those short of time is to get up to Ladakh as soon as possible after arriving in India and leave your exploration of Delhi until the end of your holiday. Aim to fly back from Leh about five days before you are due to fly home. If all goes well, this will give you plenty of time to see Delhi and maybe fit in a trip to the Taj Mahal in Agra as well. If, on the other hand, your flight from Leh is cancelled, you still have plenty of time to make it back to Delhi by road.

If you are one of the lucky few who has no need to be back home by a set date, then there's almost no end to the number of trails that can be walked and discovered in Ladakh.

Route options

Ladakh is criss-crossed by a complex network of mountain trails which, even in these days of motorised transport and roads, still provide the only link between the majority of valleys, villages and high pastures. Some of these were the highways of the centuries-old caravan trade, while others are hardly ever used except by a few shepherds each year. These provide the trekker with wonderful routes ranging from gentle undulating hikes to demanding expeditions over wild mountain passes.

PLANNING YOUR ROUTE

The following pages give an overview of the trekking possibilities to help you plan your trek according to the length of time you have, your ability and where your interests lie. The well-known 'classic' trails are covered in detail, both in this section and also in Part 7 where you will find extensive maps and trail descriptions. This level of detail has been extended to one or two other trails, which because of their proximity to Leh and the easing of restrictions, have already become popular. These detailed route descriptions provide the core of this book and amply reflect the wonderful variety of trekking Ladakh has to offer.

As your experience and confidence grows it's inevitable you will start to get curious about other possible routes. Perhaps in the Markha Valley you noticed an alluring trail disappear up a narrow side valley and wondered where it led, or was it that dotted line on your map which no one knew much about which sparked your imagination? To reveal some of the opportunities available I have included some other routes in sufficient detail for you to make preliminary plans but not so much that it spoils one of the greatest joys of travelling in remote mountains: that of making unexpected and unplanned discoveries for yourself. There are still hundreds of miles of trails that rarely see the tread of a visitor's boot. There are hints within the text of some of these, but many special places remain unmentioned. If you have the ability

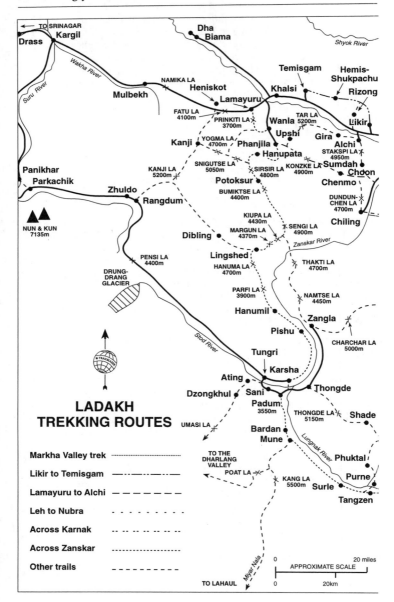

LADAKH TREKKING ROUTES

Markha Valley trek ....

Likir to Temisgam ———·———·———

Lamayuru to Alchi — — — — — —

Leh to Nubra · · · · · · · · · ·

Across Karnak ·· —·· —·· —·· —

Across Zanskar ....

Other trails — — — — — — —

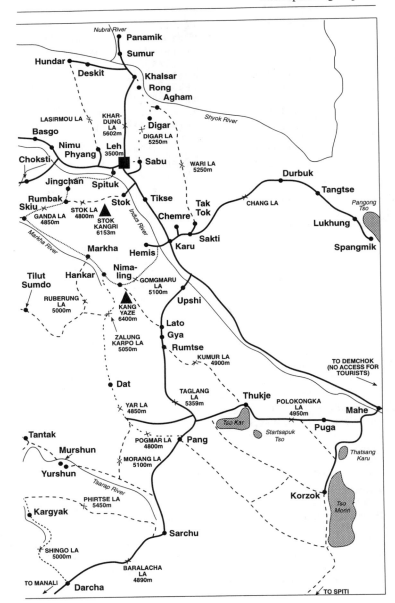

to walk the wilder treks, detailed route descriptions would be superfluous anyway; far better to go with a knowledgeable local guide, whatever map you can get hold of, and mountain sense gained from previous experience in remote places.

Finally, don't make the common mistake of trying to cram too much into too little time. Getting to know one area in depth is so much more rewarding than rushing on to the next just so it can be ticked off that list of 'must be seen' places. The number of days it takes to walk each trek is given as a rough guide only and doesn't take into account the all-important rest days. For sample itineraries for the most popular treks see p270; for the **Route Planning Map** see the previous pages.

The treks are arranged into regions, starting with central Ladakh and then radiating out in a clockwise direction. At the end is some basic information on mountaineering in Ladakh. A page reference is given to routes covered in further detail in Part 7.

CENTRAL LADAKH

Ease of access from Leh and the rich cultural heritage along the Indus Valley have ensured the popularity of treks in the region between the Zanskar Mountains and the Ladakh Mountains. If this is your first visit to Ladakh the wide variety of treks of various lengths and for different abilities make it an ideal place to start your explorations.

The Markha Valley Trek (6-10 days)   pp176-92

This is Ladakh's most popular trek attracting about 60% of all trekkers. Its length, accessibility and variation of landscape have ensured its classic status. People usually take eight or nine days to complete it; doing it in less time would involve some very long days and being well-acclimatised before you start. It can be walked any time from mid-June to mid-October providing there isn't too much snow on the passes.

● **Direction** The trek is usually walked from west to east, beginning in either Spituk or Stok and finishing in Karu, near Hemis. This way the first two days are relatively gentle, taking you to the lowest point of the Markha Valley and making acclimatisation easier. Consider starting at the other end only if you are fit and well-acclimatised, as the steep and difficult route from Karu to the Gongmaru La takes you quickly to 5100m/16,730ft.

● **Route** Spituk or Stok are a short bus or taxi ride from Leh. Karu is about an hour and a half to the east of Leh and can also be reached by bus or taxi. If you are starting from the west you have two options: the most popular is to start from Spituk and ascend the Jingchan Nala; the other is to begin in the village of Stok, cross the Stok (or Namling) La (4800m/15,750ft) and then descend to Rumbak where the two trails converge. The latter involves a steep ascent and descent of the Stok La and usually takes an extra day if you're acclimatised and longer if you're not.

The trail crosses the high but gentle Ganda La (4850m/15,910ft) and descends via a magnificent gorge to the Markha Valley. The next few days are spent following the Markha River upstream, passing through small and under-populated villages until you climb to the high-altitude valley of Nimaling, where villagers graze their livestock beneath the snow covered peak of Kang Yaze. You then cross the Gongmaru La (5100m/16,730ft), which reveals views as far as the Karakoram, and descend back down to the Indus Valley.

● **Safety** A tent and enough food to last the whole trip are essential on this trek. During the main trekking season of July and August it's sometimes possible to supplement your supplies with chocolate, biscuits, instant noodles and cigarettes bought from the tea tents/shops which are set up along the trail, but you can't depend on these as they are not always there.

Backpacking with over a week's food and camping equipment while walking at high altitude is only for fit and experienced trekkers. Even a French mountain guide from Chamonix, whom I once met, was finding backpacking this route extremely hard work and not very enjoyable. It makes sense to hire pack animals.

Route finding is generally easy, although it can become difficult over the passes if there's been recent snowfall. If you are travelling without pack animals which you can hang on to or ride, take either a stick or some rope to cope with the river crossings; these are usually straightforward but demand extra care if there has been any rain.

Altitude, as always, is a problem. Whichever direction you decide to start from, you have to cross a high pass to gain access to the Markha Valley. The only answer is to allow enough time in your itinerary to acclimatise before each pass. Beginning in Spituk helps because the altitude gain is not so rapid, and after crossing the Ganda La you descend to the lower end of the Markha Valley.

● **Pros and cons** This is one of the easiest treks to organise because of its proximity to Leh. Practically all the local pony-men and guides know the route, so finding one to suit your needs is easy. The scenery is stunning and very varied. You pass close to two of the most regularly climbed peaks in Ladakh, Stok Kangri and Kang Yaze, and there is a good chance of seeing interesting wildlife, particularly bharal (blue sheep), Ladakh urial (a rare species of wild sheep) and marmots, the trek being within the Hemis National Park. This does, however, mean you will sometimes have to pay a national park entrance fee of Rs20 per person per day (reduced to Rs1 if you are a student). The trek can be linked with others to make it as long as you wish: you can combine it with the Lamayuru to Alchi trek by crossing the Zanskar River at Chiling, and with the trail to Pang by continuing up the Markha River above Hankar rather than going to Nimaling. There is also much of cultural interest at Spituk, Stok and Hemis as well as some small monasteries along the route.

All this contributes to its main drawbacks: it can get busy in July and August; and some of the camp-sites have become filthy because of too many unthinking and uncaring trekkers. Solutions to this problem are discussed in Part 6 – please help make a positive change.

Stok to Spituk via the Stok La (2-4 days)   p193

This short trek follows the two alternative starts to the Markha Valley trek. From Stok you begin by following the trail towards Stok Kangri. The trail divides and you climb to the 4800m/15,750ft Stok La before descending to Rumbak and then on to Spituk via Jingchan. Being short, and close to Leh, it is easily organised and an ideal acclimatisation trek to see how you cope with trekking at high altitude. Take plenty of time to acclimatise before crossing the Stok La.

Likir to Temisgam (2-4 days)   p193-9

Also known as the 'Sham Trek', this short, low-altitude trek through historical villages is an easy introduction to trekking in Ladakh. It is Ladakh's one and only tea-house trek where a tent is not essential as there are guest-houses in some of the villages. It can easily be completed in two days, but taking longer would allow you to make side trips and have time to explore each village properly. The best months to walk this route are May, June, September and October, when the temperatures are lower.

● **Direction** This route can be walked in either direction.

● **Route** Likir is a two-hour bus ride from Leh. The trail runs parallel to but north of the Leh-Srinagar highway, passing through six relatively prosperous villages and over five low passes. It follows part of the old Leh to Khalsi road between Likir and Temisgam, which was the main pony trail along the Indus Valley before the motor road was built. You can add on a side trip to Rizong Gompa and an extra stage by extending the trek to Khalsi.

● **Safety** Rudimentary guest-houses allow you to walk this route without the encumbrance of a tent and all the associated camping paraphernalia. You will still need a sleeping bag and possibly a mat but an evening meal and breakfast will be provided. The shops on the trail have limited supplies so bring from Leh some food for lunches. Generally this is a safe and easy walk with no large gains in altitude or dangerous river crossings but, as always in the mountains, you should be prepared for the worst.

● **Pros and cons** Its short length and low altitude (under 4000m/13,120ft) make this trek an ideal proposition for the novice trekker or for those looking for a short acclimatisation trek. With gompas at Likir, Rizong, Hemis-Shukpachu and a ruined fort at Temisgam there's plenty of cultural interest. If you stay in the guest-houses along the route it is an excellent way of seeing village life at close quarters. It can also be walked at any time of year making it suitable for off-season visits.

Points against it are that it can get very hot in mid-summer and the jeep road connecting Likir to Hemis-Shukpachu has the occasional bus travelling along it. This is not really a problem as the traffic is so infrequent.

Lamayuru to Alchi (4-6 days) pp199-209

High passes, rough ground and some complicated route finding make this a short but challenging trek through stunning mountain scenery. It's possible to walk in four long days but the pony-men prefer to take at least five. One commercial trekking company takes nine days over this trek so, as always, it depends very much on the individual. It can be walked from June to October as long as there isn't too much snow on the passes.

● **Direction** It's best to tackle this trek from west to east as this gives you longer before you have to climb your first major pass, allowing you to gain height gently. If you need further persuasion, one look at the mountain barrier behind Alchi should send you hurrying on to Lamayuru. Starting at Alchi would involve an immediate, steep climb of nearly 2000m/6560ft with no good places to camp until you're over the pass and down the other side, a minimum of 10 hours walking. In addition it is easier to find guides and pack animals in Lamayuru than in Alchi.

● **Route** The traditional start is Lamayuru, at least six hours from Leh by bus or truck. The first section follows the well-worn trail between Lamayuru and Phanjila going over the Prinkiti La (3700m/12,140ft) and through Wanla. This is also the start of a popular route into Zanskar.

From Phanjila it branches up the secluded Ripchar Valley to the Konzke La (4900m/16,080ft) then descending to the isolated village and monastery of Sumdah-Chenmo. (It is possible to continue east to Chiling via the Dundunchen La from here. You can then either trek down the Zanskar River to Nimu or cross the river on a cable-car and walk up the Markha Valley, see p209). The route to Alchi goes down the narrow and complicated Sumdah Chu and then heads north-west to Sumdah-Choon with its beautiful monastery perched above the village. It's a long, hard climb over the Stakspi La (4950m/16,240ft), from which you descend to Alchi.

There is an alternative route to Alchi from Phanjila, which takes you over the difficult Tar La and then through the villages of Tar, Mang Gyu (where there is a gompa), Gira and Lardo which all lie close to the Indus River. This route is roughly the same length and is not described in further detail in this book.

● **Safety** You will need a tent and all your food with you as there is nowhere after Wanla where you can restock. You'll be thankful if you hire pack animals in Lamayuru as the two major passes involve stiff climbs of over 1000m/3280ft and the pony-man can also act as a guide on the more complicated sections. The trail can be hard to follow between Sumdah-Chenmo and the Stakspi La.

There are several rivers to be forded and gorges to walk through so extreme care should be taken if there is any rain. If you plan this trek properly you can camp below 4000m/13,120ft every night. However, much of the walking is above this and there are two passes of almost 5000m to cross. Should you suffer any altitude-related problems after crossing the first major pass, emergency evacuation is almost impossible, so careful acclimatisation is essential and is made easier if you start in Lamayuru.

● **Pros and cons** This is a wonderful way to get between the two historical sites of Lamayuru and Alchi. The scenery is dramatic and never dull and there are several beautiful villages and gompas which can be visited along the route. If all you need is pack animals and a guide, organising the trek yourself in Lamayuru is straightforward. However, if you want an organised trek with food, tents, guide and cook included, it is best to make arrangements in Leh. Because it is some distance from the capital, this trek avoids the intense visitor pressure that the Markha Valley attracts.

Although it can be strenuous and difficult at times, going with a good guide and taking your time makes this a most rewarding trek.

Across Karnak (8-10 days)   pp210-21
Between the Indus Valley and Zanskar, on the western edge of Rupshu lies a remote region called Karnak, an area sparsely inhabited by semi-nomadic peoples. Their simple winter villages and tented summer encampments are the only signs of civilisation you will see on this demanding high-altitude trek. Crossing Karnak by way of its vast valleys, deep gorges and barren deserts takes a minimum of eight days. It should be possible to walk this route from June to October but this depends on how much snow is on the passes.

● **Direction** For logistical reasons this route is usually walked from north to south, beginning near Hemis, as the start is easily reached from Leh. If you wanted to start in the south, at Pang, there is nowhere nearby where you can arrange pack animals and guides, although you could get basic supplies from the tea tents here.

● **Route** From Leh you take a bus, truck or taxi to Karu, near Hemis. The first part of the trail follows the end of the Markha Valley trek, climbing steeply to the Gongmaru La (5100m/16,730ft) and then over into the high-altitude pastures of Nimaling. The scenery gets wilder as you progress south over the Zanskar Mountains via the Zalung Karpo La (5050m/16,570ft) and from here the trail stays above 4000m/13,120ft, following remote valleys and passing a few tiny winter settlements.

There are two more passes to cross, the Yar La (4850m/15,910ft) and the Pogmar La (4800m/15,750ft), before you descend to the vast plain of Kanchuthang which is often dotted with the black yak hair tents of the Changpa nomads, who come to graze their livestock on the summer pastures. The Leh-Manali road crosses this area and the trail follows it to Pang. From here you can either continue south to Manali by bus or truck, or return to Leh.

A harder alternative ending to this trek after crossing the Yar La is to head south over the Morang La and then follow the Tsarap River to the Leh-Manali road, which would add on two or three days.

● **Safety** This is a long trek through isolated country. The first climb up to the Gongmaru La is the hardest; from then on the walking itself is not particularly difficult. The altitude and remoteness, however, make this a serious undertaking and a guide and pack animals are essential.

Almost the entire route is above 4000m/13,120ft and there is no practical way of descending to lower altitude if AMS should strike. You need to be completely self-sufficient and confident that you can cope if an emergency arose – help is a long way away. Not only are the villages deserted during the summer but very few people travel through this area. There are a number of river crossings to be made but as long as there hasn't been any rain they shouldn't be too difficult. The trail is often vague and sometimes non-existent and with no locals to ask for directions, a good guide is invaluable.

Finding a guide who knows this route is harder than for the more popular treks. It is often members of the Tibetan community in Leh who know this area best because of trading connections with the Chang Tang region.

● **Pros and cons** This is a trek for those who like wild and remote places. In this little-known region of Ladakh you are unlikely to pass many other people apart from the occasional nomadic Changpa. Compared with the other treks, there is little of cultural interest along the way, apart from the tiny gompa at Dat. You walk through a landscape that combines the dramatic scenery of the Zanskar Mountains with the gentler plains of Rupshu.

You need to be well acclimatised, equipped and experienced before you set off because of the constant high altitude and isolation. If you combine this trek with the Markha Valley trek you have a wonderful long distance route with the added bonus that it allows time for acclimatisation. It can also provide an interesting start to treks in Rupshu or as an alternative to crossing Zanskar for entering or leaving Ladakh. Finding guides can be a problem but the reputable trekking agencies in Leh should be able to help you with this.

Combining treks

Many of the treks in central Ladakh can be linked to provide longer routes. One of the most obvious is to link the Lamayuru to Alchi trek with the Markha Valley trek as explained on p209. This, in turn, can be combined with the route Across Karnak to Pang, making an interesting but demanding 11- to 15-day traverse of the Zanskar Mountains from Lamayuru in the west to Pang in the east. You can, of course, come down to the Indus Valley anywhere in between: Nimu, Spituk, Stok, Hemis; or continue into Rupshu.

NUBRA

This region north of Leh, on the north side of the Ladakh Mountains, encompasses the Nubra and Shyok river valleys. It is one of Ladakh's 'protected areas' which means trekking is complicated by various restrictions (see p66). If you are willing to comply with these there are some interesting routes which are being rediscovered since this area was opened to tourists in 1994.

Most trekkers exploring this region in the last few years have concentrated on routes from the Indus Valley into Nubra. All these are fairly intimidating as they involve short, steep ascents to over 5000m/16,400ft to cross the frequently snow-bound passes of the Ladakh Range. You then trek along the beautiful broad valleys of the Nubra and Shyok rivers, with the vast east-ern Karakoram Mountains towering over you to the north. Exploration of these, Ladakh's highest mountains, has been restricted to one or two fortu-nate expeditions a year. All the exciting trekking possibilities which exist in the Indian Karakoram, and also further west towards Baltistan and east into the Aksai Chin will have to wait until relationships improve between India and its two posturing neighbours, Pakistan and China.

Leh to Nubra via the Digar La (4-6 days)   pp221-230

This route follows a trail often used by the inhabitants of eastern Nubra as a way of getting to and from the markets of Leh. In the past it was used by the caravans when the shorter trail over the Khardung La was blocked by snow: the English explorer, William Moorcroft, followed the same route during his travels in the early 1820s. It provides an exciting way into the area and explores the remote and rarely visited Shyok Valley. It's a tough trek involv-ing rapid ascent to high altitude which is usually walkable from July to September, depending on how much snow is on the Digar La.

● **Direction** The route is best walked from east to west, starting from Sabu. This direction involves less ascent and also makes organising the trek much easier. Guides and pack animals are very hard to find in Nubra so it makes more sense to arrange these in Leh.

● **Route** From Leh, you can either walk over the hills to Sabu (three hours) or take a 20-minute bus ride. The route from Sabu follows the small Sabu River up through pastures then climbs steeply to the Digar La (5250m/ 17,230ft). From here you descend gradually to the pretty village of Digar and then down to the barren floodplain of the Shyok River. The route continues west along the river, sandwiched between the Ladakh Mountain Range to the south and the eastern Karakoram to the north. Eventually you reach the fer-tile village of Rong; it's just a short distance to Khalsar from where you can either carry on your explorations of Nubra or return to Leh by road over the Khardung La.

● **Safety** You need to be completely self-sufficient as the villages you pass through have only enough for themselves. A tent is essential as many of the camps are in exposed and remote places. The route is used mainly by locals rather than trekkers, so finding pony-men and guides who know the way can be hard. However, with time, perseverance and perhaps some help from a trekking agency, you should be able to find someone.

The main problem on this trek is the rapid altitude gain at the beginning. From Leh you go quickly up to over 5000m/16,410ft, so you need to be

---

(Opposite) Top: Acting as tutor, translator and companion, a Ladakhi guide or pony-man will help make trekking in Ladakh a fascinating experience. **Bottom**: Ponies and pony-men crossing the Markha River near Umlung (p186) on the Markha Valley trek (see p26). Rivers are a frequent obstacle on many treks in Ladakh.

acclimatised to these altitudes before you embark on this trek. It's best to do an easier trek before this one or to spend about two nights acclimatising at Pulu before crossing the Digar La. If you have problems with the altitude you can quickly descend back to Leh. If you experience AMS on the other side of the pass (unlikely if you've acclimatised properly) you can descend rapidly to the Shyok River at 3300m/10,830ft.

There are no difficult river crossings but some of the walking is very strenuous. The Digar La is both steep and high, whilst the Shyok Valley has long, tiring sections across sandy alluvial deposits. This latter stage can also get very hot because of the lower altitude. This is exacerbated by the shortage of places where you can find potable water. Route finding can be a bit tricky up to the Digar La but after that it is quite straightforward.

● **Pros and cons** It's a little travelled route through remote and challenging country passing only two small, isolated villages. Finding guides or ponymen may be hard as few know the route well. For those who are physically prepared and have the time to deal with the logistics it's a wonderful way to experience this harsh but majestic landscape close up; an aspect of Nubra that most travellers can't fully appreciate from the comfort of their jeeps.

A road and irrigation project is currently under construction along the south side of the Shyok River near the village of Rong. If this progresses up river as is planned, it could substantially alter the enjoyment of this route. At the time of this update, however, the majority of this trek was unaffected.

Other possibilities in Nubra

There are two other main passes over the Ladakh Range which are used by trekkers; the Lasirmou La north of Phyang and the Wari La near Sakti. There are some other interesting possibilities marked on the AMS U502 maps in addition to these but bear in mind that the more westerly passes will take you into prohibited areas. All these passes along the Ladakh Mountains hold snow on their northern slopes well into the summer months which can make them difficult if not impossible to cross. Ask locally about the condition of the pass you intend to cross before embarking on your trek.

● **Phyang to Hundar via the Lasirmou La (4-5 days)** This pass is notorious for snow build-up on its northern flank and in a good year can only be crossed in August and September when the worst of the snow has melted. If you don't want to travel by road to or from Nubra this route can provide an excellent start or finish to a walking tour of Nubra. For instance, start by following the Digar La or the Wari La routes into Nubra, walk around the sites of interest in the Nubra and Shyok valleys for a few days (see p149) and return to the Indus Valley over the Lasirmou La.

(**Opposite**) **Top:** Stok Kangri (see p43) is clearly visible from Leh and has become a popular mountaineering objective. **Bottom:** The summit of Stok Kangri (6153m) is within reach of experienced trekkers with basic mountaineering skills. The ascent normally requires the use of crampons and an ice axe.

● **Sakti to Khalsar via the Wari La (5-7 days)** From Sakti you ascend to the Wari La (5250m/17,220ft) and then descend to the Shyok River at Agham. From then on the route west to Khalsar follows that outlined in the Digar La trek above.

PANGONG

At the time of writing there is word on the grapevine that more of Pangong Tso and some of the area to the south may soon be opened up in the government's eternal quest for tourism's elusive golden egg. If this goes ahead, regulations will be the same as for other 'protected areas' (see p66) and trekking in the Pangong and Ladakh Ranges should be possible on a more legal footing than is allowed at present. A glance at the AMS U502 maps, particularly sheet NI 44-9, shows some of the options which might become viable.

RUPSHU

The Rupshu region in the south-east of Ladakh is the western fringe of the Chang Tang, a huge plateau that spreads hundreds of kilometres east across Tibet. It is a starkly beautiful region of high-altitude arid plains, gentle mountain ranges and salt-water lakes, such as Tso Kar and Tso Moriri. As on the Chang Tang its inhabitants are largely pastoral nomads.

The Rupshu region in the south-east of Ladakh is another of Ladakh's 'protected areas', open to foreign tourists since 1994. If you want to trek here you must comply with various government restrictions (see p66) while also bearing in mind that this is one of Ladakh's most fragile environments where uncontrolled tourism is causing serious problems, particularly around Tso Moriri (see p153). As with all of Ladakh, a sensitive, informed and low impact approach to trekking is essential.

Rupshu does not have established trekking routes yet. Simply choose your own way and itinerary, making use of the nomad and traders' paths which have been around for centuries. This is mountain wandering as it should be. I have outlined some of the trails I know exist to help you plan; undoubtedly there are countless more.

Hints for trekking in Rupshu

Don't underestimate a trek in Rupshu; the remoteness, high altitude and vague trails all demand respect. For a safe and enjoyable trek you need to be experienced and adaptable. If you take a few maps and go with horses and a knowledgeable local guide you'll have a fascinating experience.

The AMS U502 maps are reasonably reliable; NI 43-12, NI 44-9, NI 44-13 cover most of the region, although for completeness you may want to include NI 43-16. Although these show most of the principle routes, also get hold of the more recently published *Trekking Map of Ladakh* by Sonam Tsetan and Henk Thoma. This shows plenty of other possibilities, as well as marking the new jeep roads.

As there is no public transport in the region most people begin a trek from the Leh-Manali road or from Mahe on the River Indus. The other option is to rent a jeep to Tso Kar or Tso Moriri and then trek from there.

Bring all your food and fuel with you as there is nowhere to restock. Water can be a problem in some areas. If you are ever in any doubt about where the next water is, take plenty with you as there are some long stretches without fresh water. Just because water is marked on a map does not mean it will necessarily be there; the streams do disappear at various times of the year. One area notorious for this is along the shores of Tso Moriri. There are lots of streams marked on the AMS map but, apart from the Korzok Phu, they are almost all seasonal. Don't forget, Tso Moriri is brackish; a case of 'water, water, everywhere, nor any drop to drink', as several trekkers have found to their cost.

Grazing is also in short supply in many areas of Rupshu; the situation is particularly acute around Tso Moriri. Not only does trekking put pressure on the nomads' pastures but if your ponies are not properly fed they will wander for miles in search of food, or go back the way they came at the first opportunity. Encourage your pony-man to bring lots of extra fodder if you want to have a peaceful trek.

Routes to Tso Kar
● **Rumtse to Tso Kar (3-4 days)** From Rumtse follow the Kyamar Lungpa south-east to the 4900m/16,000ft Kumur La (Kiameri La on AMS map). From here either cross the Shibuk La or the Thatsang La (4900m/16,000ft) to take you down to Tso Kar. This is a far more interesting route than the two below but make sure you are fully acclimatised before crossing the Kumur La.
● **Km338 to Tso Kar (1-2 days)** Trek east to Tso Kar along the jeep road which leaves the Leh-Manali road at the 338km marker post.
● **Mahe to Tso Kar (3-4 days)** Follow the jeep road west from Mahe, past the hot springs in the Puga Valley, over Polokongka La (4950m/16,200ft) to Tso Kar.

Routes from Tso Kar to Tso Moriri
● **The jeep road (4 days)** The least inspiring route is to follow the jeep road east to Sumdo and then south to Tso Moriri.
● **Via the Polokongka La and Nakpo Gozing La (3 days)** Follow the jeep road as far as the Polokongka La and then head south-east to cross the 5000m/16,400ft Nakpo Gozing La (Nanak La on AMS maps). You then descend to rejoin the other jeep road just north of Tso Moriri.
● **Via Kyamayuri La (3-4 days)** From the south side of Tso Kar cross the 5400m/17,700ft Kyamayuri La. Then follow the Gyamsharma/Yan River to Tso Moriri, or head south over the Yalung Nyau La (5300m/17380ft) to Korzok, a route not marked on the AMS maps though it does exist.

Routes from Tso Moriri
In addition to the above three routes which can be reversed:
● **Korzok to Pang via Lanyer La; Gyama La; or Barma La (3-4 days)** One way to Pang from Tso Moriri is to trek north-west from Korzok across the Yalung Nyau La (not on AMS maps) and descend into the next valley. From here it's a big climb west over the 5700m/18,700ft Lanyer La into the

Zogoang Valley. Follow the valley north-west over the Thelakung La and descend through gorges to Pang. Two alternative passes to the Lanyer La are the Gyama La and the Barma La (see *Trekking Map of Ladakh*)

● **Korzok to Pang via the Phirse Phu (5-6 days)** Another possible route is to follow the western shore of Tso Moriri to its southern end before striking north-west up the Phirse Phu and then continuing as above up the Zogoang Valley.

● **Tso Moriri to Spiti (10-13 days)** This long and arduous route goes south from Tso Moriri, then south-west following the Para Chu to the glaciated Parang La (5600m/18,300ft). The trail descends to the village of Kibber in Spiti.

Route from Ladakh to Mt Kailas

For those trekkers who love to dream, there have been rumours in the last couple of years that the frontier post with Tibet, at Demchok, may be re-opened. This would allow pilgrims and possibly foreign tourists to reach Mt Kailas in Tibet, probably the world's most sacred mountain. Unfortunately these plans suffered another setback in 1998 when India and Pakistan carried out nuclear tests, increasing the tension once again between China and India. It looks as if this route will remain a dream for sometime yet.

ZANSKAR

Zanskar lies south of the Indus Valley and north of the Great Himalaya Range, its boundaries being loosely defined by the drainage basin of the Stod, Zanskar, Lungnak, Tsarap and Kargyak rivers. Rich in traditional culture and breath-taking landscapes, it remains a draw for trekkers who can put up with strenuous mountain days or long uncomfortable bus journeys to get to its isolated valleys.

Across Zanskar (15-21 days)   pp231-63

A classic trail crossing Zanskar from south to north, taking in some of its finest scenery from the Great Himalaya on the border with Lahaul to the jagged Zanskar Mountains in the north. The whole journey can be walked in 15 to 21 days if you keep your head down, but it seems a shame not to spend longer dawdling in villages, deviating up quiet valleys or scrambling up ridges and small peaks. If you haven't time to complete the whole trek it is possible to start or finish in Padum, the capital of Zanskar, which conveniently splits the route in half. The northern half takes 8-11 days while the southern stretch is marginally shorter taking 7-10 days.

Despite its popularity, it is not an easy trek. There are eight passes to cross between Lamayuru and Padum which gives this section a reputation for being particularly difficult. Those coming up from the south will find the Shingo La (5000m/16,400ft) a real test of their acclimatisation. The trek can be walked as soon as the Shingo La is free of snow; usually the end of June through to October. The snow disappears more quickly on the other passes.

● **Direction** The route can be walked in either direction. Pack animals and guides for small groups of trekkers can easily be arranged in Lamayuru, Padum and Darcha (or failing that, nearby Keylong).

● **The route** Starting from the south, the trek begins at the small village and road-side halt of Darcha on the Manali-Leh road, north of Keylong in Lahaul. From here you follow the Barai Nala upstream into the mountains to a pasture called Zangskar Sumdo. A tributary stream is followed to the Shingo La (5000m/16,400ft) amid fine mountain scenery. The trail drops into Zanskar to a beautiful high-altitude valley inhabited by marmots, wolves and grazing yak. Gentle walking takes you past the sheer-sided Gumburanjon Mountain to the first village, Kargyak. Several more small villages follow before the trail enters the Lungnak Gorge. Most trekkers make the side trip to the beautiful Phuktal Gompa suspended above the Tsarap River on a vertical cliff face, before continuing on to Padum.

The large village of Padum is joined by a rough and long road to the Suru Valley and Kargil (see warning p79). It is, therefore, a convenient place to start or finish your trek, or to stock up with more supplies to continue on foot into the mountains.

The second half of the trail continues past Karsha, the largest gompa in Zanskar, and then follows the Zanskar River downstream, heading gradually north. The first of the eight passes to be crossed between Padum and Lamayuru is the Parfi La, not too much of a struggle at 3900m/12,790ft. Beyond lies a corrugated landscape to test your stamina. Having crossed the Hanuma La (4700m/15,410ft), relax by the gompa in Lingshed before summoning strength to cross the Margun, Kiupa and Sengi passes. The latter is known as the Lion Pass and is the highest on this half of the trek at 4900m/16,070ft. Easy walking takes you over the Bumiktse La (4400m/14,430ft) to the spectacularly-located village of Potoksur, below a vast rock wall. The trail winds over the Sirsir La (4800m/15,740ft), down to Hanupata, and through a spectacular gorge to Phanjila and Wanla. A small canyon rises to the Prinkiti La (3700m/12,140ft) from which you descend to Lamayuru.

This is the standard route which the majority of trekkers follow. If you prefer to walk off the beaten track, there are several other trails which can be used as alternatives to some of the sections mentioned above. The trek can be started further north along the Leh-Manali road near Sarchu, and by crossing either the Phirtse La or Sarichan La you join the main trail near Kargyak. From Phuktal it is possible to continue up the Tsarap River to cross the Thongde La and down to Thongde, before following the road to Padum.

On the second half of the trek, you can walk up the east side of the Zanskar River, rather than the west, and join the main trail beyond Lingshed. Between Potoksur and Lamayuru there are two other options: one is to follow the gorges to Phanjila rather than via the Sirsir La and Hanupata; the other is to cross the Sirsir La and then continue west over the Snigutse La and descend down the Shillakong River.

● **Safety** You need a tent and basic supplies for each half of this trek. Padum has a few shops where it is possible to stock up on the basics (rice, dal, biscuits, noodles, kerosene etc) but don't expect the choice you would find in the Leh or Manali bazaars. Vegetables are sometimes hard to come by and petrol isn't available for your stove, unless you can persuade a taxi driver to siphon some out of his vehicle for you. If you are trekking in the main season (July and August) you should be able to buy some luxuries along the way. Most villages have opened a tea tent or a tea shop specifically for trekkers. Some entrepreneurs even set up tea tents at remote camp-sites where big trekking groups regularly stop for the night. These all offer simple sustenance (biscuits, noodles, chocolate, dal and rice, tea, beer, fruit juice) and Western trekking 'essentials' (lavatory paper and cigarettes).

An informal guest-house system is beginning to develop in a few villages along this route so that you can unroll your sleeping bag in a family home, tea shop or tea tent for a fee and be given a simple supper and breakfast. Some travellers have made the most of this, walking the route without a tent or cooking equipment. However, the villagers are under no obligation to let you stay with them and you should not expect this hospitality as a matter of course. You will spend several nights in remote places far from any villages and unable to guarantee any shelter or food. You must, therefore, come equipped for nights in the open and carry a few days' supplies. This option is definitely only for the hardy, at least until a more dependable system is established.

Considering you need to take over a week's food with you on either half of the trek, it makes sense to employ a guide and horses. A local guide would prove very useful on any of the alternative trails. If at all possible employ someone who is from Zanskar. The people of Zanskar are fed up with self-sufficient groups trekking through the valley year after year, using up the valuable grazing, leaving litter and disturbing their peaceful way of life without giving anything in return. If you are travelling independently in a small group it is possible to make amends. Rather than organising everything in Manali or Leh, wait until Lamayuru, Darcha or Padum to find a pony-man who comes from Zanskar. You will also be doing yourself a favour: Zanskaris know the region better; will probably own Zanskari horses which are renowned for their strength, endurance and climbing ability (far better than the often overworked ponies from Manali); are able to communicate in the local dialect; and will probably introduce you to friends and family along the trail. This, of course, doesn't deal with all the problems trekking causes, but by travelling sensitively (see Part 6) you can improve the situation.

High altitude is encountered early on whichever end you start and evacuation from this remote area is difficult. Particular care must be taken if you're starting in Darcha (3400m/11,150ft) and have just come from Manali (2050m/6730ft), as the process of acclimatising will have only just begun. Spend about two days in Darcha and please take it very slowly up to the Shingo La – there have been altitude-related fatalities here. Descending from the Shingo La into Zanskar should not be regarded as a safe option if you aren't fully acclimatised as you can only descend rapidly to about 4500m/14,760ft. It takes a couple of days' walking to drop below 4000m/13,120ft.

● **Pros and cons** This is one of the longest treks in the region and an exciting way to travel between Manali and Leh. You pass through a variety of Himalayan cultures and scenery from central Ladakh in the north to Lahaul in the south, while Zanskar itself has some fascinating villages and gompas.

Its length, plus several difficult and demanding sections, means that you need to be in good physical shape before setting off. It's also a very popular trek, particularly with large commercial groups; if you're looking for solitude avoid the peak season (mid-July to mid-August).

Padum to Zangla to Padum (3-4 days)

This is an easy trek around the principal villages of the Padum plain and central Zanskar. It is quite possible to walk this route without camping equipment by staying in village guest-houses or with villagers. The route goes up one side of the Zanskar River via Karsha and comes back the other via Zangla and Thongde. For route details, follow the appropriate sections in the Across Zanskar trek (p231).

Wild treks in Zanskar   pp264-5

The physical geography of Zanskar makes for some excellent adventurous treks. The high glaciated passes of the Great Himalaya Range to the south and the deep narrow gorges of the Zanskar Mountains are just some of the difficulties encountered. These routes are not for the inexperienced and this is one of the reasons detailed route descriptions were felt to be unnecessary. There is enough information here to nudge you into making the right decisions but, I hope, not so much that it detracts from the mystique of these trails.

The AMS U502 maps along with one or two of the other options (see p55) will help you find your way, but as always, there's no substitute for a local guide.

● **Zangla to the Markha Valley via the Jumlam (5-6, 9-11 days)** The trek takes five to six days from Zangla to the Markha Valley or nine to eleven days from Padum to the Indus Valley. Passing through uninhabited country, it has the reputation of being one of the hardest treks in the whole of Ladakh, and rightly so. Not only are there high passes to cross, but there are many complicated gorges to navigate, and over 100 stream crossings to be made. It is really only safe to attempt during September and October when the streams are at their lowest, before the winter cold sets in. If you attempted it any earlier you could get stranded in the gorges, unable to cross the raging torrents. It can get very cold as sunlight rarely penetrates as far as the gorge bottom. Pack animals can negotiate the route, although it is far from easy, with steep scree slopes and difficult river crossings to be negotiated. One section requires a squeeze through a $1^1/2$m gap which will be impassable to animals if the stream is running high. Walkers can take a very precipitous high route to avoid this; which is not an option for your ponies. Whether or not you take them, a local guide is essential. There is a complicated section through the gorges where it would be easy to become thoroughly lost.

● **Thongde to Phuktal to Padum (5-6 days)** Although this looks an appealing circuit, it is a hard trek with difficult river crossings and precipitous trails. Between the Thongde La and Shade there are numerous river crossings which may be impossible to cross before August. There are also difficult sections of trail across steep scree slopes and on paths built on to cliff faces. These can be difficult for pack animals. From the small gompa at Tantak the path heads south to Phuktal where you join up with the well-trodden trail back to Padum.

● **Phuktal to Leh-Manali road via Tsarap River (5-6 days)** A difficult route following the Tsarap River to the base of the Lachalang La on the Leh-Manali road. It makes an interesting alternative to the popular trail over the Shingo La to Darcha. The hardest section of trail is between the confluence of the Shade and Tsarap rivers and the village of Murshun where you spend between one and two days traversing cliffs high above the Tsarap River. The consequences of a slip here don't bear contemplating, so this is not a trek for those with unsteady feet. These steep slopes and several traditional suspension bridges made from ropes of twisted vegetation make it impossible to take pack animals along this route.

● **Zanskar's southern passes** Zanskar is usually approached from the west via the Pensi La, the north via the Sengi La, or the east over the Shingo La. There are also several rarely-used passes to the south over the Great Himalaya which provide exciting routes into or out of Ladakh for the adventurous trekker/mountaineer. All involve crossing glaciers and should only be attempted by those with the necessary mountaineering experience. Apart from the Kang La into Lahaul, these passes cross into the regions of Kashmir and Jammu, both of which are considered unsafe for foreign travellers because of militant activity (see warning p79).

● **Padum to Rangdum via Dibling (8-10 days)** This is a seldom-walked route running parallel to but north of the road over the Pensi La. The beginning of the route follows the main trail towards Lamayuru, as described in Across Zanskar (see p36). It then heads west from the Parfi La along a choice of trails, which all join up at the village of Dibling. The route continues over the Puzdong La to the Kanji Nala which descends to Rangdum.

● **The Zanskar River Gorge in winter – the Chadur (5-8 days – not covered in Part 7).** During the middle of winter, when the passes are blocked by snow, the only way in and out of Zanskar is along the frozen Zanskar River, between Hanumil and Chiling. This is a traditional trade route used by the Zanskaris every year to trade butter in Leh. It is a particularly hazardous journey with temperatures regularly below -30°C and on which the solidity of the ice can change rapidly. The route is possible only when the river is at its coldest, this is for about six weeks during January and February.

Since 1977 when James Crowden made the first recorded passage by a non-Ladakhi, several foreign expeditions have successfully completed the journey. It is becoming an increasingly popular objective and most winters now see one or two Western parties on the ice. If you are considering walking this route, do not underestimate the difficulties. It is a full-blown winter mountaineering expedition with many dangers for which you must be phys-

❏ The Chadur Route

The word *chadur* means blanket and is used to refer to the trek along the frozen Zanskar River. The most amazing thing about the frozen river is how unfrozen it is! Spring water prevents the blanket from completely smothering the river which in some places retains its rapids, all the more fearsome in temperatures of -30°C. On one traverse, we and our Zanskari companions removed gloves and hugged a blank wall, arms splayed, while the toes of our boots shuffled precariously along a 5cm-wide ledge of ice plastered on to the gorge wall. Everyone knew the consequences of a slip at that moment. Further up the gorge, flowing water had flooded the river's frozen crust. Boots and socks were removed to save them from becoming wet and then freezing, and the Zanskaris waded through the river, sliding numb feet over the treacherous ice, often razor sharp in places. Western feet are not so well accustomed to such punishment and so our laces were kept firmly tied. Speedily our Zanskari friends pulled their boots back on, laughing in the cold, and we shuffled along our icy path. **Ben Stephenson** (UK)

ically and mentally prepared. You need to be flexible with your time so that you can wait for the best conditions and should be aware that if the ice melts you could get stranded in the gorge. You must be completely self-sufficient as the villagers will not be able to spare any of their food which only just sees them through the winter. It would be madness to attempt this route without a Zanskari guide who knows whether the ice is safe, the location of caves and where the few escape routes are.

WESTERN LADAKH

Western Ladakh, the heartland of Ladakh's Muslim population, lies between the Fatu La and the Zoji La on the Leh to Srinagar road and includes the Suru, Drass and Wakha river valleys. It is a forgotten corner, largely ignored by trekkers and tourists alike who tend to concentrate on central Ladakh now that travel to Kashmir is discouraged (see warning p79). It is a beautiful region which deserves more attention. Magnificent wind-sculpted mountains surround the Wakha Chu and its tributaries, while the upper Suru Valley is dominated by Nun Kun (7135m/23,400ft), the highest mountain in the western Himalaya. For more routes in this area take a look at the Carte Artou/Editions Olizane map, *Ladakh – Zanskar*.

Rangdum to Heniskot, Lamayuru or Khalsi (4-7 days)   pp265-6

Although the Buddhist villages around the gompa at Rangdum, on the western side of the Pensi La are geographically in western Ladakh, the inhabitants consider themselves Zanskari. This route provides a much shorter way out of or into Zanskar than the well-travelled Lamayuru to Padum trail and may well be preferable to the tedious and uncomfortable bus journey. It's a little-used trail through remote country with some difficult sections and is best walked at the start of autumn when the streams are not so powerful.

For the first three days all the routes follow the same trail from Rangdum to Kanji. You then have to decide whether to drop down to the Leh-Srinagar road near Heniskot (four to five days); continue over the Yogma La and then follow the Shillakong stream to Lamayuru (six days); or from the Yogma La carry on over the Snigutse La to join up with the main trail to Padum. From here you can either follow this via Wanla to Lamayuru (six to seven days) or to the Leh-Srinagar road near Khalsi (six to seven days).

Panikhar to Parkachik (1 day)

Between the villages of Panikhar and Parkachik in the Suru Valley, the road from Kargil to Padum forms a large 'U' as it follows the Suru River around the base of a spur. For those not restricted to road travel there is a path which climbs across this spur by way of a small pass called the Lago La. From this summit there are wonderful views of Nun Kun, denied to those on the road. The whole walk takes about five hours and it is possible to pick up a lift from Parkachik to continue your journey to Padum. If you have time it is worth shunning mechanised transport, continuing to Rangdum on foot. This takes two days; the first follow the road for most of the way, while on the second you have the freedom to make your own way across the broad and beautiful upper Suru Valley, avoiding areas of boggy ground as best you can.

MOUNTAINEERING IN LADAKH

There are some excellent mountaineering objectives in and around Ladakh which have been well documented in the usual sources (see p57) and are beyond the scope of this book. However, one mountain has been included because it provides an ideal introduction to Himalayan mountaineering. In **good conditions**, the summit is within the grasp of experienced trekkers with basic mountaineering skills. This is Stok Kangri (6153m/20,188ft), also known as Kang La Cha. It is the highest peak visible south of Leh. Even if you have no desire to climb the mountain, a trek to advanced base camp makes an excellent three to four-day excursion amid impressive mountain scenery.

All over Ladakh there are lower peaks accessible to adventurous trekkers, which are typically passed without a second glance. If you have the time and energy, make the effort to climb them and be rewarded with spectacular views denied to those left in the valleys.

Unfortunately mountaineering has not escaped the jaws of Indian bureaucracy. Theoretically you need to apply to the Indian Mountaineering Foundation (IMF, see p57) at least three months before arriving in India for a permit to climb any peak in the Indian Himalaya, whether it's a 4000m bump or 7000m giant. The cost escalates with height and is biased towards large groups. It's the same price for two people as it is for twelve. Currently, peak fees for all mountains in Ladakh, except Stok Kangri, range from US$1500-4000.

Stok Kangri has been designated one of four 'trekking peaks' within India which means that it has a cheaper peak fee of US$300. Other costs for climbing the mountain are the same as any other peak: the expedition has to be accompanied by a liaison officer who must be provided with mountaineering equipment (US$500) and the expedition has to pay a non-returnable environmental levy of US$400. For more information on the paperwork and other rules and regulations contact the IMF. Some climbers get away without a permit each year and the general opinion in Leh is that if you are a small independent party, you are less likely to be noticed on the mountain. The main contributing factor for this permissiveness is the red tape and the length of time it takes to make arrangements.

Registered mountaineering guides can be hired through the trekking agencies in Leh for Rs600 per day.

Stok Kangri ascent (4 days minimum) pp266-8

● **Route** Most people ascend the mountain from the village of Stok, just south of Leh, which is served by several buses a day from the capital. A trail continues south from the village climbing steadily through a gorge and then out into open pasture where several camp-sites can be found. The gradient increases as you climb higher to the main base camp. There's a steep pull up onto a ridge and the advance base camp is situated among grand mountain scenery on top of the glacier's lateral moraine. A simple glacier walk takes you to the base of the mountain from where you have several options of ascent depending on your level of mountaineering competence.

Most people return to Leh along the same route but you could make an interesting round trip by crossing the Stok La (see p193) and descending to Spituk.

● **Safety** While not technically difficult, you will need to be proficient at using crampons and an ice axe on steep snow, relish ridge scrambling on snow and rock and be able to cross glaciers safely with knowledge of crevasse rescue techniques. Some may find the security of a rope reassuring both on the glacier and on the more exposed sections. Glacier glasses, good sun-block and warm clothes are also essential.

The real determining factors for your success are how well you have acclimatised and how good the conditions are. You must acclimatise slowly and properly while remembering that at this altitude conditions can deteriorate rapidly turning your ascent into a serious climb. Even in mid-summer you can sometimes get over a metre of snow, freezing winds and blizzard conditions that will wipe away any trace of your ascending footsteps. Coping with this at 6000m calls for a high level of experience.

If several parties have ascended before you, the route across the glacier will be obvious. If snow has obliterated their footsteps you will need enough mountaineering sense to make your own way safely across the glacier avoiding the crevasses. At all times you should be able to assess the possible dangers of rock-fall and avalanche on your climb to the summit and on your descent.

● **Pros and cons** Trekkers with mountaineering experience in glacial terrain will find little difficulty with this climb. Those unsure of their experience would be wise to hire a registered mountaineering guide through a trekking agency in Leh.

What to take

The sense of having one's life needs at hand, or travelling light, brings with it intense energy and exhilaration. Simplicity is the whole secret of well-being.
Peter Matthiessen *The Snow Leopard*

KEEP IT LIGHT

How much you take with you is a very personal decision. Some trekkers love to travel as light as the locals (rarely more than a shoulder bag), while others are only happy when they have countless bits of equipment for every possible occasion, most of which they'll never use. It takes experience to know what you'll find useful but if you are in doubt about anything on your list, be ruthless and leave it at home. Even if you are planning to hire ponies for your trek, you've still got to get your luggage to Ladakh. You'll find that you'll be much freer with a light pack as it allows you to wander easily around towns or to jump on a bus with the minimum of fuss. If you are going on an organised trek with a company from your home country, you'll be given an exhaustive equipment list when you book. How much you take is not so important since taxis or minibuses will be arranged to get you around.

BUYING GEAR

Equipping yourself for a trek can cost a considerable amount of money and if you don't really know what you are looking for, you can make expensive mistakes. There is no substitute for a knowledgeable mountaineering shop where all your questions can be answered by people who know what they are talking about. If this trek is not a one-off it's usually a false economy to go for the cheapest products. Stick to respected and well-known manufacturers and use price as a reasonably reliable guide to quality, although you should be careful not to buy something packed full of features that you are unlikely ever to need – they simply add cost and weight.

HOW TO CARRY IT

Backpackers will obviously need a **large rucksack** (65-80 litres capacity) in which to carry all their camping gear and food. This should have a stiffened back system and be fully adjustable for a perfect fit. The idea is to have the load high and close to the body with a large proportion of the weight carried on the hips by means of a padded hip belt. It's also handy to have a **bum/waist bag** or a light **day-pack** in which you can carry your camera, guidebook etc when you're sightseeing.

If you will be hiring ponies or going on an organised trek a **large hold-all** will do the job just as well as a rucksack when you are trekking but it's not quite as convenient for carrying your luggage around town or to the start of the trek. You'll also need a **day-pack** for carrying the things you need with you throughout the day, such as your camera, a water bottle, some food, waterproofs and a fleece or jumper. All this takes up quite a lot of room, so a day-pack of 30-40 litres will probably be about right.

Pack similar things (such as clothes, washing things, camping equipment) in separate **stuff-sacks** so that they are easier to pull out of the dark recesses of your rucksack. All of these can be put inside a **waterproof rucksack liner**, or tough plastic bag, which then slips inside your pack. Everything will then be well protected from rain or leaking kerosene, a hazard of Asian bus travel.

FOOTWEAR AND FOOT CARE

Boots

Your boots are probably the single most important item of gear that can affect the enjoyment of your trek. Most of the trails in Ladakh involve crossing fairly rough and steep ground from time to time. You should therefore look for a boot which provides good ankle support, has a reasonably stiff sole, has an upper which is substantial enough to provide protection from knocks, and is waterproof enough for crossing shallow streamlets and walking through late lying snow on high passes. If you are carrying your own pack you will need even more support. If you plan to climb Stok Kangri you'll need boots that are stiff enough to accept articulated crampons.

Leather boots are generally more supportive, offer greater protection, are more reliably water resistant (if regularly treated), and will last longer than Gore-tex or Sympatex fabric boots. However, the latter will be instantly comfortable, lighter and require less 'walking in' – the choice really depends on where your priorities lie. Whatever the material of the upper, you should have few problems if you choose a well-made, three-season hill-walking boot from a respected company.

The most important thing is to make sure they fit properly. When fitting boots, try lots of different makes and models, and wear the same socks as you would when walking. Make sure you have enough room in front of your toes (so that they don't keep hitting the end when you descend a steep slope), by pushing your foot forward in the boot before lacing up and checking that you can easily slide a finger down between your heel and the back of the boot. Then slide your foot to the back, lace them up and pace around the shop to get a feel of what they are like in action. If your heel lifts off they are too loose but if you feel pressure points they may be too tight. Before assuming they are the wrong size, try lacing them up in a different way. Once you've bought them, wear them in thoroughly before trekking; this is very important.

Insoles

Good quality boots either have a dual density sole or a shock-absorbing insert in the heel to reduce the effects of jarring with each step. However, insoles can be bought to reduce the shock even more and can be useful for taking up any excess room in the boot.

Socks

The traditional wearing of a thin liner sock under a thicker wool sock is no longer necessary if you choose a high quality modern sock specifically designed for walking. The ones with thick spongy pads around the ball and heel of the foot are particularly comfortable. Three pairs are ample.

Extra footwear

If you're hiring pack animals you can afford the extra weight of a pair of sports sandals. These are invaluable for crossing the countless streams you will come across and are good for lounging around camp. It also means you have an alternative to wearing your hiking boots in Delhi and Leh. Lightweight trainers are a good substitute.

Foot care

Keeping your feet dry and clean is the best way to keep them healthy and blister-free. When you stop for lunch, take off your boots and socks and pull the footbeds out of the boots so you can let everything dry in the sun. Washing your feet every evening will prevent any nasty fungus growing, so will keeping your socks reasonably clean. (See p277 for information on how to deal with blisters).

CLOTHES

There has been a revolution in outdoor clothing (in technology as well as in fashion) and finding an outfit that can cope with the wide range of conditions that you can expect in Ladakh (see p106) is easy and doesn't have to weigh a ton. Most trekkers pick their clothes according to the versatile layering system, which consists of a base layer to transport sweat away from your skin; a mid-layer or two to keep you warm; and an outer layer or 'shell' to protect you from the wind, rain and snow.

You must take care to wear clothes that don't offend the local people, see p157 for further guidance.

Base layer

This is the least exciting layer but is important if you want the system to work well. Too much moisture next to the skin is not only uncomfortable but can rapidly cool your body, making you feel cold. A cotton T-shirt, for instance, will absorb your sweat and trap it next to your skin. A thin thermal layer made from a synthetic material, on the other hand, will draw that moisture away and keep you dry. A thin and lightweight **thermal top** can therefore keep you cool and dry when worn on its own, modern designs being now styled with this in mind; or warm and dry when worn under other clothes. The other major advantages are that the material still feels warm when wet and it dries extremely quickly. This means that you can wash it often and let it dry on you if the weather is reasonably warm. Buy one with long arms and a collar if at all possible, as this will help keep the sun off. As this shirt will be worn all day every day it's nice to have something clean to put on in the evenings. Another thin thermal is ideal, but if your budget does not run to that, a light **cotton shirt** or T-shirt is useful.

Mid-layers
These layers provide the insulation and so anything that is warm will do. From July to late August a medium thickness **woollen jumper**, or a mid-weight **fleece top**, along with another thinner layer (a thin jumper or a light-weight fleece top) will suffice. If you really feel the cold or will be trekking at other times in the year, substitute the thinner of these layers with a **down jacket**. These are expensive but provide unbeatable warmth for very little weight. They are wonderful in the cold evenings and can substantially boost the warmth of your sleeping bag. A cheaper and less effective alternative is a fibre-pile jacket or pullover.

Outer layer
This is the final layer between you and the elements so it must be capable of keeping out the wind, rain and snow. The emphasis nowadays is on **jackets** made from waterproof, windproof and breathable fabrics, (such as Gore-Tex, Aqua Dry, Triplepoint Ceramic etc), which prevent the build up of conden-sation on the inside of the jacket. However, as this technology doesn't come cheap (£150/US$225 or more) and since it's unlikely to rain that much when you're in Ladakh, a cheaper neoprene or polyurethane-coated nylon jacket will suffice.

   If you go for the latter option then consider bringing a **windproof top** (made from Pertex or a similar fabric) as well, as these are highly breathable while keeping out the wind and protecting you from a light shower. They weigh next to nothing, take up hardly any room and can also be used as a rather inefficient but adequate towel. Many trekkers swear by an umbrella or poncho but as both become worse than useless in a high wind with driving rain or snow, their value in high mountains is limited.

Leg wear
It can get quite chilly at night and at high altitude, so a pair of thermal **longjohns** or thick tights is pretty much essential. Cotton trousers and skirts are easily bought or made up for you in India and are great for trekking. **Poly-cotton trousers** are even better as they are extremely light, hard wear-ing, relatively windproof and dry very quickly. Jeans should not be worn as they take ages to dry and can restrict movement.

   Many women find long **skirts** useful, as they are more culturally accept-able than trousers. They also have the advantage that they can double as a 'port-a-loo' when there aren't any bushes to crouch behind.

   A lightweight pair of **waterproof over-trousers** can help keep you warm as well as dry but is not vital, particularly if you've got quick-drying poly-cotton trousers.

Other clothes

A **sunhat** that protects the back as well as the front of your head and **sunglasses** which offer 100% UV protection are necessary to combat the strong sunlight during the day (glacier glasses with side protection flaps are useful when there's snow around). A warm **woolly hat** and a pair of warm mittens or **gloves** are welcome accessories for the cold evenings and cooler days. If you are prone to bathing in freezing streams bring a **swimsuit** – you must never swim or wash in the nude. **Towels** never dry when trekking and soon start to smell awful. Many trekkers find that a tea-towel, light sarong or even an item of clothing is just as handy and takes up far less room in your pack. A large **handkerchief** or bandanna has many uses from mopping your brow to keeping the sun off your neck. Don't forget your **underwear**! Three pairs are fine.

SLEEPING BAG

A good quality sleeping bag is indispensable as many guest-houses don't have blankets and the ones for hire in Leh are usually dirty and lacking in insulation. The temperatures plummet at night, even in Leh, so your bag should be warm. A three-season bag is fine for July and August, but if you are trekking before or after this you will find a four-season bag preferable, unless you have an excellent circulation. Any bag can be upgraded simply and cheaply by wearing more clothes when you're in it.

Down-filled bags are far superior to synthetic ones because though just as warm, a down bag will pack down smaller, will be much lighter and although more expensive will far outlast a synthetic bag. Their only drawback is that they lose most of their insulating properties when wet and take an age to dry; keep yours in a sealed plastic bag.

A cotton, silk or synthetic sleeping bag **liner** helps keep the bag clean and is useful on its own for Delhi's hot and humid nights.

TOILETRIES

Viewing the contents of many trekkers' rucksacks, you could be forgiven for thinking you were looking at a travelling pharmacist, rather than a lover of the great outdoors getting back to the simple things in life. Most toiletries (soap, shampoo, toothbrushes, toothpaste, loo paper, razors, sanitary towels and washing powder) can be bought in Delhi and Leh, so there is no need to worry about how much you need. A small amount of what you usually use should be ample: one bar of **soap** in a plastic container; a few sachets of **shampoo**; a small tube of **toothpaste** and a **toothbrush**; one roll of **loo paper** in a plastic bag, along with a **lighter** for burning after use (if the left-hand-and-water method does not appeal); a **razor** and a tiny bottle of **shaving oil** is much more compact than foam; **deodorant**; **tampons/sanitary towels**, bring plenty of your own as the local brands are antiquated; good quality **aftersun** and **lip balm** to combat the drying effect of the sun and dry air; a high factor **sun screen** or **sun block** is vital and should be liberally applied at high altitude (it's hard to find in India so bring enough); and finally **condoms/contraceptive pills**.

MEDICAL KIT

Deciding what to include in a medical kit for remote areas is never easy and no two people will agree. If you don't have much experience in this area have a look at a good book on the subject (see p53) or talk to an expert. The problems you're most likely to encounter are discussed in the health section on p271. The list below should be seen as a basic kit to which you may want to add.

If you're trekking with an organised group the company will probably have their own extensive medical kit. Check to see what it includes in case you want to bring along any extra items.

First aid

Ready-made **first aid kits** for outdoor activities are a sensible investment, as they solve the problem of deliberating about what to take and should include detailed and clear instructions on how to cope with the most common emergencies. If you want to make up your own, it should include **plasters/Band-Aids** for minor cuts; **Steri-strips** for closing larger wounds; **moleskin**, **Compeed** or **Second Skin** for blisters; **bandages** for holding dressings, splints and limbs in place, and for supporting a sprained ankle or a weak knee; various-sized **sterile dressings** for wounds; **non-adherent dressings** for burns; porous **adhesive tape**; **antiseptic wipes**; **antiseptic** cream and liquid (eg Dettol); **safety pins**; **tweezers**; **scissors**; and a **thermometer**.

Pills and potions

Bring **paracetamol** for treating mild to moderate pain and fever; **co-proxamol** for severe pain; **loperamide** (Imodium) for emergency relief of diarrhoea; *ciprofloxacin* and *metronidazole* for treating diarrhoea; *acetazolamide* (Diamox) for altitude sickness; and a broad-spectrum antibiotic such as *amoxycillin* for urinary tract, skin, sinus and throat infections. Don't forget your **anti-malarial** tablets and bring along a small amount of **insect repellent** to keep the mosquitoes away while you are in Delhi (the best available contains a high percentage of diethyl-toluamide – DEET). Some travellers like to bring **multi-vitamin tablets**, particularly if they fear they won't be eating healthily for a while; and **oral rehydration powder** can be useful if you become dehydrated.

Note that the drugs in italics need a doctor's prescription in the UK and USA. All these drugs are available in Delhi and you can usually buy the antibiotics in Leh. They are available without a prescription and are much cheaper than in the West. However, you should be warned that counterfeit drugs are not uncommon in India and it's therefore much safer to buy them in the West before you leave. Wherever you decide to buy them, you should have discussed your requirements with your doctor first, as these drugs have side effects and can be dangerous if taken by some individuals.

❏ **Alternative medical kit**
For those who wish to supplement their medical kits with some natural alternatives here are a few 'broad-spectrum' suggestions:
● **Tea-tree oil** – antiseptic/antifungal. Use for cleaning minor wounds, treating acne, athlete's foot, soothing bug bites etc.
● **Nutribiotic/citricidal** – antibiotic. Use tablets at onset of symptoms of any illness, or in low doses for strengthening immune system. Drops can be used for mouth-wash, face-wash, vegetable wash etc.
● **Echinacea** – strengthens general immunity when taken on a daily basis. Recommended to begin taking several months before starting travels. Can also take at onset of a cold or flu.
● **De-activated charcoal**, taken at onset of diarrhoea will concentrate foreign material in intestines and draw it out. Don't be alarmed by black stools as a result!
● A **combination supplement** of blue-green algae (eg *Spirulina*) and 'friendly bacteria' (eg *Lactobacillus acidophilus*) taken daily is recommended for strengthening immunity and preventing digestive ailments. Take a high dose of 'friendly bacteria' after a course of antibiotics to replace vital intestinal flora.
Elana Vollen (USA)

Aids avoidance kit

Important for anyone travelling to developing countries, the kit should be carried with you at all times to reduce the risk of your contracting blood-borne diseases. It contains syringes, needles and suture material and is designed to be given to a qualified person looking after you in an emergency. The kits are sold by travel clinics and some pharmacies in the West.

Water purification kit

No water in India can be considered safe to drink unless you have purified it yourself. The various methods are described on p271 and you should choose whichever appeals the most. **None of these treatments is available in Leh** (including iodine), so make sure you bring enough plus some extra in case of breakage or loss.

GENERAL ITEMS

Other essential items include a litre **water bottle** (see camping gear below); a watch with an **alarm** for catching those early buses; a **torch/flashlight**, head torches are the most convenient as your hands are left free (don't forget a spare battery and bulb, as Indian batteries are next to useless and tend to come only in AA and C sizes); a longlife **candle** (but take extreme care if using it in your tent – put it in a saucepan so that it won't set the tent alight if knocked over; keep a bottle of water and an open penknife handy so you can cut your way out of the tent if it does go up in flames); **matches** or a reliable **lighter**; **large and small plastic bags** (they aren't available in Leh) so you can pack out any rubbish you accumulate in the mountains; spare **boot**

laces or a length of **cord**; a **sewing kit**; a small **padlock** for locking your room with the knowledge that you are the only one with the key, and for safeguarding your luggage on buses; a **compass** for following some of the directions in this guide and for exploring off the beaten track; and a Swiss Army **penknife** which will become your friend for life.

There are lots of other odds and ends that some people find indispensable and others totally useless: a **frisbee** is a good way to integrate with the local kids and can also be used as a plate; **ski/trekking** poles can significantly decrease the stress on joints and the spine, especially if you are carrying your own pack (one manufacturer calculates a 250-ton reduction in an eight-hour hike), and they can also help you power over those high passes – whether you use one or a pair is up to you; some people find an **umbrella** useful to protect you against rain, wind, sun and fierce dogs, or as a walking stick; a **collapsible bucket** is convenient for washing clothes and yourself in the mountains without polluting streams; writing a **diary** is the best way to keep memories fresh; a paperback **book** will help you wile away the time on long bus journeys, as will pocket **games** or a pack of **cards**; and lastly, an **altimeter** is a fun if expensive way to disprove the heights I calculated for this book!

PHOTOGRAPHIC EQUIPMENT

Modern compact cameras are the answer for those who don't want to fuss with all the paraphernalia of an SLR or be lumbered with its weight. Those taking an SLR should restrict their equipment to a minimum to keep the weight down. Whatever your camera, treat it to a padded carrying case so that it is protected from all the knocks it will inevitably get. Bring a spare set of batteries as they are hard to come by in India. Lens tissues and a brush are vital in Ladakh's dusty and dry atmosphere and a polarising filter can be useful in the bright light. Slide and print film can sometimes be found in Leh, but as you have no idea how they have been treated it is better to bring all you need from home. Airport X-ray machines are generally considered safe in the West, but you should be more cautious in India. Airport officials are usually prepared to check film by hand; pack the canisters in a clear plastic bag so that they can see the contents. You could even consider leaving your camera at home – you'd be surprised how liberating it can be.

CAMPING GEAR

It's possible to arrive in Leh without any camping equipment and make do with what's available there (see p168). However, if you've got good equipment already, definitely bring it along with you, as it will perform far better than anything you can obtain in Leh.

Tent

As rain or light snow is quite possible, some kind of shelter is necessary. A few ultra-lightweight trekkers make do with a Gore-Tex bivi bag or a basha (a waterproof sheet that can be used to rig up a make-shift shelter), but a tent provides much more privacy, comfort and safety, and as most people hire ponies, weight is not the main importance. A three-season tent is fine for Ladakh in summer as heavy snowfall is very rare.

Sleeping mat
This is essential. Not only will it make sleep more comfortable but it'll also insulate you from the cold ground. Closed-cell foam mats are fine, but for the ultimate in five-star luxury try a Thermarest self-inflating pad.

Cooking equipment
If you are hiring a cook there's no need for this equipment, as he will either have his own, or you can buy it cheaply in the bazaar if he doesn't.

It is almost impossible to buy gas canisters in Leh or Delhi so you have to rely on either **kerosene** or **petrol** for fuel. As both are dirty and of low quality, you need a **stove** which can be easily cleaned and is fully maintainable in the field. One of the best on the market, which has proved its worth over the years, is MSR's XGK stove. Take along a **maintenance kit**, a small **funnel** for filling up the fuel bottle and some coffee **filter papers** for filtering the fuel (also useful for getting rid of sediment in river water). Buy good quality **fuel** and **water bottles**; cheap ones tend to leak.

Unless you enjoy knocking up cordon bleu meals in the wild, one **pan** and one **frying pan** that can double as a lid/plate is fine for two people. You'll also need a **mug**, **spoon** (more useful than a fork), **pan handle**, and a **wire scrubber** for the washing up (there's no need for washing up liquid). Bring along lots of **plastic food/freezer bags** for dividing up and storing your food.

MOUNTAINEERING EQUIPMENT

If you are planning to climb Stok Kangri you can equip yourself in Leh. Serviceable ice axes, rope and articulated crampons (make sure your boots are stiff enough to accept them) are all available; but if you need anything more specialised for harder climbs, bring your own.

MONEY AND DOCUMENTS

Travellers' cheques are the best way to carry your money as they are much safer than cash and you get a better rate of exchange in the banks. Buy cheques from a well-known company such as Thomas Cook or American Express in either US dollars or pounds sterling, as other currencies can be hard to change outside big cities. It's sometimes worth having cheques from two different companies as some banks don't accept every variety (for instance, the bank in Manali won't change Visa travellers' cheques).

A **credit card** can be useful in Delhi and for buying souvenirs elsewhere but there is nowhere in Leh to get cash advances on cards. Keep your **passport** with you at all times as there are several army and police checkpoints along the major roads and close to any border areas. If you are considering driving or riding a motorbike, bring an **international driving licence**.

All these things can be kept reasonably safe in a **money belt**, or a pouch that goes around your neck. You should, however, make photocopies of any important documents in case you do lose them.

FINDING OUT MORE

Books

● **Guidebooks** The best general guides to the whole of India are those from Lonely Planet and Rough Guides. Lonely Planet also publishes a more specific guide, *Indian Himalaya*, which has a section on Ladakh. For seeing the potential for trekking throughout the Himalaya you should get hold of Hugh Swift's wonderfully anecdotal *Trekking in Pakistan and India* (Hodder and Stoughton), or Lonely Planet's *Trekking in the Indian Himalaya*. Two guidebooks published by Artou are *Hiking in Zanskar and Ladakh* by Chabloz and Cremieu, which contains 13 separate treks throughout the region written on individual pull-out sheets, and *Ladakh, Zanskar* by Charles Genoud, which is a good introduction to the region. Both of these books can usually be bought in Leh if you have difficulty finding them in the West.

● **Flora and fauna** The only guide directly relevant to the area is *The Wildlife of Ladakh* by JN Ganhar which you are unlikely to find outside India. Ornithologists will find the various books by Salim Ali useful: *Indian Hill Birds* (Oxford University Press)*; A Pictorial Guide to the Birds of the Indian Sub-continent*; and *Field Guide to the Birds of the Eastern Himalayas*), or Charles Vaurie's *Tibet and its Birds*. *The Book of Indian Animals* by SH Prater is good for identifying mammals, as is *Mountain Monarchs – Wild Sheep and Goats of the Himalaya* by GB Schaller. *Stones of Silence* by the same author is a fascinating account of his various expeditions to the Himalaya to study the wildlife and reveals much about the natural wealth of the region. The best book for the botanist is *Concise Flowers of the Himalaya* by Oleg Polunin and Adam Stainton (Oxford University Press).

● **Phrasebooks** *Getting Started in Ladakhi* by Rebecca Norman (Melong Publications) is the best introduction to the language and is widely available in Leh. Those wanting to delve deeper may like to try the *Ladakh-English-Urdu dictionary* by Abdul Hamid which is also available in Leh. Lonely Planet's *Hindi/Urdu phrasebook* is very useful for the rest of India.

● **Medical books** Trekking in Ladakh can take you a long way from medical help and although only large-scale expeditions can afford to take extensive medical supplies, even the lightweight backpacker can carry a book which will help diagnose the more common medical emergencies. One of the most detailed self-help books on the subject is *Medicine for Mountaineering and Other Wilderness Activities* by James Wilkerson (The Mountaineers), but at half a kilogram it's a little on the heavy side for the backpacker.

With the weight factor in mind, Drs Jim Duff and Peter Gormly have written the superb *Himalayan First Aid and Survival Manual* which is small and light enough to slip unnoticed into a pocket, but weighty enough in content to help you manage most accidents and illnesses which you may encounter trekking. What's more, profits go to a Himalayan environmental project and the price is low – about £3/US$5/A$6. For more information and for ordering: in Europe contact Paul Braithwaite (UK ☎ 0161-627 5036, 🖹 0161-627 5590, 🖳 vertaccess@aol.com); in USA and Canada contact Denis Guay (Canada ☎ 418-833-6064, 🖹 418-835-5415, 🖳 emiiil@total.net); in Australasia contact Jim Duff (Australia ☎ 02-6653 4241, 🖹 02-6655 0266, 🖳 duffbel@omcs.com.au, www.users.omcs.com.au/duffbel).

Another excellent little book that takes up hardly any room in your pack is Stephen Bezruchka's *Altitude Illness – Prevention and Treatment* (Cordee), which makes diagnosing this potentially lethal sickness relatively easy.

● **Other books** One of the most readable and informative books on Ladakh's history and culture is Janet Rizvi's *Ladakh – Crossroads of High Asia* (Oxford University Press). If you are after a detailed guide to the main monasteries in Ladakh and Zanskar get hold of *The Cultural Heritage of Ladakh* by David Snellgrove and Tadeusz Skorupski. *Himalayan Buddhist Villages* by John Crook and Henry Osmaston (obtainable from the University of Bristol, UK) is an impressive book resulting from a holistic study of the environment and culture of Zanskar. For those wanting an in-depth explanation to the landscape and way of life they see around them in Zanskar and much of Ladakh, this book is unbeatable.

A fascinating and important book is *Ancient Futures – Learning from Ladakh* (Rider). This is written by the founder of the Ladakh Project (see p56), Helena Norberg-Hodge, who paints a vivid picture of traditional Ladakhi culture and describes how this is being changed by inappropriate modernisation. The example of Ladakh is used throughout the book to challenge the Western notion of development and to point a way towards a more compassionate and sustainable way of living.

One of the best known travel books to the region is *A Journey in Ladakh* by Andrew Harvey (Picador), which is as much about the author's spiritual journey as it is about his travels. *Zanskar – the hidden kingdom* by Michel Peissel, describes a trek the author made through the region soon after Zanskar was opened to foreigners in the mid-1970s. Another trek across Zanskar from Darcha to Padum is described in Mike Harding's *Footloose in the Himalaya* along with many fine photographs. *Nomads of Western Tibet – the survival of a way of life* by Melvyn Goldstein and Cynthia Beall (University of California Press) is a fascinating book on the lifestyle of the Chang Tang nomads and much of the information, as well as many of the superb photographs, are in their article in *National Geographic* (June 1989). *The Yogins of Ladakh* by John Crook and James Low (Motilal Banarsidass, Delhi) is an account of the authors' adventurous travels in Ladakh which unlocks many of the spiritual secrets of this part of the Himalaya.

William Moorcroft and George Trebeck's *Travels in the Himalayan Provinces of Hindustan and the Panjab* is the classic account of what Ladakh was like in the early 19th century, while *Himalayan Tibet and Ladakh* by A Reeve Heber and Kathleen Heber, *The Himalayan Letters of Gypsy Davy and Lady Ba* by Robert and Katherine Barrett, and *Peaks and Lamas* by Marco Pallis are all interesting accounts of treks at the beginning of the 20th century. Further exploits of the extraordinary and sometimes eccentric early explorers of the western Himalaya can be read in *When Men and Mountains Meet* by John Keay.

There are several coffee-table books full of wonderful photographs of the region, most of which you can buy in Delhi or Leh. Olivier Follmi's photographs are hard to beat and he has several books on the region: *Zanskar – a Himalayan Kingdom* is the most widely available.

If you've enjoyed Ladakhi cuisine on your travels and wish to recreate some of the dishes back home, buy a copy of *Ladakhi Kitchen* by Gabriele Reifenberg (Melong Publications) while in Leh – many of the recipes are delicious and translate well to a Western kitchen.

Maps
Even the most detailed route descriptions in this book have been designed to be used alongside large-scale sheet maps of the area. These will not only be useful if you want to explore further afield but would become vital if you are forced by circumstance to change your itinerary.

For navigation purposes the **US Army Map Service (AMS) series U502 (1:250,000)** is by far the best. The maps are not entirely accurate and certainly very out of date, being based on surveys conducted in the 1920s, 30s and 40s, so many of the new roads are not marked. They do however, have contours and the position of most villages, trails and rivers are accurately marked. Most of the treks are included on sheets NI 43-8 *Leh* and NI 43-12 *Martselang*, but you may also need NI 43-11 *Anantnag* and NI 43-7 *Kargil* for western Zanskar, and possibly NI 43-16 *Palampur* for the southern end of the 'Across Zanskar' trek. Sheets NI 44-9 *Pangong Tso* and NI 44-13 *Tso Morari* could be useful if you wanted to explore these two lakes. A few of the maps in this series are currently out of print. You may be able to obtain photocopies of these from a specialist map library; in the UK try the Royal Geographical Society (see below).

Carte Artou/Editions Olizane publish a good overview map, *Ladakh – Zanskar* (1:350,000), which covers the most popular treks and some less-known routes. However, it has no coverage of Nubra, Pangong or Rupshu. It is based on a Landsat image so it accurately portrays physical features, making it a very useful navigation tool alongside the sometimes misleading AMS maps. The same map is also published by Nelles Verlag if you have difficulty finding it under the former publisher.

Another very useful map is the *Trekking Map of Ladakh* by Sonam Tsetan and Henk Thoma (no scale given but roughly 1:350,000) which can be bought with a useful accompanying booklet. This is a very comprehensive and accurate portrayal of most of the known trails and is particularly detailed for central Ladakh, Rupshu and Zanskar, but has no coverage of western Ladakh. At present it is available only in Leh, so make it one of your first purchases there, especially if you are considering anything off-beat.

One of the above is all that's required if trekking along a popular route, but if you are planning to explore some of the lesser known trails I would use the AMS maps in conjunction with one or both of the others – they all complement each other well. Until the rumoured large scale Indian army maps are declassified you'll just have to put up with the extra weight in your backpack.

Another series is the **Leomann Trekking Maps** which at 1:200,000 offer the largest scale available. They include brief trekking information on the reverse side, mark the principal trekking routes and name most of the mountains, but they are not entirely accurate as to trails or the position of villages and they don't include contours. The relevant sheets are: Sheet 2 – *Kargil, Zanskar and Nun Kun Area*; Sheet 3 – *Nubra Valley, Leh and Zanskar Area*; and Sheet 5 – *Kulu Valley, Parbati Valley and Central Lahaul*.

If your local travel bookshop can't obtain any of these maps try Stanfords in London (☎ 0171-836 1321, 🖷 0171-836 0189), who have a mail order facility.

India tourist offices

The Government of India's foreign tourist offices are good for general background information and glossy brochures: **Australia** (☎ 02-9264 4855) Level 2, Piccadilly, 210 Pitt St, Sydney, NSW 2000; **Canada** (☎ 416-962-3787) 60 Bloor St West, Suite 1003, Toronto, Ontario M4W 3B8; **France** (☎ 01-45 23 30 45, 🖳 info.fr@India-Tourism.com) 11-13 Bis Boulevard, Haussmann, 75008 Paris; **Germany** (☎ 069-242 9490, 🖳 info@India-Tourism.com) Baseler Str 48, 60329, Frankfurt-am-Main 1; **Israel** (☎ 03-510 1407, 🖳 info.il@India-Tourism.com) Sharbat House E5, 4 Kaufman Street, Tel Aviv 68012; **Italy** (☎ 02-80 49 52, 🖳 info.it@India-Tourism.com) 9 Via Albricci, Milan 21022; **Netherlands** (☎ 020-620 8991, 🖳 info.nl@India-Tourism.com) Rokin 9-15, 1012 KK, Amsterdam; **Spain** (☎ 01-345 7339, 🖳 info.es@India-Tourism.com) Avenida Pio XII 30-32, Madrid 28016; **Sweden** (☎ 08-21 5081, 🖳 info.se@India-Tourism.com) Sveavagen 9-11, 157, Stockholm 11157; **UK** (☎ 0171-437 3677/8) 7 Cork St, London W1X 2AB; **USA** (☎ 212-586-4901, 🖳 www.tourindia.com) 1270 Avenue of Americas, Suite 1808, New York, NY 10020; (☎ 213-380-8855) 3550 Wilshire Blvd, Room 204, Los Angeles, California 90010.

Organisations

● **International Association for Ladakh Studies** (c/o Francesca Merritt, Hon Membership Sec, 254 West End Rd, Ruislip, Middlesex, HA4 6DX, UK; 🖳 ibm.rhrz.uni-bonn.de:80/~upp701/IALShome.html) provides contacts between all who are interested in the study of Ladakh, disseminates information about research and publications, and publishes *Ladakh Studies*, an occasional newsletter with information on Ladakh.

● **International Society for Ecology and Culture (ISEC)/Ladakh Project** (UK: ☎ 01803-868650, 🖷 01803-868651, Apple Barn, Week, Totnes, Devon

TQ9 6JP; or USA ☎/🖹 510-527 3873, PO Box 9475, Berkeley, CA 94709, USA; 🖥 www.ecovillages.org/india/ladakh/). ISEC is a small international organisation which seeks to promote sustainability and community regeneration in various countries throughout the world, both North and South. Through campaigns, videos, books, seminars and local community groups, ISEC raises awareness of the social and environmental impact of economic globalisation and explores long-term systemic solutions. Much of their work has been carried out over the last 20 years in Ladakh where they have worked to support methods based on Ladakh's own values and its human-scale economy. One of their achievements was the setting up of LEDeG (see p132). Part of this 'counter-development' work is a Farm Project run in association with the Women's Alliance of Ladakh, which allows Westerners to experience and support Ladakhi life by working on Ladakhi farms. Contact ISEC for more information on this and other volunteer opportunities.

Mountaineers and adventurous trekkers may find the libraries, journals, expedition reports and information services provided by the following organisations helpful:
● **Alpine Club**, (☎/🖹 0171-613 0755, 🖥 sec@alpine-club.org.uk, www.alpine-club.org.uk), 55/56 Charlotte Rd, London, EC2A 3QT.
● **British Mountaineering Council**, (☎ 0161-445 4747, 🖹 0161-445 4500, 🖥 info@thebmc.co.uk, www.thebmc.co.uk), 177-179 Burton Rd, Manchester, M20 2BB.
● **Himalayan Club**, c/o Mr JC Nanavati (President), Eastern Bunkerers Ltd, Scindia House, Ballard Estate, Mumbai, 400 001, India.
● **Indian Mountaineering Federation (IMF**, ☎ 011-467 1211, 🖹 011-688 3412, 🖥 indmount@del2.vsnl.net.in, www.indmount.com), Benito Juarez Rd, Anand Niketan, New Delhi, 110 021.

❑ **Websites**
In addition to the sites mentioned in the main text, check out some of the following. Two of the most useful sites for practical information concerning the whole of India and containing many links are: **www.mahesh.com** and **www.tourindia.com**. For up to date news try **www.timesofindia.com**.
    Two well-produced websites devoted to the Himalaya with informative sections on Ladakh alongside good pictures can be found at **www.geocities.com/Yosemite/5112/index.html** and **library.advanced.org/10131/start.shtml**.
    There is usually some up to date travel information on Lonely Planet's 'Thorn Tree'. Their 'Destination Indian Himalaya' is also worth a look. Both these sites can be found at **www.lonelyplanet.com**.
    Updated information for this guide will be placed on the Trailblazer site at **www.trailblazer-guides.com**. If you notice any changes we'd like to hear from you at info@trailblazer-guides.com.

• **Royal Geographical Society**, (☎ 0171-591 3000, 📄 0171-591 3001, 🖳 info@rgs.org), 1 Kensington Gore, London, SW7 2AR.
• **The International Mountaineering and Climbing Federation (UIAA)** (☎ +41-31-370 1828, 🖳 UIAA@compuserve.com, www.mountaineering.org), Postfrach, CH – 3000 Bern 23, Switzerland.

Health precautions and inoculations

Travelling to Ladakh does not necessarily involve greater risk to your health than life in the West, but many of the hazards that you may be exposed to will be different from those you're used to dealing with. Most risks are totally avoidable – it's simply a matter of learning what they are and taking the relevant precautions.

WHO SHOULD AVOID HIGH ALTITUDE TREKS?

Travel to Ladakh demands a little more respect than many other high-altitude destinations because the whole region is considerably higher to start with (all above 2600m/8860ft). Therefore there is no way of reaching lower altitudes without going over a high pass first. In addition to this, when you are on your trek, you will almost certainly be several days away from the nearest hospital (Leh, Kargil or Manali). People in reasonably good health should not get alarmed by this but the altitude and lack of medical facilities can create problems for certain groups. If you have a medical condition such as high blood pressure, heart or lung disease, before going you should get the advice of a doctor who is familiar with the effects of altitude.

Infants and young children are more likely to be susceptible to altitude than adults and it is usually recommended that if they are to go above 3000m or 10,000ft, there should be a means of getting them rapidly and easily to lower altitude if the need arises. As this is not possible anywhere in Ladakh it is best to find a more suitable destination. Teenagers are also more at risk than adults and should allow a few extra days for acclimatisation.

People on specialist medication should check with their doctor before travelling to altitude. Probably the greatest risk is not being able to replace your medication should you lose it or run out. If you have any niggling complaints that are worrying you, get them examined by a doctor before you go, if only to put your mind at rest. The effects of altitude on pregnancy are not known but if you are at all concerned it is better not to go.

PRE-TREK PREPARATIONS

Getting fit – before or during your trek?

Being fit will not lessen your chances of getting altitude sickness, in fact it may well increase the risk as fitter people are more likely to climb higher and faster than those who aren't so well prepared. Having said that, you will enjoy your trek far more if you are in good physical shape. Walking for up to seven hours a day each day is demanding anywhere in the world but in high mountains it is even more so. Anyone going trekking in Ladakh will greatly benefit from an exercise programme starting about three months before going. If you are used to a sedentary life, start gently, build up gradually and try to get out every other day for at least 20 minutes. Any exercise will do: swimming, jogging, aerobics, cycling are all good, but the best of all is to go for long walks in hilly country.

Plenty of people go trekking with no physical preparation at all, but should you spend your whole holiday in agony you've only yourself to blame. If your body is used to a bit of exercise before you leave, you can build on this throughout the trek and come home feeling wonderfully fit and healthy.

Visit your dentist
Few people think about their teeth before going away, but as dental care in Ladakh is rudimentary and dental problems can develop because of the altitude, (the lower pressure can cause air in cavities to expand), you would be well advised to have a check-up before you leave. Allow enough time for any treatment that may be necessary.

INOCULATIONS

Officially you do not need any inoculations before entering India unless you have just come from a country where yellow fever is endemic (Africa and South America). You would be very unwise, however, not to get yourself vaccinated against some of the diseases listed below.

Up to date information on the recommended vaccinations for Delhi and Ladakh is best got from specialist travel clinics who are usually better informed than your local doctor. As they keep most vaccines in stock they can provide on-the-spot inoculations. **British Airways** have travel clinics throughout the UK (☎ 0800-600900 for the nearest), or try **Trailfinders** in London (☎ 0171-938 3999, 194 Kensington High St). Prices vary, so shop around and compare the prices of travel clinics with those at your local doctor's surgery.

As some inoculations cannot be given at the same time and others need boosters to be fully effective, you should start making enquiries about two months before you leave. Make sure the inoculations are recorded in a booklet which you should be given at the time.

● **Hepatitis A** This is prevalent in areas of poor hygiene and it is essential that you are vaccinated against it. The newer vaccine, Havrix, gives long term immunity (up to 10 years) and is less painful than the gamma-globulin injection, but it is more expensive and requires two initial injections and a booster a year later. Gamma-globulin should be given as close to the departure date as possible and will last for two to six months depending on the size of dose.

● **Typhoid** This disease is caught from contaminated food and water and is prevalent in India. Vaccination is highly recommended.

● **Meningitis** Epidemics of this disease regularly break out in India and so vaccination is recommended.

● **Tetanus-diphtheria** A low dose diphtheria vaccine is now available combined with tetanus. You should check that your protection against both of these easily-preventable diseases is up to date. You may need a booster before you travel.

● **Polio** Boosters are recommended every 10 years so check your records.

● **Rabies** There is a minimal risk of being bitten by a rabid animal and you may wish to consider the vaccination, particularly if you are going for a long time. The course of three injections is expensive and you will still need a course of follow-up injections should you get bitten.

● **Cholera** The vaccination gives only limited protection and is not necessary unless you are travelling on to a country which demands evidence of vaccination on entry.

Malaria prophylaxis

This serious and potentially fatal disease is caused by a parasite that is transmitted to humans by the bite of an infected *Anopheles* mosquito. Malaria transmission does not take place above 2000m or 6500ft, so Manali and Ladakh are theoretically safe. Unfortunately, malaria is prevalent in Delhi and lowland India, so you will be exposed to the risk while you travel to Ladakh. Delhi airport, in particular, is noted for its clouds of mosquitoes.

Anti-malarial drugs are a sensible precaution against the disease. The drug of choice for different areas changes as the parasite becomes resistant to the drugs; check which is being recommended before you leave. It is essential that you begin taking the drugs one week before entering a malarial zone and for four weeks after leaving it. It is, therefore, highly likely that you will have to continue taking the drug throughout your stay in Ladakh, in order to ensure that you are still protected when you go back to the lowlands. As the drugs can cause nausea they are best taken last thing at night.

Anti-malarials are not 100% effective, so it is vital that you take adequate precautions to avoid being bitten. The *Anopheles* mosquito is active only between dusk and dawn, so you should cover up as much of your body as possible during those times and use a powerful insect repellent on any exposed skin.

TRAVEL AND HEALTH INSURANCE

Trekkers should seriously consider a combined travel/health insurance cover. Some companies rate trekking in the Himalaya as a hazardous sport which will mean you won't be covered if you haven't paid an extra premium; check this before you part with your money. Also ensure that you are covered for emergency helicopter evacuation. The military helicopters which operate emergency airlifts won't leave the ground unless they are guaranteed payment of their operational costs (see p279). In view of this, it is also wise to register with your embassy in Delhi as they will often be contacted to see if anyone will cover the cost.

For further health information, see p271-80.

PART 2: INDIA

Facts about the country

GEOGRAPHICAL BACKGROUND

India's 3,287,590 sq km can be split into three distinct geographic zones. Running across the far north of the country, along the borders of China, Nepal and Bhutan, are the mountains of the Himalaya, which effectively separate most of India, excluding Ladakh, from the Tibetan Plateau. South of this mighty mountain range is the Indo-Gangetic plain which stretches from Pakistan in the west to Bangladesh and Burma in the east, while encompassing the Thar Desert and the drainage basins of the River Indus (mostly in Pakistan but from which India derives its name), the River Ganges and the Brahmaputra River. To the south of this is the huge Deccan Plateau which is flanked by two lines of hills called the western and eastern Ghats.

CLIMATE

The climate of most of India, apart from Ladakh (see p106) and to a lesser extent Lahaul and Spiti, is governed by the monsoon. This arrives in the south-west of India at the end of May and slowly moves up the country reaching the north by July. Although it rains heavily, it doesn't rain incessantly, with most areas getting one or two heavy downpours a day interspersed with bright sunshine. The south-west monsoon begins to withdraw in September, then follow a few months of comfortably cool weather between October and January. This is the best time to visit anywhere south of the Himalaya, although the extreme south-east of the country is affected by a brief north-east monsoon. The heat increases from February to May, when it's almost intolerable – temperatures of 40°C and above are common, and everyone awaits the beginning of the monsoon to start the cycle again.

HISTORICAL OUTLINE

The people in the Indus Valley (now in Pakistan) formed India's first important civilisation. This incredibly ordered and stable culture survived for 1000 years before its rapid decline in the wake of the Aryan invasion in about 1500BC. It was during this Aryan civilisation that Hinduism evolved, although during the following Mauryan Empire (321BC to 184BC) and the beginning of the Gupta dynasty (4th-6th century AD) it was largely superseded by Buddhism, until Hinduism gained many followers once again at the end of the Gupta era.

Muslim raiders invaded northern India in the 12th century and managed to unify much of India from their sultanate in Delhi. A subsequent Muslim invasion heralded the beginning of the great Mughal Empire (1526-1761), and the start of a golden age for building, arts and literature, as epitomised by the Taj Mahal. It was during this era that various Europeans began to arrive: the Portuguese, British, French, Danes and Dutch. As the Mughal Empire began to collapse, the British East India Company and the French started to fight for a hold on Indian trade. British supremacy was established in 1757 after Robert Clive's victory at the Battle of Plassey.

British India

Throughout the next century power gradually moved from the East India Company to the British government. Those areas directly controlled by the new imperial power became known as British India, while the rest was administered by a number of compliant Indian princes.

Among the achievements of British India were the creation of a stable system of government and law, and a massive rail infrastructure. However, their main raison d'être for colonising the country was to increase wealth for the British Empire. Their trading arrangements had a damaging effect on the Indian economy by allowing British goods into India duty free while imposing high tariffs on Indian exports to Great Britain. Other policies helped to create a landless population of peasants in many parts of the country, and these, coupled with the widespread enforcement of English as the main administrative language, provoked social and political unrest. The Indian Mutiny of 1857-59, also known as the First War of Independence, in which about 35,000 Indian soldiers rebelled, developed into a bitter war between the British and the Indians. When the conflict was finally resolved, the East India Company handed its remaining administrative powers over to the British government. There then followed a slow transition of more and more power to the Indian people. In 1919 an elected parliament was formed, which allowed the Indian National Congress greater freedom to demand home rule. This independence movement gathered momentum under Mahatma Gandhi's non-violent policy of civil disobedience, which led to his frequent imprisonment. Congress was not prepared to support Britain during WWII unless demands for independence were met.

Independence

Independence finally came in 1947 but not without bloodshed. The majority of Muslims, under the leadership of the Muslim League, wanted a separate state for themselves. The problems of such a split were immense but as no other solution seemed possible the creation of Pakistan was reluctantly approved. Millions of Hindus and Muslims moved east and west across the border and in the bloody process about 500,000 people were slaughtered. The maharaja of one of the last remaining princely states, Kashmir, couldn't decide whether to join India or Pakistan, and it wasn't until he was pressed by their two advancing armies that he chose India. Ever since, the region has been the scene of conflict between the two countries, Pakistan claiming it is geographically and culturally theirs with its mainly Muslim population, while the Indian government believes it legitimately and politically belongs to India. The militants' demands have now escalated to one of complete independence for Kashmir from both India and Pakistan, one that is not popular with either nation.

This intractable problem still simmers away, made worse by the likely funding and arming of Kashmiri militants by Pakistan, unconfirmed reprisals by the Indian military, and a series of nuclear tests carried out by both sides in 1998. In May 1999 there was an upsurge in hostilities between the two countries and Pakistan shot down two Indian MiG fighter planes.

Modern India

India's prime ministers, Jawaharlal Nehru, Indira Gandhi and Rajiv Gandhi have all been dogged by the inherent difficulties of dealing with the world's second largest population of over 970 million people in a country where 40% of the world's most desperately poor people live, surrounded by economic difficulties, inefficient administrations, corruption and the continued threat from separatist and terrorist organisations. This is, however, a country that can feed its rapidly expanding population without relying on outside help, is the tenth greatest industrial power and, perhaps most significantly, is the world's largest democracy.

After a succession of fragile coalition governments, India is now led by the right-wing Bharatiya Janata Party under Prime Minister Atal Bihari Vajpayee.

RELIGION

All the world's major religions can be found in India. As well as about 700 million Hindus there are approximately 100 million Muslims, 20 million Christians, 18 million Sikhs, 6.5 million Buddhists and several other minor religious groups including Jains and Zoroastrians.

Hinduism

Hinduism has developed from about 5000 years of continuous cultural evolution. As a result it has no formal creed but has instead absorbed much wider influences, including those of Christianity, Islam, Buddhism and Sikhism and is, therefore, one of the most tolerant of religions in theory if not in practice.

Central to Hinduism is the belief in *karma* – the sum of your life's good and bad actions that determines whether you'll be reincarnated at a higher or lower level of life, a rich businessman or an ant. Hindus also adhere to a rigid caste system. The four main castes consist of the **Brahmins** at the top, traditionally the priestly caste; **Ksatriyas** or warriors; **Vaisyas**, the merchants; and **Sudras**, the serfs and artisans. Outside these castes are the 'untouchables' or **Dalits**, who carry out menial and unclean chores.

Countless rebirths lead to eventual release, or *moksha*, from the constant cycle. However, depending on your karma, you can as easily move further away from moksha with each life as closer towards it. Hindus, therefore, try to increase their karma in a variety of ways: by good deeds, through meditation or asceticism, or by worshipping a popular god. The three main gods (*Trimurti*) are **Brahma** the creator, **Vishnu** the preserver and **Shiva** the destroyer and god of reproduction. Most Hindus are either Vaishnavites following Vishnu or are Shaivites following Shiva.

Buddhism

Buddhism is more of a philosophy for life than a religion as it does not worship a god. It was founded in the 6th century BC in north-east India by the Indian prince Gautama Siddhartha who was later given the title, Buddha, or awakened one. He was brought up in a life of royal luxury but by his late twenties had become disenchanted with this indulgent lifestyle.

Endeavouring to find the reasons behind the endless suffering of human life, he abandoned his wife and son to become an ascetic. For six years he deprived himself of all comforts until he eventually came to the realisation that this, too, was not the path to real happiness. He sat down alone under a banyan tree in what is now Bodhgaya in Bihar to meditate on his predicament. In meditation he discovered the Middle Way, moderation in all things, and in so doing attained enlightenment. For the rest of his life he taught the principles of enlightenment, *dharma*, to his disciples around northern India.

The Buddha's teachings Central to Buddhism is the belief that all living things can reach enlightenment. Unfortunately we are all tied to the endless wheel of existence and therefore, through reincarnation, are stuck in a cycle of rebirth. Like Hindus, Buddhists also believe that karma determines your next life. The only way to be set free from constant rebirth is to cease to desire, for it is desire that makes us permanently dissatisfied. If we cannot obtain what we desire we are unhappy, but if we get what we desire we soon grow bored with it and turn to something else. This is inevitable because, as the Buddha taught, all things are impermanent, including ourselves.

The Four Noble Truths These are: that life is characterised by suffering; that desire causes this suffering; that it is possible to bring an end to this suffering; and that this can be achieved by following the Eight-Fold Path of right understanding, right thought, right speech, right action, right livelihood, right effort, right mindfulness and right meditation.

By thorough comprehension of the Four Noble Truths we can gain enlightenment and reach *nirvana*, a state in which we are free from the cycle of rebirth and in which desire and the self are annihilated.

Theravada and Mahayana Buddhism Over its long history Buddhism has split into many schools. The two main branches are Theravada and Mahayana. **Theravada** is the old conservative school of Buddhism, also

---

(Opposite) Top: The large Buddha statue at Likir Gompa (see p140).
Bottom: Young monks from Chemre Gompa (see p147).

known as the Hinayana (or 'lesser vehicle'), which is popular in Sri Lanka and South-east Asia. This school maintains that the only way to enlightenment is through your own efforts as a monk. **Mahayana** on the other hand is more adaptable, believing that everybody will eventually gain enlightenment. So that this can be achieved a few enlightened beings called *bodhisattvas* refuse the bliss of nirvana so that they can return again and again to the world in order to help all other living things gain enlightenment. This feature has widened the appeal of the Mahayana school because gods from other religions can be incorporated into Buddhism as bodhisattvas. This is the school of Buddhism which is dominant in Ladakh (see p116) and also in Nepal, Tibet, Mongolia, China, Korea and Japan.

Islam
Muslims, as the followers of Islam are called, believe in only one God, Allah, whose prophet, Mohammed, established the religion in the 7th century AD in Arabia. The visions that Mohammed received are recorded in the Muslim holy book, the Koran, which also sets out the basis of Islamic belief, practice and law. Much of the Koran relates to parts of the Bible, particularly the Books of Moses and the Gospels of Christ, and Muslims believe that Moses and Jesus were prophets of Allah.

Muslims must follow five basic obligations: to state and believe that there is only one God, Allah, and that Mohammed was his prophet; to recite the five daily prayers at set times, facing Mecca; to make the pilgrimage, or *haji*, to Mecca once in a lifetime if they are financially able; to fast and abstain from sex during daylight hours for the month of Ramadan; and to pay a special tax for charity. The rapid conversion to Islam throughout the Middle East and north Africa in the 7th and 8th centuries AD was aided by means of *jihad*, or holy war. The religion soon spread to sub-Saharan Africa, India, China, SE Asia, the Balkans and Spain. Early on in its history, Islam divided into two major sects which still remain today, the majority Sunnites, the rest Shiites.

Sikhism
With their beards and turbans, Sikhs are one of India's most unmistakable peoples. They are recognisable by their five outward symbols, or *Kakkars*, which stem from the belief in *Khalsa*, a chosen race of warrior holy men. In addition to uncut hair and beard, they include shorts, a sword, a comb and a steel bracelet. The religion was founded by Guru Nanak in the 15th century with the aim of combining Hindu and Islamic ideals. Sikhs reject the Hindu caste system and the vast pantheon of gods, believing instead in one universal God, but they believe in karma, reincarnation and that devotional singing, the repetition of God's name and meditation can all help free the self from the endless cycle of rebirths. Since the 16th century, when Guru Gobind Singh militarised the religion, the majority of Sikhs have taken the surname Singh, meaning lion.

(Opposite) Masked dancer at Phyang festival. Spectacular monastic festivals occur throughout the year (see p73).

Practical Information for the visitor

VISA VALIDITY AND EXTENSIONS

Tourist visas are theoretically non-extendable, although in practice it is sometimes possible to gain an extension. If you succeed, the length of time granted is in the hands of the official you are dealing with, and it can vary from about two weeks to three months. Apply to the Foreigners' Registration Office in Delhi (☎ 331 9489, Hans Bhavan, Tilak Bridge, open 9.30am-1.30pm and 2-4pm Monday to Friday) or in Bombay (Mumbai), Calcutta and Madras (Chennai), or alternatively to the Superintendent of Police at any district headquarters (see p135 for Leh).

If you stay in India for more than 120 days you are required to get an income tax clearance exemption certificate from the foreign section of the Income Tax Department in Delhi, Bombay, Calcutta or Madras before you leave the country.

TREKKING RESTRICTIONS

There are few restrictions on trekking in Ladakh, which comes as a pleasant surprise in a country which is usually over-keen on wrapping things up in red tape. Apart from a few sensitive border areas (see below), trekkers are free to walk where they like and for as long as they like, providing they have a valid visa.

The Inner Line

The restricted areas in Ladakh (or protected areas as the government now likes them to be known) are all beyond what is known as the Inner Line. Travellers are not allowed to cross this without special permission. The position of this line sometimes alters but at the time of going to press it runs parallel to but 1.5km north of the Zoji La-Drass-Kargil-Khalsi road in the west of Ladakh; it then moves 6km to 8km north of the Khalsi-Nimu-Leh-Upshi road to allow visitors to reach the various monasteries in that area; and in eastern Ladakh the Inner Line runs along the Upshi to Manali road, thereby restricting access to all the areas further to the east.

Since 1994 the government has opened up several of these areas to tourists – Nubra, Pangong Tso, Dha-Hanu, Tso Moriri and Tso Kar. You still need permission to visit them but this is easily arranged in Leh (see p131) as long as you comply with certain conditions: you must travel in a group of four or more; you can't stay longer than seven days; and you should stick to the identified tour circuits. Permission to enter the other Inner Line areas is rarely granted to foreigners but if you want to try, contact the Ministry of Home Affairs (☎ 469 3334), Lok Nayak Bhavan, Khan Market, New Delhi, well in advance of your intended visit.

LOCAL TRANSPORT

Air

Indian Airlines (IA), the government-run domestic carrier, has an extensive network of routes throughout India (timetables are available from IA offices) and is the only airline flying to Leh. Air India planes fly between Bombay (Mumbai), Delhi, Calcutta and Madras (Chennai), and there are also a number of smaller operators, of whom **Jagson** and **Archana** are the most useful for the Himalayan-bound trekker, as they fly from Delhi to Kullu.

There are Indian Airlines offices or agents in most major towns and cities and making a booking is a simple affair provided there are seats available. Many routes, Leh-Delhi being one of them, get heavily booked in summer, so try to plan as far ahead as possible. If economy class is full there may still be seats available in first class. If you don't manage to get a confirmed flight you can be put on the waiting-list. You can be wait-listed for up to four different flights, so make the most of this until one is confirmed. The waiting-list works in mysterious ways – even if you're told that there are a couple of hundred people ahead of you on the list, you may still get a confirmed seat in the end.

Tickets can be paid for in hard currency (cash or travellers' cheques) or rupees in Leh, or by hard currency, rupees or credit card elsewhere. There is an excellent youth fare entitling you to 25% off if you are aged 30 or under, children under 12 get a 50% discount, while those under two pay 10%. If you cancel your ticket before your flight you will get a full refund but IA will not refund you if your ticket is lost. You can also lose all rights to your ticket if you are not at the airport at least 30 minutes before the flight is due to leave, so it is advisable to turn up at least an hour before departure. As Indian Airlines has a habit of changing its flight timings without warning it's a good idea to check flight details a day or two before you fly. Finally, don't pack lighters, batteries or knives in your hand luggage; they will be confiscated. Put them in the hold baggage.

Train

Travel by rail is one of the great Indian experiences. Unfortunately Himachal Pradesh and Ladakh are two of the few regions that aren't served by the railway.

Bus

The bus system in India can get you almost anywhere cheaply and generally quickly (barring, of course, breakdowns). Buses come in varying degrees of dilapidation and comfort. On rock-bottom priced **ordinary** or **B class** buses you will be squashed on to a hard seat with as many people as possible but the journey will be an entertaining insight into local life. At the other end of the scale is **deluxe** or **supercoach**, which are a bit faster and have reclining seats. On some popular long distance routes, such as between Delhi and Manali, and Manali and Leh, you will find luxury **tourist** buses operating. While these are comfortable, if a little expensive, they don't provide quite the same level of cultural exchange as a bus full of locals.

For the faster and longer distance services you'll usually need to book in advance; tourist buses insist on it but for local services you just need to turn up and pay on the bus. At large bus stations, as at railway stations, women should make use of the separate (women only) ticket counter since the queue is usually shorter. If there doesn't appear to be one you can go straight to the front of any other queues. Luggage goes on the roof of the bus (no charge), along with any passengers who can't fit inside. The cramped seats on some services help explain why the roof 'seat' is the most favoured by many Westerners but you should realise that it is illegal to be up there and if you are asked to come down, do so as the conductor can be fined. Keep an eye out for low power cables and branches if you want to stay on!

City buses, particularly in Delhi, are horrendously crowded and trying to find out which buses run on which routes is difficult if your Hindi isn't good enough to translate the timetables. As a result, most visitors opt for the more expensive but less complicated auto-rickshaws.

Taxi

The main vehicle used for the job is the classic Hindustan Ambassador, a copy of the 1950s Morris Oxford, complete with sofa-like bench seats. In Delhi they are easily identified as they are painted yellow and black. In the mountains you will also find a number of Gypsy and Mahindra jeeps which cope better with the difficult roads. Taxis in Delhi have a meter, rarely switched on for tourists even if it is working. The best policy is to agree on a price before getting in. If the driver won't agree on a fair price, find another. In Leh, fares are set by the Taxi Operators' Union and there is a list available detailing these.

Auto-rickshaw

These three-wheeler scooters are much cheaper than taxis and faster for short distances in traffic. You are guaranteed an exhilarating ride. You may occasionally be able to persuade the driver to use his meter but expect to pay more than the fare indicated as the meter is unlikely to have been recalibrated to the latest tariff. It's often easier to follow the same advice as for taxis. There are no auto-rickshaws in Leh.

Tempo

The auto-rickshaws' big brother with seating for up to eight people, tempos are often propelled by the front half of a Harley-Davidson. They are mainly found in Delhi where they operate along fixed routes.

Cycle-rickshaw

These operate in Old Delhi and are a cheap, environmentally sound but slow way of getting around. While you may feel pity for the rickshaw wallahs' physically demanding work, it is far better to use their services than to deny them your money. Always agree on a price before setting off.

Hire car

If you are looking for a more independent way of travelling around it is possible to hire self-drive cars in Delhi and other major cities but once you've seen the conditions on the road you'll understand why most people hire a car with driver. This can be done either through a specialist firm (ask the tourist office or your hotel), or with a taxi driver. It's an expensive way to travel long distances, often costing more than flying, but it does allow you to stop wherever you like.

Motorbike

India is a dream for the classic motorcycle enthusiast and the lure of the stunning high-altitude road between Manali and Leh is too much for many to resist. Hundreds of travellers each year tour around on Indian Enfield 350cc or 500cc Bullets, copies of the British Royal Enfield Bullet. There are also smaller bikes available, such as scooters and the ubiquitous 100cc Japanese two-strokes. You'll find the widest range of bikes for sale or hire in Delhi but hiring them in Manali and Leh is also possible. If you plan to buy a bike look on the notice-boards of popular travellers' hang-outs or start your enquiries at a mechanic's. One such recommended person who hires and sells bikes is Lali Singh at Inder Motors (☎ 011-572 8579, 🖹 011-575 5812), 1/44/55 Hari Singh Nalwa St, Abdul Aziz Rd, Karol Bagh, Delhi.

Bicycle

Cycling is an excellent way to explore local areas and it's possible to hire bikes in Leh and Delhi. For those with more time there can be few better ways of travelling further afield. You are totally free to go where you like; it costs you next to nothing and should your legs give up on you, it's a simple matter to put the bike on to a bus, train or plane. Those after the ultimate challenge should consider cycling between Manali and Leh along the world's second highest road (see p101) or even continuing up and over the Khardung La above Leh, the 'highest motorable road in the world'. For this sort of adventure you will need to bring your own machine.

The CTC (Cyclists' Touring Club) (☎ 01483-417217, 🖹 01483-426994, 🖳 cycling@ctc.org.uk, www.ctc.org.uk), Cotterell House, 69 Meadrow, Godalming, Surrey, UK, produces fact sheets covering almost every aspect of cycle touring, including India.

Hitching

This is not an easy option and the only people likely to stop for you are truck drivers. Expect to pay as much as you would on the bus and make sure you agree on the amount before you set off. You should also find out when the driver expects to reach your destination. He may be planning to spend the night at a village just down the road, or popping in to visit friends or relations on the way. Women should never hitch alone in India. The Western thumb-up gesture that says 'give me a ride' is not understood in India. The way to stop any vehicle is to pretend you're a one-winged bird trying to fly, a gentle up and down waving of the hand and arm.

LANGUAGE

The most widespread spoken language in India is English and it is perfectly possible for the traveller to get around without any knowledge of any of

India's other languages, although a few words of Hindi are useful. Officially India has 14 languages, but if minor languages are included this rises to over 700. There have been attempts to make Hindi, which is the most widely spoken of Indian languages, into the official national language but so far this has not succeeded.

The Ladakhi language is a form of Tibetan. While much of the spelling is the same, the words are pronounced so differently that Ladakhis and Tibetans can find it hard to understand each other. The Ladakhi language is hardly ever written down in the same way as it is spoken, because the 'correct' written language is a scholarly Tibetan, comparable to Shakespearean English. As a result very few people outside monasteries read or write in their own language.

English is commonly understood, particularly around Leh, as is Urdu (similar to Hindi) but trekkers should try to learn a little Ladakhi so that they can talk to people particularly in rural areas. You'll provide a great source of entertainment for those listening. It's not hard to pick up a few basic words (see p282-3), and to help you learn, buy a copy of Rebecca Norman's excellent little yellow book, *Getting started in Ladakhi*, which is widely available in Leh.

TIME

Indian Standard Time is 5 hours 30 minutes ahead of Greenwich Mean Time (GMT). Time calculations for the following cities are:
- **London**: -5 hours 30 minutes (Oct-Mar), -6 hours 30 minutes (Apr-Sep).
- **New York**: -10 hours 30 minutes.
- **Los Angeles**: -13 hours 30 minutes.
- **Sydney**: +4 hours and 30 minutes.
- **Auckland**: +6 hours and 30 minutes.

MONEY

Currency

There are 100 paise (p) in the Indian rupee (Rs). Coins come in denominations of 5, 10, 20, 25, 50 paise and 1, 2 and 5 rupees. Notes come in denominations of 1, 2, 5, 10, 20, 50, 100, and 500 rupees. Make sure the notes you are given have no ripped edges as you will find it almost impossible to get rid of them again. Holes left by staples do not matter.

> ❏ **Rates of exchange**
> There's a slightly better rate of exchange for travellers' cheques than for cash and you'll get more for your money in Delhi than in Leh. Current rates for travellers' cheques in Delhi are:
> | | |
> |---|---|
> | Euro 1 | Rs45 |
> | US$1 | Rs43 |
> | £1 | Rs69 |
> | CHF1 | Rs28 |
> | Can$ | Rs29 |
> | Aus$ | Rs28 |
> For up-to-the-minute rates of exchange check the Web on **www.xe.net/currency**.

Changing money

This can be time consuming and frustrating, especially in smaller towns. The best solution is to change as much as you feel happy carrying before you leave Delhi. You'll get a better rate of exchange than in Leh or Manali and you will be able to change most foreign currencies or travellers' cheques – pounds sterling and US dollars are often all you can change outside the capital or other big cities. American Express, MasterCard and Visa **credit cards** can be used to obtain cash rupees in several banks but there is nowhere in Leh that offers this facility. Credit cards can also be used in large hotels, restaurants and shops. There are several **foreign banks** which have branches in India; ANZ Grindlays has the most branches.

Hang on to the **encashment certificates** that the banks give you, because you will need them if you want to change more than Rs10,000 back into hard currency when you leave. Taking rupees out of or into India is illegal.

Changing money on the **black market** is illegal and does nothing to help India's national debt. Now that the Indian rupee is a convertible currency you will get only a marginally better rate than at the bank, your best chances being with US$100 or £50 bills. The black market in Leh is almost non-existent, though it is alive and well in Delhi.

Bargaining

This is an important part of buying souvenirs or things from a market and some negotiating will also take place when you are hiring a pony-man. Approach it as a light-hearted game and not as a means of getting the lowest possible price. You should have an idea of how much you are prepared to pay for an item before you begin haggling and never begin bargaining if you are not interested in buying the item. Once you've quoted a figure you are committed to it, there's no backing out. Although bargaining is important, don't lose sight of the fact that 10p or 15 cents is nothing to you, but could be a lot to the vendor.

ELECTRICITY

The voltage is usually 220 volts AC, 50 cycles but some areas also have DC supply. Always check the voltage before plugging in. Socket sizes vary but

---

❏ **Baksheesh**

This is the term used for giving small amounts of money as a 'thank you' for good service, to help get things done or to beggars. Baksheesh applies equally to Indians as to visitors, so don't assume you are being picked on just because you are a Westerner. Although it is not really necessary to tip taxis, cheap restaurants or small hotels, it is often expected and the small amount of five rupees will keep everyone happy. A similar amount to whoever helps you with your bags will be appreciated, while those who achieve the seemingly impossible deserve a little more. Large restaurants and hotels will expect 10%.

Genuine pleas from desperate beggars are an inevitable, heart rending, part of travel in India. These people depend to a large extent on donations from the public (there is no social security) and the best course of action seems to be to follow what other Indians do and give them your small change. Alternatively you can give to the various charities who help the poor. Giving to children who reserve their pestering for tourists, demanding 'one pen', 'one bon-bon' or 'one rupee' should on no account be encouraged (see p158).

the most commonly found are two or sometimes three round-pin type. Take a universal adaptor if you're going to be using the supply.

Mains electricity has not affected the majority of Ladakh and is generally restricted to Leh, Kargil and a few villages along the Indus Valley. Leh's inadequate supplies are provided by the Hydro-electric Project at Stakna and a couple of diesel generators in the town which you can hear humming away at night. Power cuts are very common so always have a torch or some candles on you after dark. Even when it's working properly, the light given off by the bulbs can be so dim that it's hard to read at night.

HOLIDAYS AND FESTIVALS
Opening times
All **shops** are generally open between 10am and 5pm, Monday to Saturday but many keep longer hours. **Banks** are open 10am-2pm Monday to Friday, 10am-12pm on Saturday. **Post offices** are open 10am-5pm on weekdays and 10am-12pm on Saturday, while **government offices** are open 9.30am-5pm Monday to Friday and 9.30am-1pm on Saturday (sometimes closing on alternate Saturdays).

In Leh some shops are open on Sundays as well. Official times sometimes alter during winter in Ladakh.

National public holidays
● **Republic Day** (26 January) This is in celebration of the day India became a republic in 1950. The main events are in New Delhi and include a huge parade to the Red Fort.
● **Independence Day** (15 August) Marks the anniversary of India's independence from Britain in 1947.
● **Gandhi's birthday** (2 October)
● **Christmas Day** (25 December)

Festivals
There is a festival somewhere in India almost every day of the year. They are colourful and noisy occasions to which visitors are generally welcomed. The principal Hindu, Buddhist and Islamic festivals are listed below. The dates are complicated to work out as they change each year. Buddhist, Hindu and Sikh festivals being determined by the lunar calendar, while Islamic festivals are determined by the Islamic year which is shorter than the Gregorian calendar (contact a tourist office for dates).
● **Id-ul-Fitr** (December to February) The end of Ramadan, the month in which Muslims have to abstain from sex and must not eat, drink or smoke between sunrise and sunset, is celebrated with a large feast and festivities.
● **Tibetan New Year** (late February or early March) While most Tibetans will be celebrating their New Year now, the Ladakhis will have beaten them to it by two or three months. (See Losar).
● **Holi** (March) A slightly anarchic Hindu festival that marks the end of winter and the beginning of spring. Don't wear smart clothes on this day as the

streets are full of people throwing coloured powder and water. Tourists are a popular target but it's all good fun.

● **Rama Navami** (March-April) The Hindu festival which celebrates the birthday of Rama, the main character of the epic *Ramayana*. It is auspicious to read from and act episodes of this great story.

● **Id-ul-Zuha** (March-April) The Muslim festival commemorating Abraham's attempt to sacrifice his son on the command of God. Animals are sacrificed and mutton traditionally eaten.

● **Buddha Purnima** (May-June) The Buddhist festival that conveniently celebrates Buddha's birthday, enlightenment and attainment of nirvana, all at the same time. Full celebrations are held in Leh.

● **Ladakh Festival** (1-15 September) This cultural festival takes place mainly in Leh. It's a good opportunity to see polo matches, archery, music recitals, crafts and other things Ladakhi and succeeds in its aim of extending the short tourist season a few more weeks.

● **Janmashtami** (August-September) Krishna's birthday is celebrated by Hindus all over the country.

● **Dussehra** (September-October) This popular 10-day Hindu festival celebrates the triumph of good over evil, usually represented by Rama's destruction of Ravana, or the goddess Durga's victory over the demon Mahishasura. Try to be in Kullu (just south of Manali) for this festival, where it is celebrated in great style.

● **Diwali** (October-November) Rama's homecoming after 14 years of exile is celebrated by Hindus all over India by the lighting of oil lamps and firecrackers. It ranks as India's noisiest and brightest festival.

● **Nanak Jayanti** (October-November) The major Sikh festival which celebrates the birthday of Guru Nanak. It is marked by processions and the continuous reading of the holy book.

● **Losar** (December-January) Ladakhis celebrate their new year, Losar, before the actual Tibetan new year (in February). According to popular history this was because of a decision made by the Ladakhi king, Jamyang Namgyal, at the beginning of the 17th century. The impatient king was keen

❑ Monastic festivals in Ladakh
Ladakh's monasteries put on spectacular dramatic festivals each year to re-enact the story of each gompa's particular divinity. These used to take place in the winter when they provided a much needed diversion from the drudgery of the long, cold months. In a shrewd financial move, however, several have changed their dates to make the most of the summer visitors. The most famous of these masked dance festivals is the one at Hemis but Lamayuru, Karsha, Phyang and Tak Tok all now have their festivals in the tourist season. The dates of the festivals are governed by the Tibetan lunar calendar so vary from year to year. For details of when they will be, contact the India Tourist Office in your country (see p56).

to lead a military campaign to western Ladakh but was advised to wait until after the new year celebrations. Rather than waste a couple of months he decided to bring the date of the celebrations forward. However, many historians believe it was the Tibetans who were forced to change their new year date to celebrate the invasion of Genghis Khan in 1227. So, perhaps it is the Tibetans who are out of step with the Ladakhis.

POST AND TELECOMMUNICATIONS
Postal services
The Indian postal service is generally reliable, with letters from Europe taking one or two weeks to arrive, even in Leh. Most travellers use the Poste Restante service at all main post offices to receive mail. Letters should be addressed with your surname in capital letters and underlined (so that it is sorted properly), Poste Restante, GPO, the name of the town and the state. If you can't find a letter that you were expecting, check under the first letter of your first name, in case it's been mis-sorted. Airmail rates are currently Rs11 for a letter, Rs6.50 for an aerogramme and Rs6 for a postcard.

Sending parcels home is a convenient way to shed some of the weight in your pack. The parcel needs to be wrapped in cheap white material and then stitched up. Most tailors will perform this service for you. Leave one end open so that the post office can inspect what you're sending. This way you can also take things out, or put things in the parcel so that it fits into the kilogram bracket (0-1kg, 1-3kg, 3-5kg etc) that gives you the best value for your money. Take a needle and thread to the post office so that you can sew it up. If you want to be extra safe seal the seams with wax (available at stationery shops).

Phone, fax and email
Telephoning anywhere from India is simple at one of the many private STD/ISD offices available in every town. Many of these now have fax machines which you can use as well. The international **dialling code** for India is 91, Delhi is 011, Kargil is 01985, Leh is 01982, Manali is 01901 and Srinagar is 0194 (leave off the first 0 if calling from outside India).

Check **http://cybercaptive.com** for places to collect email in India. If you don't already have a free address with one of the companies such as hotmail, rocketmail or yahoo you can easily set up an account at a cybercafé.

THE MEDIA
Newspapers and magazines
Indian newspapers are excellent value, rarely costing more than Rs2. The *Times of India* and the *Indian Express* are the most popular English language papers. Also available are the *Hindustan Times*, the *Independent* and the *Statesman*.

Look out for *Ladags Melong* in Leh. This excellent magazine is the only locally-produced journal and covers a wide range of topics. Most articles are written in English, but the magazine has also taken on the admirable task of trying to extend the use of written Ladakhi beyond religious texts. It therefore includes a few articles in Ladakhi that are written as closely to the spoken language as possible. The other regional papers are the *Kashmir Times* and the *Daily Excelsior* but as both are based in Srinagar they carry little news relevant to Ladakh.

Radio and TV
All-India Radio broadcasts news in English at 9pm every night while Doordarshan, the national TV channel, broadcasts news at 9.30pm.

Satellite TV has hit India by storm. Programmes from BBC World Service TV and numerous American soaps are available. The effect of rose-tinted images of the West, as portrayed by *Baywatch* and *Beverly Hills 90210*, on remote areas like Ladakh remains to be seen.

FOOD
Indian
India is rightly famed for its unique cuisine but that wonderful food is really only available in smart restaurants and private houses. Make the effort to eat in a really good restaurant once in a while as the food is incomparable. Such a meal may take a large chunk (£7/US$10) out of your daily budget yet it's superb value when compared with the cost of a restaurant meal in the West. Travellers generally make do with the run-of-the-mill food that is provided by small restaurants and *dhabas*, the cheapest and most numerous of India's eateries. The basis of the meal is a plate of rice or Indian bread such as *chapatis*, *rotis*, *parathas* or *puris* to which is added *dal* (lentils) and a vegetable curry. This is filling and tasty and shouldn't set you back more than Rs30. Meat dishes are sometimes available and cost a little more, but the meat (usually mutton) often consists of little more than bone. There is no need to worry if you can't stand hot and spicy food as there are several milder dishes which are generally available.

Chinese
Chinese food, or at least attempts at it, is widely available in Delhi; fried rice or chow mein can make a pleasant change from curry. Most of Leh's restaurants also offer a wide selection of Chinese dishes.

❏ **Popular Indian dishes**
- **Bhindi bhaji** Fried okra or ladies' fingers
- **Biryani** Mild dish of saffron or turmeric coloured rice with meat or vegetables
- **Dal bhat** India's basic meal of lentils and rice
- **Dhansaak** Meat and lentil curry with rice
- **Dum alu** Potato curry
- **Kofta** Vegetable or meat balls with curry
- **Korma** Mild curry with a yoghurt sauce
- **Malai kofta** Lamb in a rich creamy sauce
- **Mattar panir** Peas and cheese
- **Pakoras** Small deep-fried batter balls filled with vegetables
- **Pulau** Mildly-spiced rice
- **Rogan josh** Classic mild Kashmiri lamb
- **Saag alu** Spinach with potatoes
- **Samosas** Fried triangles of pastry filled with curried meat or vegetables
- **Tandoori chicken** Marinaded chicken cooked in a clay oven, mild and dry
- **Vindaloo** Vinegar-marinaded meat in hot curry

Western

In restaurants popular with Western travellers spaghetti, pizzas, pancakes, porridge, muesli and other Western dishes are on all the menus. Elsewhere, chips and omelettes are usually easy to find and you will almost always be able to get toast and jam for breakfast.

Ladakhi/Tibetan food

The Ladakhi staple is roasted barley flour called *ngamphe* or *tsampa*. The raw barley is roasted in hot sand (to prevent it from burning) until it pops. It is then separated from the sand and ground to a fine flour. This can be mixed with tea (*kholak*, or *phemar* if it's sweetened), put into soup, or made into a porridge. Other popular dishes include various soups or *thukpa*, and *skyu* or *chhu tagi*, both of which are thick stews with different-shaped noodles in them.

One of the most popular Tibetan delicacies is *momos*. These are like miniature Cornish pasties filled with meat, cheese or vegetables. The dough is steamed rather than baked and they are often served in a soup called *rhuchotse*. Fried momo are called *khotay* and are particularly delicious when they have been put into a simmering soup until all the soup has been absorbed by the momo. Soups figure heavily on any Tibetan menu and include *tsam-thuk*, which is tsampa in a soup, and *than-thuk*, a flat noodle soup.

DRINK

If you want to stay healthy in India, it is wisest to assume that all **water** needs to be purified before it's safe to drink (see p271). Reasonably safe bottled **mineral water** (Rs15 to Rs30) is available almost everywhere but make sure the seal hasn't been tampered with. Most of it is simply treated tap water and as the bottles are generally not recycled it's far cheaper and more environmentally friendly to purify your own.

India grows some of the best **tea** in the world though lovers of English tea may be disappointed when they drink a glass of sweet and milky *chai* (Rs2 to Rs5). This ubiquitous beverage is made by boiling water, tea, milk powder and sugar (and occasionally cardamom or ginger) together in a pot and straining the resulting liquid into a glass. It's a safe, cheap and refreshing drink that's available everywhere, so it's worth learning to like it. Other teas such as lemon and ginger, jasmine, mint, and cardamom make a delicious change when you are sick of chai. **Coffee** is also popular but by far the best is made in south India. The favourite Ladakhi hot drink is **butter tea**, or *gur-gur cha*, which is made by mixing salt and brick tea together, and adding a little butter after it has boiled. This is churned in a special cylindrical barrel with the onomatopoeic name *gur-gur*. Well-made butter tea is delicious; think of it as weak soup rather than as tea.

Soft drinks (Rs10 to Rs15) are safe thirst quenchers. Coke and Pepsi are inevitably found in most places, as well as a range of interesting domestic makes such as Limca, Thums Up, Campa Cola and Gold Spot. There are also lots of **fruit juices** available either in bottles, such as the delicious apple juice in Ladakh (Rs28 for a large bottle), or cartons, such as mango, lemon and apple flavoured Frooti (Rs7). **Lassi** is a traveller's favourite; you should take note that the curd is often mixed with ordinary tap water, so if you wouldn't drink the water, don't drink the lassi.

Beer is widely available in India with Kingfisher and Godfather being popular brands. It's comparatively expensive (Rs50-80), probably just as well as the wide use of chemical additives will ensure a heavy head the next morning if you drink too much. Indian imitations of whisky, brandy and rum are also available and usually drinkable though they bear little resemblance to the originals. William Moorcroft pointed out in *Travels in the Himalayan Provinces of Hindustan and the Panjab* (in the 1820s) that the Ladakhis were 'apt to be addicted to intoxication' and large quantities of *chang*, a delicious and mild home-brewed barley beer, are always consumed at any excuse for a celebration.

THINGS TO BUY

Delhi, Manali and Leh are literally brimming with irresistibly cheap things to buy. Silks, textiles, carpets, rugs, metalwork, woodwork, ceramics, leather, paintings, musical instruments, books and even cassettes of Indian or Western music can all be bought at bargain prices. However, it's best to wait until the end of your stay before you splash out, otherwise you'll end up lugging the contents of a souvenir shop across the Himalaya with you. Once the initial euphoria has worn off, you'll also have a better feel for what's available and what a sensible price is. During the tourist season, Manali and Leh fill up with Kashmiri and Tibetan souvenir sellers whose wares can often be found more cheaply in Delhi. Having said that, each region also has its own specialities which are certainly best bought locally – shawls, woollen goods and Kullu pill-box hats in Manali, or butter tea churners, Tibetan carpets, *thankas*, traditional Ladakhi clothes and locally knitted woollens in Leh. Wherever you buy, make sure you bargain.

❏ **Alternative and natural medicines**
India is a cornucopia of alternative and natural medicines. **Ayurveda** is an ancient tradition of healing based on personal constitution and herbalism. Ayurvedic medicines are widely available in India but good Ayurvedic doctors are harder to find – ask around. Tibetan 'Amchis' practising **Tibetan medicine** can be found wherever there is a sizeable Tibetan community (Delhi, Manali, Leh). They prescribe herbal treatments based on a diagnosis of the patients' morning urine and pulse and the treatment is usually long-term (several weeks). **Homeopathy** originated in Europe but is surprisingly widespread in India. Remedies are prescribed on an individual basis concerning personal symptoms, but there are also remedies for specific ailments that work for the majority of people. These treatments are natural, effective and safe. **Elana Vollen** (USA)

❑ Women travellers

Women in Ladakhi society are well respected. They make many key decisions at the household level and are the guardians of the family's wealth in the form of jewellery and their turquoise-studded head-dresses (*peraks*) which are passed down from mother to daughter. Ladakhi women may be shy of Western men, but with women they are friendly and helpful and can give you a unique insight into Ladakhi life.

Travelling alone in India is generally a safe and fascinating experience. Unfortunately, the increasing exposure to Western-style television programmes has led a small minority of Indian men to believe that Western women are 'easy to get'. As a result, a few travellers have experienced unwanted attention. This rarely amounts to more than a quick grope; a yell should frighten them off and attract help from passers-by. This type of situation is almost unheard of in Ladakh, although there have been recent reports of incidents involving soldiers.

There are a few simple ways you can avoid unnecessary scrapes and at the same time help to restore Western women's image. Modest dress is highly recommended if you want to be respected. In Ladakh the art of subtlety is alive and kicking – flaunting your feminine attributes will not be appreciated! Avoid tops that show your shoulders, stomach or back, and keep your legs covered – long skirts and loose trousers are ideal. In Leh, the elegant and practical Tibetan *chubas* are popular among travellers.

With regard to trekking it is best not to go alone as you will rarely see local women on their own outside their village. If you are travelling alone, hire a guide for your trek or team up with other Westerners in Leh. **Tor Loram** (UK)

SECURITY

India is a reasonably safe country to travel in and big cities are certainly less violent than those in the West. As with travel anywhere you should be particularly aware of theft; travellers have been popular targets throughout history and things haven't changed. Keep the receipt for your travellers' cheques, details of your insurance policy, some spare cash and a photocopy of the personal information and Indian visa pages of your passport in a very safe place, so that you're not completely stuck if your wallet and passport get stolen. Pickpockets abound in busy places (bus stations) and on buses and trains. Keep hold of your valuables at all times. Bring a padlock to safeguard your luggage on buses and trains and also to securely lock your hotel room. Unfortunately you are probably as much at risk from fellow travellers as from anyone else.

Ladakh, however, has a very low crime rate and when trekking you are far more at risk from the natural elements than from man. There have been occasional thefts from unattended tents in areas such as around Padum and the Markha Valley, so even in the mountains keep your valuables on you all the time.

Hashish (*charas*) is widely produced in the Himalaya and is readily available. It is illegal, however, as are all other drugs. Possession carries a minimum 10-year sentence. Police in tourist areas are particularly vigilant; if you're arrested you may spend months in jail simply waiting for your case to come to trial. This is a travel experience that is best avoided.

PART 3: DELHI, MANALI, KEYLONG

Delhi to Leh – travel options

Regular flights to Leh have made it all too easy to forget that Ladakh is still one of the most remote regions in the Himalaya. Travel to such a place is bound to have inherent difficulties and although most visitors have no problems, it's not

---

❏ Warning

Owing to continued militant activity, it is advisable not to visit **Kashmir** – in other words, anywhere west of the Zoji La, Ladakh's western boundary. There is a serious risk to travellers' safety in this area. In recent years foreigners have been involved in kidnappings, robbery and murder. In 1994 two Britons were kidnapped in the Vale of Kashmir, while an American tourist was shot dead in Srinagar and then in 1995 five Western trekkers were kidnapped and a Norwegian member of the group was subsequently executed. In 1996 six Indian tourists were murdered after being abducted from their houseboat in Srinagar. Frequent demonstrations and bomb blasts in public places in **Srinagar**, **Jammu** and the **Jammu region** make this an unsafe place to travel. Trains and buses en route to Jammu are frequently targeted.

If you are travelling to Ladakh by road, you should go via the Kullu Valley and Manali, rather than via Jammu and Srinagar. Be aware of travel agents in Delhi who are trying to convince tourists that Kashmir is a safe and rewarding place to travel to. They will even go as far as to say that the route to Ladakh between Manali and Leh is closed, so you must go via Srinagar. No matter how convincing they seem, their advice should not be followed. Kashmir remains a dangerous place for travellers. Flights via Srinagar or Jammu are reasonably safe because security at these airports is some of the tightest in the world. However, if you leave the airport the dangers are as above.

Kargil, the westernmost town in Ladakh, came under frequent attack from Pakistani artillery shells in 1997, 1998 and 1999. This town is very close to the Line of Control and presents an obvious target to the Pakistani army outposts nearby. However, this is the first time the civilian population has been attacked and as the Leh to Srinagar road was also specifically targeted, travellers should avoid the area until the situation improves. This will affect those travelling by road from Leh to Zanskar via the Suru Valley and also anyone intending to go by road to Srinagar. Whether Pakistani troops will employ similar tactics in the future is unknown, but it would be wise to check locally before visiting the Kargil area. Accurate and up-to-date information on the situation is hard to get outside Ladakh.

For the latest official line contact your embassy in Delhi or the Foreign and Commonwealth Office (☎ 0171-238 4503/4504, 🖳 www.fco.gov.uk/).

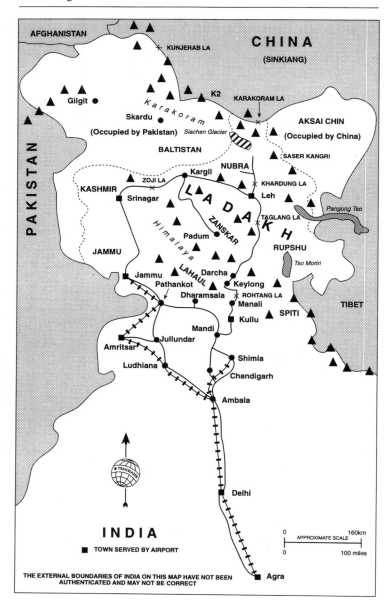

AFGHANISTAN

CHINA

(SINKIANG)

KUNJERAB LA

Gilgit

K2

KARAKORAM LA

Skardu

AKSAI CHIN

(Occupied by Pakistan)

Karakoram

Siachen Glacier

(Occupied by China)

BALTISTAN

SASER KANGRI

NUBRA

Kargil

KHARDUNG LA

ZOJI LA

KASHMIR

Leh

Srinagar

L A D A

TAGLANG LA

Pangong Tso

ZANSKAR

K H

Padum

Himalaya

RUPSHU

JAMMU

Tso Moriri

LAHAUL

Darcha

Jammu

Keylong

Pathankot

ROHTANG LA

Dharamsala

Manali

TIBET

SPITI

Kullu

Mandi

Jullundar

Amritsar

Shimla

Ludhiana

Chandigarh

Ambala

INDIA

Delhi

■ TOWN SERVED BY AIRPORT

0   160km
APPROXIMATE SCALE
0   100 miles

THE EXTERNAL BOUNDARIES OF INDIA ON THIS MAP HAVE NOT BEEN
AUTHENTICATED AND MAY NOT BE CORRECT

Agra

PAKISTAN

unknown for planes to be delayed because of bad weather and buses to be held up because of landslides or snow.

Most travellers choose either to fly directly from Delhi to Ladakh or to go by bus via Manali. Continued unrest in Kashmir means that the once popular overland route to Ladakh via Srinagar is not recommended until the situation changes. If you have the time and are not averse to a little discomfort, the three-day bus journey via Manali is a must. Although you get superb views of the Himalaya from the air, it is only by travelling overland that you can fully appreciate the awesome scale of the mountains, the variety of scenery and cultures that are found here, and just how cut off from the rest of India Ladakh really is.

It is possible to fly into Ladakh all year round but the roads are open only for the brief summer. The principal route into the region, the Manali to Leh road, is officially open from the first week of July to 15 September each year and the government guarantees to keep it open for that period. It occasionally opens earlier and often remains open for considerably longer but if you are travelling along it outside the official period you will not be rescued if the road gets blocked.

Many travellers find that the best way to travel to and from the region is a combination of flying one way and taking the bus the other. Whichever way you decide to travel, you must take your rate of ascent into account to prevent the onset of altitude illness (see p272-5 for more information). If travelling to Ladakh by road, use the altitude figures on the map on p149 to plan your journey.

Delhi

Delhi is the ideal gateway into India for Himalayan-bound trekkers. The city is well served by international flights and also by a vast network of road, rail and domestic air services, which make onward travel to Ladakh straightforward.

The capital of India is steeped in history and culture which reflect the diversity of the subcontinent. This provides travellers with many fascinating sightseeing possibilities, while enabling them to put India's disparities into context. With its many national and international services and shops, it's also a convenient place to make any final arrangements. However, Delhi's pollution, noise and crowds can quickly become too much to bear, and trekkers heading for Ladakh in the summer months will be keen to exchange the heat and humidity of the city for the cool of the mountains as soon as possible.

HISTORY

The location of the modern city of Delhi encompasses more than eight previous sites under various names. The first recorded city is that of Indraprastha, which is thought to have been near the Purana Qila until the 4th century AD and is the city of a similar name mentioned in the Hindu epic poem *Mahabharata*. The city officially recognised as the first Delhi was that of the Tomora and Chauhan kings (8th and 12th centuries) which was first called Lal Kot and then became Qila Rai Pithora. Muslim invaders from Afghanistan established a Sultanate here at the beginning of the 13th century.

The prosperous 14th century commercial city of Siri, near modern-day Hauz Khas, was the next to be built, followed rapidly by the fortress of Tughlaqabad to the south-east, which was only inhabited for five years before being replaced by Jehanpanah, also near Hauz Khas.

All these cities were situated to the south of modern Delhi. The next Delhi was founded in 1354 to the east of Connaught Place on the banks of the Yamuna, and was called Ferozabad after the sultan, Feroz Tughlaq. With the coming of the Mughals the capital was moved to Agra, but the second Mughal emperor, Humayun, moved it back to Delhi in 1534, where he built the Purana Qila as his fortress. However, he was soon ousted by the Afghan Sher Shah who added to the fort and renamed it Shergarh. Humayun regained power in 1555. After his death his son, Akbar, moved the capital back to Agra.

Delhi came back to prominence in 1638 under the great monument builder, Shah Jehan, who founded Shahjehanabad (officially the seventh city of Delhi). Today's Old Delhi has grown around this former city and much of it, such as the Red Fort and the Jama Masjid, is well preserved. New Delhi became the eighth Delhi, conceived by the British when they decided to move their capital from Calcutta in 1911. However, it wasn't inaugurated as the capital until 1931, so the British colonial enjoyment of the grand buildings was short lived.

Delhi has remained the administrative and political capital of India since Independence in 1947 and has now become one of India's fastest-growing commercial centres. As is common in many Third World cities, social and environmental problems, such as pollution, traffic congestion, overcrowding and poverty have followed in the wake of this rapid economic growth. Delhi's population of over ten million continues to rise daily as people are lured by the prospect of work and money, yet almost one third of these people live in the pitiful conditions of the shanty towns on the outskirts of the city, largely unnoticed by the Western visitor or the Delhi élite.

INTERNATIONAL ARRIVAL AND DEPARTURE

Arrival

Indira Gandhi International Airport is 20km to the south-west of the city centre. You pass through immigration and customs into the arrivals hall where there are **foreign exchange counters** (State Bank of India and Thomas Cook), open 24 hours. There's also a **hotel reservations counter** where you can book accommodation in the more up-market hotels, and a **Government of India tourist counter** (☎ 569 1171) for any other information.

The cheapest way to get into Delhi is by **bus**. The most reliable is the **Ex-Servicemen's Airlink Transport Service (EATS)**. Buses leave regularly from outside the arrivals hall, going via the domestic airport to Connaught Place, (Rs30, 45 mins) and they will usually drop you off at the major hotels if you ask. Otherwise there are Delhi Transport Corporation buses which go via the domestic terminal, Connaught Place and the railway stations, to the Inter-State Bus Terminus. Your other option is to get a **taxi**, which will be marginally quicker. Ignore all the taxi drivers who demand your custom and go straight to the **pre-paid taxi desk** in the arrivals hall, where you pay a fixed rate for your destination (Rs200-300).

Departure

Don't forget to confirm your flight 72 hours before leaving. **EATS** (☎ 331 6530) have buses that go first to the domestic and then on to the international airport (Rs30, 45 mins). They leave from their small office, just past the Wimpy restaurant in Connaught Place, regularly from 4am to 11.30pm. If you are leaving at night it's easier to take a **taxi** (Rs200-300, 30 mins); make sure you book it the previous afternoon as it's almost impossible to find one in the middle of the night.

You need to arrive at the airport two hours before your flight leaves. If you arrive earlier there is a pleasant **visitors' lounge** (Rs10, open 24 hours) opposite the main terminal building where you can relax before joining the throng in the departure hall. **Departure tax** will have been pre-paid at the time of booking your ticket. In the **departure hall** there are **foreign exchange counters** (State Bank of India and Thomas Cook), a **post office**, **phone booths**, an over-priced **food counter** and a 24-hour **cafeteria**. After you have checked in you can move through to the **departure lounge** where there are several **duty-free shops**, another over-priced **food counter** and two expensive **restaurants/bars**.

❏ **Taxi scams**
Many international flights arrive in Delhi late at night which can pose a few problems for the unaware traveller. Most of the budget guest-houses are closed from midnight to sunrise so either check into a more up-market hotel for your first night or hang around the airport until it gets light – there is a pleasant visitors' lounge at the international terminal which is open 24 hours. If you are taking a taxi in the early hours of the morning be on your guard for unscrupulous taxi drivers who may take you for a ride in more ways than one. The usual con trick is to be told that it's not possible to go to the hotel of your choice and instead you will be taken to a hotel where the taxi driver gets paid a commission and you get badly ripped off. One way of avoiding this is to telephone your hotel in advance from the airport to make sure they are open and have a vacancy. Once you've got into the taxi act as if you know Delhi like the back of your hand, even if this is your first time in Asia.

ORIENTATION

Delhi is situated on the west bank of the River Yamuna and is two cities in effect, New Delhi and Old Delhi.

The most important landmark for getting your bearings is **Connaught Place** (officially renamed Rajiv Place, although still generally referred to by its former name) in the north of New Delhi, around which runs a busy ring road called **Connaught Circus** (officially renamed Indira Circus). Among the beautiful colonnades of Connaught Place you will find banks, shops, airline offices, restaurants, hotels, tourist offices and a host of other services useful to the traveller.

Running south from here is the important tree-lined road called **Janpath**, along which you will find the Government of India tourist office, a few more airline offices and plenty more guest-houses and hotels.

Further south from here are the government buildings centred around **Rajpath** and among the parks and wide avenues are the expensive residences of the Delhi élite. Far out to the south-west, about halfway between Connaught Place and the airport, is the diplomatic area called **Chanakyapuri** where most of the embassies can be found.

North of Connaught Place, the streets get narrower and more crowded as you approach Old Delhi. Between the two cities are **New Delhi railway station** and **Paharganj**, where there are lots of popular budget guest-houses.

The main street of **Old Delhi** is Chandni Chowk, a seething mass of noise, smells and colours, off which run the narrow alleys and bazaars that this part of the city is famous for. The Red Fort and the Jama Masjid are here and just to the north is **Old Delhi railway station** and the main **Inter-State Bus Terminus**. (Note that there's a second bus terminus, Sarai Kale Khan, in the south of New Delhi, for buses to Agra).

WHERE TO STAY

Hotel areas

● **Connaught Place** There is a wide range of places to stay near Connaught Place, including budget guest-houses around the top of Janpath, the YMCA and YWCAs around Sansad Marg, moderately-priced hotels in Connaught Place itself and five-star international hotels slightly further south. The main reason for staying here is its proximity to Delhi's main shops, airline offices, banks, tourist offices and restaurants. Although very popular with budget travellers, the cheaper guest-houses are overpriced and cramped when compared with similar accommodation in Paharganj.

● **Paharganj** This area around the Main Bazaar is about a ten-minute walk from Connaught Place and has a large selection of budget guest-houses which attract Indian and Western travellers alike. The busy and narrow streets are conveniently located near New Delhi railway station and give the traveller a better understanding of Indian city life than by staying in the more sedate and commercially-orientated area around Connaught Place. When the

Main Bazaar's noise, exhaust fumes and chaotic traffic of rickshaws, cows, bicycles and people get too much, it's always possible to retreat to a shady rooftop restaurant.

● **Other areas** There are several guest-houses and hotels in other areas of Delhi which offer excellent value if you are just biding time in the city. They are not so convenient, however, if you've got a lot of organising or shopping to do in the centre.

Prices
Prices given below are for single/double rooms, with common (**com**) or attached (**att**) bathrooms, and air-conditioning (AC) as indicated. Rooms without AC almost always come with a ceiling fan, which is essential in summer. The budget, moderate, and expensive categories are based on the price of the cheapest double room. As is often the case with capital cities, accommodation in Delhi is far more expensive than elsewhere in the country and not nearly as good value for money.

Camping
The popular *Tourist Camp* [3] (☎ 327 2898) in Old Delhi (on Jawaharlal Nehru Marg, near Delhi Gate, and opposite the JP Narayan Hospital, or Irwin Hospital, as it is sometimes called) has ample lawn space for pitching your own tent and at Rs50 per tent it's one of the cheapest places to stay in Delhi. There are clean communal washing and toilet blocks, a restaurant, laundry service and left-luggage facility on site, and if you don't have a tent, you can stay in the very basic huts for Rs125/180 (com), or 'delux' double for Rs390 (att). The main drawback of the camp is that it's about 2km from all the facilities in Connaught Place.

Budget guest-houses and hotels (£7/US$10 or less)
Places to stay below are [keyed] to the Connaught Place and Paharganj map on p87 or the main Delhi map on p86.

● **Connaught Place** At the top of Janpath, down a side street heading off to the east, are two very popular budget hang-outs. The first is the *Ringo Guest House* [36] (☎ 331 0605, 17 Scindia House), where you can stay in a cramped dorm for Rs90, have a single for Rs125 (com) or a double from Rs250 (com) or Rs350 (att). The *Sunny Guest House* [37] (☎ 331 2909, 152 Scindia House), a little further on, offers much the same. Just around the corner from here is the slightly more expensive but rather dirty *Asian Guest House* [35] (☎ 331 3393, 14 Scindia House), above the Air France offices. Double rooms without a bathroom are Rs125-225; rooms with attached bathroom are Rs250/300, or Rs450/495 if you want air-conditioning.

If you are after something quieter try looking down the small residential street called Janpath Lane, on the west side of Janpath, where you'll find *Mr SC Jain's Guest House* [41] (☎ 332 3484) at 7 Pratap Singh Building, costing Rs100 for a bed in a small dormitory, or Rs150/300-350 (com) for simple rooms. In Connaught Place, at 85 M Block, is *Hotel Bright* [27] (☎ 332

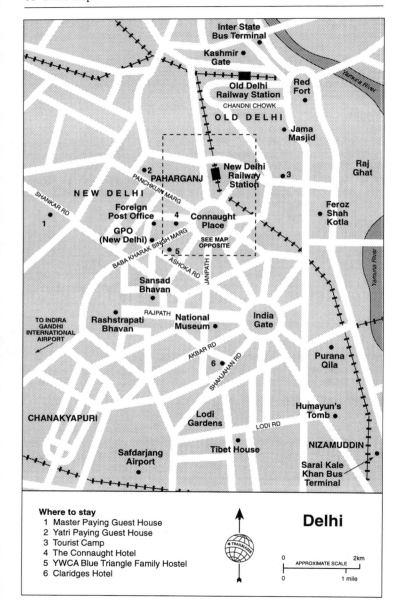

Inter State
Bus Terminal

Kashmir
Gate

Old Delhi
Railway Station

Red
Fort

CHANDNI CHOWK

O L D   D E L H I

Jama
Masjid

Raj
Ghat

SHANKAR RD

PANCHKUIN MARG

2
PAHARGANJ

N E W   D E L H I

New Delhi
Railway
Station

3

Feroz
Shah
Kotla

Foreign
Post Office

4

Connaught
Place

1

GPO
(New Delhi)

BABA KHARAK SINGH MARG

ASHOKA RD

JANPATH

5

SEE MAP
OPPOSITE

Sansad
Bhavan

RAJPATH

National
Museum

India
Gate

TO INDIRA
GANDHI
INTERNATIONAL
AIRPORT

Rashtrapati
Bhavan

AKBAR RD

SHAHJAHAN RD

6

Purana
Qila

CHANAKYAPURI

Lodi
Gardens

LODI RD

Humayun's
Tomb

NIZAMUDDIN

Safdarjang
Airport

Tibet House

Sarai Kale
Khan Bus
Terminal

Where to stay
1 Master Paying Guest House
2 Yatri Paying Guest House
3 Tourist Camp
4 The Connaught Hotel
5 YWCA Blue Triangle Family Hostel
6 Claridges Hotel

Delhi

TRAILBLAZER

0   2km
APPROXIMATE SCALE
0   1 mile

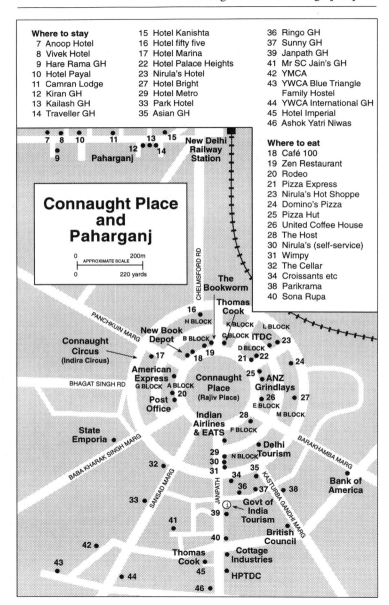

Where to stay
7 Anoop Hotel
8 Vivek Hotel
9 Hare Rama GH
10 Hotel Payal
11 Camran Lodge
12 Kiran GH
13 Kailash GH
14 Traveller GH
15 Hotel Kanishta
16 Hotel fifty five
17 Hotel Marina
22 Hotel Palace Heights
23 Nirula's Hotel
27 Hotel Bright
29 Hotel Metro
33 Park Hotel
35 Asian GH
36 Ringo GH
37 Sunny GH
39 Janpath GH
41 Mr SC Jain's GH
42 YMCA
43 YWCA Blue Triangle
   Family Hostel
44 YWCA International GH
45 Hotel Imperial
46 Ashok Yatri Niwas

Where to eat
18 Café 100
19 Zen Restaurant
20 Rodeo
21 Pizza Express
23 Nirula's Hot Shoppe
24 Domino's Pizza
25 Pizza Hut
26 United Coffee House
28 The Host
30 Nirula's (self-service)
31 Wimpy
32 The Cellar
34 Croissants etc
38 Parikrama
40 Sona Rupa

Connaught Place and Paharganj

0 ___ 200m
APPROXIMATE SCALE
0 ___ 220 yards

New Delhi Railway Station

Paharganj

The Bookworm

Thomas Cook

CHELMSFORD RD

H BLOCK   K BLOCK   L BLOCK
New Book Depot   B BLOCK   G BLOCK   ITDC
Connaught Circus (Indira Circus)   D BLOCK
PANCHKUIN MARG
American Express   G BLOCK   A BLOCK   Connaught Place (Rajiv Place)   ANZ Grindlays
BHAGAT SINGH RD
Post Office
Indian Airlines & EATS   M BLOCK
F BLOCK
State Emporia   Delhi Tourism
N BLOCK
BABA KHARAK SINGH MARG
BARAKHAMBA MARG
Bank of America
JANPATH
KASTURBA GANDHI MARG
SANSAD MARG
Govt of India Tourism
British Council
Thomas Cook   Cottage Industries
HPTDC

3456, 🖹 373 6049), where decent-sized though gloomy rooms cost Rs350/450-600 (com) and Rs475/660 (att) or Rs950 (double att/AC). A little further round in D Block is *Hotel Palace Heights* [22] (☎ 332 1419) which has a pleasant terrace to sit out on. Rooms are Rs250/375 (com) or Rs605 (double/AC/att).

● **Paharganj** All the places to stay in this area fall into the budget category. Starting at the east end of the Main Bazaar (by New Delhi railway station) and heading west, you come first to *Hotel Kanishta* [15] (☎ 52 5365) which has clean double rooms for Rs200 and Rs250 (att).

Not far after, on the other side of the road, is the very clean and pleasant *Traveller Guest House* [14] (☎ 354 4849) with doubles for Rs180-200 (att) and all but the cheapest rooms come with a TV. Almost next door are the *Kailash Guest House* [13] (☎ 777 4993) with rooms costing Rs110/175 (com) or Rs200-225 (double/att, and the similarly priced *Kiran Guest House* [12] (☎ 52 6104) Rs120/175 (com), or with a bathroom for Rs150/225. Both are cheap but OK.

Further west, the *Camran Lodge* [11] (☎ 73 0618, 🖹 777 9906) offers cheap and interesting accommodation with its vaguely Mughal-look décor for Rs75/140 (com) and attached doubles for Rs175. *Hotel Payal* [10] (☎ 52 0867) has rooms for Rs150/200-250 (att). Towards the west end of the Main Bazaar is the popular *Vivek Hotel* [8] (☎ 52 1948, 🖹 753 7102), which has plenty of large rooms at Rs200-400/250-450 (att), and Rs600/700 (att, AC).

Down a side alley to the left is a very popular travellers' haunt called the *Hare Rama Guest House* [9] (☎ 52 1413, 🖹 753 2795), where rooms with attached bathroom are Rs120/220, or Rs350 with AC as well. Part of its appeal is the busy open-air restaurant on the roof. The *Anoop Hotel* [7] (☎ 52 1451, 🖹 753 2942) also has a rooftop restaurant with great views over Delhi. The clean rooms are similarly priced at Rs230 (double/att) and Rs375 (AC/att).

Moderately priced guest-houses and hotels (£7-20/US$10-30)

● **Connaught Place** *Janpath Guest House* [39] (☎ 332 1935, 🖹 332 1937, 82-84 Janpath) is conveniently situated near the tourist office and Connaught Place. The carpeted rooms are Rs425/495 (att), or Rs900, 1650/1100, 1950 (att, AC). If you don't want air-conditioning choose a room with a window as the others get very hot in summer.

Around Sansad Marg there are two YWCAs and one YMCA, all of which accept men and women. Despite the institutional atmosphere they are extremely popular. The *YMCA* [42] (☎ 336 1915, 🖹 374 6032, Jai Singh Rd) has large, airy and clean rooms for Rs375/645 (com) and Rs735/1230 (att, AC) plus a membership fee of Rs30 per person. A free breakfast is provided and there's a swimming pool (Rs50). The *YWCA International Guest House* [44] (☎ 336 1561, 🖹 334 1763, 🖳 YWCAind@del3.vsnl.net.in, 10 Sansad Marg), is similar, but all rooms have attached bathrooms and air-conditioning and cost Rs720/990. The large **YWCA *Blue Triangle Family Hostel*** [5/43] (☎ 336 0133, 🗎 336 0202) on Ashoka Rd is a bit further away from Connaught Place than the other Ys and has clean, reasonably priced rooms: Rs400 for a single (att) or Rs550 with air-con, and Rs750 for a double (att) or Rs850-1000 (AC/att). It is only possible to book a room here by letter or in person. Equally far from Connaught Place, at 19 Ashoka Rd near the junction with Janpath, is the ***Ashok Yatri Niwas*** [46] (☎ 334 4511, 🗎 336 8153). Rooms in this government-run tower block are reasonably priced at Rs500/650 (att).

In Connaught Place is the ***Hotel Metro*** [29] (☎ 331 3805, 49 N Block) which despite the grotty entrance hall has surprisingly nice rooms with attached bathrooms for Rs650/800 and Rs800/1000-1200 with air-con. At 55 H Block, Connaught Circus, is the fully air-conditioned ***Hotel fifty five*** [16] (☎ 332 1244, 🗎 332 0769) where attractively decorated, clean rooms cost Rs900/1350 (att). There's a lovely balcony on the top floor, an ideal place to enjoy your breakfast and read the morning papers.

● **Other areas** If you don't mind the inconvenience of being further away from Connaught Place and are looking for a bit of peace and quiet, there are two wonderful guest-houses that deserve a mention. The first is the homely ***Master Paying Guest House*** [1] (☎ 574 1089) at R 500 New Rajendra Nagar, which is a few kilometres west of Connaught Circus. Immaculately clean rooms are from Rs250 to Rs800, all with shared baths. The other is the ***Yatri Paying Guest House*** [2] (☎ 752 5563, 🖳 yatri@nde.vsnl.net.in) which is only 1km to the west of Connaught Place at 3/4 Punchkuin Rd (Radial Rd No 3). It's at the western end of this road, down a small residential side street. This has well-furnished, clean double rooms for Rs600 (com), Rs900-1000 (att), or Rs1200 (att, AC). Both of these places get booked up quickly; it's advisable to phone ahead to check vacancies.

Expensive hotels (more than £20/US$30)
Delhi's smarter hotels are found mainly around Connaught Place and are spread out to the south. The ***Hotel Marina*** [17] (☎ 332 4658, 🗎 332 8609) at 59 G Block, Connaught Circus, contains a restaurant, coffee shop, travel agency and laundry facilities in its plush surroundings. The comfortable rooms are from Rs2600 for a single and between Rs3200-6000 for doubles. On the opposite side of Connaught Place is ***Nirula's Hotel*** [23] (☎ 332 2419, 🗎 335 3957, 🖳 delhihotel@nirula.com, website: www.nirula.com) in L Block, which is surrounded by Nirula's various eateries, ranging from an ice-cream bar to a Chinese restaurant. This popular four-star hotel has pleasant, well-equipped rooms costing Rs1199 for a single and Rs2399 for a double. Just a stone's throw from Connaught Circus is the modern and uninspiring ***Park Hotel*** [33] (☎ 373 3737, 🗎 373 2025) at 15 Sansad Marg. Single rooms in this five-star hotel are US$260 and doubles from US$275.

Five minutes' walk to the west, at 37 Shaheed Bhagat Singh Marg, is ***The Connaught Hotel*** [4] (☎ 373 2842, 🗎 334 0757, 🖳 prominent.hotels@g ems.vsnl.net.in) where single rooms are US$120 and doubles between US$130 and US$145. If you can afford a little more the *Hotel Imperial* [45] (☎ 334 1234, 🖹 334 2255) is centrally located on Janpath, sheltered from the traffic noise by its extensive grounds. Plush doubles range from US$170-$500 and within its old-style façade you will find several restaurants, a swimming pool and all the usual five-star facilities.

To the south of the city centre is *Claridges Hotel* [6] (☎ 301 0211, 🖹 301 0625, 12 Aurangzeb Rd), one of Delhi's legends. This beautiful hotel has four restaurants and a swimming pool and prices start from US$175.

WHERE TO EAT

Connaught Place has a wide choice of good restaurants which cover all budgets and palates. There are several fast food restaurants popular with young Delhi-ites and Western travellers alike, such as *Wimpy* [31] and *Nirula's* [30] in N Block, *Café 100* [18] in B Block and *Croissants Etc* [34] at 9 Scindia House. Pizzas have also hit the capital in a big way; *Domino's Pizza* [24] on M Block does take-away and deliveries, while *Pizza Hut* [25] and *Pizza Express* [21] cater for those who want to eat in.

There is a selection of places to eat by Nirula's Hotel which include *Nirula's Pastry Shop* [23], the *Hot Shoppe* (pizzas, burgers and curries), *Pot Pourri* (burgers, tandoori, pizzas and snacks) and an ice-cream bar. If you want a Mexican experience in India, try *Rodeo* [20] on A Block where there's live music and waiters in costume. The *United Coffee House* [26] in E Block is popular for reasonably-priced south Indian, Chinese and European food. *The Cellar* [32] on the corner of Sansad Marg and Connaught Circus offers a variety of Eastern and Western food and at 46 Janpath you will find *Sona Rupa* [40], which specialises in good-value south Indian vegetarian food.

For something more up-market try *The Host* [28] in F Block, or the ritzy *Zen Restaurant* [19] in B Block, which serves high class and expensive Japanese and Chinese food. *Parikrama* [38] on Kasturba Gandhi Marg offers first-class Indian food with excellent views of Delhi (at a price) from its revolving perch on top of a tower block.

Paharganj has lots of cheap eateries along the main street and several of the guest-houses have rooftop restaurants which are popular with travellers.

SERVICES

Airline offices

● **Domestic airlines** **Archana Airways** (☎ 684 4215), 41A Friends Colony East, Mathura Rd; **Indian Airlines** have 24-hour booking at their office at Safdarjang Airport (☎ 462 0566). More convenient offices are at the Malhotra Building (☎ 331 0517, F Block, Connaught Place), and at the PTI Building (☎ 371 9168, Sansad Marg) both of which are open daily, except Sunday, 10am-5pm; **Jagson Airlines** (☎ 372 1594), 12E Vandana Building, 11 Tolstoy Marg.

• **International Airlines Aeroflot** (☎ 331 2843), BMC House, 1st Floor, Middle Circle, 1 N Block, Connaught Place; **Air Canada** (☎ 372 0043), 5th Floor, Hindustan Times Bldg, Kasturba Gandhi Marg; **Air France** (☎ 373 8004), 7 Atma Ram Mansion, Scindia House, Connaught Place; **Air India** (☎ 373 1225), Jeevan Bharati Bldg; **British Airways** (☎ 332 7428), DLF Centre, Sansad Marg; **Emirates** (☎ 332 4665), Kanchenjunga Bldg, 18 Barakhamba Rd; **Gulf Air** (☎ 332 4293), 12 G Block, Hotel Marina Arcade, Connaught Circus; **KLM** (☎ 335 7747), Prakash Deep, 7 Tolstoy Marg; **Lufthansa** (☎ 332 7268), 56 Janpath; **Quantas** (☎ 332 1434), Mohan Dev Bldg, 13 Tolstoy Marg; **Royal Jordanian** (☎ 332 7418), 56 G Block, Connaught Circus; **SAS** (☎ 335 2299), 1st Floor, Ambadeep Bldg, Kasturba Gandhi Marg; **Singapore Airlines** (☎ 332 0145), Ahoka Estate Bldg, 9th Floor, Barakhamba Rd; **Swissair** (☎ 332 5511), DLF Centre, Sansad Marg; **Thai** (☎ 623 9133), Park Royal Hotel American Plaza, Nehru Place; **United Airlines** (☎ 335 3322), c/o Interglobe Enterprises Ltd, Ambadeep Bldg, 14 Kasturba Gandhi Marg.

Banks
Among the many banks for foreign exchange are: **American Express**, A Block, Connaught Place; **ANZ Grindlays**, E Block, Connaught Place; **Bank of America** and **Banque Nationale de Paris**, Barakhamba Rd; **Thomas Cook**, Imperial Hotel, Janpath and also at C-33 Connaught Place. There are 24-hour foreign exchange services at the State Bank of India and Thomas Cook at the airport and also at the Ashoka Hotel in Chanakyapuri.

Bookshops and libraries
There are many good bookshops and stalls around Connaught Circus; books are often cheaper than in the West. Good places to browse are the Bookworm, Radial Rd 4, Connaught Place, and New Book Depot, B Block, Connaught Place. For a good read of the foreign newspapers, visit the British Council Library, 17 Kasturba Gandhi Marg.

Communications
• **Telephone, fax and email** You can make direct dial calls from any of the many STD/ISD booths around the city. Some will allow incoming calls and many have a fax service and email facilities as well.
• **Post** Have your poste restante letters addressed to 'GPO New Delhi', as letters addressed to 'GPO Delhi' may end up in the Old Delhi post office. The poste restante is at the Foreign Post Office on Bhai Vir Singh Marg (Market Rd) to the west of Connaught Place.

Medical clinics
The East West Medical Centre (☎ 469 0429, 🖹 469 0428, 38 Golf Links Rd) is a highly recommended private clinic and, failing that, you can try the All India Institute of Medical Sciences (☎ 66 1123, Ansari Nagar). There are several pharmacies in Connaught Place and in most other main shopping areas. An ambulance service is available by dialling ☎ 102.

Shopping

The best place to start looking for souvenirs is at the **Central Cottage Industries Emporium** on Janpath (open 10am-7pm Monday to Saturday). This huge government-run centre has high quality goods from all over India and is a good place to get an idea of what's available. The prices are fixed and are generally slightly more expensive than in the bazaars. The **state emporia** along Baba Kharak Singh Marg, each stocked and operated by a different state, are also worth visiting for fixed-price shopping.

Small boutiques continue all the way down **Janpath** to the Imperial Hotel, finishing with the Tibetan Market. There are more shops, emporiums and pavement traders all around **Connaught Place** and if you prefer shopping in a more authentic environment, try the small alleys around **Chandni Chowk** in Old Delhi.

Tourist information

While you are in Delhi, you will be approached by many people offering tourist information. These people are touts for tourist agents and are only after your money. There is only one main Government of India tourist office in Delhi and that is at 88 Janpath (☎ 332 0005, open Monday to Friday 9am-6pm and 9am-2pm on Saturday). This is an excellent place to find out any information and to pick up a free map of the city.

State Government tourist offices can provide more relevant information for their regions: Himachal Pradesh (☎ 332 5320) have their offices at Chandralok Building, 36 Janpath; Jammu and Kashmir (☎ 334 5373) are at Kanishka Shopping Plaza, 19 Ashok Rd.

Most news stalls sell the excellent weekly *Delhi Diary* (Rs8) which gives listings of all the current films, exhibitions, plays and lectures, while also providing an invaluable city directory and map.

WHAT TO SEE

If you are short of time join an organised tour of the city. These are very good value for money and avoid the hassle of using the public transport system. Many companies will offer to guide you around Delhi; the two official companies, **ITDC** (☎ 332 2336, L Block, Connaught Place) and **Delhi Tourism** (☎ 336 5358, 36 N Block, Middle Circle, Connaught Place), are generally thought to be the best. Both offer morning tours of New Delhi and afternoon tours of Old Delhi (Rs90-125 each or Rs175-200 if booked together), and also run day tours to Agra (Rs535-600).

Red Fort

This was the centre piece of Shahjehanabad (Old Delhi), the great city built in under ten years by the Mughal emperor, Shah Jehan, in the 17th century. The whole city was surrounded by an 8.8km wall in which there were fourteen gates, five of which survive today: Delhi Gate, Kashmiri Gate, Turkman Gate, Ajmeri Gate and Lahori Gate. On the eastern edge of the city was the huge Red Fort (Lal Qila), so named because of its massive red sandstone walls. The building of this impressive palace took place between 1638 and 1649, and the design is similar to the Agra Fort, where Shah Jehan's original capital was based.

The modern visitor enters through the **Lahori Gate** which takes you into **Chatta Chowk**.There would once have been gold and silver for sale here; now it's full of souvenir sellers. Some of the important buildings within the fort are: the **Diwan-I-Am** (the hall of public audience) where the emperor would settle judicial matters of the general public; the **Rang Mahal**, or Palace of Colour; the **Khas Mahal**, which was the emperor's personal palace; and the **Moti Masjid**, Aurangzeb's personal mosque.

The most impressive of the buildings is the **Diwan-I-Khas** (hall of private audiences) where the emperor would meet his nobles and ministers. In its former glory visitors were in no doubt that it was an attempt to create a copy of paradise as it is described in the Koran. There was once a ceiling of silver and gold; a Stream of Paradise that cooled the air as it trickled through the building; a Peacock Throne made of gold and marble and inlaid with precious gems; still remaining are columns inlaid with semi-precious stones and the inscription on the north and south walls which translates as, 'If there is paradise on earth, it is here, it is here, it is here.'

The Red Fort (entry Rs2) is open daily from sunrise to sunset. There's an excellent hour-long **sound and light show** each night (Rs20). The English commentary starts at 8.30pm September to October, 7.30pm November to January, 8.30pm February to April, 9pm May to August.

Jama Masjid

India's largest mosque is another of Shah Jehan's triumphs. It reportedly took 5000 masons six years to construct, starting in 1650 and costing Rs1,000,000. It was designed to hold the whole population at prayer and today has a capacity of 25,000 which is sometimes reached on Fridays and other holy days. It's worth climbing the southern minaret for the excellent views you get over Delhi (Rs10).

Entrance costs Rs10. You must remove your shoes and if you are wearing shorts, hire a robe to wrap around your legs.

Raj Ghat

In this green park, just south of the Red Fort and by the River Yamuna, is a black marble plinth where Mahatma Gandhi was cremated after his assassination in 1948. Prayers take place here every Friday evening.

India Gate

This majestic 42m high arch is a memorial to the Indian soldiers killed in WWI. It stands at the eastern end of Rajpath and provides the best views of Rashtrapati Bhavan and the symmetrical buildings of the Secretariat.

Rashtrapati Bhavan and Sansad Bhavan

Originally designed as a symbol of British colonial power by the ambitious English architect, Edwin Lutyens, **Rashtrapati Bhavan** was the former residency of the viceroy and is now the home of India's president. The building was erected between 1921 and 1929 and is a blend of European and Eastern styles. The huge gardens, however, are strictly Mughal in style and are open to the public once a year, in February. **Sansad Bhavan** (Parliament House), at the end of Sansad Marg, is another of Lutyens' vast creations, although Sir Herbert Baker actually supervised the construction. The circular building now houses a library, chambers for the Council of State, an assembly chamber and a chamber for the Council of Princes. Today the two Houses of Parliament, the Lok Sabha and the Rajya Sabha, meet here.

National Museum

This large museum gives an excellent overview of Indian culture with exhibits dating from Neolithic times to the 20th century. It is located a little over halfway down Janpath. It's open Tuesday to Sunday, 10am-5pm, Rs0.50.

Tibet House

Discussion groups, lectures and retreats are held at the Tibet House (☎ 461 1515), 1 Institutional Area, Lodi Rd, on the south side of Delhi. There's also a small museum with a collection of Tibetan art and artefacts, and a handicraft shop. It's open Monday to Friday 9.30am-1pm, 2-5.30pm.

Purana Qila

The 'Old Fort' is said to have been built on the legendary site of Indraprastha, the capital of the Aryans of 1000BC. In the 16th century it was part of Emperor Humayun's capital and known as the sixth city of Delhi. The building was completed during the brief rule of the Afghan ruler Sher Shah (1538-45). Humayun came back to power after defeating Sher Shah's weak successor but died in 1556 as a result of falling down the steep steps of the Sher Mandal. You can still climb these for good views of the city. The fort is on Mathura Rd, not far to the south-east of India Gate.

Nizamuddin

This small village, just south of the Purana Qila, has grown up around the shrine of the 14th century Islamic Sufi saint, Sheikh Nizam-ud-Din Auliya. Try to visit on a Thursday evening when *qawwali* singers gather to perform religious songs. There are several other important monuments in the area including the Jana-at-Khana mosque, west of the shrine.

Humayun's Tomb

It was usual for the Mughal rulers to build their tombs before they died. Humayun's accidental death prevented this tradition from being followed, so his widow, Haji Begum, built it in the 1560s. Its grand architectural style has led many to suggest that it was the forerunner of the Taj Mahal in Agra. The tomb is in Nizamuddin, just south of the Purana Qila.

Qutab Minar Complex

Fifteen kilometres to the south of Connaught Place is a group of buildings which date from India's first Islamic rulers. The most well known of these is the Qutab Minar, a 72.5m high, red sandstone tower topped in marble, that dates back to 1199 when Qutab-ud-din started building the tower as a symbol of Islamic victory over Delhi. Next to the tower is the first mosque founded in India, the Quwwat-ul-Islam Masjid, which was built at a similar period out of the remains of 27 Hindu and Jain temples which the Muslims destroyed. Also in the complex is a fourth century iron pillar of the Gupta period, which has mysteriously remained virtually rust free despite its age. There is a local belief that if your arms can encircle the pillar with your back to it, your wishes will be granted.

It's open daily from sunrise to sunset (Rs3). You can get there on bus No 505 from Ajmeri Gate.

Day trip to the Taj Mahal, Agra

India's most famous building is 200km from Delhi, close enough for a day trip. No matter how many times you've seen its image in print, nothing can prepare you for the visual impact of seeing the mausoleum itself. It is perhaps the greatest monument ever built for love, standing in memory of Shah Jehan's wife of 17 years, Mumtaz-I-Mahal, after she died in childbirth in 1631. Work started on the building in the same year, but it took 20,000 workmen 22 years to complete this masterpiece of white marble symmetry. It's open Tuesday to Sunday from 6am-7pm (closed on Mondays), and costs Rs10.50 (8am-4pm), or Rs105 for entry at sunrise or sunset (before 8am or after 4pm).

● **Getting there** There are several trains each day to Agra; the most convenient is the fully air-conditioned Shatabdi Express (2002) which departs New Delhi railway station at 6.15am (1 hour 55 minutes, Rs370) and leaves Agra at 8.10pm. There are also regular buses (five hours) which leave from Sarai Kale Khan, the new bus terminal in south Delhi.

GETTING TO LADAKH

By air

The regular Indian Airlines flights into and out of Leh get heavily booked in the tourist season – book as far in advance as possible. Whichever way you're flying, try to book your tickets in Delhi, as the Indian Airlines office in Leh invariably has long queues and the computers are frequently down. Delays and cancellations are common because the high mountains that surround Leh airport make the approach difficult if there is any cloud cover. For this reason, flights will leave Delhi only if they can be assured of clear weather on arrival in Leh. If you can't get a seat on a direct flight, you could go via Jammu or Srinagar instead (but see the warning on p79), or via Chandigarh.

It's also possible to fly to Bhuntar, near Kullu, 40km south of Manali, with either Archana Airways or Jagson Airlines most days of the week.

All these operators have a habit of frequently changing their services – check the flight schedule with a travel agent or with the airline (see p90) before making rigid plans.

Indian Airlines flights from Delhi to Leh

● **Direct** Indian Airlines fly direct from Delhi to Leh (US$105, 1¼ hours) daily at 6.10am from mid-May to the end of August. Throughout the rest of the year there are four flights a week departing at 5.40am.

● **Via Jammu** There are flights to Jammu (US$105, 70 minutes) every day, leaving at 9.50am. Onward flights to Leh (US$65, 55 minutes) depart Jammu on Thursday and Sunday at 9am.

● **Via Srinagar** There are direct flights from Delhi to Srinagar (US$115, 1¼ hours) on Monday, Wednesday and Friday leaving at 9.30am. Flights from Delhi to Srinagar via Jammu depart every day at 9.50am (2¼ hours). There's only one onward flight a week to Leh (US$55, 40 minutes) which operates on Saturday at 9am. Don't be tempted to break your journey and stay overnight in Srinagar.

● **Via Chandigarh** Flights to Chandigarh (US$65, 40 minutes) leave Delhi on Monday, Wednesday and Friday at 11.20am. The weekly flight to Leh (US$70, 55 minutes) leaves Chandigarh on Tuesday at 9am.

Flights from Delhi to Bhuntar, Kullu

● **Archana Airways** have daily flights at 7am (US$150, 1½ hours).

● **Jagson Airlines** have daily flights at 7.30am (US$150, 1 hour 50 minutes).

By bus

Getting to Manali or Srinagar from Delhi is possible all year round but the two roads on to Leh from there are free of snow only during the summer. If you are entering Ladakh from Srinagar, the main obstacle is the Zoji La which is usually snow-free from the beginning of June to the end of October, but bad weather can significantly shorten this season. The Rohtang La and the Taglang La, between Manali and Leh, usually remain snowbound for longer and this route is only guaranteed to be open from the first week in July to 15 September.

● **Via Manali** Buses from Delhi to Manali take about 16 hours. See p100 for details of onward buses to Leh. Himachal Tourism (HPTDC) have comfortable buses to Manali leaving from their office at the back of Chanderlok Building, 36 Janpath, at 7pm daily (Rs450) and they also allow you to book a seat for the Manali to Leh section of the journey from their office in Delhi. Private buses to Manali are available from many of the tourist agents around Janpath for Rs350 but standards vary widely. There are also several state-run buses to Manali every day which leave from the Inter-State Bus Terminus (ISBT) near Kashmiri Gate. Prices vary between Rs220 and Rs450 depending on what class of bus you choose. Make sure you give yourself plenty of time, as you've got to book a seat at the relevant counter before you can board the bus.

● **Via Srinagar** Because of militant activity, overland travel in Kashmir is **not recommended** (see warning p79).

(Opposite) Buses will transport you cheaply around much of Ladakh; trekking is the only way to get truly off the beaten track. **Top**: Leh bus stand. **Bottom**: Trekking towards Tso Kar (see p35). (Photo: © Victoria Loram).

Manali

It takes 16 hours to travel the 840km from Delhi to Himachal Pradesh's alpine playground of Manali. Situated at an altitude of 2050m (6730ft) on the west bank of the Beas River, it makes an idyllic stop before heading on over the Rohtang Pass to the barren mountain landscapes beyond. This rapidly expanding resort caters for both Western and Indian tourists with its many and varied hotels and restaurants. Although the town itself is not particularly attractive, it is surrounded by lush orchards and dark forests, typical of the fertile Kullu Valley, and it has enticing views to the north, of snow-capped 6000m peaks.

ORIENTATION

The bus stand is on the main street called the Mall. Tourist information is available from the small office by Hotel Kunzam. Most of the town's restaurants line the western side of the Mall and behind them is the area known as Model Town, where many of Manali's less interesting but conveniently-placed hotels are situated. The chaotic market above the bus stand is called the Manu Market. It's a good place to find fresh fruit and vegetables and also one or two cheap restaurants.

Three kilometres north is the attractive village of **Old Manali**. Its peaceful surroundings, good views and budget guest-houses have made it a popular place to stay. There's also some accommodation at **Vashisht,** 3km northeast of Manali although the main reason for visiting is to soak in the hot springs. There are public baths in the centre but the HPTDC baths (run by the tourism department, Rs100 for two people for 30 minutes), by the road into Vashisht, are better.

WHERE TO STAY

Prices below are for double rooms with common (com) or attached (att) bathrooms. The 'budget', 'moderate' and 'expensive' categories are based on the price of the cheapest double room. Most of these places do not reduce their prices much outside the high season of April to June and September to November. You can, however, expect discounts of up to 50% in July or August from hotels which cater primarily to Indian tourists. Places to stay below are [keyed] to the Manali map on p99.

(**Opposite**): Magnificent natural colours of the Tsarap Gorge near Phuktal Gompa, Zanskar (see p241).

Camping

At Rs200 for 'luxury' tents *Camp Freedom* [9], near the bridge to Old Manali, offers few advantages over staying in a guest-house. If you've got your own tent you can pitch it here for Rs100 and make use of the hot showers.

Budget guest-houses and hotels (£4/US$6 or less)

For 'Homely, Airy & Sanitary Accommodation' there's the *Su-kiran Guest House* [4] (☎ 52178), just off the Mall. This very basic place is convenient for the main bus stand; beds in the dormitory cost Rs30 and doubles are Rs125 (att). One of the most peaceful places to stay in Model Town is the *Hotel Yamuna* [3] (☎ 52506) whose southerly facing double rooms have good views and a balcony, Rs100 (com) and Rs150 (att). Just down the road is *Hotel Sunflower* [2] (☎ 52419) with clean rooms for Rs150-200 (att).

Some of the best budget guest-houses are found in Old Manali. *Hotel Krishna* [14] (☎ 53071) has clean and quiet double rooms for Rs100 (com). The *Veer Paying Guest House* [13] (☎ 52410) costing Rs100 (att) is particularly good value with wonderful mountain views across the valley. Just next door is the smarter and slightly more expensive *Tourist Nest Guest House* [12] with clean, comfortable rooms for Rs225-250 (att). There are numerous clean but soulless places to stay near the HPTDC Club House, such as *Hampta Guest House* [11] which has adequate rooms for Rs100 (att) and *Hotel Neelgiri* [10] with rooms for Rs200 (att).

The other accommodation area that's popular with travellers is the village of Vashisht, 3km from the bus station. Although the guest-houses here are generally not quite as pleasant as those in Old Manali, Vashisht does have an added attraction with its hot springs.

Moderately priced guest-houses and hotels (£4-8/US$6-12)

Most hotels in Manali are aimed at the large number of Indian tourists that the town attracts. You'll find the central area, Model Town, packed with places that charge about Rs450 for a double (att). The most pleasant mid-range hotels are along the road between the new town and Old Manali. The first you get to is *John Banon's Guest House* [5] (☎ 52335, 🖹 52392) which has become a bit of an institution in mountaineering circles as the proprietor is the Honorary Local Secretary of the Himalayan Club; double rooms are Rs500 (att). *Sunshine Guest House* [7] (☎ 52320) is full of old world charm with dusty books, fireplaces and dressing rooms in each double room. The proprietor and family are very hospitable and doubles cost Rs350 (att). Higher up the valley side is *Hotel Kalpana* [8] (☎ 52413) which has fantastic views and a nice garden. Double rooms cost Rs200-300 (att) in the low season, rising to Rs450-550 (att) in the high season.

More expensive hotels (above £8/US$12)

In the forest between Old and new Manali is *Negi's Mayflower Guest House* [6] (☎ 53104, 🖹 52182) which offers attractive double rooms with a glass-

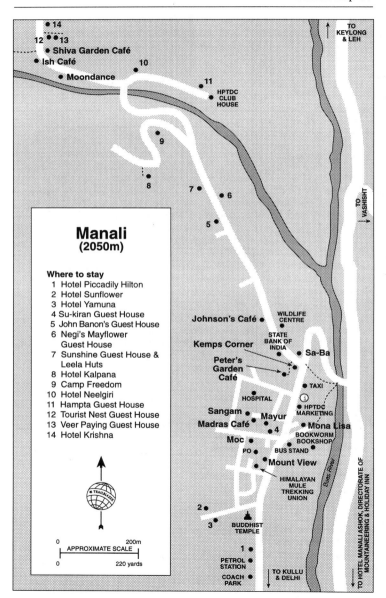

TO
KEYLONG
& LEH

● 14
12 ● ● 13
● Shiva Garden Café
● Ish Café
● 10
● Moondance
● 11
HPTDC
CLUB
HOUSE

● 9

● 8

7 ●   ● 6

5 ●

TO
VASHISHT

Manali
(2050m)

Where to stay
1 Hotel Piccadily Hilton
2 Hotel Sunflower
3 Hotel Yamuna
4 Su-kiran Guest House
5 John Banon's Guest House
6 Negi's Mayflower
  Guest House
7 Sunshine Guest House &
  Leela Huts
8 Hotel Kalpana
9 Camp Freedom
10 Hotel Neelgiri
11 Hampta Guest House
12 Tourist Nest Guest House
13 Veer Paying Guest House
14 Hotel Krishna

WILDLIFE
CENTRE

Johnson's Café ●

STATE
BANK OF
INDIA

Kemps Corner
● **Sa-Ba**

**Peter's
Garden
Café**

● TAXI

● HPTDC
MARKETING

HOSPITAL ●

Sangam ●
Mayur
● **Mona Lisa**

Madras Café ●
● 4
BOOKWORM
BOOKSHOP

Moc ●

PO ●
BUS STAND

Mount View

HIMALAYAN
MULE
TREKKING
UNION

2 ●

3 ●
BUDDHIST
TEMPLE

1 ●

PETROL ●
STATION

COACH ●
PARK

TO KULLU
& DELHI

TO HOTEL MANALI ASHOK, DIRECTORATE OF
MOUNTAINEERING & HOLIDAY INN

Beas River

TRAILBLAZER

0   200m
APPROXIMATE SCALE
0   220 yards

enclosed balcony facing the trees for Rs815 (att). At the bottom of the main town is the newly refurbished *Hotel Piccadily Hilton* [1] (☎ 52114, 📠 52113) with rooms for Rs2000-3000 (att). On the other side of the River Beas, about 1km downstream from the bridge is the *Hotel Manali Ashok* (☎ 53103, 📠 53108) with doubles from Rs1000 (att). Two kilometres south is the *Holiday Inn* (☎ 52262, 📠 52562), which has doubles from Rs2800 (American plan – ie with all meals). Off season, there are good discounts at these hotels. If you are travelling in a group you could consider renting the cosy *Leela Huts* [7] (☎ 52464, 📠 54035) which cost Rs3000 for a two-bedroom cottage or Rs4000 for one with three bedrooms.

WHERE TO EAT

If you're staying in Old Manali most of the guest-houses offer basic meals for reasonable prices. The potato dishes at the Veer are heavenly. There are also several popular travellers' cafés above the river, such as *Ish Café*, *Shiva Garden Café* and *Moondance Garden Restaurant* all offering typical travellers' food.

Back in the main town there are numerous places to choose from. At the top of the town is *Johnson's Café* which serves delicious fresh trout among other dishes. In the main part of town the *Mayur*, *Mount View* and *Mona Lisa* restaurants are deservedly popular and packed with Westerners. *Moc Restaurant* is an atmospheric place with good Tibetan and Chinese food, as well as some Japanese dishes such as tempura.

For good Indian food the *Madras Café* has a choice of dishes from the south, or try the purely vegetarian *Sangam Restaurant* next door.

For fast food visit *Kemps Corner* (pizzas, ice cream etc), or the *Sa-Ba Restaurant*. For slow food there's *Peter's Garden Café*, a hippy hangover from the 70s which also sells home-made bread and pots of jam.

MOVING ON

By air

The nearest airport is at Bhuntar, 10km south of Kullu (40km south of Manali). Archana Airways and Jagson Airlines have flights every morning to Delhi (US$150, 1½ hours). Contact travel agents in Manali for information on schedules; they are liable to change. There are lots of buses between Kullu and Manali.

By bus

● **Leh** For a description of the route see p148. The journey to Leh is possible only during the summer months with the road being officially open from the first week in July to 15 September. Himachal Tourism buses will travel this route only while the road is officially open, but many of the privately-operated buses will continue to ply the route until it is physically impossible because of landslides or snow.

The least painful bus on this bumpy two-day ride is that operated by Himachal Tourism (HPTDC) which departs every other day at 6am. Tickets are available from the HPTDC Marketing office and cost Rs700. For an extra Rs300 you have the dubious privilege of a bed in HPTDC's overpriced tented accommodation at Sarchu along with a basic evening meal. An alternative is to bring your own food and sleep on the bus. These get heavily booked

❑ Cycling from Manali to Leh

Every year sees more and more cyclists attempting this high-altitude cycle ride which must rate as one of the most spectacular in the world. If you don't feel up to going it alone there are several adventure travel companies who run fully-supported tours along the route (see p14).

Route

The 485km journey through desolate and remote country involves climbing four major passes up to a height of 5328m (17,480ft), so both you and your bike must be in good condition. The route is slightly easier from north to south, but most cyclists find the objective of going to Leh more appealing and this direction is far better for acclimatisation. If you've got the time, start your trip in the populated and gentler foothills: Chandigarh for instance. This will allow you to build up faith in your own capabilities and those of your bike.

Equipment

The right machine for the journey is really a question of preference. Mountain bikes with knobbly tyres seem to be the most popular, but plenty of people have completed the trip on touring bikes, or mountain bikes fitted with road tyres which will have you speeding along on the paved sections (about 50% of the road is sealed). A small 20-teeth chain-ring on the front with 28 teeth on the rear will help you master the last kilometres to the top of a pass with all your gear. Long-lasting brake pads are especially important. Keep your machine simple and low on maintenance and give it (particularly the chain) loving attention every night.

Come prepared for all possible weather from scorching sunshine to freezing blizzards, even in mid-summer. Tight lycra cycling clothing and shorts are not appreciated by the locals. The best solution is to take cycling underwear and wear trousers over the top. There are several dhabas along the way where you can sleep and eat, but to be on the safe side, you need to bring camping equipment and several days' supplies. Water is not generally a problem, except on the dry and barren More Plains between Pang and the southern base of the Taglang La; take plenty with you on this stage.

Itinerary

A punishing but possible eight-day itinerary would be: Manali-Rohtang La-Koksar; Koksar-Keylong; Keylong-Patseo; Patseo-Baralacha La-Sarchu; Sarchu-Lachalang La-Pang; Pang-Taglang La-Rumtse; Rumtse-Tikse; Tikse-Leh (see p149). Most cyclists prefer to take two more days over the journey, plus a rest day. If it all gets too much, jump on the next passing bus or truck.

(Thanks to **Marcel Schouten** (Netherlands) for supplying much of the above information).

in July and August; buy your ticket as early as possible. Several travel agents operate similar private services. Local HPSRTC and J&KSRTC buses also run on this route, leaving from the bus stand. Although not as comfortable they're much cheaper. Ordinary buses cost Rs350 and stop in Keylong for the night where decent hotel accommodation is available. Semi-deluxe buses (Rs520) continue on to Sarchu for the night which considerably cuts down the next day's travel.

● **Keylong** There are frequent buses to Keylong every morning from 4.30am onwards (Rs57).

● **Delhi** HPTDC have daily buses to Delhi at 5pm which arrive in Delhi at 10am the next morning (Rs450). Tickets are available from the HPTDC Marketing office. There are also plenty of state-run buses to Delhi throughout the day from the bus stand (Rs240-454).

By taxi
A taxi into which you can squeeze between four and six people will cost Rs11,000 to Leh.

Trekking to Ladakh
The 21-day trail from Darcha takes you across Zanskar right into the heart of Ladakh (see p230). Trekking agencies in Manali will separate you from your cash by organising everything for you but if you are a small group it is relatively simple to arrange the trek yourself, either here in Manali, or in Darcha. The Tourist Information office can be a good source of information, or go directly to the pony-men at the Himalayan Mule Trekking Union office in Model Town. If hiring ponies from Manali you will need to allow three days for them to get to Darcha; you can go by bus. Buy all your supplies in Manali or Keylong as little is available in Darcha.

Keylong

Keylong, the capital of Lahaul and Spiti, is a small and peaceful town surrounded by impressive mountains, six hours north of Manali on the main highway to Leh. It is the only town on this long road and makes a convenient resting place if you want to break your journey for a night or more. It's also an ideal base for preparing a trek into Zanskar as the tiny village of Darcha, the usual start of this trek, is only 1½ hours further north.

Buses stop above the town by a collection of dhabas which all offer good, cheap food. Walk along the road to some steps which descend to the main part of the town. Turn left at the bottom of the steps to find the hotels. The first you reach is *Hotel Lama Yuru* which offers simple accommodation for Rs125/150 (att) and there's reasonable food available in the restaurant. *Hotel Gyespa* is a little further on and has pleasant double rooms for Rs150 (att), some of which have good views across the valley to Kardang Gompa. The restaurant provides good Western, Indian and Chinese food. The *Tourist Bungalow* across the road has dorm beds for Rs45 and doubles for Rs300. Up on the hillside above the other hotels is *Hotel Snowland* (☎ 019002-2219) which has clean rooms with good views for Rs300 (att).

WHAT TO SEE

Kardang Gompa, the golden-roofed monastery across the river from Keylong, makes a nice excursion to help you acclimatise. The concrete path to this Gelukpa monastery begins below the hospital. The walk one way takes about 1½ hours.

An alternative outing is the one-hour walk to **Shashur Gompa**. Take the path that leads up some steps from the bus stand and keep heading straight up.

ORGANISING YOUR TREK

If your trekking requirements are simple you should have little difficulty organising a trek into Zanskar from here. There are several general stores and a vegetable market so buying enough food and kerosene is no problem. However, don't expect as wide a variety of items for sale as you would in Manali. The hotels can help with finding ponies and a guide and if you require petrol for your stove it is available at Tandi, a small village 8km south of Keylong where the road to Manali crosses the Bhaga River.

MOVING ON

There are frequent buses in both directions along the Manali-Leh highway so getting to Manali, Darcha (for the start of the Across Zanskar trek, see p230) or Leh should present little difficulty.

If you want to reach Leh without another night on the road you need to catch a local bus which is going all the way to Leh without a night stop at Sarchu. These depart very early in the morning – check the times locally. A taxi to Darcha will cost Rs800.

❏ **Bihari road menders**
Travellers on Himalayan roads are often struck by the image of these tough, dark skinned workers, whose camps resemble something out of a *Mad Max* movie. The occasional memorial stone on the side of the road is a testament to one of the hardest jobs in India. Yet the Rs80 per day plus food and lodging that they receive is enough to lure them away from the poverty-stricken lowlands of Bihar to the high altitude and appalling weather of the western Himalaya.

PART 4: LADAKH

Facts about the region

GEOGRAPHICAL BACKGROUND

Ladakh lies in the eastern half of Jammu and Kashmir State in the far north of India. It shares its much disputed north-western border with Pakistan, while to the north lies the Chinese province of Sinkiang, and to the east, Chinese-occupied Tibet.

Covering an area of about 60,000 sq km and ranging in elevation from 2600m to 7670m (8500ft to 25,165ft), it is the largest and highest district in India. A further 37,000 sq km of north-east Ladakh, an area called the Aksai Chin is currently illegally occupied by China.

Ladakh is sandwiched between two vast mountain systems: the Himalaya to the south and the Karakoram to the north. It is the latter range which provides the region with its highest peak, Saser Kangri (7670m/ 25,165ft). Between the two ranges are the Ladakh and Zanskar Mountains, north and south of the Indus Valley respectively. These run north-west to south-east, almost as far as Nepal in the case of the Zanskar Mountains and have peaks mainly between 5000m and 6000m.

Geographic regions of Ladakh
● **Central Ladakh** Ladakh's heartland is the central Indus Valley. This runs from Khalsi in the west to Upshi in the east, bounded by the Ladakh Mountains to the north and the Zanskar Mountains to the south.
● **Nubra** This region of deep valleys and high mountains, to the north of the Ladakh Range, encompasses the Nubra and Shyok river valleys and the eastern end of the Karakoram Mountains. It can be reached by road from Leh over the 5602m (18,380ft) Khardung La, reputedly the highest motorable road in the world.
● **Pangong** The area east of Upshi and north of the Indus River around the vast and brackish Pangong Tso.
● **Rupshu** This dry, high-altitude plateau (4000-5500m) is in the south-east of Ladakh. If you're travelling up from Manali by bus, it's the first region you see. It's the western fringe of the much larger area of Chang Tang, which spreads east into Tibet for about 1500km to the province of Qinghai in China, and whose landscape is characterised by vast plains, rolling mountains and brackish lakes.
● **Zanskar** Between the Great Himalayan Range and the jagged mountains of the Zanskar Range is the 300km long valley of Zanskar. Access can be

gained only by crossing high passes which effectively cut off the valley from the rest of the world during winter. With an average valley bottom altitude of 4000m (13,000ft), it's one of the highest inhabited regions of the world. The two major rivers are the Stod and the Lungnak which join to form the mighty Zanskar. This eventually merges with the Indus having cut an impressive gorge through the Zanskar Mountains.

● **Western Ladakh** The area around the town of Kargil is sometimes referred to as Lower Ladakh. It comprises a number of river valleys, principally the

❏ The geology of Ladakh

In recent geologic history the Indian subcontinent was a separate land mass to Asia, separated by a vast ancient ocean called Tethys. During the Mesozoic the Indian tectonic plate was moving northwards at roughly 15cm per year, Tethys was closing and its oceanic plate was subducted, or 'taken below', the Asian continental block. Melting occurred deep in the earth, associated with this subduction, resulting in a series of granite bodies all along the southern margin of Asia. The Ladakh Range north of the Indus Valley is formed from one such granite body.

It was 55 million years ago that the last marine sediments in Tethys were deposited. This ocean closed forever and the Indian and Asian continental plates collided along a suture zone, tracked today by the path of the Indus River. A mountain belt began to form due to the thrusting of Indian-plate rocks to the south, back onto the subcontinent. Prior to this collision however, a slice of oceanic plate, an 'ophiolite', was thrust onto the Indian continent and is now preserved near Lingshed, where the black and green crystalline rocks, including dykes and pillow lavas can be seen. During and after the collision, distinctive red conglomerates and sandstones – the 'Indus molasse' – were deposited on the north side of the Himalaya, now superbly exposed near Chiling and in the Rumtse and Stok La gorges, where they have been tilted upright.

As India continued its northward motion, crustal thickening occurred both in Asia, creating the expansive high-altitude plateau of Tibet, and more spectacularly in India, forming the Himalaya ranges. This thickening and associated shortening of the Indian crust is clearly seen from the km-size folds and thrusts throughout the limestones of the Zanskar Range.

About 25 million years ago the convergence of the two continental masses caused movement along a huge fault – the 'Main Central Thrust', seen south of Zanskar near Atholi. This thrust uplifted hard, crystalline metamorphic rocks from 35km depth to the surface, rocks which now form the Great Himalaya Range. At the same time large extensional or normal faults, situated right along the Zanskar Valley removed the overlying sediments. One such low angle fault can be seen from Padum in the cliffs above Karsha Gompa. Concomitant with crustal thickening, Indian continental rocks melted to form white garnet-tourmaline granites in the Greater Himalaya, such as those of the spectacular Gumbaranjun mountain spire near the Shingo La.

Convergence continues today and the Himalaya are still rising. To date India has bulldozed a dent some 2400km long into Asia, four times the length of Great Britain!   **Dr Ben Stephenson** (UK)

Suru, Drass, Wakha and the Indus, downstream of Khalsi. The altitude here is lower than the rest of Ladakh so vegetation is much more varied. Further to the west is the Zoji La, Ladakh's western gateway, which takes you over the Great Himalayan Range into Kashmir.

CLIMATE

Extremes of temperature

There's a saying that anyone whose head is in the sun and feet are in the shade in Ladakh will endure both heat stroke and frostbite at the same time. While this is something of an exaggeration, in summer the sun is incredibly powerful but step into the shade and you may need an extra layer of clothing. Night temperatures are comfortably cool. Altitude also plays a strong role in regulating the temperature. One day you can be trekking at 3000m in the stifling heat, the next you can be battling over a 5000m pass in a blizzard. Generally, summer days are a warm 20-25°C.

Winter is a different matter. Even in Leh the thermometer rarely rises above freezing and has been known to drop as low as -35°C. In Zanskar and the far west of Ladakh temperatures as low as this are more frequent.

Rain and snow

Ladakh is dry in the extreme; a typical year sees under 150mm of rainfall which produces the characteristically barren landscape. This is because the Great Himalayan Range forms an almost impenetrable barrier for the monsoon clouds that sweep up from the south across the rest of the subcontinent. Recent years have seen a slight change in the normal weather pattern with some rain-bearing clouds crossing the mountains in August and early September producing a few days of light rain.

In central Ladakh little snow falls in winter while in Zanskar and the far west of Ladakh, especially around Drass, substantial falls are common. Valley travel becomes arduous without skis in the deep unconsolidated snow, and avalanches are a constant hazard in narrow steep-sided valleys.

HISTORICAL OUTLINE

The first mention of the country seems to have been made by Herodotus, who describes a land of wonderful ants, who in burrowing out their homes in the earth threw up gold. These ants were said to be nearly as large as dogs, and still more ferocious, with a keen sense of smell and great fleetness of foot. This made it very difficult for the Indians who wanted the gold to obtain it, and the only method found possible was to fetch the gold day by day when the ants slept, and bear it away on swift horses.
A Reeve Heber and Kathleen Heber *Himalayan Tibet and Ladakh*

Prehistory

Neolithic rock carvings have been found in many parts of Ladakh, from Zanskar to Nubra, showing that the area has been inhabited from the earliest of times. As in many Himalayan regions, these carvings are often of ibex, an animal given divine status throughout the Himalaya by the early inhabitants.

Tribal herdsmen from the west and east slowly settled in Ladakh over the centuries. Traces of these early influxes are still evident in the people in parts of Ladakh today. The Aryan Dards, who came to Ladakh from Kashmir and northern Pakistan, preserve their unique culture in the Dha-Hanu area, while the Rupshu region is largely populated by Tibetan herdsmen, whose semi-nomadic way of life has changed little in the intervening centuries. Other races also trickled into the region, notably from central Asia and Baltistan. Gradually this ethnic hotchpotch integrated into the more unified culture you see today.

The emergence of a nation
From the 6th to the 9th century, the area now known as Ladakh was influenced by the greater powers that surrounded it. Kashmir, Tibet and China were all keen to increase their territory and it seems likely that they all invaded the region at one time or another. Eventually Tibet won the struggle but only held a loose claim on the area. A more direct interest wasn't shown until the collapse of the Tibetan dynasty in 842. This resulted in a power struggle among the ruling classes, which led to some members of the ousted royalty, notably Nyimagon, travelling to western Tibet in search of new dominions. They took control of Ladakh, Guge, Perang, Zanskar and Spiti. Ladakh was allocated to Pelgigon, Nyimagon's eldest son, who installed himself as the first king in the mid-10th century.

Buddhist influences
Buddhism was flourishing in western Ladakh well before the Tibetans arrived, possibly taking root as early as the 2nd century while much of eastern Ladakh and western Tibet was still practising the ancient Bon religion, an animistic belief presided over by shaman priests. The Buddhist influence came via India and, in particular, Kashmir. The rapid rise of Hinduism throughout India forced Indian Buddhist monks to seek sympathetic areas to which they could migrate. Many travelled to Ladakh bringing with them their artistic skills and religious beliefs. The 8th century rock carving of the Maitreya, or future Buddha, at Mulbekh is a fine example of Buddhist art in the Indian tradition, prior to the Tibetans.

Nyimagon's dynasty was keen to nurture Buddhism and help encourage its revival in Tibet, a move which became known as the **second spreading** (see p108). By the 12th and 13th centuries Buddhism was well established in Tibet but had been replaced by Hinduism in India and Islam in Kashmir. Ladakh, unable to rely on its traditional religious and cultural guides, turned instead to Tibet. A strong bond developed between their monasteries with young Ladakhi monks being sent to Tibet to be trained in the finer points of monastic life. This tradition continued for over 700 years until the Chinese occupation of Tibet put a stop to it.

The Namgyal dynasty
Continual raids on Ladakh by the plundering Muslim forces of central Asia and Kashmir were a feature of the 15th and 16th centuries. The more accessible

```
┌─────────────────────────────────────────────┐
```

❏ The second spreading

The protagonist of this movement was a scholar named Rinchen Zangpo, sometimes referred to as 'the great translator', who had the onerous task of making Indian Buddhism accessible to the Ladakhi and Tibetan people.

Modern-day visitors to Ladakh will see his name again and again in connection with various monasteries. While many claim to have been founded by him, it's unlikely that he was as productive as they would like you to believe. It's true that many monasteries were built at this time, and although Rinchen Zangpo was not personally responsible for all of them, he was probably the inspiration behind this building frenzy. Unfortunately, only a handful of gompas, of which Alchi is the finest, remain intact from this era.

```
└─────────────────────────────────────────────┘
```

western part of Ladakh took the full brunt of this aggression and was partially converted to Islam. Ladakh, as a result, was divided and weakened, with Lower Ladakh ruled by **King Takpabum** from Basgo and Temisgam, and Upper Ladakh by **King Takbumde** from Leh and Shey. It took **Bhagan**, the grandson of the Basgo king, to unite Ladakh by overthrowing the king of Leh. He took on the surname Namgyal (meaning victorious) and founded a new dynasty which still survives today. This new lineage was not immune from Islamic attack either: during the 1530s and 40s Ladakh was constantly besieged by central Asian forces under the intrepid warrior, Mirza Haidar.

The strong rule of the brutal **King Tashi Namgyal** (1555-1575) strengthened a flagging and low-spirited country and managed to repel most of the central Asian raiders. He is best remembered for the imposing royal fort he built on top of Namgyal Peak and the Gonkhang just below. The fortunes of Ladakh continued to flourish under his nephew, **Tsewang Namgyal**, an eminent soldier who temporarily increased his kingdom as far as Nepal.

The Muslim invasion

It was at the beginning of the seventeenth century, during the reign of **Jamyang Namgyal**, Tsewang's brother, that the proponents of Islam made the most concerted effort to convert Ladakh once and for all. The Baltistan army under **Ali Mir** stormed through the country destroying all Buddhist artefacts that they came across and thwarting the Ladakhis' attempts to stop them. Today there are few gompas that date from before this catastrophic episode as most were razed to the ground. Alchi and a few hill gompas are the exception.

Jamyang Namgyal was forced to marry Ali Mir's daughter, **Gyal Katun**, and to promise that any offspring from this union would be first in line for the throne, thereby ensuring future Islamic kings. However, in an ironic twist of fate, her subjects saw the new queen not as a Muslim but rather as the manifestation of a Buddhist goddess! Buddhism was resurrected with increased vigour.

Sengge Namgyal

The son of Jamyang and Gyal Katun, Sengge Namgyal, the 'lion' king (1616-1642), is perhaps the best remembered of Ladakh's kings. In an effort to bring Ladakh back to its former glory he embarked on an ambitious and energetic building programme which produced several gompas, the most famous of which is Hemis, many mani walls, the huge statue of Buddha at Shey and the skyscraping palace overlooking Leh.

He was also a courageous soldier, expanding the kingdom into Zanskar, Spiti and the west Tibetan province of Guge. He had less success in the west, being badly defeated by the Mughal army that had already taken Kashmir and Baltistan. Peace was restored only by his agreeing to pay the Mughals a regular tribute; a promise that he never honoured. Although he is constantly praised in the chronicles, his extravagant and overambitious reign had negative consequences for the future of Ladakh.

The loss of independence

His son and heir, **Deldan Namgyal** (1642-1694), had to pay for his father's defiance by building a mosque in Leh in order to placate the powerful Mughal emperor, Aurangzeb. He was also supposed to pay the tribute but, like his father, either paid infrequently or not at all. He led a successful campaign against the Baltis in the west and defeated a Mughal army that came to their aid. However, he made a grave mistake with his allies on the eastern border by going against the Dalai Lama, siding instead with Bhutan in a religious dispute. A combined Tibetan and Mongol force descended on the impudent king and forced him to take refuge in the fortress at Basgo, where he was held for three years. The Tibetans were finally forced to withdraw by an advancing Kashmiri army but this help from Deldan's former enemies did not come cheap.

While Ladakh remained internally autonomous, the Kashmiris now assumed overall power. The king was made to convert to Islam, all Ladakh's valuable pashmina wool had to go to Kashmir, and the long-ignored tribute had to be paid. As with the other attempts to convert Ladakh to Islam it was the people who were impossible to win over, remaining true to their Buddhist roots.

The **Treaty of Temisgam** in 1684 settled the dispute between Ladakh and Tibet but by means of various trade and religious agreements it ensured that Ladakh became partially controlled by its eastern neighbour as well. Sandwiched between Kashmir and Tibet and answerable to both, Ladakh was severely restricted in what it could do beyond its borders.

The Dogra invasion

By the beginning of the 19th century the Mughal empire had collapsed and Sikh rule had been established in Kashmir. Meanwhile, Ladakh had been weakened by a series of inadequate kings and seemed an obvious target for the expansionist ambitions of the Sikh ruler, **Ranjit Singh**. His commander-in-chief, Zorawar Singh, invaded Ladakh with 5000 men in 1834, meeting little resistance from the poorly equipped and trained Ladakhi army. **King Tshespal Namgyal** was dethroned and the royal family exiled to Stok, where they still live. Ladakh came under Dogra rule and it was incorporated into the state of Jammu and Kashmir in 1846. However, Ladakh was allowed to maintain considerable autonomy and to keep its links with Tibet.

Partition and the Indo-Pakistan wars

The tragic events that swept over India in the run-up to partition in 1947 mercifully avoided Ladakh. Buddhists and Muslims continued living side by side, without any major incidents, as they had done for centuries. Partition left Ladakh as part of the Indian state of Jammu and Kashmir with the result that it would be administered from Srinagar.

In 1948, just after partition, Ladakh was invaded yet again. This time by Pakistani raiders who managed to take Kargil, occupy Zanskar and get to within 30km of Leh. The capital was badly defended and volunteers were hastily sought and trained. Fortunately, reinforcement troops were sent in by air and a battalion of Gurkhas made its way slowly to Leh on foot from the south. Both reached Leh in time to expel the raiders and return Ladakh to India. Kargil was the scene of fighting again in 1965 and 1971 during the two Indo-Pakistan wars, when both nations challenged the position of the cease-fire line. This ran extremely close to Kargil thus involving it in the skirmishes. In 1971, the Indian army managed to push it back to 12km from the town, where it still remains.

Chinese aggression

The events that took place on Ladakh's northern and eastern borders had much wider repercussions for the region than the series of Indo-Pakistan wars. The first blow to Ladakh was the Chinese closure of the border between Nubra and Sinkiang Province in 1949. This effectively stopped the traditional trade route between India and central Asia and starved Ladakh of

❑ Siachen Glacier war

The most constant and least talked about conflict between India and Pakistan has been going on for over 15 years at the head of the Nubra Valley. This extraordinary war on the longest glacier in the Karakoram is the highest in the world with fighting at up to 6500m (21,000ft). The exact position of the cease-fire line in this remote part of the Karakoram has never been fully agreed. When rumours started circulating that Pakistan might try to stake a claim on the Siachen Glacier and the surrounding peaks, Indian troops swiftly occupied the area in 1984. Fighting soon broke out and skirmishes have continued ever since.

The severe cold restricts the fighting to the summer but this hasn't limited the casualties. Far more people have died as a result of the environmental conditions (altitude, crevasses, avalanches and exposure) than from the actual fighting. Nubra is quite safe to visit as the fighting is going on far away from the places that tourists are allowed to go.

the 1000-year-old business that had been generated from the caravans. In 1950 the Chinese authorities invaded Tibet. For a decade the Tibetans were assaulted with violence and propaganda which culminated in the brutal suppression of the Lhasa uprising in 1959. The Dalai Lama sought refuge in India and has since been followed there by thousands of refugees. The Chinese then continued their expansionist programme into Ladakh by occupying 28,500 sq km of the Aksai Chin, a high desolate plain in the north-east of the region, where they promptly built roads connecting Tibet with Sinkiang. In 1962 the Chinese launched a massive attack on the borders of Ladakh but were repelled by Ladakhi and Indian troops. The loss of the worthless land of the Aksai Chin was not an important issue but the proximity of the Chinese, who by now were working closely with the Pakistanis, posed a real threat to India. This was demonstrated by the joint construction of the Karakoram Highway.

Suddenly, the strategic importance of Ladakh was recognised by the rest of the subcontinent. The region's isolation was swiftly brought to a close by the rapid completion of the 434km Srinagar to Leh highway, cutting the journey from 16 days to two, and enabling a massive military build up to ensue. Simultaneously, China closed the Tibetan border and brought to an end the 700-year-old paternal link between the gompas of Ladakh and Tibet.

Towards autonomy

Since partition, Ladakh has been governed by the State Government based in Srinagar. This has never been a wholly satisfactory arrangement and Ladakhis feel that they have often been neglected by the politicians in Kashmir. Calls for a Union Territory, separate from Jammu and Kashmir State and directly governed from New Delhi, have circulated since the early 1970s but have met with little success. Among the few efforts designed to help develop the region was the opening up of Ladakh to foreign tourists in 1974. In 1979, allegedly for the convenience of administration, Ladakh was divided into the so-called Buddhist Leh District and Muslim Kargil District of which Zanskar was a sub-division. This upset many people, not least the Zanskaris, who were justifiably concerned about who was going to represent their Buddhist interests. This unnecessary division started to rock the centuries-old cohesiveness between Buddhists and Muslims.

In the early 1980s the State Government mishandled several simple, localised problems, sparking off demonstrations throughout Ladakh. Continued apathy, corruption and Muslim bias from the State Government throughout the decade provided the catalyst for violent riots in Leh in 1989 between Buddhists and Muslims. This culminated in the police opening fire on a peaceful demonstration, killing three innocent people. More subtle agitation ensued, provoking the Ladakh Buddhist Association (LBA) to call for a social and economic boycott of Muslims.

In 1989 there were further calls for a Union Territory which were soon toned down to a more realistic demand for autonomous status within the state. Pressure from within Ladakh increased and the process gathered pace.

The LBA lifted the boycott against the Muslims in 1992 and since then there has been greater co-operation between the two religious groups.

Ladakh Autonomous Hill Development Council

In October 1993 the central Indian Government and the State Government agreed that Autonomous Hill Council Status would be granted for Ladakh. Under this proposal, only control over law and order would remain with the Kashmir government. Responsibility for almost everything else, including development, education, culture, the staffing of government posts and the collection of local taxes, would be placed in the hands of the Ladakhis. In September 1995 the decentralised and democratic Ladakh Autonomous Hill Development Council became reality, and a new era for Ladakh began.

ECONOMY

For centuries Ladakh has enjoyed a stable economy based on self-reliance. But over the last 50 years, the region has shifted away from this sustainable economy towards one based on dependence on outside forces and is slowly being drawn into a much wider economic sphere over which it has little control.

Misguided policies to 'help' this 'deprived and backward' region, along with the build-up of a large population of Indian troops and the influx of foreign tourists, have all contributed to encouraging a money economy. A materialistic culture where the notion of having a job and buying what you need, rather than producing it yourself, is now becoming more widespread. While change is inevitable, it doesn't have to take the form of rapid Western-style modernisation.

Fortunately Ladakh is the home of several forward-thinking indigenous organisations who are swimming against this tide of inappropriate change (see p132). By encouraging ecological and sustainable development which preserves and builds on traditional practices, it is hoped Ladakh will avoid the pitfalls which so many other blindly modernising, developing countries have suffered.

Agriculture

Ladakh has traditionally been an agricultural subsistence economy based on growing barley, wheat and peas and the keeping of yak, *dzos* (yak-cow crossbreeds), cows, sheep and goats. At lower elevations fruit is grown successfully, while the high-altitude Rupshu region is the preserve of nomadic herders. Surplus produce is traded for tea, sugar, salt and various luxuries such as the semi-precious stones that adorn women's head-dresses, or *peraks*.

There is little that can be exported for economic gain. Two exceptions, however, are apricots from western Ladakh and pashmina (see opposite).

Sustainable agriculture In many ways it's amazing that the harsh environment of Ladakh can support any agriculture, and yet a highly productive subsistence system has provided the population with most of their needs for centuries. In fact, when average crop yields are compared, they are almost as high as those of intensive, high input farms in Europe. The success of this system is due to the refinement of techniques to suit the environment and a social structure that supports agriculture. For example:

● **Water** The lack of water is overcome by diverting melt water from mountain streams along sophisticated irrigation channels.

● **Fuel** The shortage of fuel wood is overcome by using dried animal dung. The hardy local breeds of livestock also provide farmers with power for ploughing and threshing while producing useful by-products such as milk, cheese and wool.

● **Fertiliser** As the animal dung is used mainly for fuel and not for fertiliser, human 'nightsoil' is collected in dry latrines and spread on the fields instead.

● *Langde* An extensive system of sharing resources throughout a village, called *langde*, evolved so that the labour-intensive activities, such as sowing and harvesting, can be completed without having to hire labourers.

● *Rares* Another system called *rares* means that each family has to take it in turn to herd all the animals in the village for a day.

● **Polyandry** Both the tradition of passing on land only to the eldest son and the practice of polyandrous marriages (whereby brothers share a common wife) prevent the fragmentation of family land.

In recent years, several trends have started to undermine this integrated agricultural system and destroy the fragile environment on which farming depends: more people are leaving the villages to seek employment in Leh; those that remain are moving towards growing single cash-crops; polyandry and other social structures are becoming relics of the past; people are beginning to perceive farming as a lowly occupation; and the government is promoting highly subsidised hybrid seeds, chemical fertilisers and pesticides, while distributing subsidised food at half its actual price to the markets of Leh.

❏ **Pashmina**
This incredibly fine wool from the underbelly of the Chang Tang goat (*Capra hircus*) is the basis for Srinagar's cashmere shawl weaving industry. This industry has been vital to Srinagar's economy since the 17th century and goes some way towards explaining Kashmir's obsession for control of Ladakh. Cashmere fabric is notoriously expensive because each goat produces only small quantities of this soft hair and its processing is incredibly time-consuming. Cheaper wool is available from Mongolia and Iran, but is thought to be of inferior quality.
Since the 1684 Treaty of Temisgam, Ladakh has had a monopoly on the purchasing of this valuable product from the nomads of Rupshu and Chang Tang, although the agreement also stipulated that it could be sold only to Kashmiri traders. The monopoly still exists today, and although it has kept the price of pashmina artificially low, it has supported a unique way of life on the Chang Tang plateau.

❏ Population control

Living in a landscape where resources are severely limited encouraged the Ladakhis to adopt customs which kept the population stable and prevented the fragmentation of family land. Central to this was the right of primogeniture, whereby all the land was inherited by the eldest son and could never be split or sold. Naturally, this left the remaining sons without an inheritance. It was therefore the custom that at least one son would become a monk, while the others were free to seek their fortune in any way that they saw fit without the support of the family, or alternatively, to enter into a polyandrous marriage with their eldest brother's wife. In this way, the celibate monks would require only minimum support from the community in return for religious duties, while one family could live off the same land for centuries without increasing the size of the population; a polyandrous family is unlikely to produce any more offspring than one husband and one wife.

Fraternal polyandry was a remarkably effective solution which, perhaps surprisingly, resulted in few problems. The younger brother or brothers accepted their eldest brother's authority, and the question of who was the genetic father of the children was thought irrelevant. The children called the head of the household, 'big father' and the other brothers, 'little father'.

If there were no sons, the land would go to the eldest daughter and the exact opposite arrangement would occur. She would bring in a husband, who would have no rights over her land, and her sisters would either become nuns, would marry into another family or would join their eldest sister in a polygamous marriage. The guiding principle throughout was that the land never got divided.

The customs of polyandry and primogeniture are still occasionally practised but to a much lesser degree since they were made illegal in the early 1940s. Whilst this was done with the intention of protecting the rights of the individual, it has completely changed rural society. Now the population is increasing and the village land can no longer sustain the communities.

There is a realisation that if these trends go unchecked agriculture will suffer a demise, there will be a decline in soil and water quality and Ladakh will become dependent on imported food. Within the last decade or so, efforts have been made by various non-governmental organisations (NGOs), in particular LEDeG (Ladakh Ecological Development Group) and the Ladakh Women's Alliance, to raise awareness of the dangers of 'modern' methods, to increase the status of farmers and to harness the benefits of the sustainable and productive traditional system. There is now growing evidence that the farmers' initial excitement with the new techniques is gradually being replaced by a return to their faith in traditional agriculture.

Trade

In the past, Ladakh's geographical position at the crossroads of some of the most important trade routes in Asia was exploited to the full. Ladakh's kings happily collected tax on the goods that crossed their kingdom from Turkistan, Tibet, the Punjab, Kashmir and Baltistan, while a minority of Ladakhi people were profitably employed as merchants and caravan traders.

However, since the Chinese authorities closed the borders into Tibet and central Asia, this international trade has completely dried up. Business is now reliant on the more fickle market of the Indian army and summer tourists.

Tourism

Since 1974, when Ladakh was opened to tourists, the industry has expanded rapidly. On average it now receives 18,000 tourists a year. Although in Ladakh as a whole, tourism employs only 4% of workers, in Leh it employs 15%. It also accounts for almost 50% of the region's GNP. See p155 for information on how to limit your impact on Ladakh.

EDUCATION

For almost 50 years the education system in Ladakh has been in chaos. It is based on the Indian education system which is a poor copy of the British system. Schools are now well distributed throughout Ladakh but 75% of them are primary only (5-11 years). These are attended by about 65% of the children, but there is a high level of absenteeism, especially in the busy agricultural seasons when the children's help is needed on the farms. As there are fewer middle and high schools, study beyond the age of 11 often involves leaving home.

Low salaries (Rs1500-3500 per month) attract poor quality teachers, most of whom have to be recruited from outside Ladakh. Teacher absenteeism is also a problem and it is not unheard of for teachers to charge for private tuition on subjects that they themselves failed to teach in school.

As if this were not enough, the Western-biased curriculum teaches the pupils nothing of their own land or history and they aren't even taught in Ladakhi. Until the age of 14 they learn in Urdu and after that in English. They then have only two years to master this new language before taking the all important matriculation exam, in English. This is their passport to jobs and further education: 95% fail it. It seems that for the vast majority, schooling has served only to alienate them from their native culture.

The long-term outlook is a little more promising. In 1993 the **Students' Educational and Cultural Movement of Ladakh** (SECMOL) launched 'Operation New Hope', a campaign to provide 'culturally appropriate and locally relevant education' by a number of means which include producing Ladakhi textbooks, adopting one language for the teaching of maths and science at all ages, and the regular training of teachers. A government degree college has been opened in Leh, thus providing further education students with the option of staying in Ladakh, rather than having to move to Delhi or Kashmir.

THE PEOPLE

The 200,000 strong population of Ladakh is a result of the blending of many different races, in particular the Tibetans and the Dards.

Tibetans

The nomadic and semi-nomadic **Changpa** people of the Rupshu plateau are pure Tibetans and it is probably herders like them who first populated

Ladakh. Through centuries of experience they have mastered the art of not only living but thriving in one of the most hostile environments on earth. Since the early 1960s their numbers have increased as Chang Tang nomads from across the Tibetan border flee the occupation of their homeland by the Chinese. Leh has also provided a home from home for about 3500 **refugees** who live in the various camps around the city.

The looks and the way of life of both the **Ladakhis** of central Ladakh and, perhaps even more so, the **Zanskaris**, reflect a strong influence from central Tibet. Moving west, this influence diminishes and is replaced by that of the Dards. The one exception to this is the **Baltis** who live around Kargil and the Suru Valley. They have Tibetan origins, speak a language that has Tibetan links and were once Buddhists, though today they are devout Shiite Muslims.

Dards

These people originate from Gilgit in Pakistan. They now live in Drass and the Dha-Hanu area. Although originally Buddhist, the Dards around Drass have embraced Islam and have been strongly influenced by their Kashmiri neighbours. Those in the Dha-Hanu area, known as **Brokpa**, have preserved their Buddhist faith and retain many of their original customs and traditions.

In most villages in Ladakh you'll find another group of Dards, the **Mons**, descendants of Ladakh's early settlers. Whilst these people represent Ladakh's lower class the segregation is nothing like as severe as that found in the Indian caste system. Their traditional roles as musicians, blacksmiths and carpenters are highly valued in the community.

Others

Some of the constant visitors to Ladakh over the centuries have inevitably settled here. This is particularly true of Leh, where you can find small communities of Kashmiris and central Asians whose forefathers came when it was an important city on the great trade routes across Asia. Thousands of Indian military personnel are the most recent incomers.

RELIGION

Tibetan Buddhism

Ladakh is one of the few places where you can see this branch of Mahayana Buddhism (see p64), sometimes also called **Lamaism**, being practised as it would have been in Tibet before the brutal Chinese suppression. Buddhism has permeated Ladakhi and Tibetan culture since the 7th century AD.

Tibetan Buddhism is a mystical religion which absorbed many of the magical and superstitious features of Tibet's previous shamanistic Bön religion, along with elements of Hindu Tantrism. With an array of deities, beliefs, rituals and symbols it's incredibly complex, but to most Ladakhis, who don't concern themselves too much with these difficulties, it becomes a practical and down-to-earth philosophy which emphasises one thing – compassion.

Lamas It is usual for most families to have at least one son who is a lama (monk). At an early age he will be sent to the **gompa** (monastery) to which his village is attached where he will be educated in the religious teachings. Monks are highly respected in the community and spend a lot of their time away from the gompa performing religious ceremonies in the villages. The heads of gompas are called *kushoks* and are reincarnations of previous venerated lamas. The head of Tibetan Buddhism and traditional political ruler of Tibet is the **Dalai Lama**, an incarnation of Avalokiteshvara, the bodhisattva of compassion. The current Dalai Lama is the 14th in a succession that originated in the 14th century and lives in exile in Dharamsala, Himachal Pradesh.

The lamas of Tibetan Buddhism are divided into four main sects. The oldest is the **Nyingmapa** (the Ancient Order or Red Hat sect) and was founded by the great sage Padmasambhava in the 8th century. Next came the **Sakyapa** sect, followed by the last of the Red Hat schools, the **Kagyupa**. The most recent order is the **Gelukpa**, more commonly known as the Yellow Hat sect, who came from a reform movement in the 1400s and which is led by the Dalai Lama. All these sects are represented in Ladakh, but the most common are the Kagyupa and Gelukpa.

Islam

Although Ladakh is usually described as a Buddhist region, there is a large minority of Muslims (about 45%). Constant invasion by Islamic forces in the west of Ladakh gradually led to the conversion of the previously Buddhist people. Most Ladakhi Muslims still live in Kargil District where they account for 85% of the population. Here they are puritanical Shiites. Leh also supports a small population of Muslims, mainly Sunnis, who are descended from immigrant Kashmiri and central Asian traders.

Christianity

There is a small community of Christians in Leh. Most belong to the top rungs of Ladakhi society and were converted by Moravian missionaries who first came to Ladakh in 1885. They built two churches, one in Leh and one in Shey.

❏ Om mani padme hum

This is the great mantra of Avalokiteshvara (or Chenresig, to give the Tibetan name), the bodhisattva of compassion. It flows from the lips of devout Tibetan Buddhists at all times of the day and is a constant affirmation of the compassion of all the Buddhas. *Om* is the auspicious syllable which precedes most mantras, *mani* means jewel in Sanskrit and *padme* means lotus, *hum* has no literal meaning but may infer 'holding'. This syllable also rhythmically ends the mantra. The mantra helps people visualise Chenresig and the compassion he represents, as he is always seen holding a jewel and a lotus. Prayers in Buddhism do not call on an outside force for help, but remind the speaker of the powers within themselves, which can be utilised when we are free from selfish desires.

You will see the mantra inscribed on prayer flags, mani stones, prayer wheels and even carved into rocks throughout the Buddhist Himalaya. These remind the passer-by to repeat the mantra to realise their own potential for love and good will.

PART 5: LEH AND BEYOND

Leh

There is nothing whatever to do. That is Leh's charm...nothing to do but to slow down, relax, laze, to become one vast transparent eye. **Andrew Harvey** *A Journey in Ladakh*

Leh, the capital of Ladakh, lies nestled among low hills on the north side of the Indus Valley, between the Stok Mountains to the south and the Ladakh Range to the north. For centuries it has been a place where travellers of different nationalities have rested, before continuing over the mountains along the ancient trade routes that radiate from the city. Today, Leh is popular with a different kind of mountain wanderer and makes an ideal base for treks in the region.

The town's activities still centre on the bustling Main Bazaar. Indian soldiers, Kashmiri souvenir sellers and Western tourists have now replaced the exotic traders from Turkistan, Afghanistan and Tibet, while the load-bearing camels and horses have given way to diesel-belching Tata trucks. There have been many changes as a result of wider contact with the rest of the world but much goes on as it always has: Ladakhi women sell vegetables along the shady side of the Main Bazaar; old men and women spin hand-held prayer wheels in the narrow side streets; Muslims congregate in animated conversation around the mosque; and every shop in town closes early when the final polo match of the season is played.

It's worth spending a few days in Leh before embarking on your trek, not only to acclimatise to the rarefied air but to give yourself time to explore the fascinating villages nearby. If you've just come up from the south, the dry,

---

❏ **Beware of the altitude**
Most people who ascend rapidly to Leh by plane or bus will feel some effects of the altitude. At 3500m (11,500ft) it is vital to take it easy for the first few days: don't overexert yourself; drink lots of water, soup or tea; avoid alcohol at least until you're acclimatised; and look out for any symptoms of altitude illness (see p272). If you are in any doubt about symptoms, assume that it is AMS and act quickly and appropriately. Twenty-four hour medical help is available by phoning ☎ 52360.

Being at such high altitude is not all bad news. What could be nicer for the first few days of your holiday than having to submit to lethargy and self-indulgent laziness?

---

hot days and cool nights will come as a welcome relief after the summer humidity of the Indian plains. The town is brimming with excellent guest-houses run by welcoming Ladakhi families and the only difficulty with eating out is deciding which of the many good restaurants to choose.

Leh is a small town with a population of about 25,000. Because of this it's easy to escape from the vibrant chaos of the centre by walking out into the surrounding fields along poplar and willow-lined paths. Peace is readily found in the cool dark of a nearby gompa.

HISTORY

In the 15th century both Leh and the village of Shey shared the responsibility of being the capitals of Upper Ladakh. Shey was the more fortified of the two, while Leh was in a prime position for trade. The town's growth in importance is reflected by the building of the first royal residency on top of Namgyal Peak by Tashi Namgyal in the 16th century and then the building of the majestic Royal Palace by Sengge Namgyal a century later. Since then Leh has remained the administrative and commercial capital of Ladakh.

Leh's prosperity derived from its location at the foot of the Khardung La, the gateway of the infamous trade route to Yarkand in Turkistan (see p229). The trade involved the people of Leh at all levels: a few undergoing the rigorous journeys over the mountains themselves, some merely setting up as merchants, while others profited indirectly by providing services to the constant stream of visitors.

Since the Chinese closure of the trade routes in 1949, Leh's economic base has shifted. It now concentrates on providing services to the new incomers, notably the thousands of Indian troops who have moved into the area since the 1960s and the influx of foreign tourists since 1974. Leh has come face to face with a world with which it had little previous contact, a world in which technological advances and economic gain are the driving forces. Leh is gradually adopting this inappropriate model of development and is beginning to suffer from corresponding environmental and social problems. However, all is not bleak. The changes that have been brought about are relatively recent and are not irreversible. What's more, Leh is the home of several excellent grass roots organisations who are striving to stem this tide, and adopt a more sustainable and appropriate way forward for this fascinating city.

ARRIVAL

By air

Leh's small airport is 2½ km to the south of the town. There is a tourist information desk in the arrivals hall, and you are required to fill in a registration form while waiting for your luggage to arrive. By far the easiest way into Leh is by taxi (Rs70). There is no bus from the airport but if you persevere you may be able to stop one by the main gates.

By bus

Most buses will drop you at the main bus stand, a 10-minute walk from the centre of town. Himachal Tourism buses are usually more obliging and will drop you by their centrally located office on Fort Rd.

ORIENTATION

Everything is within walking distance. The central focus is the Main Bazaar, a wide and straight street with the Royal Palace above it at one end. The majority of shops are found along this road at ground level and popular restaurants take up the first floor space. The old town, a fascinating network of rabbit-warren streets, is immediately beneath the Palace, while the rest of Leh sprawls away downhill from here.

The main bus stand, hospital, Tourist Reception Centre and post office are all outside the centre along the road leading south to the airport.

LOCAL TRANSPORT

Hiring a **motorbike** is an ideal way to get around Ladakh and gives you incomparable freedom. The most popular is the 350cc Enfield Bullet (Rs600-800 per day); smaller 100cc Yamahas are also available (Rs500-600). You should be able to find one through most travel agents. You will be required to leave some kind of deposit behind, usually your passport or air ticket. The roads are generally good and relatively free of traffic although you should ride very defensively as nobody will give way to you. Take plenty of petrol if you're venturing far; there are few petrol stations outside Leh.

You can pick up a **taxi** from the Taxi Operators' Union rank, ☎ 52723, (open 6am-6pm) on Fort Rd in the centre of town. While most places in Leh, apart from the airport, are within easy walking distance, taxis provide a convenient if expensive way to get around the Indus Valley. None of the taxis are metered but this shouldn't cause any problems as there are official rates to most places in Ladakh. Most drivers should have a rate list on them, or you can check the rates at the Union office. If you're catching a plane early in the morning be sure to book a taxi the night before, as there is never much activity at the taxi rank first thing.

Buses are the cheapest and often most enjoyable means of transport for travelling around the principal towns and villages of Ladakh, but they can be over-crowded. (See 'Places of Interest Beyond Leh', p139 for bus times). Both the J&KSRTC buses and the privately operated buses leave from the main bus stand. The private buses have their destinations written on the front, but finding out destinations and departure times of the others is a matter of asking as many people as you can find and going with the consensus. The bus timetable posted in the Tourist Information Office in town can also be useful.

WHERE TO STAY

Hotel areas

● **Leh** There is a wide range of accommodation in Leh from cheap guest-houses (under Rs100) to expensive hotels (over Rs2000). Restaurants, shops, trekking agencies, buses and taxis are all nearby making it the most convenient place to stay. Guest-houses and hotels are dotted all around the town.

● **Chanspa (Changspa)** This village lies on the west side of Leh along the road to the Shanti Stupa. There are places to stay for all budgets and tastes; the majority are at the cheaper end. It's a good 10-15 minute walk from the town centre and well away from the noise and crowds but it's not ideal if you've got a lot to organise.

● **Sankar** is a quiet village 10-15 minutes walk to the north of Leh. There are only a few guest-houses here and no other facilities. It's the perfect place to stay when you want to get away from it all.

Prices and seasons

Prices vary enormously depending on the time of year. The high season of July and August is when the hotels are at their most expensive; the prices quoted below refer to these months and are for single and double rooms with attached (**att**) or common (**com**) bathrooms. Prices for the more expensive hotels often include some meals and where this is the case the cheapest option is shown.

Discounts of 25% are often available at the beginning and end of the season, particularly in the hotels (rather than guest-houses), and it's sometimes possible to get a slight reduction if you're staying in the same room for a long time. Many places are closed between November and May. Two or three of the big hotels stay open all year round and many of the guest-houses will let you stay even though they're not officially open.

Hotels are **[keyed]** to the map on p122-3.

Budget guest-houses and hotels (£4/US$6 or less)

Private guest-houses are the most popular places to stay in Leh. Not only are they the best value for money but also the most interesting. They tend to be run by Ladakhi families who convert their homes into guest-houses for the summer and back into their homes for winter. The accommodation is usually simple, comfortable and clean; you will need to bring your own sleeping bag or bedding. Many places have solar-heated showers and those that don't can provide hot water by the bucketful (Rs5). There is usually a choice of Western or Ladakhi-style toilets and where possible you should use the latter. Unfortunately these are increasingly being replaced by flush systems, a worrying trend in a town with no proper sewage infrastructure and a severe shortage of water.

Near the centre of town, above the polo ground by the Mani Sarmo chortens is *Namgyal Guest House* [72] (☎ 53307), one of the cheapest and friendliest guest-houses in Leh. The Namgyal family go out of their way to make you feel at home and offer clean double rooms for Rs80-150 (com) and

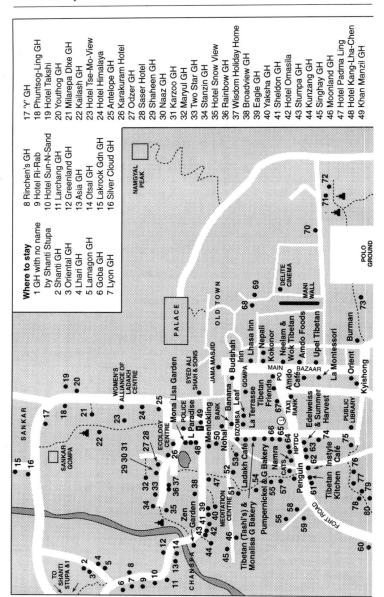

Where to stay
1 GH with no name by Shanti Stupa
2 Shanti GH
3 Oriental GH
4 Lhari GH
5 Lamagon GH
6 Goba GH
7 Lyon GH
8 Rinchen's GH
9 Hotel Ri-Rab
10 Hotel Sun-N-Sand
11 Larchang GH
12 Greenland GH
13 Asia GH
14 Otsal GH
15 Lakrook Gdn GH
16 Silver Cloud GH
17 'Y' GH
18 Phuntsog-Ling GH
19 Hotel Takshi
20 Youthog GH
21 Milarepa Dixe GH
22 Kailash GH
23 Hotel Tse-Mo-View
24 Hotel Himalaya
25 Antelope GH
26 Karakuram Hotel
27 Odzer GH
28 Saser Hotel
29 Shaheen GH
30 Naaz GH
31 Karzoo GH
32 Maryul GH
33 Two Star GH
34 Stanzin GH
35 Hotel Snow View
36 Rainbow GH
37 Wisdom Holiday Home
38 Broadview GH
39 Eagle GH
40 Yaksha GH
41 Sheldon GH
42 Hotel Omasila
43 Stumpa GH
44 Kunzang GH
45 Singhay GH
46 Moonland GH
47 Hotel Padma Ling
48 Hotel Kang-Lha-Chen
49 Khan Manzil GH

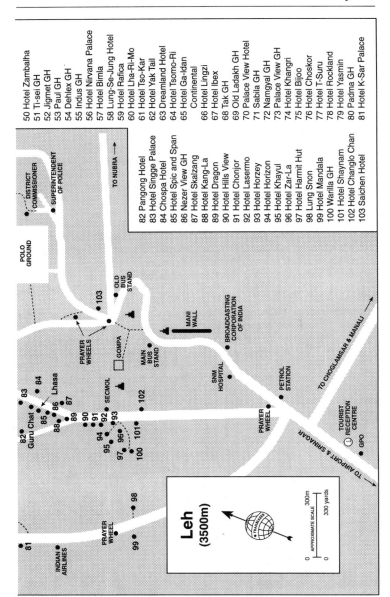

50 Hotel Zambalha
51 Ti-sei GH
52 Jigmet GH
53 Paul GH
54 Dehlex GH
55 Indus GH
56 Hotel Nirvana Palace
57 Hotel Bimla
58 Lung-Se-Jung Hotel
59 Hotel Rafica
60 Hotel Lha-Ri-Mo
61 Hotel Tso-Kar
62 Hotel Yak Tail
63 Dreamland Hotel
64 Hotel Tsomo-Ri
65 Hotel Ga-ldan
   Continental
66 Hotel Lingzi
67 Hotel Ibex
68 Tak GH
69 Old Ladakh GH
70 Palace View Hotel
71 Sabila GH
72 Namgyal GH
73 Palace View GH
74 Hotel Khangri
75 Hotel Bijoo
76 Hotel Choskor
77 Hotel T-Suru
78 Hotel Rockland
79 Hotel Yasmin
80 Padma GH
81 Hotel K-Sar Palace

82 Pangong Hotel
83 Hotel Singge Palace
84 Chospa Hotel
85 Hotel Spic and Span
86 Nezer View GH
87 Hotel Skalzang
88 Hotel Kang-La
89 Hotel Dragon
90 Hotel Hills View
91 Hotel Chonjor
92 Hotel Lasermo
93 Hotel Horzey
94 Hotel Horizon
95 Hotel Khayul
96 Hotel Zar-La
97 Hotel Harmit Hut
98 Lung Snon
99 Hotel Mandala
100 Warilla GH
101 Hotel Shaynam
102 Hotel Changlo Chan
103 Saichen Hotel

Leh
(3500m)

APPROXIMATE SCALE

0   300m
0   330 yards

Rs200 (att). They are always willing to have people in the winter. The *Old Ladakh Guest House* [69], in the interesting old town below the Palace, has nice double rooms for Rs120 (com) and Rs200-300 (att).

On the other side of town up a small alley off Fort Rd are a collection of popular places. *Dehlex Guest House* [54] (☎ 52755) is particularly good value with rooms for Rs150-200 (com), some of which have views to the mountains. On the other side of Fort Rd is the ever-popular *Padma Guest House* [80] (☎ 52630, 📠 53072) which has accommodation in both the guest-house and a modern extension. Double rooms with shared bath cost Rs150-200, while those with their own bathroom range from Rs250-600. Traditional Ladakhi food is served most evenings to guests in the beautiful family kitchen. Nearby is the utilitarian *Hotel Choskor* [76] which offers good value double rooms with attached bathrooms for Rs150-200. Much further down Fort Rd, on a path opposite Hotel Mandala, is the friendly, family-run *Lung Snon Guest House* [98] (☎ 52749). They have peaceful rooms for Rs120 (com) and Rs200-250 (att) and food can be provided.

There's a wide choice of places in Chanspa village. After crossing the bridge there is *Asia Guest House* [13] with its beautiful garden by the stream. Clean rooms cost Rs150/200 (com). If you don't mind a long walk the *Oriental Guest House* [3] (☎ 53153), below the Shanti Stupa, is another wonderful place to stay. This large traditional house has views to the Palace and to Leh and Tsemo gompas. The rooms are Rs120-170 for a double (com) and Rs200 (att) and the cheerful family provides delicious communal meals every evening. The best views in Leh are without a doubt from the *guest house* (no name) [1] by the Shanti Stupa. The rooms for Rs130 (com) look out over the town and the Indus Valley to the Stok Mountains.

On the road up to Sankar you will find the attractive *Antelope Guest House* [25] (☎ 52086), with double rooms for Rs200 (com) and rooms with attached bathrooms from Rs250. Further on up is the secluded *Hotel Himalaya* [24] which has double rooms in an orchard for Rs200-250 all with attached bathrooms. In Sankar itself, *'Y' Guest House* [17] (☎ 52180) provides budget accommodation for Rs150 (com). Those looking for peace and a very long walk into town could try *Lakrook Garden Guest House* [15] (☎ 52987) where you can 'enjoy organic vegetables and herbal teas' straight from the garden. Double rooms cost Rs150 (com) and Rs300 (att).

Moderately-priced guest-houses and hotels (£4-8/US$6-12)

Many places in this price range still retain the charm of the budget guest-houses while providing a few extra comforts such as an attached bathroom. If you want to be in the centre of the town, *Dreamland Hotel* [63] (☎ 52089) is very convenient yet quiet, being set back from the road. Double rooms are Rs350 (att). Further down Fort Rd is the *Hotel Tso-kar* [61] (☎ 53071) which shares the same flower-filled courtyard as the Tibetan Kitchen.

LIST OF GUEST HOUSES AND HOTELS IN LEH – IN PRICE ORDER

Prices given are for single/double rooms with common (c) or attached (a) bathroom. Listed in ascending order based on the price of the cheapest double room, places below are **keyed to the map on p122-3**.

Budget guest houses/hotels (£4/US$6 or less)
72 Namgyal GH (53307) dbl: Rs80-150 (c) Rs200 (a)
73 Palace View GH, Kiddar dbl: Rs100 (c)
71 Sabila GH Rs60/100 (c)
68 Tak GH Rs70/100 (c)
27 Odzer GH dbl: Rs100 (c)
45 Singhay GH dbl: Rs100 (c)
34 Stanzin GH dbl: Rs100 (c)
88 Hotel Kang-La dbl: Rs100,150 (a)
7 Lyon GH (53361) Rs75/100-150 (c)
49 Khan Manzil GH dbl: Rs100-150 (c)
90 Hotel Hills View dbl: Rs100 (c), Rs300 (a)
30 Naaz GH dbl: Rs120 (c)
4 Lhari GH dbl: Rs120 (c)
98 Lung Snon (52749) dbl:Rs120 (c), Rs200-250 (a)
36 Rainbow GH dbl: Rs120-150 (c)
31 Karzoo GH dbl: Rs120,150 (c)
3 Oriental GH (53153) dbl: Rs120-170 (c), Rs200 (a)
69 Old Ladakh GH dbl: Rs120 (c), Rs200-300 (a)
1 GH with no name by Shanti Stupa dbl: Rs130 (c)
18 Phuntsog-Ling GH (52267) dbl:Rs130 (c), Rs150 (a)
46 Moonland GH dbl: Rs150 (c)
14 Otsal GH dbl: Rs150 (c)
5 Lamagon GH dbl: Rs150 (c)
41 Sheldon GH dbl: Rs150 (c)
44 Kunzang GH dbl: Rs150 (c)
20 Youthog GH (53056) dbl: Rs150 (c)
6 Goba GH dbl: Rs150 (c)
8 Rinchen's GH dbl: Rs150 (c)
17 'Y' GH (52180) dbl: Rs150 (c)
38 Broadview GH dbl: Rs150 (c)
43 Stumpa GH dbl: Rs150 (c)
29 Shaheen GH (52636) dbl: Rs150 (c)
70 Palace View Hotel dbl: Rs150 (c), Rs200 (a)
86 Nezer View GH dbl: Rs150 (c), Rs200 (a)
54 Dehlex GH (52755) dbl: Rs150-200 (c)
40 Yaksha GH dbl: Rs150-200 (c)
2 Shanti GH dbl: Rs150-200 (c)
76 Hotel Choskor dbl: Rs150-250 (a)
52 Jigmet GH dbl: Rs150 (c), Rs250 (a)
11 Larchang GH dbl: Rs150-200 (c), Rs250 (a)
51 Ti-sei GH dbl: Rs150 (c), Rs200-250 (a)
97 Hotel Harmit Hut (52707) dbl: Rs150-300 (a)
53 Paul GH dbl: Rs150 (c), Rs 275 (a)
15 Lakrook Garden GH (52987) dbl: Rs150 (c), Rs300 (a)
80 Padma GH (52630) dbl: Rs150 (c), Rs250-600 (a)
100 Warilla GH dbl: Rs150 (c), Rs300 (a)
87 Hotel Skalzang (53407) dbl: Rs200 (a)
84 Chospa Hotel dbl: Rs200 (a)
24 Hotel Himalaya dbl: Rs200-250 (a)
96 Hotel Zar-La (52672) dbl: Rs200-300 (a)
13 Asia GH Rs150/200 (c)
102 Hotel Changlo Chan dbl: Rs200 (c)
39 Eagle GH dbl: Rs200 (c)
12 Greenland GH dbl: Rs200 (c)

32 Maryul GH dbl: Rs200 (c), Rs 250 (a)
94 Hotel Horizon (52602) dbl: Rs200-400 (a)
25 Antelope GH (52086) dbl Rs200 (c) Rs250-400 (a)
33 Two Star GH (52250) dbl: Rs200 (c), Rs275 (a)
50 Hotel Zambalha dbl: Rs250 (a)
103 Saichen Hotel (52586) dbl: Rs250 (a)
37 Wisdom Holiday Home (52427) dbl Rs250-300 (a)
23 Hotel Tse-Mo-View (52296) dbl: Rs150 (c), Rs250-300 (a)

Moderately priced hotels (£4-8/US$6-12)
57 Hotel Bimla (52754) dbl: Rs250 (c), Rs450 (a)
67 Hotel Ibex (52281) dbl: Rs250-350 (a)
79 Hotel Yasmin (52405) dbl: Rs250-350 (a)
55 Indus GH (52502) dbl: Rs250-400 (a)
16 Silver Cloud GH (53128) dbl: Rs250-400 (c), Rs500-600 (a)
58 Lung-Se-Jung Hotel (52193) dbl: Rs250-400 (a)
21 Milarepa Deluxe GH (53218) dbl: Rs250-500 (c)
77 Hotel T-Suru dbl: Rs300 (a)
61 Hotel Tso-Kar (53071) dbl: Rs300-500 (a)
35 Hotel Snow View dbl: Rs300-500 (a)
22 Kailash GH (52210) dbl: Rs300 (c), Rs700 (a)
63 Dreamland Hotel (52089) dbl: Rs350 (a)
28 Saser Hotel (52654) dbl: Rs350-500 (a)
9 Hotel Ri-Rab (53108) dbl: Rs350-600 (a)
91 Hotel Chonjor (53165) Rs300/400 (a)
82 Pangong Hotel (52300) dbl: Rs400-500 (a)
95 Hotel Khayul (52321) dbl: Rs400-500 (a)
64 Hotel Tsomo-Ri (52271) dbl: Rs400-600 (a)
19 Hotel Takshi (53130) dbl: Rs600

More expensive hotels (above £8/US$12)
47 Hotel Padma Ling (52530) Rs700/800 (a)
78 Hotel Rockland (52589) dbl: Rs800 (a)
75 Hotel Bijoo (52153) Rs900/1100 (a)
56 Hotel Nirvana Palace (52834) Rs1000/1200 (a)
99 Hotel Mandala (52943) dbl: Rs1200 (a)
92 Hotel Lasermo (52313) Rs1000/1200(a)
93 Hotel Horzey (52454) Rs1000/1200 (a)
74 Hotel Khangri (52311) Rs1035/1265 (a)
85 Hotel Spic and Span (52765) Rs1265 (a)
59 Hotel Rafica (52258) Rs1035/1265 (a)
62 Hotel Yak Tail (52118) Rs1000/1300 (a)
42 Hotel Omasila (52119) dbl: Rs1700 (a)
65 Hotel Ga-ldan Continental (53173) Rs1450/1725 (a)
83 Hotel Singge Palace (53344) Rs1725/2070 (a)
66 Hotel Lingzi (52020) dbl: Rs2070-2340 (a)
60 Hotel Lha-Ri-Mo (52101) Rs1720/2070 (a)
81 Hotel K-Sar Palace (52348) Rs1720/2070 (a)
10 Hotel Sun-N-Sand (52468) Rs1740/2070 (a)
48 Hotel Kang-Lha-Chen (52144) Rs1720/2070 (a)
26 Karakuram Hotel (53154) Rs1720/2070 (a)
101 Hotel Shaynam (52345) Rs1625/2070 (a)
89 Hotel Dragon (52139) dbl: Rs2070 (a)
[In Stok] Ladakh Sarai (42013) dbl: US$120 (a)

Rooms cost Rs300-500 (double, att). Just to the north is the very homely *Hotel Bimla* [57] (☎ 52754) which has large double rooms for Rs250 (com) and Rs450 (att). Down the track on the opposite side of Fort Rd, *Pangong Hotel* [82] (☎ 52300) has airy doubles (att) with good mountain views for Rs400-500.

If you follow the footpath to Sankar Gompa you eventually reach the beautiful *Kailash Guest House* [22] (☎ 52210). Although it seems expensive at Rs300 for a double sharing a communal bathroom or Rs700 for a double (att), it's an extremely comfortable and peaceful place to stay. The rooms are immaculately clean, there are wonderful views to the mountains and the walled garden is a riot of colour. *Milarepa Deluxe Guest House* [21] (☎ 53218) on the road to Sankar is a similar place surrounded by its wonderful vegetable garden. Beautiful rooms with good views to Namgyal Peak cost between Rs250 and Rs500. All have communal bathrooms.

More expensive hotels (above £8/US$12)

There are plenty of hotels at the upper end of the market that are cheap by Western standards but poor value for Leh. They cater predominantly for groups and getting a room as an individual can sometimes be difficult. Almost all of them have a restaurant on the premises and the prices include breakfast. All rooms have attached bathrooms with hot running water.

In the heart of Leh on Fort Rd is *Hotel Yak Tail* [62] (☎ 52118), one of the few hotels to stay open all year. Rooms surrounding the central courtyard cost Rs1000/1300 (att) some of which have balconies to sit out on. Away from the noise and with good views to the Stok Range is the smart *Hotel Nirvana Palace* [56] (☎ 52834) which has rooms for Rs1000/1200 (att). In Chanspa *Hotel Omasila* [42] (☎ 52119) is deservedly popular with double rooms for Rs1700 (att).

There are several places to choose from at the top end of the price range. The *Karakuram Hotel* [26] (☎ 53154), next to the Ecology Centre, is attractive in its mature gardens and has rooms for Rs1720 single (att) or Rs2070 double (att). To the south of the town centre is the efficiently run and very clean *Hotel Singge Palace* [83] (☎ 53344, 🖹 52042) which has doubles for Rs2070 (att). Its Ladakhi-style dining hall and garden with tables and chairs make it a pleasant place to stay. One of the more impressive looking hotels in Leh is the *Hotel Lha-Ri-Mo* [60] (☎ 52101); bedecked with prayer flags, it looks more like a gompa than a hotel. Rooms cost Rs1720 single and Rs2070 for a double with breakfast. The complex even has its own gift shop. *Hotel Dragon* [89] (☎ 52139, 🖹 52720) competes on style with its intricately decorated rooms at a similar price.

The most exotic place to stay in Ladakh is the *Ladakh Sarai* (☎ 42013 or Delhi ☎ 011-752 5357) at the village of Stok (14km from Leh). This is a collection of 15 luxurious *yurts* (round tents) in a willow grove overlooking the Indus Valley; prices are from US$120.

WHERE TO EAT

Eating in

Most guest-houses and hotels can provide you with a simple breakfast of bread and jam, an omelette and maybe some porridge along with tea or coffee. Others go much further than this and provide their guests with an evening meal as well. The usual format in such guest-houses is for the family to cook one dish which is served at about 7pm. Anyone is welcome to share the meal (about Rs40) as long as they have given sufficient notice. This can be a great chance to sample some traditional Ladakhi dishes which are hard to find in Leh's restaurants.

Most of the more up-market hotels have restaurants as part of their complexes and it is possible to get your accommodation and meals covered under one tariff. However, considering Leh's range of excellent and reasonably priced restaurants it seems a shame to always have to eat at the same place.

● **Bakeries** The bakeries are a good place to stock up for home-made breakfasts, lunches and for those in-between times. The most popular are the *Pumpernickel German Bakery* and the *Monalisa German Bakery*, which are almost next door to each other, and the *German Bakery* at *Instyle Café*.

They all sell similar fare which seems quite expensive considering you could get a full meal for the price of a slice of cake, but the mouth-watering choices such as 'choco banana cake' (Rs22) or plum crumble (Rs40) are hard to resist, especially if you've been away trekking for a few days. If someone you know has a birthday they will make and decorate a cake to order. If you are just off on a trek stock up with some of their long-lasting bread which remains edible for up to six days (wrap it in some cloth and don't let it get wet). Muesli (Rs55 for 250g) and energy-giving muesli biscuits (Rs5 each) are also good buys.

Behind the mosque there are several Muslim bakeries selling Kashmiri bread for Rs2 a piece – wonderful for breakfast with apricot jam.

● **Snacks** A favourite local snack known as *yos* is available from Dzomsa. It consists of roasted barley grains, which are sometimes mixed with apricot kernels, dried peas and walnuts – it makes superb trekking food. Delicious fresh and dried apricots are abundant in the summer and can be bought from sellers on the Main Bazaar along with other fruit.

Every evening between 7pm and 8pm the Main Bazaar becomes a hive of activity. It's at this time that you will find roadside vendors selling charcoal-grilled sweetcorn and fried spicy nibbles.

Eating out

● **Ladakhi, Tibetan and Chinese** The majority of restaurants in Leh fit into this wide-ranging category. Prices don't vary enormously wherever you go and are generally between Rs30 and Rs60 for a main meal. Standard dishes on the menus include soups, chop-suey, chow mein, momos and all manner of rice dishes, all of which can be ordered with meat or vegetables. Most will also have a go at some easy Western dishes in an attempt to satisfy everyone's palate. There are a number of such places along the Main Bazaar, all of which are above street level. *The Wok Tibetan Kitchen* is always popular, as is *Amdo Foods*. The entrance to the latter is off a small side alley with two butcher shops on it. If the sight of dismembered carcasses hasn't killed your appetite you should enjoy the good food here. Its nicely decorated sister restaurant, *Amdo Café*, is on the other side of the road. Their food is superb and the 'Amdo special noodles' come highly recommended. (Amdo is the eastern province of Tibet. There is a legend that the people of this remote region, over 5000km away, were originally from Ladakh). Further along the street is *La Montessori Restaurant* which has a similar menu and is very popular with locals. On the other side of the street is the friendly *Upel Tibetan Restaurant* serving good Tibetan and Chinese food. The family-run *Nohal Restaurant* specialises in Tibetan food but can also do popular Chinese and Western dishes.

If you're on a tight budget try some of the smaller Tibetan restaurants where the food is tasty and the prices low. The atmospheric *Kyishong Restaurant* is very popular with Tibetan locals and its extensive menu is one of the few that includes *tsampa* among more usual dishes of fuyong, sweet and sour spring rolls and bamboo shoots. It's very good value and the prices include unlimited cups of black tea. The *Tibetan Restaurant (Devi)*, known locally as Tashi's, is a simple place sandwiched between the two German bakeries. The very friendly owners have made it popular with travellers and locals alike. Another small and popular place is the *Tibetan Friends Corner Restaurant*. This again serves Tibetan and Chinese food and is good value. For dessert, try the spectacular 'chocolate custer with fire' – it's sure to turn a few heads.

For fine Tibetan cooking *The Tibetan Kitchen* is hard to beat. Here's your chance to try authentic dishes such as *tingmo* and *fingsha*, *shabagleb*, *peshee* as well as some continental favourites, tagliatelli alla spinati, ravioli and gnocchi. It's closed between 3pm and 6pm.

● **Indian** Good Indian cuisine is surprisingly hard to find in Leh. The popular *Summer Harvest Restaurant* specialises in Indian and Kashmiri dishes and has Tibetan and Chinese food as well. The *Budshah Inn Restaurant*, on a top floor to the left of the mosque, makes up for its lack of atmosphere with a wide selection of delicious Indian, Kashmiri and tandoori dishes. *Edelweiss Restaurant and Bar* has also been recommended for its Indian cooking.

● **Western** Most places have a few easy-cook Western meals on their menus. Fried egg and chips to satisfy the most homesick Brit are available almost everywhere, as are other travellers' favourites such as banana and honey pancakes, mashed potato and cheese and various styles of spaghetti

---

(Opposite) Top: The imposing 17th century Palace overlooking Leh was the home of Ladakh's Royal Family until they moved to Stok after the Dogra invasion in the mid-19th century. **Bottom:** Leh viewed from Namgyal Peak looking south to the Indus River and the Stok Mountains.

(thinly disguised noodles!). If you are really craving some Western food the dark and intimate *German Bakery Coffee House* has lasagne, pizza and 'burgers for health freaks'.

● **Garden restaurants** Leh enjoys a warm summer climate, as do the tourists who can lounge in one of the town's many outdoor eateries whose cuisine falls into the 'have a go at anything' category. *Instyle Café* is very popular and manages to cook most types of food with reasonable success. Unfortunately the New Age music instils a laid-back atmosphere which is reflected in the speed of service. There's a large and well-used noticeboard here to leave messages on. Nearby is the *Penguin German Bakery Restaurant and Bar* where you can treat yourself to a bowl of 'penguin soup'. Also on Fort Rd is *Hotel Yak Tail* [62] where you can enjoy well-cooked Chinese and Indian dishes whilst relaxing in their beautiful court-yard. If you want to watch the world go by, perch yourself under the rooftop umbrellas of *La Terrasse* opposite the State Bank of India.

Mona Lisa Garden Restaurant and Bar has taken over a willow grove near the Ecology Centre to provide shade for its tables and chairs. As well as providing standard travellers' fare, it also goes out of its way to cater for the large number of Israeli travellers and offers falafel and hummus on its menu. The *Mentokling Restaurant and Bar* in its big walled garden offers pizzas and snacks as well as Chinese and Indian dishes. Along the road into Chanspa are two other popular places with a similar ambience. The first is the peaceful *Sheldon Green* [41] which is one of the few places to serve tra-ditional Ladakhi dishes like *skyu*, *chhu tagi* and *phemar* (see p76 for expla-nations). *Zen Garden Restaurant* is further along by the stream and has a very good tandoori menu.

● **Vegetarian** Every restaurant in Leh serves vegetarian food and most have as wide and varied a menu as the non-vegetarian choices.

Drinking
● **Water** The environmental costs of buying expensive bottled mineral water that's been trucked across the Himalaya and then sold in non-return-able, non-biodegradable plastic bottles have been widely documented, but until recently there were few alternatives for travellers without the means to purify their own. That was until a small business called **Dzomsa** set up in Leh to provide, among other things, pressure-boiled water which, having been boiled at 121°C, is 100% safe to drink; it costs only Rs7 a litre and is sold either straight into your water bottle or in re-used mineral water bottles.

● **Local specialities** The innovative Dzomsa also sells locally produced **apricot juice** for Rs5 a glass or Rs25 a litre which makes a change from the

(Opposite) Many Ladakhis dress up in their finery for the annual Ladakh Festival. This woman is dressed in the traditional *goncha* (long coat) and *tibi* (hat), while the woman in the background is wearing a turquoise-studded *perak* (head-dress).

ubiquitous soft drinks. Look out for **Tsestalulu juice**, a healthy home-grown fruit drink made from the berries of the sea buckthorn plant which grows naturally in many parts of Ladakh. The small-scale local production of this high-vitamin C drink by the Indus Tsestalulu Society aims to provide a source of income for previously unemployed, uneducated and economically deprived rural people through an all-Ladakhi product. It is hoped that this will help prevent country to town migration, while providing a delicious and healthy drink for Ladakhis and thirsty trekkers. It costs about Rs25 for a 650ml bottle.

● **Liquor store** The small shop opposite the main taxi stand sells beer, rum and whisky.

● **Bars** Leh begins to quieten down once it gets dark. You can get a drink at a few of the garden restaurants such as the *Penguin Bar*, which has a variety of bottled beers, and the popular *Mona Lisa Garden Restaurant and Bar* which in addition to the usual beverages also stocks champagne and wine. *Hotel Ibex* [67] has a good selection of beer for the late-night drinker.

SERVICES
Airline offices
Indian Airlines has an office a long way down Fort Rd (open 10am-1pm, 2-5pm). Get there early to avoid long queues during July and August. If you're booking a flight make sure you have enough money with you as they do not accept credit cards.

Banks
The State Bank of India has a foreign exchange counter at the Tourist Office in town (open 10.30am-1.30pm Monday to Friday, 10.30am-12pm Saturday). In July-August turn up very early or you'll have to queue for an hour or more. You can avoid this long wait by changing money at some of the large hotels (eg Hotel Khangri), but you won't get such a good rate of exchange. There is nowhere in Leh where you can get a cash advance on a credit card, so make sure you have plenty of travellers' cheques or cash.

Barber
A haircut will set you back all of Rs20 and with it you'll receive a complimentary scalp massage. A shave with a cut-throat razor is Rs10, but make sure they use a fresh blade: AIDS is on the increase in India. There are barbers on Naw Shar (the alley east of Main Bazaar) and also near the bus stand.

Bookshops, newsagents and libraries
There are several good bookshops in Leh. On the Main Bazaar near the post office is the friendly **Lehling Bookshop** and on the other side of the road, **Lost Horizon Bookshop**. **Artou Bookshop**, opposite Hotel Zambalha [50], has a good selection of books on Ladakh, the Himalaya and a wide range of other titles. If you've just finished your novel you can trade it in for another

at **The Book Worm** by Hotel Lingzi [66]. Newspapers, magazines and books are sold at **Parkash Sales Corporation** below the Pumpernickel German Bakery.

The town **library** has a very limited selection of books and will gladly accept any you wish to donate. A few books on the Himalaya and Buddhism may be of interest. The **Ecology Centre** has an excellent library which is open to anyone (10am-4.30pm). It has a vast range of books and journals on sustainable development, ecology, philosophy, religion, Himalayan history and culture, and Himalayan travelogues. The **Tibetan Library** in Choglamsar has books on Buddhism.

Dentist
The best dentists can be found in Choglamsar.

Horse riding
Ladakhi horses are used more as beasts of burden than for riding but most have also been schooled for riders. Ask at the trekking agencies and expect to pay about Rs300 per day. You may find it hard to get a horse in July and August because they'll all be out on treks.

❏ **Protected area permits**
Visitors need a permit to get into any of the recently opened areas in Ladakh. These are Nubra, Pangong Lake, Dha-Hanu, Tsomoriri and Tsokar. This allows you to stay in the area for a maximum of seven days. Officially you must travel in a group of at least four people and follow one of the several identified tour circuits (unofficially the regulations seem to be fairly flexible). You can either apply directly in person to the District Commissioner's office or go through one of the many travel agencies who will charge you about Rs100 per person for the privilege. The latter is by far the easier option. You will usually need to take along photocopies of your passport and visa.

If there are fewer than four of you, do not worry. Many of the travel agencies will tag your names onto the bottom of another group's application and get round the regulations that way. Alternatively, if you can produce photocopies of four people's passports you will be issued with a permit, whether the owners of the other passports are coming with you or not. It will be assumed that you are travelling by bus or jeep. While it's perfectly legal to get there by other means, the authorities are understandably suspicious of independent trekkers, cyclists or motorcyclists wandering around their sensitive border areas. So if you are planning an alternative way in, it's best to keep your plans quiet unless specifically asked. If you are trekking get your permit dated from the day you are entering the protected area, not the day you are leaving Leh. This will give you an extra day or two to explore the region.

You should be aware that the travel agent who issues you with a permit is responsible for your safe return to Leh. You owe it to them not to overstay your seven days and not to go missing! Occasionally the regulations tighten up, so find out the latest situation when you arrive in Leh.

❑ NGOs (non governmental organisations)

Ladakh is the base for several indigenous organisations doing extremely worthwhile work in the development field. They are not tourist attractions but if you have something to offer, they may welcome your support.

● **Ladakh Ecological Development Group** (LEDeG, Leh, Ladakh 194101, ☎ 52646). LEDeG, probably the most well known of Ladakh's indigenous NGOs, aims to promote 'ecological and sustainable development which harmonises with and builds on the traditional culture'. This is achieved by regular campaigns on environmental matters; encouraging local education; improving and raising the status of traditional organic agriculture; spreading the use of appropriate technologies, including solar ovens, micro-hydro plants and Trombe wall solar space heaters; and by nurturing local, small-scale handicraft production in rural areas. Volunteers are always welcome and there are often informal study groups on development and ecology for visitors. Their headquarters is at the Centre for Ecological Development.

● **Leh Nutrition Project** (LNP, PO Box 59, Leh, Ladakh, 194101, ☎/🖹 52151) aims to address development needs of women and children in rural Ladakh by empowering local communities, strengthening village institutions, influencing government policy and running a series of projects from health and sanitation to vocational training.

● **Students' Educational and Cultural Movement of Ladakh** (SECMOL, PO Box 4, Leh, Ladakh, 194101, ☎ 52421, 🖹 52735, 🖳 secmol.leh@gems.vsnl.net.in) works to restore pride in Ladakh's unique culture and to improve the chaotic education system by promoting culturally appropriate and locally relevant education. Between 2pm and 5pm, Monday to Friday, it welcomes visitors who are genuinely interested in real cultural exchange. Also interested in volunteers who have experience in teaching, carpentry, farming, forestry, computers, art and illustration. Occasionally they run trekking tours with the aim of increasing cultural exchange.

● **Tibetan Environment Network** (Yeshi Lhundup, TEN, Sonam Ling Tibetan Settlement, PO Choglamsar, Leh, Ladakh 194104, or: TEN UK, 10 Dunstable Rd, Richmond, Surrey, TW9 1UH, UK, ☎/🖹 +44 181-940 3166, 🖳 dalha@aol.com). Set up in Choglamsar in 1994 as a grassroots self-help group for the Tibetan refugee population in Ladakh. Works in environment, ecology, health, agro-forestry and appropriate high-altitude farming. Practical/financial support is always welcomed.

● **Womens' Alliance of Ladakh** (Leh, Ladakh, 194101) Set up to counter the negative consequences of development and the increasing participation of Ladakh in the global economy. They aim to encourage respect for women and farming and to preserve Ladakhi culture. Membership is over 3500 women from 65 villages.

● **Zanskar Development Project Society** and **Zanskar Ski School** (Mohd Amin Zanskari, Padum, ☎ 01983-45018, 🖹 01985-2575, or: Ben Stephenson, Laburnum Cottage, Broomheath Lane, Tarvin, Chester, CH3 8HD, ☎ 01829-740747) **ZDPS** is a Zanskari NGO committed to raising the standard of living in Zanskar. With the increasing influence of the modernised world on the region, ZDPS sees its role as crucial for its ecological development. **ZSS** is a joint Zanskar/UK NGO under the umbrella of ZDPS working to provide opportunities for the people of Zanskar through skiing. As Zanskar is covered in snow for eight months of the year this is a very effective way of travelling, enabling children to get to school quickly, providing communication for remote villages, as well as creating opportunities for sport and tourism. You can help by donating skiing equipment, acting as an instructor in the winter, or using a Zanskar ski guide summer or winter.

Laundry

The best place to have your washing done is at Dzomsa where care for your clothes goes hand-in-hand with care for the environment. Instead of the waste water being poured into Leh's streams, the water is filtered into a hole in the desert.

Left luggage

You can safely store the things you don't want to lug into the mountains at your guest-house or hotel. There's rarely a charge.

Medical clinics

Medical help phone numbers: ☎ 52360 (24 hours) or ☎ 52012 (10am-4pm). For serious medical and altitude-related problems go to the **Sonam Narbu Memorial** (SNM) hospital. Stool tests are available and treatment is free. Consultations are from 10am-2pm. The various clinics around Leh can help with minor complaints. Otherwise see **Dr Tsering Narboo** at the Kunsoi Medical Hall (open 9-10am and 4-7pm).

The army has a hospital equipped with a **pressure chamber** for those suffering from AMS, but as it runs off the unreliable mains electricity you are safer going to the SNM hospital which has supplies of oxygen.

Doctors specialising in **Tibetan medicine** can be found in Choglamsar and there is a **homeopath clinic** below Hotel Zambalha [50].

Meditation

Mahabodhi International Meditation Centre (☎ 44025, 🖹 44155), Devachan (near Choglamsar) runs residential courses and the occasional meditation-cum-trekking camps for those who want to improve their spiritual as well as their physical well-being. During the week they run daily group meditation classes at their sub-centre in Chanspa from 5-7pm. Both centres are open Monday to Saturday, 10am-5pm.

Photography

It's best to wait until you get home to have your films developed. For the impatient, **Gemini Lab** on Fort Rd processes print film adequately. The nearest processing place for slides is in Delhi. Both **Dijoo Studios**, on the Main Bazaar, and **Syed Ali Shah & Sons' Postcard Shop**, have a reasonable stock of print and transparency film. Shah & Sons also sell excellent pictures of Ladakh and Ladakhis that the late owner took himself; these are very good value for money at Rs200 for a large print, especially when you consider the cost of enlarging a print in the West.

Post and telecommunications

There is a **post office** on the Main Bazaar open 10am-5pm, but there is no Poste Restante facility here. Your letters will have been kept at the **main post office**, next to the Tourist Reception Centre, inconveniently situated on the road to the airport. The address is: Poste Restante, GPO, Leh, Ladakh, 194101, India. Alternatively you can have your mail sent to one of the communications agencies which will charge you a small commission.

There are lots of communication agencies in Leh (look for the yellow signs) where you can make national and international **phone calls** and send and receive **faxes**. An international phone call will typically cost you Rs80 per minute or Rs90 to the USA. Most places operate a call-back system which is Rs10 per minute. Sending an international fax costs Rs3 per second and Rs20 to receive; Gypsy's World (📠 +91-1982-52735), on Fort Rd is a reliable place to have faxes sent. **Email** is also available from Gypsy's World (📧 matin.chunka@gems.vsnl.net.in) at their White House office further down Fort Rd; it costs Rs100 to send and receive a page.

Calling Delhi or abroad during the day or early evening can be frustratingly difficult. You'll have more success in getting through if you try ringing late at night when fewer lines are in use.

Rafting

Several companies offer rafting on both the Indus and the Zanskar. There are sections to suit all abilities from a gentle, grade two float, up to a white-knuckle ride on a grade five rapid. Day trips are available (from Rs800 per person) but the best way to see the river is to make a three- or four-day excursion, camping on the beaches and visiting a few sights along the way. Perhaps the ultimate trip for those trekking to Zanskar is to arrange for the rafts to meet you at Padum, and then ride the river back down to Nimu – surely preferable to the long and dusty road journey.

Shopping

If you are buying souvenirs you can make sure your money goes towards a good cause at the **Tibetan Children's Village Handicraft Centre** in Choglamsar. They also have a shop beneath Upel Restaurant in the Main Bazaar. This has a large selection of clothes, thankas, Tibetan carpets, jewellery and trinkets, all at reasonable prices. Much of what's on sale is made at the centre and all the profits go back to helping the children.

There are two **LEDeG craft shops**, one at the Ecology Centre and the other below La Terrasse restaurant. They sell the handicrafts produced from their various projects as well as books, T-shirts and postcards. Other good buys in Leh are traditional clothes which you are unlikely to find elsewhere, such as the stovepipe hats or *tibi*; the long coats that are worn by men and women called *kos* or *gonchas*; the elegant Tibetan pinafore dresses favoured by younger Ladakhi women known as *pumet* in Ladakhi, or *chuba* in Tibetan; a *stodtund*, which is a short jacket; or the traditional pointed shoes called *thigma pabu*. These can all be found in Ladakhi shops in and around the Main Bazaar.

Tourist information

There's a tiny and poorly stocked Tourist Information Office (☎ 53462, open 8am-8pm Monday to Saturday) in town and also the Tourist Reception Centre (☎ 52297, open 10am-4pm Monday to Saturday) on the road to the airport. They can give you a free map and a vaguely useful tourist directory.

Trekking agencies

Leh's many trekking agencies should be able to help you organise anything from a single pony-man to a full-blown luxury trek. Many also have a certain amount of equipment for hire. The standard of the agencies varies enormously, so it's well worth visiting several to give you an idea of what you'll get for your money.

Trekking equipment rental

While most trekking equipment can be hired in Leh, the quality leaves a lot to be desired. Many of the trekking agencies have equipment for hire as does The Travellers' Shop on Fort Rd which can provide almost everything you may need including insulating pads (Rs30), stoves (Rs30), crampons (Rs30), and ice axes (Rs40). They occasionally have plastic mountaineering boots and dehydrated food as well, but don't count on it. The Tourist Reception Centre also occasionally has equipment for hire.

Visa extensions

You can extend your visa for up to 14 days in Leh and the length of stay granted seems to depend on the mood of the official you see. On a bad day he may well give less than 14 days. If you need longer you'll have to go to Delhi (see p66). The office is in the Superintendent of Police building, open 10am-4pm.

ENTERTAINMENT

Ancient Futures – Learning from Ladakh

When you first arrive in Leh and the altitude is making you feel lethargic, go one afternoon to watch the excellent one-hour video, *Ancient Futures*. This is shown at the new Women's Alliance of Ladakh Centre on Sankar Rd; check the posters to verify the time. The film provides a valuable insight into the culture of Ladakh and the problems that the region faces today as it struggles to come to terms with recent changes. It should be compulsory viewing for every visitor. Lively and thought-provoking discussions are held after each viewing.

Cinema

The latest releases from Bollywood (as Bombay's huge film industry is known) are screened at the Delite Cinema near the old town. Showings are at 2pm and at 7.15pm.

Cultural shows

There are two cultural shows most evenings. One given by the **Cultural and Traditional Society** (CATS) near the Instyle Café, while the other is up by the Palace and is performed by the **Ladakh Artists Society of Leh** (LASOL). Both last an hour and cost Rs50. Programmes include folk music and dances, an explanation of traditional dress and the serving of chang and salt butter tea. They're very professionally performed and well worth seeing.

Festivals

Festivals in and around Leh occur throughout the year and are a fascinating insight into Ladakhi culture. During the summer look out for the **monastic**

festivals at Hemis, Lamayuru, Karsha, Phyang and Tak Tok; the other monasteries hold their festivals at the traditional time of winter. (Please remember these are religious ceremonies and must be shown the proper respect – see p158). The **Ladakh Festival** is another interesting cultural event worth attending at the beginning of September and if you're around for **Buddha Purnima** (May-June), or **Losar** (December-January) the town is sure to be alive with celebration. See p72 for more information on festivals.

Polo
There are lots of matches on the highest polo ground in the world. Keep an eye out for posters advertising the next game. They attract a huge crowd, are very exciting and free.

WHAT TO SEE

Leh Palace
Majestically overlooking the town, the Palace allowed the king to survey his subjects at all times. Today it stands empty, as it has since the mid-19th century when the royal family moved to Stok Palace after they were besieged by Kashmiri forces. It was built by King Sengge Namgyal in the 17th century in the same style as the Potala Palace of Lhasa. Although not on quite the same scale, it still stands nine storeys high. The upper floors were used by royalty, while the store rooms and stables took up the lower floors, hence the larger windows at the top.

There is very little to see as the whole building is in a poor state of repair but there are good views across Leh and it's a fascinating walk through the alleys of the old town to get there. The old town is full of traditional architecture and many households have retained some of their rural values, keeping livestock in their backyards and drying fodder on the roofs. The alternative way up is to take the gentle track that begins above the polo ground.

Namgyal Peak
Namgyal Peak is crowned by the now ruined **fort of Tashi Namgyal** that sits high above the Palace, along with the **Gonkhang** and the **Maitreya temple**. Some of the best views of the locality are from this vantage point. The red Gonkhang was built in the 16th century by Tashi Namgyal and is where he offered the bodies of the defeated Mongols to the deities. There's a portrait of the king here, in which he's seen drinking chang. Just below this building is the temple of the Maitreya which may date from the first king of Leh, King Takbumde. There are various ways up to the peak; the most straightforward is to follow the steep path that can be seen snaking down from underneath the buildings. Visit early in the morning to avoid the heat and to be certain that you'll find a monk there who can show you around.

Jama Masjid
This Sunni mosque is at the end of the Main Bazaar. The muezzin's call to prayer soon becomes a familiar sound as it drifts out across the town. The

threat of military action by the Mughal Emperor Aurangzeb prompted King Deldan Namgyal to build the mosque in about 1661. The building, which is in the Ladakhi style of architecture, can accommodate more than 500 people. It's open throughout the day but try to avoid visiting during prayer times. Shoes must be removed and women should cover their arms, legs and hair.

Sankar Gompa
This colourful gompa belongs to Spituk and is the residency of their kushok. Entry is permitted only early in the morning or late in the afternoon but there is nothing to stop you wandering around the peaceful courtyard at other times of day. You get to the gompa by taking the stream-side path just before the Antelope Guest House. This is a pretty 2km walk through fields which takes you past some interesting ornate chortens.

Shanti Stupa
Visible from most of the town, this new stupa was officially opened in 1985. The peace pagoda is part of the legacy of the Japanese Fujii Guruji who, as part of his mission to promote world peace through Buddhism, built pagodas and temples all over the world. It stands above Chanspa overlooking Leh and the Indus Valley. It's possible to take a taxi all the way to the top but a good test of your acclimatisation is to walk up the 554 steps. The stupa may be a bit garish but the views are spectacular.

Centre for Ecological Development
The centre is the headquarters of LEDeG (see p132) and has an excellent library, a shop selling locally produced handicrafts and demonstrations of various appropriate technologies such as solar ovens, Trombe wall solar space heating units (on the side of the library), and solar water heating systems. There are frequent study groups for visitors on subjects such as globalisation, tourism and development held throughout the summer. It's open 10am-4.30pm, daily.

Mani Sarmo
This yellow stupa above the polo ground is said to date back to the time of Rinchen Zangpo and is reputed to have magical properties; if you have an illness you should rub the affected part against the stupa and then walk away without looking back. You should be better within five days.

MOVING ON

By air
The high mountains, altitude and strong winds around Leh airport mean that departing planes are restricted to carrying 75% of their total capacity. The other problem here is that flights may have to be cancelled owing to bad weather, a not infrequent occurrence. As a result getting a confirmed flight during the summer can be very difficult, so book as far in advance as possible even if you're not 100% sure you'll be leaving by plane. You can get your money back as long as you ask for a refund before your flight date;

make sure you get your refund in Leh: you enter a bureaucratic minefield if you wait until you reach your destination. If you can't get a seat on a direct flight, you could go via Jammu or Srinagar instead, (but see the warning on p79), or via Chandigarh. If you're on the waiting list for a flight, no matter what your number is, it's still worth turning up at the airport in time as the number of passengers that can be carried varies with the weather.

● **Direct flights** (US$105, 1¼ hours) Indian Airlines fly direct from Leh to Delhi daily at 8.15am from mid-May to the end of August. Throughout the rest of the year there are four flights a week departing at 10.35am.

● **Via Jammu** There are IA flights to Jammu every Thursday and Sunday at 7.30am (US$64, 55 minutes). Onward flights to Delhi depart Jammu every day at 1.50pm (US$105, 70 minutes).

● **Via Srinagar** There is only one IA flight a week to Srinagar, which leaves on Saturday at 7.30am (US$55, 40 minutes). Direct IA flights from Srinagar to Delhi leave at 10.30am on Monday, Wednesday and Friday (US$115, 1¼ hours). IA flights from Srinagar to Delhi via Jammu depart daily at 12.45pm (US$115, 2¼ hours).

● **Via Chandigarh** There is one IA flight to Chandigarh from Leh on Tuesday departing at 7.30am (US$70, 55 minutes). Onward flights to Delhi depart Chandigarh on Monday, Wednesday and Friday at 12.30pm (US$65, 1 hour 50 minutes).

Security is comfortingly tight at Leh airport. You and your bags will be thoroughly searched as you leave; this is partly to stop the export of antiques, (it's illegal to leave Ladakh with anything over 100 years old), but mainly to stop terrorist attacks.

By bus

The journey to Manali is possible only during the summer months with the road being officially open from the first week in July to 15 September. Himachal Tourism buses will travel this route only while the road is officially open, while many of the privately operated buses will continue to ply the route until it is physically impossible because of landslides or snow.

The road to Srinagar is open from about the beginning of June to the end of October and is likewise dependent on the weather.

● **To Manali** The most popular and comfortable bus for the two-day journey to Manali is that run by **Himachal Tourism** (HPTDC). Tickets cost Rs700 and are available from the Himachal Tourism office (open every day from 10am-7pm) in Leh. It's recommended that you buy your ticket three or four days in advance. The bus leaves from outside the office at 5.30am daily. The overnight stop is at Sarchu where reasonably comfortable, tented accommodation is available. As there are no alternative places for you to stay, Himachal Tourism gets away with charging the exorbitant rate of Rs300 per person for a shared tent, supper of dal and rice and a packed breakfast. Several travellers have succeeded in sleeping on the bus for free; a sleeping bag is needed as it gets very cold. A few tour operators in Leh run similar private buses for Rs800, also with tented accommodation. The other possibility is to take a **local bus** to Manali. Although these leave extremely early (4am daily from the main bus stand) and are less comfortable, they go all the way to Keylong. The advantage of this is that there are some good places to stay in this interesting small town (see p102) for far less than you'd pay for a grotty tent in Sarchu. The bus departs Keylong for Manali at 6am the following morning and reaches its destination at 12 noon. These buses are cheaper; B class Rs356 and semi-deluxe Rs530. Tickets just to Keylong are Rs285 (B class) and Rs440 (semi-deluxe). Always book in advance.

● **To Delhi** See p102 for details of onward transport from Manali to Delhi. It is possible to book a seat on the HPTDC bus from Manali to Delhi at Himachal Tourism's office in Leh.

● **To Srinagar** Because of militant activity, travel in Kashmir is **not recommended** (see warning p79).

By taxi

If you can't get a flight out of Leh and you can't face the thought of another bus journey, taking a taxi to Manali may be the answer. When the road has been damaged by landslides, jeeps are sometimes the only vehicles that can get past. A one-way trip costs Rs11,850 to Manali. You can squeeze four to six passengers into a jeep.

Places of interest beyond Leh

Scattered along the Indus Valley, both east and west of Leh, are other fascinating towns, villages, monasteries and palaces. Some are visited by almost every traveller who comes to Ladakh while others remain the preserve of the dedicated few.

A **tour of the gompas** is high on most people's lists. Whether you decide to see as many as possible or to spend more time at one or two is up to you. Buses connect most of the principal villages and provide a cheap means of transport – confirm the departure times at the Tourist Information Office as they are liable to fluctuate. If your time is limited it may be more convenient to hire a taxi for a day between three or four people. A round trip taking in Shey, Tikse, Hemis and Stok will cost Rs1045, or if you've got the energy you could add Chemre, Tak Tok, Matho and Stakna for Rs1950. A tour to the west stopping at Basgo, Likir, Alchi and Lamayuru is Rs2225 one way or Rs2640 return. Go to the taxi office for other alternatives. You can usually visit gompas between 8am and 5pm and most now charge an entrance fee of Rs10-20.

Interesting places further afield include the **Suru Valley** and **Zanskar** (but see the warning on p79 about the Kargil area), and now that entry has been allowed into the former restricted areas (now called 'protected areas') the choice is wider than it has been for decades. The government is trying to develop the tourism potential of these areas but at the moment the infrastructure is minimal and permits are still required. **Nubra** and **Dha-Hanu** are the easiest to visit as they can be reached by public transport and have several guest-houses. The simplest way to get to **Pangong Tso, Tso Moriri** and **Tso Kar** is with an organised tour.

WEST OF LEH (see map p143)

Spituk
This was the first Gelukpa (Yellow Hat) monastery to be established in Ladakh. Rinchen Zangpo predicted that a monastery would be founded here that would set an example to other monasteries in the land. The monastery you see today was built in the 15th century on the site of an 11th century temple. As it's situated on top of a small hill there are good views over the Indus Valley. There are buses to and from Spituk (20 minutes) every 30 minutes throughout the day.

Phyang
The building of this 16th century gompa was ordered by the king, Tashi Namgyal. It's thought that he was trying to seek forgiveness for blinding his elder brother, a devious act that made him heir to the throne and soon after, king. The gompa sits on a small hill above the attractive village and like Lamayuru belongs to the Kagyupa (Red Hat) order of monks.

There are at least three buses a day (45 minutes, Rs12) from Leh at 8am, 2pm and 4pm and returning at 9am, 3pm and 5pm. A taxi costs Rs495 return.

Likir
This impressive monastery is about an hour's walk from Likir village where there are several good places to stay (see p193). The land was given to the gompa in 1065 but the original structure was destroyed by fire so the buildings you see today are about 200 years old. The monks are of the Gelukpa order, and the kushok is the Dalai Lama's younger brother. As well as looking after this monastery, the monks also take responsibility for Alchi Gompa and several of the smaller gompas in the area. There is a small museum with interesting royal artefacts, arms and armour on show.

There's a privately-operated bus everyday to Likir (two hours, Rs25) which leaves from the main bus stand at 4pm and returns at 7am the next morning. A taxi costs Rs795 one way, Rs890 return.

Alchi
The *Choskor*, or religious enclave, is one of the most important cultural sites in Ladakh. Built in the 11th century, it is a treasure trove of early Buddhist art in the Kashmiri tradition, a style quite different from the Tibetan art found in Ladakh's other monasteries. Also unlike other gompas, it is hidden down by the river rather than in the more usual elevated position. This may explain why it wasn't destroyed by the various invaders who have passed by throughout the centuries. It was constructed under the supervision of Kaldan Shesrab, a follower of Rinchen Zangpo, the man responsible for reviving interest in

Buddhism at that time. Alchi is one of the few remaining examples of that era. As this is a popular stop on the tourist circuit there are a variety of **places to stay** (see p209). The village and gompa are reached by crossing the Indus just beyond Saspol and doubling back on yourself for about 2km. If you are walking it takes about one hour from the bridge. There are daily buses from Leh at 4pm (three hours, Rs30). They return to Leh the following morning, leaving Alchi at 7am. Taxis cost Rs935 one way, Rs1155 return.

Rizong

The solitary Gelukpa monastery at Rizong lies up a remote side valley to the north of the main road between Nurla and Saspol. Take any bus from Leh going to Khalsi or beyond and get off at the turning to the gompa. If coming from Alchi this is 20 minutes by bus or truck from the Alchi bridge. A taxi from Leh will cost Rs1138 one way, Rs1330 return. From the turn-off it's a nice 1½ hour walk to the gompa. Follow the rough motorable track lined with poplar, willow and apricot trees and after about 50 minutes you'll reach the small Chulichan nunnery. Continue up the valley for about 40 minutes taking the left fork where the valley divides and climb up a desolate gorge until you reach the magnificent monastery which spans the narrow valley.

Gelukpa monasteries are known for their strict discipline but Rizong is reputed to be the strictest of them all. The 30 or so monks own nothing more than the robes they are wearing and all eat the same food from the monastery kitchen. The gompa, just over 160 years old, contains little of historical interest but its location in this quiet valley is worth the walk.

Lamayuru

The gompa at Lamayuru is one of the most immediately striking in Ladakh. Its position on top of a beautifully eroded crag, complete with rock pinnacles and caves, gives it an almost fairy-tale quality as it stands over the small village below. There is a local legend that the whole valley was under a deep lake until the holy man, Nimagou, prayed for a monastery to be founded here. With that, the lake drained away. The site of the monastery is probably the oldest in Ladakh with the first temple, like so many others, being built at the time of Rinchen Zangpo. The monastery is officially called Yung-dung Tharpa Ling, or 'place of freedom', after it was declared a holy site in the 16th century. In such places even criminals could be safe from persecution if within one square mile. It now belongs to the Kagyupa sect. There are several places to stay in the village (see p199). To get there take any bus or truck that is going to Kargil or Srinagar (see below), as the village is on the main road. The journey takes about six hours. A taxi costs Rs1952 one way, Rs2365 return.

Kargil (2650m/8700ft)

Travellers should be aware that Kargil is very close to the Line of Control between India and Pakistan and throughout the spring and summer of 1997, 1998 and 1999 became the target of frequent artillery attacks from Pakistani troops – please read the **warning** on p79 before visiting.

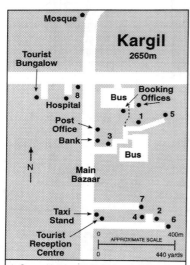

1 Crown Hotel – dbl Rs80 (com), Rs100 (att)
2 Hotel Evergreen – dbl Rs100 (com)
3 Hotel Tourist Marjina (☎ 2540)
     dbl Rs100-150 (att)
4 Hotel Greenland (☎ 2324) – dbl Rs100-400
5 Hotel International – dbl Rs150 (att)
6 Hotel Broadway Suru-View (☎ 2304)
     dbl Rs600-700 (att)
7 Hotel Siachen (☎ 2221) – dbl Rs700-800
8 Hotel Scons (☎ 2424) – dbl Rs1050 (att)

This uninspiring Muslim town is the overnight halt for all buses travelling between Leh and Srinagar and is the jumping off point for journeys up the Suru Valley and into Zanskar, so the hotels are used to travellers arriving late and leaving early the following morning on the next bus out. One of the most convenient hotels for the bus stand is *Hotel Tourist Marjina* (☎ 2540) which has double rooms with attached baths for Rs100-150. *Hotel Green-land* (☎ 2324) is another comfortable place to stay in a quieter part of town with a range of rooms from Rs100-400 (att). If you are looking for something more up-market try the *Hotel Broadway Suru-View* (☎ 2304) around the corner, with doubles for Rs600-700 (att).

There are several **places to eat** along the Main Bazaar and most hotels provide food. It is possible to change money at the State Bank of India and there are many STD/ISD booths in town. The Tourist Reception Centre near the taxi stand can provide suggestions for trekking itineraries in the area.

Buses leave Leh daily at 5am reaching Kargil at 4pm. Prices are Rs145 for an A class bus and Rs110 for B class. Buses from Kargil to Leh leave at about 5am. Taxis between Leh and Kargil cost Rs3355 one way.

Buses to Padum in Zanskar depart Kargil at 3am and cost Rs150 (14-15 hours). If you wish to explore the Suru Valley or trek some of the way to Zanskar there are two buses a day to the villages of Panikhar and Parkachik. A taxi to Padum will set you back Rs7000, plus an extra Rs1100 if you want to take two days over the journey to enjoy some of the sights along the way.

Buses to Srinagar depart daily at 4.30am and arrive in Srinagar at 5pm. Taxis cost Rs3000 one way.

❏ Leh-Srinagar Highway

(See warning p79) *(Distances given are from the place last mentioned; and are approximate.* This 434km highway leaves Leh passing the airport and **Spituk** gompa. After the army camps the road rises to a plateau and passes the turning to **Phyang**. The gompa lies about 2km north of the road. Just before **Nimu** (36km from Leh) the Indus and Zanskar rivers meet at an impressive confluence.

The next 60km are a culture vulture's dream, passing the temples and derelict fort at **Basgo** (6km); the large monastery at **Likir** (10km); painted caves at **Saspol** (10km); the historic gompa at **Alchi** (2km); if you follow the track heading north off the main road in 7km you will reach the gompa at **Rizong**; or get off at Nurla (15km) and walk the 4km north to the ruined castle and temples at **Temisgam**.

At **Khalsi** (11km) there is a police check post where you'll be required to show your passport. One road continues west along the Indus to the Dard villages of **Dha** and **Biama**, while the main highway crosses the river and slowly winds its way up to the beautiful gompa at **Lamayuru** (27km from Khalsi). On the left, just before reaching the village, there are great views of the 'moonlands'. You continue climbing for 15km to the highest pass on the route, the **Fatu La** (4100m/13,450ft). After crossing another pass, the **Namika La** (3900m/12,800ft) (36km), the road descends to the village of **Mulbekh** (15km) where there is a beautiful gompa. Just before the village, at the side of the road, there's an ancient nine-metre sculpture of the Maitreya, or future Buddha, carved into the rock. If you leave the highway and follow the Wakha River upstream from here you can visit the tiny cliff-face gompa at **Gyal**. Beyond Mulbekh there is a turning on the left that takes you to the small cave gompa at **Shergol** (7km).

The formerly important town of **Kargil** (34km) marks the transition to a predominantly Muslim area and from here you can either continue west to Kashmir or take the rough road south, up the **Suru Valley** to **Zanskar**. Fifty-six kilometres further along the main highway is **Drass**, the last major village in Ladakh, whose hardy Dard inhabitants have to put up with appalling winter weather of continuous heavy snowfall and temperatures as low as -40°C. Some 40km on, the road crosses the **Zoji La** (3530m/11,580ft), leaving behind the arid mountains of Ladakh to descend through the lush, wooded Sind Valley to the Vale of Kashmir and **Srinagar** (110km).

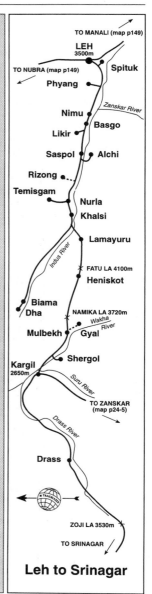

Leh to Srinagar

ZANSKAR (see map p24-5)

South of the main Indus Valley on the northern edge of the Great Himalaya Range lies Zanskar, one of the most isolated inhabited valleys of the Himalaya. Enclosed by giant mountains, this spectacular region is accessible in summer only by crossing high passes, or for about six weeks in the depths of winter when you can travel on foot along the frozen surface of the Zanskar River through a long narrow gorge. Until recently the valley was relatively untouched by the modern world and although a rough road now connects Padum with Kargil, much of Zanskar is still a fascinating working example of traditional self-supporting communities. The small villages, surrounded by highly productive fields, nestle in the valleys and magnificent gompas cling defiantly to the crags and ridges above. Most visitors to this remote Buddhist region are trekkers as the main town of Padum is the starting point for several strenuous but spectacular treks across the convoluted Zanskar Mountains, or across the Himalaya to Lahaul.

From mid-July to the end of October the road over the Pensi La, opened in 1980, provides convenient if long and uncomfortable summer access to Padum and the main Zanskar Valley. From **Kargil** (see p142), it runs south up the predominantly Muslim **Suru Valley** for 67km to **Panikhar**. The lush fields of the Balti settlements along this valley support a wide variety of crops and fruits. As you gain height the mighty snow-capped twin peaks of Nun Kun (7135m/23,410ft and 7077m/23,220ft) become visible and soon dominate the view. The road swings east and then north, through the last Muslim settlement of **Parkachik**, and then east again past the snout of the Nun Kun glacier which fills the bus with icy air. Most buses stop for a welcome tea-break at **Zhuldo** (Jildo). Leaving Zhuldo the road skirts around the Buddhist Gelukpa monastery at **Rangdum** (63km from Panikhar) which sits astride a small hill in the middle of this verdant plain. Founded about 250 years ago it has about 40 monks in residence.

As you climb towards the **Pensi La**, only 20km on from here, south leading side valleys allow glimpses of glaciers and snow-draped peaks but the most impressive view of all welcomes you at the summit of the pass (4400m/14,440ft). Carving its way through the Himalaya and surrounded by sheer-sided mountains, the Drung-Drang glacier is a spectacular sight; you descend past these wonderful mountain vistas towards the upper reaches of the Stod River. The road follows the river east past well cared-for Zanskari villages. On the opposite (right) bank near the village of Ating, a trail leads south to the Umasi La through a gorge in which the small Kagyupa monastery of **Dzongkhul** (Zongkul) is situated. This rock-face gompa was founded by the great Buddhist scholar Naropa almost 1000 years ago and is now an important retreat for meditation.

At a junction in the road, the way to Padum crosses on to the south bank of the Stod, while the road ahead leads to Gelukpa Gompa at **Karsha**, the largest monastery in Zanskar (see p251). Continuing on to Padum you soon reach the village of **Sani** (a gentle two-hour walk from Padum if you're coming in the other direction), where there is a low-lying gompa belonging to the Kagyupa sect. The site is particularly sacred because it is said the great sage Padmasambhava visited and blessed the area. If you have eagle eyes you may be able to spot the white cave high on the cliff on the other side of the river where he is supposed to have meditated for several years; it is still used for the same purpose. Behind the gompa is the 1000-year-old Kanishka Stupa, one of the most sacred monuments in Zanskar which possibly contains the remains of Naropa. Continue along the road for just a few more kilometres to the capital of Zanskar, **Padum** (90km from Pensi La) – see p246 for information on accommodation, food and transport.

Two roads continue from Padum, but as yet are little used and carry no public transport. One goes to the temple and village of **Pipiting**, crosses the Lungnak River and continues via **Thongde**, where there is an attractive Gelukpa monastery high on a cliff, to **Zangla**. Here a ruined fortress, once the royal residency, sits high above the current village on top of a precipice. The Hungarian scholar, Csoma de Koros, spent a cold and miserable winter studying Tibetan here in 1823. The other road is steadily forcing its way up the Lungnak River past **Bardan** to **Mune** (see p246).

SOUTH-EAST OF LEH (see map p149)

Choglamsar
This is a Tibetan refugee village where the Dalai Lama has his beautiful temporary residence (not open to tourists) and where the Central Institute of Buddhist Studies is based. There are lots of buses going east from Leh, all of which pass through Choglamsar. Taxis charge Rs145 one-way; Rs120 return.

Shey
This was the old capital and the home of the kings of Ladakh before the new capital became established in Leh. The palace sits in a strategic position on a spur jutting out into the Indus Valley. The main temple contains a large Buddha statue sculpted by Nepalese craftsmen. It is believed that after its completion they settled in the area of Chiling and started the now famous metal-working industry there. In the courtyard there's an impressive gold-topped stupa, best viewed from above. The top of the palace is reached by some very dilapidated steps and from here there are wonderful views across to Stok and Spituk, and also of the hundreds of stupas on the desert to the north-east.

It is possible to stay in Shey at the *Hotel Shilkhar* below the palace. They have double rooms for Rs150 (att). There are buses to Shey every hour from Leh. Taxis cost Rs210 one way or Rs265 return.

Tikse
If you're going to see only one monastery, make it Tikse (Thiksay/Thekse). This large gompa is an impressive sight, situated on top of a craggy hill while the rest of the complex sprawls down beneath it. It was founded in the 15th century by Gelukpa monks. The temple on the right of the courtyard houses a 15-metre statue of the Maitreya, or future Buddha, which was fin-

ished in 1981, while at the back of the Dukhang there is a Buddha statue dating from the 15th century. The monks here are helpful and friendly and the whole gompa is well cared for. There is accommodation available at the *Skalzang Chamba Hotel* for Rs150. Buses via Tikse leave Leh every hour, or you can get a taxi Rs330 one-way, Rs400 return (30 minutes).

Stok

This has been the royal palace since the king was dethroned by the Dogras and is now the home of the last king's widow. There's an interesting museum that contains an odd collection of exhibits including the king's teacup holder, the queen's turquoise head-dress, some armour and a stuffed yak. It is open 8am-8pm and costs Rs20. The nearby gompa is worth visiting. There are buses to Stok at 7.30am, 2pm and 4.30pm which return at 8am and 3.15pm (Rs10). A taxi will cost you Rs285 one way or Rs405 return.

Matho

This is the only Sakyapa gompa in Ladakh and has become famous for its annual festival, during which specially chosen monks become the vehicle for an oracle. For several days they answer people's questions and predict the following year's events while in a trance. Occasionally their superhuman powers are put to the test. They have been known to sprint along the thin outer wall of the gompa and over the roofs without falling and have been seen to cut their mouths and hands with knives until they bleed profusely; the next morning there are no scars to be found.

The main temple isn't particularly interesting but there is a tiny museum on the left side of the courtyard which is worth seeing. It contains a stuffed yak, old masks, skulls and costumes that are used at the festival. Right at the top of the gompa there's the highly revered Room of the Oracles. Women are not allowed into this tiny room and photographs must not be taken. The floor is covered in grain, taken from every field in the village to ensure a harvest for the next year. It's almost pitch dark inside but you can just make out the walls which are covered in grotesque and frightening masks. It's not a place for the easily scared. The monastery is situated at the foot of the Stok Mountains midway between Hemis and Stok. Buses leave Leh at 7.30am, 2pm and 4.30pm and return at 8am and 4pm (Rs10). Taxis cost Rs565 one way, Rs725 return.

Stakna

This Kagyupa gompa is sited in a commanding position on its own plug of rock in the centre of the Indus Valley. It was repainted in 1982 and is now one of the most bright and colourful gompas in Ladakh. It lies between Hemis and Matho and is reached by taking the bumpy road that runs along the left (W) bank of the Indus. Taxis cost Rs515 one way, Rs630 return; the bus is Rs13.

Hemis

This monastery has become famous because of its spectacular annual festival. It's even more special if you can co-ordinate your visit with the unfurling of the monastery's vast thanka, thought to be the biggest in the world. However, as this is only displayed at every 12th festival you'll have to wait until 2004 for the next showing. Although it is the largest and richest of Ladakh's monasteries, it is not the most beautiful and much of the gompa looks run-down and in need of restoration. Unfortunately the gompa's wealth is held mainly in land and not in cash.

The gompa was founded in the 17th century and is sometimes called Chang Chub Sang Ling, 'the solitary place of the compassionate ones'; it belongs to the Kagyupa sect. Try to see the impressive image of Guru Padmasambhava which is in a temple behind the Dukhang (the temple on the right). This huge statue is 12 metres high and was completed in 1984.

The village and gompa lie tucked up a little side valley south-west of Karu. As you drive up to it you pass two enormous mani walls. There are guest-houses, a camp-ground and various places where you can eat in the village.Buses leave Leh at 9.30am daily and sometimes at 4pm as well (two hours) and return at 6.30am and 12 noon. Taxis cost Rs750 one way and Rs860 return (1¼ hours).

Chemre
This gompa looks more impressive from afar than close up, sitting astride a hill high above the village. It's situated about halfway along the quiet road from Karu to Tak Tok and is worth a visit if you are passing. The Kagyupa monastery was built in 1645 in honour of Sengge Namgyal after his death. Taxis cost Rs750 one way, Rs860 return.

Tak Tok
Tak Tok (Thak Thak/Trakthok/Tak Thog) means 'rock roof' and this interesting little monastery is built around a cave where it is believed Padmasambhava lived and meditated for a while. The cave is now a cool dark temple. This is the only gompa in Ladakh of the Nyingmapa sect, the oldest Tibetan order. It's 20km up a side valley north-east of Karu.

❑ Prayer wheels and mani walls
Ritual and symbolism are an intrinsic part of Tibetan Buddhism which help reinforce the processes involved in gaining liberation. **Prayer wheels** are one example, representing the Wheel of Dharma, or the Buddhist truth, and also the rotation of the universe. These vary in size from the small pocket versions which revolve with the flick of a wrist to the huge cylindrical drums needing all your weight to set them in motion. They contain many scrolls of paper on which the mantra *om mani padme hum* is written. The creative act of turning a prayer wheel in a clockwise direction (never spin it anti-clockwise) helps focus the mind on the qualities of the Buddha and his teachings.

Mani walls, made up of intricately carved mani stones act in a similar way when passed in a clockwise direction, keeping the wall on your right. They are a relatively new concept, first introduced in the 15th century to honour the death of a king. The building of mani walls soon became popular, particularly as a way of punishing criminals, and they can now be found even in the remotest parts of Ladakh, ranging in size from a pile of stones to massive structures over 1000m long.

❑ Leh-Manali Highway   [see map opposite]
(Approximate distances given are from the last place mentioned)

This 483km highway descends from Leh to the village of **Choglamsar** (see p146) and then follows the River Indus in a south-easterly direction passing the historic sites of **Shey** and **Tikse** (17km from Leh). The royal palace at **Stok** (see p146) is reached by branching off at Choglamsar and taking the road over the Indus up to the village at the foot of the mountains. There's an alternative and little-travelled route on this side of the Indus which takes you past the gompas at **Matho, Stakna** and **Hemis** (p146) before rejoining the main highway. At **Karu** (19km from Tikse), it's worth making a short diversion up the quiet side valley to the north-east, to see the less tourist-visited gompas of **Chemre** and **Tak Tok** (see p147).

At **Upshi** (11km from Karu) you will be asked to show your passport at the police checkpoint. The road then leaves the Indus Valley to head south along the west bank of the tumbling Kyammar Lungpa to the military camp at **Rumtse** (31km), before climbing to the **Taglang La** (32km). The concrete urinals rather detract from the experience of standing at 5359m (17,582ft) on top of the highest pass on the route, but the road sign prompts you into the correct frame of mind by exclaiming UNBELIEVABLE IS NOT IT?

Ten kilometres of unpaved hairpins take you down to the wide and windswept More Plains (4700m/15,420ft), the summer grazing grounds for the sheep, yak and goats of the Changpa nomads. A track to Tso Kar and Tso Moriri leaves the highway at km339. The 47km plateau comes to an abrupt end when the road descends for 7km into a wide gorge to the army and road builders' depot at **Pang** (see p220) where there is a collection of dhabas and tents for benighted travellers. There are 24km of truly awe-inspiring scenery between Pang and the **Lachalang La** (5060m/16,600ft). The road descends briefly to **Whiskey Nullah** before rising to the smaller Nakeela Pass. An incredible descent of the 21 'Gata Loops' brings you to the tented camp at **Sarchu** (53km) where most of the tourist buses pull in for the night.

There's another small collection of dhabas at **Bharatpur** (22km), which you pass before climbing to the bleak summit of the **Baralacha La** (10km, 4890m/16,040ft). The road continues south-west past the road builders' camp at **Zingzingbar** and the tea tents and army camp at **Patseo** (31km from the Baralacha La), to **Darcha** (14km, see p230), where there are some dhabas and a camp-site. The small town of **Keylong** (32km, see p102) is a convenient place to break your journey as there are several small hotels.

The road crosses the Bhaga River at **Tandi** (8km), just before it joins with the Chandra to form the Chandra-Bhaga River, or Chenab, and this same water eventually flows into the Indus in Pakistan. The route veers round to the east, passing through the prosperous Lahauli villages of Gondla (10km) and Sissu (15km) along the Chandra Valley, until it reaches the ramshackle collection of dhabas and a police checkpoint at **Koksar** (13km) where you will be asked to show your passport.

As you climb the looping road towards the **Rohtang La** (16km, 3978m/13,052ft) there are wonderful views to White Sail Peak (6446m/21,149ft) and its smaller neighbours. The road is rough to Marrhi (12km) and then improves dramatically as you hurtle down past Kothi (24km) and Palchan (15km) to **Manali** (10km, see p97). The abundance of greenery and trees makes a dramatic change from the arid mountains that you've left far behind.

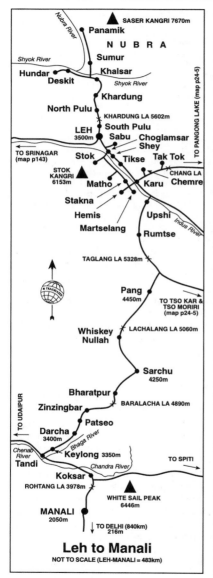

Leh to Manali
NOT TO SCALE (LEH-MANALI = 483km)

PROTECTED AREAS

All travellers visiting these areas must get a **permit** in Leh (see p131).

Nubra

(See map opposite). After years of speculation, the sensitive border region of Nubra was finally opened to foreigners in 1994. Access is possible all year round as the army endeavours to keep the road over the Khardung La free of snow, even in winter.

The district is characterised by spectacular deep, sheer-sided valleys, high mountains and long glaciers. It is here that you will find the highest peak in Ladakh, Saser Kangri, (7670m/25,165ft) which was first climbed in 1973, and also one of the longest glaciers in the region, the 70km Siachen Glacier, which is still the scene of fighting between India and Pakistan (see p110). Sandwiched between the Karakoram Mountains to the north and the Ladakh Range to the south lie the Shyok and Nubra rivers. The fertile villages are scattered along these two valley floors.

Because of the lower altitude a wide diversity of fruits, vegetables and grains are grown, creating the impression of abundance. Yet this is one of the poorest areas of Ladakh and facilities for the traveller are few and far between. Although accommodation and food can be found, you should bring anything else you need with you. Don't forget to pack your Ladakhi phrase book as few people speak English.

❏ **The world's highest motorable road – or is it?**
It's a hair-raising ride over the Khardung La with no shortage of heart-stopping moments. You feel your fears are justified as you pass the mangled wrecks of vehicles that took no notice of the road sign, SPEED THRILLS BUT KILLS, and plummeted over the edge. However, the stunning views help to divert your attention. It takes three hours to cover the 39km from Leh to the top, with one stop at the checkpoint at South Pulu (25km from Leh). Between here and North Pulu the road is unpaved and very rough. You are invited to take a free cup of tea when you reach the Khardung La (5602m/18,380ft). It is not clear whether this is designed to help you cope with the altitude or to soothe frayed nerves!

The views over the Zanskar Mountains are fantastic and if the altitude measurements are to be believed (personal altimeters have read as much as 500m lower!), you are now 100 metres higher than Mount Everest base camp and 795m above Mont Blanc; not bad for a local bus journey! Although it claims to be the highest motorable road in the world, that accolade should really rest with the road up the Uturuncu Volcano in Bolivia which reaches the dizzy height of 5900m (19,360ft).

From the pass you descend a bumpy 14km to North Pulu where there's another checkpoint and a tea stall and on through the pretty village of Khardung to the Shyok Valley floor and Khalsar, three hours and 56km from the pass.

Khalsar (3100m/10,150ft) is an unpleasant hamlet dominated by an army camp. There are several dhabas for simple nourishment and some basic guest-houses and a camp-site for accommodation. The road divides just before the bridge over the Shyok River; one route crosses the river and continues north up the Nubra Valley to Panamik, the other heads west along the Shyok Valley to Deskit and Hundar.

Deskit/Diskit (3070m/10,070ft) From the bridge, a newly paved road runs for 15km to Deskit across the immense valley floor where strong winds can whip up suffocating dust clouds. On the outskirts of the village is the Siachen Hospital, a grim reminder of the Siachen Glacier war being waged at the northern end of the Nubra Valley. The village is best known for its beautiful gompa perched on a rocky spur 200m above the village with friendly monks and breathtaking views.

Accommodation in the village is spread out. Below the gompa you will find the *Karakoram Guest House cum Camping Site* and *Olthang Guest House* which have rooms for Rs200 (att), while further along the road to Hundar is the *Sand Dune Guest House* which has rooms for Rs150 (com) and Rs200 (att). There is a shop in the village where you can buy basic supplies and a more tourist oriented shop at the gompa complete with biscuits, sweets, soft drinks and noodles.

Most people walk or catch a lift for the 7km to the next village of Hundar, but it is possible to get there on a two-humped Bactrian camel across mini sand-dunes (Rs350, ask at your guest-house). These camels are descendants of the beasts of burden which plied the trade route between Leh and Central Asia.

Hundar (Hunder/Hundat) has a small gompa by the road with ancient frescoes in the Kashmiri tradition. Above the road there are two other temples on the way up to a ruined gompa on a crag. The bridge in this village is as far west as foreigners are allowed to go; this is made perfectly clear by the armed soldiers on guard. There are two guest-houses of which the ***Moonland*** has been recommended. Camping is also possible.

Sumur North of Khalsar, over the bridge across the Shyok River, is the Nubra Valley. Sumur is one of the larger villages here with several places to stay which makes it a good base for visiting the nearby Samstanling Gompa. ***Tashis Khangsar Guest House*** and ***Stakray Guest House*** have rooms for Rs200 (com) and ***Tsewang Jorgais Guest House*** has rooms for Rs150 (com).

One kilometre along the road is the small village of **Tegar** (Tiger) where the more exclusive ***Hotel Yarab-Tsa*** charges an extortionate Rs950 for clean double rooms with bathroom. There are a few dhabas and a couple of shops in this village as well as two small gompas, one by the road and an old dilapidated building on the hillside above. The more impressive Samstanling Gompa is reached by taking a small road just after the village which winds up the hill for 2km. The monastery is situated at the mouth of a small ravine and is surrounded by poplar trees.

Panamik lies at the north end of the Nubra Valley and is unjustly famed for its hot springs. In the past they must have been a welcome sight for Silk Road traders after days of dicing with death on high Karakoram passes, but today they are not worth a special visit. The two baths are housed in a concrete building on the hillside above the PWD resthouse and can be filled up by blocking the outlet with a rag. The water issues from a spring above the baths and is almost too hot to touch. Unfortunately the whole ambience is ruined by litter, excrement and a pervading smell of urine.

There are some nice walks down by the river and a good five-hour excursion across the valley to Ensa Gompa, which can be seen from Panamik, high on the mountainside with its small willow grove and fields. Go upstream for 4km towards Takshai, cross the Nubra River at the bridge and double back for 4km on the other bank.

Panamik has a camp-site, informal guest-houses and two poorly stocked shops.

Getting to Nubra There are four **buses** a week from Leh to Khalsar. From there, two travel up the Nubra Valley to Panamik (Rs80) and two head along the Shyok Valley to Deskit (Rs65). Timetables are variable to say the least so check in Leh for the latest details. Buses within Nubra travel from Deskit to Panamik one day, and return to Deskit the next. This infrequent and over-crowded public transport makes hiring a **jeep taxi** between four people a sensible option if you are on a tight schedule. This will cost Rs6000 for a three-day, two-night itinerary.

Hitching is far easier out of Nubra than the other way round. But if you want to try, trucks usually leave Leh in a convoy early in the morning. Hitching on any vehicle that is travelling around Nubra is a good way to get from one village to the next.

The hippest way to Nubra is on a **bicycle** especially as the number of people who have cycled over the 'highest road in the world' is still relatively small. If you're not a hard-core hill climber put your bike on the roof of a bus and enjoy the longest free-wheel of your life.

Pangong Tso   [see map p24-5]

This vast lake, 150km long and 4km wide, stretches from the north-east of Ladakh across the border into Tibet. The lake has no outlet so the water has a high salt and mineral content. Because of this the lake cannot support aquatic life, hence its distinctive and beautiful shades of blue, described by Gypsy Davy and Lady Ba in their *Himalayan Letters* as an 'azure sheen of turkis blew'. There are some interesting birds around the lake shore including a few pairs of the very rare and endangered black-necked crane. Although there are several villages in the area, there are no guest-houses and few shops, so bring camping equipment and all your supplies. You can reach the lake only by jeep, easily arranged in Leh (Rs5250 for two days).

Tso Kar and Tso Moriri   [see map p24-5]

These high-altitude lakes are situated in the Rupshu region of eastern Ladakh near the border with Tibet. There is no public transport so most visitors arrive by jeep (Rs8100 for three days).

The main reason people seem to visit the area is 'because it's there' and is now accessible by road. However, for the vehicle-bound tourist, the reward of seeing the so-called sights is unlikely to offset the hours of bone-jarring discomfort that must be endured to reach them. The true beauty of the region lies in its vast untamed space, silence, rare wildlife and nomadic inhabitants. None of these can be properly appreciated on a whistle-stop tour by jeep. What's more, there is mounting evidence that the increase in motorised transport (mostly tourism generated) is driving away the very wildlife that people are coming to see. Opinion among the nomadic Changpa inhabitants is also divided. The benefits of tourism do not look so rosy against a backdrop of disturbance, loss of grazing and pollution. If you do visit this area a very sensitive approach is essential.

Tso Kar is a salt lake surrounded by white heaps of saline deposits in a vast dusty bowl surrounded by barren mountains. It supports a vital salt industry that allows the Changpas to trade with merchants from the rest of Ladakh. Thukje, the small, dusty village on the northern shore of the lake, has a tiny gompa. There is a freshwater lake to the south-east of Tso Kar called Startsapuk Tso and herds of kiang (Tibetan wild ass) often graze on the plain nearby.

The road east crosses the Polokongka La and descends to the Puga Valley where there are hot springs. It then heads south past the small lake of Thatsang Karu to Tso Moriri.

Tso Moriri The brackish Tso Moriri is surrounded by snow-topped barren mountains. This unique habitat attracts many migratory water-birds including brahminy ducks and black-neck cranes and the rare barheaded geese which cross the Himalaya to breed here during the summer around the inlets of the lake. Unfortunately, tourism is doing untold damage to this, their most important breeding ground – please read the boxed text below and minimise you impact.

Walking along the road on the western shore the first sign of habitation is a scruffy camp-site with little flat ground, some toilets and a tiny, dribbling spring for water. Further on is the small village of Korzok which has a gompa and a basic dhaba, the *Tso Moriri Restaurant*.

❑ **Minimum impact**

Pangong Tso, Tso Moriri and Tso Kar all have extremely fragile ecosystems and provide habitats for some rare species of birds.

Since 1994, when foreign tourists were first allowed to visit these areas, there has been an alarming decline in the sighting of many birds and other wildlife. This is largely due to habitat disturbance by tourists' vehicles, bright clothes and the urge to get close to the wildlife to photograph it. The situation is particularly acute at Tso Moriri where the new access road to Korzok takes jeep loads of visitors along the lake shore and deposits them at a badly-sited camp close to the breeding grounds.

As Ladakh has no tourism management scheme it is up to the tourists themselves to make sure they do not destroy the very things that they have come to see. If certain simple practices are followed the damage inflicted on these unique areas can be reduced:

● Set up camp 2-3km away from the lake shore to make sure that the lakes are not polluted and that the wildlife is not disturbed. At Tso Moriri there are several excellent camping spots before you reach the lake. There are no suitable sites around the lake shore.

● Do not go to the toilet, wash your body, brush your teeth or wash your pots and pans near the lake shore. The lakes have no outlet and therefore any chemicals introduced to the water will remain there.

● Take all garbage away with you. It's not good enough simply to bury it.

● Don't allow your guide to drive to the shore of the lake. Get out and walk instead. The increase in vehicles driving close to the water's edge is doing untold damage.

● If you are trekking in this region you will need to bring fodder for your ponies. Grazing is limited and the increase in trekking is putting the nomads' grazing areas under stress.

● Encourage others to do likewise, particularly your guide and other Ladakhi helpers.

Dha-Hanu [see map p143]

Downstream from Khalsi, along the lower Indus, live a unique group of Dard people known as Brokpa. In most other areas the Dards have been strongly influenced by either the Tibetans or by the Muslims but here they have retained much of their original culture. They are the only ones to have preserved their unique form of Buddhism which is mixed with the pre-Buddhist animistic religion, Bon. They are a fascinating people who are very different from other Ladakhis, with their strong Aryan looks, language and clothing (they wear bright flowers in their head-dresses). There are five Brokpa villages and tourists are allowed to visit two, **Dha** and **Biama**. Being at relatively low altitude (2800m/9,200ft) the villages benefit from a warm climate. They produce flourishing crops of fruit and vegetables and it's amazing to see apricots, walnuts, tomatoes, squashes and flowers thriving in stark contrast to the rest of Ladakh.

The journey from Leh to Dha takes seven to eight hours and goes via Khalsi where you will be asked to show your permit. Just beyond Dha is a checkpoint which ensures foreigners don't stray too close to the Line of Control between India and Pakistan.

The village is above the road and has four guest-houses. *Skyabapa* is the first you come to on the path into the village. *Shariemo Lhamo*, *Chunu* and *Biloo* guest-houses are all in the centre. All are clean and charge Rs30-40 for a bed and Rs15-20 for a meal. There is similar accommodation in Beema which is about 3km back down the road. Apart from a small gompa at Dha there is little to see in the vicinity or few walks that are of any interest.

There are daily buses to Dha from Leh at 8am (Rs70). A taxi there and back will cost Rs3393 over two days.

❏ Chortens
These domed Buddhist monuments, also called stupas, are found all over Ladakh, especially at the entrance to villages where they are traditionally believed to ward off evil spirits. They were originally used to hold the remains of the Buddha and other saints; now they don't necessarily contain anything. There are many different types of chorten and like mani walls and prayer wheels they are deeply symbolic. Most have the features of a square or rectangular base, representing the earth, a spherical central section representing water, a spire representing fire topped by a sun and moon representing air and space – thus symbolising all five elements of the cosmos. As with mani walls, you must keep them on your right when you pass.

PART 6: MINIMUM IMPACT TREKKING

Minimum impact trekking

If a valley is reached by a high pass only the best of friends and worst of enemies are its visitors. **Tibetan proverb**

Ladakh's unique culture and amazing natural environment are what have drawn travellers to this remote region for centuries. Despite the harsh climatic conditions, the people have created a prosperous and harmonious way of life that reflects the Buddhist principle of the interdependence of all things. Not only do the Ladakhis demonstrate respect for one another, as demonstrated by the stability and fairness inherent in family and community relations, but also for the natural environment, something that many in the 'modernised' West are now trying to rediscover.

However, the last 50 years of being part of India, and in particular the last 20 or so years of having foreign tourists, has had more effect on Ladakh's culture, environment and economy than several centuries of foreign merchants and traders. The changes have been most apparent in and around Leh, where there has been a steady erosion of the traditional values in favour of Western-style materialism and an increase in environmental problems, but the effects have also been felt in the remote mountains. Short-sighted development policies of the 1950s and '60s helped to create the notion that the Ladakhis were a backward and primitive people and that the only way to modernise was to follow the Western model of economic and technological growth. This is reinforced by cinema, television and advertising which portrays a biased picture of the West with all its glamour and wealth, while nothing even approximate to the Ladakhi way of life is ever shown, making them seem absurd. Then the arrival of foreign tourists further propagated the myth that West is best. Here are people who seem to have almost limitless amounts of money, who can travel whenever and wherever they like and who never seem to work. It is not surprising that impressionable teenagers are influenced by this alluring new culture.

At the same time, however, tourism has been having a beneficial effect. Foreign visitors who show respect for Ladakh and are impressed by the resourceful culture help to create a strong feeling of identity and strengthen local pride in the face of so much derision. With increased inter-cultural understanding the real truth about the Western lifestyle starts to filter through: in tandem with the seeming benefits of modernisation go huge environmental, social and emotional problems.

Ladakh is now part of the 'developing' world. The process of change has permeated too far into Ladakhi society for this not to be so, and no matter how attractive a traditional rural society like Ladakh may seem, it is wrong and extremely damaging to make the land into some kind of museum. The Ladakhis have a choice over how their region develops and Western tourists must be aware that they play an important role in determining what this future will be.

If we travel seeking only to be thrilled and entertained, removed from our mundane lives for just a few weeks as if in some kind of fantasy, we will experience little and do much harm. If, on the other hand, we travel with respect and openness, desiring to learn, adapt and share at every opportunity, not only will we travel lightly but we will return home so much richer, with understanding of a way of life that has many lessons for the Western world.

Here then are some simple, practical steps to help us develop in a positive direction:

CULTURAL IMPACT

Interacting with Ladakhis

It is inevitable that you'll leave some impression of your culture by visiting Ladakh; instead of just consuming the country like another product, try to give something back. Tourists are in a powerful position to present a more balanced picture of life in the West and you are the ones who should actively speak out when you see something being done for the benefit of tourists which is obviously harmful or degrading to the local environment or culture. However, unless you make an effort to communicate, all that the Ladakhis will see is yet another rich tourist on holiday – probably an inaccurate picture of someone not particularly well off by Western standards, who has worked extremely hard to pay for a trip out to Ladakh and who cares for and admires the country and its people.

You will get the most out of your visit if you travel in small groups, allow lots of time to learn and try to be constantly aware. Although many Ladakhis speak good English, do try to learn a few words of Ladakhi as this will be greatly appreciated and will underline the importance of their language.

When telling somebody about your home country talk about the problems as well as the good things. The Ladakhis get a rose-tinted image of the West through the media so it is important to put across a balanced view of what life is really like in a 'developed' country. Most Ladakhis have no idea about the environmental and social costs of living in the West, and the extent of poverty, homelessness, alienation and mental illness. Things that Ladakhis take for granted, Westerners will actively seek out and pay more for: such as local, organic food and methods of natural health care. Unlike Ladakhis, few Westerners are privileged enough to own their own land and even fewer produce their own food; we don't even know how to. If you are asked how much you earn, put it in context by explaining that almost half of your income goes on paying for somewhere to live, say how much a week's supply of groceries will cost or how much it would cost to travel a short distance on a local bus.

Interaction with the Ladakhis should be a two-way process. There is much they can teach the West about community, local self-reliance and ways of living simpler, less intrusive and more compassionate lives. A holiday is the perfect excuse for learning.

● **Encourage local pride** Express an interest in all things Ladakhi and explain why you've come all this way and spent all that money to come to their country. Try to eat local food, adapt to local practices and use local services so that you can experience the culture at first hand. Make a point of letting the people know what you like about it: if you have chosen your guesthouse because it has a Ladakhi toilet or solar-heated water, tell the owners.

● **Dress and behave modestly** Too many trekkers unwittingly insult the Ladakhis by the way they are dressed, although complaints are never heard because they are too polite. It's very easy to respect local customs by not revealing your legs, shoulders, stomachs or backs. Men should always wear a shirt and trousers; shorts are not appreciated. Women should wear loose trousers or skirts below the knee and tops that cover their shoulders, stomach and back. Bright colours and body-revealing lycra are offensive to Ladakhis. If you see someone dressed inappropriately, please bring it to their attention. Never bathe in the nude; men should wear shorts and women should be more discreet and always wear at least shorts and t-shirt.

● **Respect local etiquette** Ladakhis have different ways of doing things and by following these simple guidelines you will avoid causing offence. The most useful word to learn is *Julay* which can be used at any time of the day to greet people, say goodbye or to thank someone. As you trek through villages you will be greeted by everyone in this manner and it is polite to do likewise.

When offered something it is polite to give a couple of insincere refusals before accepting. Use both hands to receive things. If you really don't want something you may have to say 'no' two or three times. If you are pointing at something use your whole hand rather than just your finger. The feet are considered unclean, so don't point them at people or step over anything such as people, food, tables or religious articles. Similarly, if you have your legs outstretched Ladakhis will be loath to step over them, so move them out of the way or, preferably, keep them folded under you if you're seated on the floor. Religious objects, including anything that contains pictures of religious objects (postcards or books), should be kept high off the floor.

In most rooms there is a subtle seating arrangement with the place of honour usually furthest from the door and close to the stove. You may be encouraged to sit at or near the seat of honour but it is polite to sit a little further down.

When in public do not display your affection for others by holding hands, hugging or kissing. This can easily offend or embarrass Ladakhis. Don't share utensils when eating or drinking or dip your used ones into the serving dish. If sharing a water bottle, learn how to drink without your lips touching it.

● **Respect religious customs** When visiting monasteries it is particularly important that you wear appropriate clothes, take off your shoes or boots before entering the temple, don't smoke, don't touch any religious objects and always remember to give a small donation. The larger monasteries now charge an entrance fee to make sure you don't forget. If you want to photograph the frescoes inside monasteries, bring a tripod or some fast film; don't use a flash as this can damage the paintwork.

Religious festivals are sacred occasions and you will upset many local people if you wander around taking photographs while the dances are going on. Recently, masked dances have been performed outside monasteries as a tourist attraction, especially during the Ladakh Festival. This is considered deeply sacrilegious and you should express your disapproval by not supporting such an exploitation of religion and by complaining to the relevant organisers.

Always walk to the left of Buddhist monuments (chortens, mani walls, prayer wheels) by keeping them on your right. Prayer wheels should be turned in a clockwise direction. Don't sit or leave your pack on mani walls or chortens and never move mani stones.

● **Respect people's privacy** Ladakhis get just as annoyed by people peering into their lives as you do. Always put yourself in their position, especially before taking someone's photograph. It is a common courtesy to ask for permission before taking a shot and if they don't want their photo taken please respect this. Don't pay people for posing for you. It is much better to take down their address and send them a copy instead. Pony-men, and others that you spend some time with, may also ask you to send them copies of the photos you've taken of them. It is a cardinal sin not to follow this obligation through; it costs you very little and means a great deal to those at the receiving end.

● **Be modest with your wealth** However poor you think you are at home, by Ladakhi standards you are very wealthy. Don't flaunt this wealth by showing off your hi-tech equipment. Leaving it lying around unattended is further proof that you could easily afford to replace it.

● **Discourage begging** Begging in Ladakh started as a children's game to see if they could get a 'bon-bon' or 'school pen' from the always obliging tourists. However, it has developed into a far more serious problem by fostering an attitude of dependency among the young. Don't give anything to people who ask for it, after all, giving sweets to children in a country which has few dentists is not an act of charity; if you want to give money it's best to ask the advice of one of the excellent NGOs working in Ladakh (see p132) as to whom it should be given.

● **Don't play doctor** While trekking you may occasionally be asked by locals for medicines or to treat wounds. Unless it is simply a case of cleaning a cut and applying a plaster you should encourage them to go to the nearest health post. There is usually one in larger villages. If you try to treat something more complicated and your efforts do not work, you may begin to undermine the people's faith in Western medicine. This will encourage them to patronise the local shaman rather than the health post.

● **Keep your sense of humour** It is considered the height of bad manners to lose your temper, and something you will almost never see a Ladakhi do. Although things can sometimes be very difficult, always try to maintain some perspective on the situation. You are not at home but in a land where things are done differently and where concepts of time are simply different from your own. See the funny side of your predicament; there will always be one.

ENVIRONMENTAL IMPACT

Litter

Litter is a very recent problem in Ladakh. It is only since the arrival of non-biodegradable consumer items from India and the rest of the world that the concept of litter has begun to take hold. Before, everything was made from biodegradable materials or continuously recycled, there was no waste. Today, however, it is a serious problem both in Leh and on the major trekking routes. In the latter case it is only the trekkers who are to blame as most locals cannot afford the luxury of consumer products. Streamers of used lavatory paper and piles of tin cans, plastic bags and containers at every camp-site are a sad reflection on people who would undoubtedly call themselves mountain lovers. The solution is simple and summed up in the often used phrase, 'pack it in, pack it out'. If consumer products are brought into the mountains by you, or for you (via a shop/hotel or by your trekking company), it is your responsibility to take any resulting litter back out with you.

The problem in Leh is immediately obvious to the visitor who can't avoid the litter that lies in the streets, but unfortunately there is no easy solution. Leh has no proper infrastructure to cope with litter. While there are litter bins situated around the town which many tourists diligently use, there are few appropriate places for its disposal after that. The facilities that are available are hopelessly inadequate as litter left in heaps is soon scattered far and wide by scavenging dogs and the wind, while the incinerators pump toxic fumes into the atmosphere. Steps are being taken to improve the situation, one of the most effective being the banning of polythene bags from the town. Goods are now sold in paper bags rather than plastic and this has already had a noticeable effect on the cleanliness of Leh.

● **Don't leave litter** When trekking it is a simple matter to bring along an extra bag in which to put all non-organic litter. This applies equally to those trekking with ponies and to those backpacking. You can significantly cut down the amount of potential waste you bring into the mountains by repacking items to avoid unnecessary packaging. Picking up other people's litter is very helpful and sets a good example to others. Burning litter is frequently claimed to solve the problem, but many items do not burn properly and the fire leaves unsightly scars on the ground. It is far better to get into the habit of taking all non-organic waste out with you. If you are trekking with an organised group it is your responsibility to ensure that the crew dispose of the litter properly and that it isn't simply buried or left. Don't just imagine that waste will biodegrade; although most organic material will break down quite quickly, other biodegradable waste can take years to break down in this cold, dry climate. Also, don't assume that you can leave litter in villages; while much of it may be recycled they don't have any facilities to deal with the rest.

Having advocated bringing all your litter back to Leh, you then have to decide what to do with it there. However, it is far better to have it concentrated in one place where there is a chance that it will be dealt with properly than left in the mountains where it will remain for generations to come. More pressure is coming to bear on Leh's authorities and it is likely that proper litter disposal systems will be introduced soon. In the meantime all you can do is try to keep your consumption of packaged goods to a minimum, reuse as much as possible and dispose of any litter in the bins provided.

● **Burn used lavatory paper** On the trail, if you can't get used to the water-and-left-hand method make sure you burn all the loo paper that you use. Keep a cigarette lighter or some matches in the same plastic bag as the loo paper specifically for this purpose. Used loo paper burns easily and there is no excuse for the 'pink flowers' of paper that decorate the trails. Not only is it unsightly, but unhygienic as well, especially when it's blown around camp-sites and into water sources.

● **Pack out used tampons/sanitary towels** Tampons/sanitary towels should be packed out as they are almost impossible to burn completely at high altitude. Condoms should also be disposed of in this way.

● **Avoid bottled mineral water** Mineral water is sold widely in India and Ladakh in non-returnable, non-biodegradable plastic bottles. As there are several other ways to make ordinary tap water safe to drink (see p271), it is unnecessary to add to the litter problem by buying mineral water. If you treat the water yourself you not only save money (Rs15-20 a litre), but you can be absolutely sure that the water you are drinking is safe (the seals on plastic bottles are not 100% tamper-proof). A forward-thinking business in Leh, called Dzomsa, sells safe pressure-boiled water for Rs7 per litre directly into your water bottle, or in re-used bottles.

● **Dispose of used batteries outside India** Most places in India have no safe means of disposing of batteries, the contents of which are highly toxic. Discarded batteries end up polluting the soil and water, or even as children's playthings. Pack batteries out for disposal in the West.

(**Opposite**) Appropriate technology harnessing solar energy. **Top**: Photovoltaics alongside drying fuel and fodder, Testa (p239). **Bottom**: Solar cookers, water heater and Trombe Wall at the Ecology Centre (p137).

Water
● **Don't pollute water sources** If you are **bathing**, **washing clothes** or **washing up** in a stream, make sure you do so downstream of any houses. If you want to use soap or shampoo (is it really necessary in the mountains?), fill a container (collapsible buckets available in outdoor shops are ideal) and wash away from the stream, pouring the waste water onto the ground far away from the water source. The need to wash clothes with soap can be minimised by rinsing them in a stream daily. The hot sun will make sure that they dry rapidly, but modern synthetic fibres can quite comfortably be wrung out and worn damp if it's not too cold. There is never any need to use soap or washing up liquid for cleaning pots and pans, as a good wire scrubber, or failing that, a handful of small pebbles, will get any pan sparkling in no time.

Defecating in the mountains is an art, one that is well worth getting good at for your sake and everyone else's. Not only is faeces unpleasant to our senses but more importantly, faecal contamination is one of the main ways of spreading disease. Faecal matter takes at least one year to disappear in good conditions (ie damp soil with active organic material in a temperate climate) but these good conditions are rarely found in Ladakh's mountains – evidence of your passing will be around for some time.

First you need to find a good site, far enough away from water sources to stop faeces being washed into the water by surface runoff caused by rain or snow-melt; this usually means at least 50m/150ft. It also needs to be above any area that is likely to receive flooding, so that secluded dry river bed is no good! Head for high ground. Dig a small hole with the heel of your boot or a convenient stone; 15-20cm (six to eight inches) is ideal as this is the most active part of the soil. Afterwards cover in the hole and if possible mix some of the soil in with the faeces to speed decomposition. Don't forget to burn your loo paper – see it as your homage to the mountain gods! This whole rigmarole is made considerably easier on some of the popular treks where the villagers have built traditional composting toilets specifically for the hundreds of trekkers passing through each year – please use them.

For more information on this lost art, get hold of Kathleen Meyer's *How to Shit in the Woods* which explains some lesser known techniques which are particularly applicable to Ladakh. 'Frosting a rock' for instance, is suitable for rarely visited regions of Ladakh where spreading your faeces thinly onto a rock to bake in the intense sun and blow away on the wind is far more efficient and hygienic than burying it where there is little or no active soil. Another method which is particularly pertinent to large groups and high-use areas is 'packing it out'...

● **Ladakhi loos** Ladakh's traditional composting toilets are ideally suited to the environment and their use should be encouraged. No water is used (or

---

(Opposite) Top: Trekking allows for real cultural exchange; nomad children near Polokongka La, Rupshu (see p35). **Bottom**: Locals watching traditional dancing at the Ladakh Festival, Leh (see p73).

wasted), the smell is negligible because of the dry climate and the end product is one of the best fertilisers around for organic agriculture. In rural areas the process saves animal faeces which, when dry, can be used more efficiently for fuel, essential in a region with hardly any wood. When using a Ladakhi toilet, usually situated upstairs and on the north side of a Ladakhi house, don't use water and remember to shovel down some earth or ash (there's normally a pile in a corner) when you've finished; this stops the smell and discourages flies. Don't throw tampons, sanitary towels, condoms etc down the hole.

Unfortunately, many guest-houses in Leh are being encouraged by government incentives to introduce flush toilets purely to please visitors. These are having disastrous effects on the local environment. First, they are using up extremely valuable fresh water supplies and second, Leh has no sewage system to deal with the waste that is produced. Instead, the groundwater supplies and the streams are becoming heavily contaminated because of poorly constructed and poorly maintained drains and septic tanks. Even if sewage-treatment works could be built and there was enough water, polluting chemicals would have to be introduced into the systems and the lavatories would still be useless in winter when they freeze over. Various local organisations have tried to make guest-house owners aware of the problem but have met with little success because the owners believe that Western loos are essential to attract guests. Therefore it is up to travellers to make them aware that you would prefer traditional toilets rather than Western-style ones. If your guest-house has a choice between a flush system and a dry toilet, please use the latter. After all, most trekkers are quite happy without flush toilets in the mountains and surely you didn't come to Ladakh to be comforted by Western 'luxuries'.

Erosion and vegetation depletion

The lack of vegetation, the gradual growth of the Himalaya by several millimetres per year; the searing heat of summer and freezing conditions of winter all combine to give the mountains of Ladakh a high rate of denudation. Although your actions may seem minuscule in comparison to these natural processes, when they are multiplied by several thousand trekkers each year they become rather more significant.

● **Stay on the main trail** Avoid taking shortcuts on steep sections of trail: your footsteps will be followed by many others. If you happen to damage walls or irrigation channels make sure you repair them as someone's livelihood may be at stake.

● **Travel light** By travelling light you can use fewer pack animals which minimises the amount of erosion you cause and reduces the grazing on valuable mountain pastures. All villages have rights over designated pastures and the use of that land by others is not allowed. An exception has traditionally been made for travellers. Unfortunately this generosity has been abused in the popular trekking areas by unnecessarily large trekking groups whose horses put too much pressure on this scant resource.

● **Don't damage plants** Leave plants alone so that they can be enjoyed by other passers-by. You won't get through Customs with a rare Himalayan specimen so don't try. Take care where you tread so that you don't disrupt fragile high-altitude ecosystems.

● **Don't light open fires** Wood is a scarce resource so don't use any for making fires. You should always bring a stove and enough kerosene to cook on and remember that a camp-fire is a selfish luxury. Fires create ugly scars on the ground that take years to fade away. While locals may well use animal-dung fires to cook on, trekkers should not copy them as the fuel is a valuable resource for other travellers and villagers.

● **No hot running water please!** Many of Leh's guest-houses now have hot running water. A few heat the water by solar panels and this should be encouraged, but most use highly inefficient wood-fuelled boilers. Very little of this wood comes from Ladakh but is instead transported at great environmental and financial cost from mostly unsustainable forests in Himachal Pradesh and Kashmir. The cheaper guest-houses take a far more environmentally-friendly approach by heating one bucket of water at a time, usually when the stove is being used for cooking anyway. A bucketful of water is ample for a good wash.

ECONOMIC IMPACT

There is no doubt that tourism is an important force in the economy of Ladakh. This is particularly valuable now that the traditional trade routes which previously provided Ladakh with a stable economic base have closed. Although tourists may spend a large amount of money in Ladakh, much of that goes straight into the pockets of non-Ladakhis only to be taken out of the region at the end of the tourist season. Thus the Ladakhis have to put up with the cultural and environmental problems that tourism brings without benefiting as much as they could from the profits.

● **Check out your trekking company** If you book an organised trek in your home country a proportion of what you pay stays in the West to cover the company's administrative costs. Try to find out how your company spends its money in Ladakh. Does it use local services, buy locally produced food and goods, or employ local staff? Some companies bring Nepalese staff over, as Ladakh's peak season coincides with Nepal's off season. If you use an agency in Leh, is the company run by Ladakhis or employing Ladakhi staff? If you trek independently you will contribute more to the local economy. For this reason you should try to find a pony-man close to the start of your trek so that the money directly benefits the local community.

● **Use local services** Be choosy about how and where you spend your money. Hotels, guest-houses, restaurants, souvenir shops and trekking agencies are increasingly being run by outsiders. This means that all the profits that they make with your money disappear with them, back to Delhi and

Kashmir at the end of September. One estimate was that only 10% of souvenir shops in Leh were run by Ladakhis. You should use local services to boost the local economy; you'll benefit as much as the Ladakhis. Trying out Ladakhi-run accommodation will soon prove to you that their guest-houses give far better value and are much more interesting than the overpriced and uniform establishments that are part of national and international chains. They may have all mod cons but are you seeking a home from home? If so, why travel?

● **Buy local products** Handicrafts have always been important in a region that has traditionally provided for its own basic needs. However, the souvenir shops of Leh are flooded with goods imported from the rest of India; sold at a higher price than in Delhi. The potential for Ladakhi crafts is slowly being realised, especially as their manufacture can provide villagers with a supplementary income during the six to eight winter months when there is little agricultural work. This, therefore, diversifies and strengthens the rural economy. Ask for Ladakhi handicrafts and try to find out where they were made. Some of the state-run handicraft centres merely compound the problem by encouraging people (mainly women) away from the farms to work in small-scale craft factories rather than their homes, thus further undermining the traditional agricultural economy.

It is illegal to buy any object that is more than 100 years old. Abiding by the law is not enough: don't buy anything which is obviously robbing Ladakh of its cultural heritage, such as old thankas, statues and other religious objects, or even personal jewellery and old traditional tools.

When buying supplies for a trek, make the most of locally produced food such as the organic vegetables sold along the Main Bazaar, or dried apricots and roasted barley. When eating in restaurants and hotels try to support the local economy by asking for traditional Ladakhi food.

● **Pay the right price** Try to get an informed idea of how much things are worth. Guest-house owners, staff at the tourist information and other travellers can all be helpful. If you pay too much you will encourage inflation but by not paying enough you will deprive people of their rightful earnings. If you would like to give money in return for staying in a local home Rs70-100 would be an appropriate amount for food and accommodation. Your hosts may be shy about accepting it, so employ the local way of offering gifts which is to place it in an envelope on a table in the kitchen in their sight.

● **Alternative economies** It is not always appropriate to bless people with your money as it can enforce the idea of a monetary economy in an area where more appropriate economic systems are operating. Particularly in remote rural areas, giving money in exchange for food or accommodation may not be accepted, in which case you should always have some useful gifts (such as tea, penknives, lighters, scarves for the women, balloons for the children, writing and drawing materials) which can be given instead.

Organising your trek

PONY-MEN AND PACK ANIMALS

One of the most enjoyable ways to trek in Ladakh, whether you are on your own or with a few friends, is to hire a few ponies or donkeys to carry your food and equipment. The pony-man (it's almost always a man) who accompanies you will do far more than just look after the animals. He can also be your guide, translator, tutor, cook and companion.

If you're travelling in a large group, you may prefer to hire an additional cook and even a guide as well. This can be done in exactly the same way as outlined below.

First, find your pony-man

● **Independently** The independent trekker in need of a pony-man/guide should have few problems in finding a competent local. For the well-known Markha Valley trek start by making enquiries in Leh and at the nearby villages of Stok, Spituk or Choglamsar where many of the pony-men live. If you are planning to follow routes such as Likir to Temisgam, Lamayuru to Alchi, or Across Zanskar which all begin a fair distance from Leh, you're better off waiting until you arrive at the trailhead village before making any arrangements. The villages of Likir, Alchi and Lamayuru, as well as Padum in Zanskar, and Darcha (or failing that, Keylong) in Lahaul, are all used to the needs of trekkers.

You will need to allow more time for finding a guide for the less well-known or remoter treks, but even in Nubra (try in Deskit or Hundar) or in Rupshu (try Rumtse, Gya and Lato, or Korzok) you should have little difficulty if you are persistent. Ask shopkeepers and the owners of restaurants and guest-houses if they know of anyone who can help. Ask as many people as possible; the quicker the news spreads around the village the sooner a pony-man will materialise. If your requirements are simple you're unlikely to have to wait more than a couple of days.

● **Through an agency** The alternative is to use one of Leh's many trekking agencies. The knowledge of a good agency can be invaluable if you can't spare the time to look yourself, want a fully organised trek, or if you are looking for someone to guide you on one of the less well-known routes. However, you'll be charged Rs50-100 more per day than if you went direct to a pony-man (more if the trek begins a long way from Leh) and you have no control over whom the agency picks for you.

Pack animals

● **Ponies, donkeys or yaks?** The most common pack animals in Ladakh are donkeys and ponies. Very occasionally you will see yaks being used but this is rare. Donkeys can carry about 30kg each, while a pony can take up to 60kg. You often won't have much choice over which you hire as it depends what animals are available. Your choice of pony-man is far more important than your choice of animal.

● **How many?** One of the quirks of using pack animals is that no matter how little gear you have, you will almost always have to hire a minimum of two. Contrary to popular opinion, this is not just the pony-man's scam for making more money: for a start it's not only your belongings that need to be carried but also those of the pony-man plus fodder for the animals. One pony on its own is likely to wander far at night, possibly even trying to return home; this is less likely to happen if it has a companion. It is also a matter of safety: if one of the animals got injured there's still another to carry the load, and if you fell ill the pony-man has a way of carrying you out of the mountains.

To work out how many animals you'll need for a trek you have to decide how many large bags you are going to take ('large' being about 15kg, or the size of a full 60- or 70-litre backpacking rucksack). Count on two bags of that size per animal plus an extra animal for your pony-man. For example, two people taking the same amount of food and gear as they would on a backpacking trip would find two animals suitable, one for them and one for the pony-man. However, most people enjoy the luxury of being able to take slightly more than you could if backpacking, especially where food is concerned. In which case an animal each may be more realistic. If you're in any doubt, show the pony-man how much gear you've got and listen to his advice.

❑ **Trekking alone**

One or two routes, such as Likir to Temisgam, won't present the experienced lone trekker with any problems, but most routes in Ladakh are a much more serious undertaking, being less travelled, at higher altitude and with fewer villages. Every year a few hardy backpackers set off alone to trek these routes and have a very rewarding experience. However, in order to do so safely, you not only have to be extremely experienced in high-altitude wilderness travel but also aware that if anything goes wrong it's very unlikely that anyone will be close enough to help you. The occasional tragic poster in Leh, appealing for any information on Westerners who have gone missing while trekking alone, serves as a sad warning of the inherent risks of such a venture. It's not advisable for women to trek alone.

However, there is no reason why you shouldn't travel to Leh on your own with the intention of trekking. It's generally easy to find trekking partners once you've arrived as there are noticeboards in the popular restaurants and at the tourist information office; these are good places to look or advertise for fellow trekkers. Alternatively, organise your own trek with a pony-man. This is a wonderful way to walk and the best way to learn a lot about what you're seeing. Your companion will probably be able to speak enough English for both of you to get by, but you will obviously get the most out of the experience if you endeavour to learn a few words of Ladakhi.

● **Packing** The pony-men are experts at loading up their animals and have a seemingly endless range of methods for getting the distribution right. This is especially important on steep sections of the trail where a slipped load can send an animal to its death. To make life easier for them, try to split your luggage into even numbers of equally weighted bags, for instance, two rucksacks and two food bags. If you don't, you may find your luggage being opened and repacked so that the best balance can be found. Smaller items such as fuel bottles and day-packs can usually be tied on or put in the middle between the larger sacks. One word of warning: even if you aren't expecting any rain make sure your belongings are well packed in plastic bags as the pony-man's fuel containers and stove have a nasty habit of leaking all over your sleeping bag. The smell of kerosene is not conducive to a good night's sleep and is almost impossible to get rid of.

Payments and responsibilities

● **Costs** The cost of a pack animal varies between Rs150 and Rs300 per day and tends to be the same whether you hire a pony or a donkey. The pony-man doesn't charge any more for tending the animals and is usually willing to act as your guide for free. However, if you want him to be your cook as well, this will cost Rs100-250 extra a day. Prices are at their highest during July and August but you should be able to negotiate a better rate before and after the peak season.

● **Negotiations** A diplomatic attitude is essential when negotiating with your pony-man. It's self-defeating to annoy him before you've even started your trek. You must first decide how long you want to hire him for. The pony-man is usually a good judge of how long a particular trek will take but most tend to be cautious with their estimate until they've seen how fast you walk. It is expected that you will also pay for each day of your pony-man's return journey at half the daily rate.

You need to make it clear from the outset the precise role you are employing him for. Is he literally just providing the animals to carry your bags, or would you like him to act as a guide and possibly a cook as well? If you would like him to guide you, ask him how many times he has walked the route before. There have been several instances of 'guides' getting lost, so you need to be confident that he knows the way before hiring him. If he is to cook for you, you need to establish what food to buy and who's going to buy it – his culinary skills may well be limited to chapatis, rice and dal. If you want to cook on your own, make sure that your pony-man brings his own stove and enough food for himself.

● **Your responsibilities** As the employer you must remember that you are ultimately responsible for his welfare.

Before you set off make absolutely sure that he is suitably equipped for the conditions that you are expecting. If he isn't, see that he either borrows or buys whatever he needs, or be prepared to lend him any of your spares, particularly at cold, high-altitude camps.

After you've finalised the agreements, it's usual to give him enough money to cover any initial expenses such as buying food and equipment. The balance, along with an appropriate tip should be paid at the end of the trek (an extra day's wage for every seven days is about right). Any equipment or unused food and kerosene is always appreciated and can be given in lieu of a full tip.

LOCAL EQUIPMENT

If you can bring good quality trekking and camping gear with you from home, then do so. If you find you've forgotten something, or you arrive in Leh without any equipment, it's quite possible to make do with what's available there.

Hiring

The entrepreneurs of Leh have been quick to capitalise on Ladakh's growing trekking industry and it's now possible to hire most items of trekking equipment that you could need (see p135). While the quality may not be quite up to the standard you'd expect in the West, most of it is perfectly serviceable, although you should check everything thoroughly before hiring it.

Buying in the bazaar

An alternative to hiring is to buy local equipment from the bazaar. The advantage of this is that it can be resold or given to your pony-man as a tip at the end of the trek. Strong canvas **rucksacks** (Rs180) make ideal holdalls for your gear but are agony to have on your back for long. You will also see fake rucksacks bearing Karrimor, Lowe Alpine or Berghaus labels. While they will probably last for a trek or two, don't forget to pack a needle and thread. For packing breakable/squashable food items, small **wooden packing cases**, available cheaply from the fruit and vegetable sellers in the vegetable market, are ideal. Robust **tin trunks** (Rs200) can also be bought but they are unnecessarily bulky for a small trekking group. **Jute sacks** are the cheapest and best receptacles for the rest of your food. They can be bought for Rs5 from most general stores who get their grains and pulses delivered in them.

❏ Pressure cookers

Water boils at a lower temperature at high altitude because of the lower atmospheric pressure – at 3050m it boils at 90°C while at 4575m it boils at 85°C. Therefore, cooking food by boiling takes much longer in Ladakh than it does at sea level. Rice and dal, in particular, can take forever. One of the ways around this problem is to buy a pressure cooker (Rs270 for a two-litre cooker) in the main bazaar. Although they are heavy and bulky, you won't need to take nearly as much fuel because things cook more quickly.

It takes a lot of faith to cook in a pressure cooker as you can't see how things are progressing inside and it's all too easy to end up with a burnt mess stuck to the bottom of your pan. From personal experience I highly recommend that you practise before you leave on your trek.

You won't have many problems finding **clothes** to keep you warm: thick woollen jumpers, hats, socks and gloves are widely available but finding decent waterproofs is much harder. Other clothes that you should be able to find are sun hats and trousers, which you can also get made up by a local tailor. Some trekkers find the army surplus stores close to the old bus stand in Leh useful for ex-army trousers, jackets, gloves, hats and sleeping bags (Rs400).

The kerosene **stoves** (Rs200) available in the bazaar are perfectly adequate if you are hiring ponies but too heavy for backpacking. **Kerosene** (Rs5 per litre) is the most widely used fuel, although **petrol** (Rs25 per litre), while harder to find, is often preferable as it's easier to light. If possible filter either fuel through cloth or filter paper as both are dirty and will clog your stove in no time if you're not vigilant about cleaning it. Buy enough fuel for your stove as it's unlikely that you will be able to re-stock in the mountains.

The fuel and water **containers** (Rs30-40) from the bazaar invariably leak from the lid, but they are better than nothing. Buy lots of **matches** and keep them in various strategic places where they can't get wet and won't get lost. **Candles**, **torches** and **batteries** can all be bought in Leh, but the batteries are of appalling quality and in very few sizes. If you intend to cook rice or dal a **pressure-cooker** is essential. Other useful items are good metal **plates**, **mugs**, **pots**, **pans** and **cutlery**, **rope** for stream crossings and **plastic sheeting** for groundsheets or makeshift tents.

FOOD FOR TREKKING

A wide range of suitable trekking food is available in Leh so there's no need to bring mountains of specialised dehydrated food from home. As it's unlikely that you will be able to buy food on the trail, it is vital that you purchase enough to last for the whole trek, plus some emergency rations, just in case.

To cope with the physical demands of trekking you need a good balanced diet that provides about 4000 calories a day, or about double the amount you need for a more sedentary lifestyle. Fat provides twice the energy of other food groups but takes a long time to digest and fatty foods are hard to take trekking. It's far better to base your diet around lots of carbohydrates (rice, noodles, breads), which provide energy more quickly and will keep you going longer. Supplement this with fats and proteins (dal, nuts, soya chunks, cheese and meat). Sugars (sweets, chocolate, jams and honey) are also useful as they are absorbed and converted into energy even more quickly than carbohydrates but their effect soon wears off and won't keep you going for long. Eating enough, however, is not always as easy as it sounds, as high altitude can sometimes have the effect of suppressing your appetite. If this is the case, you'll really have to be determined to force enough food in.

What to eat

Listed below are some ideas for what to eat while trekking. If you are an imaginative cook you will be able to dream up far more interesting meals but at least this serves as an indication of what's available in the shops. The weights given are a very rough guide to how much will be needed per person per day. It's highly recommended that you try out your chosen menu before you leave on your trek. This way you'll know if you've got enough and whether your cooking arrangements work.

Leh is the best place to stock up with food. Some of the trailhead villages have shops (see the relevant entries in Part 7) in which you could probably buy enough for a trek if you had no other option, but there won't be much choice. Leh's general stores can provide almost all your requirements apart from vegetables which are best bought from the local women who sit along the shady side of the Main Bazaar. These are usually organically grown and come from local farms. In contrast, the vegetables and fruit from the main vegetable market are mostly imported and are unlikely to be organic. Dzomsa sells roasted barley and other local produce.

● **Breakfast** Tsampa or oat porridge (100g) made with powdered milk and sugar makes a sustaining breakfast which will warm you up while the frost still hangs on the tent. Bread with the locally produced apricot jam, or peanut butter, is another good alternative, but it's bulky to store and can be difficult to keep dry and fresh. If you have any chapatis left over from the night before, these are also delicious with jam. Other possibilities are cornflakes, muesli, eggs (tricky to keep intact but excellent for protein), dried fruit or biscuits. Wash this all down with a large mug of instant coffee, tea or hot chocolate.

● **Lunch and snacks** Lunch tends to start a couple of hours after breakfast and goes on into mid-afternoon. Having a little bite to eat each time you stop to rest is a good way to keep your energy up throughout the day. Peanuts, roasted barley, dried fruits and chocolate bars are the easiest and

---

❑ **Ladakhi skyu – ideal trekking food**

Mix about 75-100g of flour per person with a small amount of water to form a stiff dough. Pull off golf-ball size chunks and roll between your hands to form a long snake of dough, about 1cm thick. Then pinch off small pieces and squeeze between your forefinger and thumb to make a flat pasta shape. Collect these on a plate until you have finished the dough.

In a saucepan fry onion, garlic, vegetables (potatoes, turnips and carrots keep well but anything will do) spices and chilli powder in a small amount of oil for a few minutes to soften. Now cover with water and add pre-soaked soya chunks (soaked for 10 minutes in hot water, or several hours in cold) if you wish. Then place the pasta shapes on top, just covered by the water and bring to the boil. Simmer for 10-15 minutes until vegetables, soya and pasta are all cooked. Serve and enjoy!

This can be varied endlessly with different vegetables and spices, or simplified for lightweight backpacking; onion, garlic, soya chunks, flour for the pasta, chilli and spices.

quickest to eat, (reckon on 150-200g of nuts or grains a day per person). Other options are bread, chapatis or biscuits with tinned cheese, tuna, peanut butter or jam. Although quite bulky, cold potatoes (cooked at breakfast), on their own or with mayonnaise, make a delicious change.

● **Dinner** The key to a simple main meal is to be able to cook it all in one pot. One of the most adaptable dishes which also happens to be local is *skyu*. This is a vegetable broth with pasta in it; (see opposite for recipe).

A more Westernised dish on the same theme would be dried noodles (150g-200g) and vegetables boiled in a pot to which you could add some spices, ginger and a packet of soup. Peanuts, coconut or tinned cheese can be added to a dish for extra variety. For the ultimate in convenience cooking, you can buy 'two-minute noodles', complete with a sachet of masala flavouring, but the ravenous trekker would easily be able to consume at one sitting two or three packets which, although light in weight, are very bulky.

Dal (80g-100g) with rice (150g-200g) or chapatis is a more traditional trekking meal. If you don't have a pressure cooker pre-soaking rice and dal for several hours will speed cooking time. The yellow *mung* dal is the quickest to cook. Chapatis are messy and time consuming to make, but if you're prepared to make the effort you can produce enough for breakfast and lunch as well.

Tinned tuna or eggs can add more variety to your meal. Don't forget to buy salt, pepper, chilli powder, spices, stock cubes or packet soups. Butter and oil can also be obtained if you want to fry anything. The whole meal can be finished off with dried fruit, chocolate and a hot drink.

● **Emergency rations** Pack some food which the body can quickly and easily convert into energy: muesli, sweet biscuits, dried fruit, nuts, chocolate bars and hot drinks – just in case you get stranded.

❏ **Ladakhi trekking diet**
The only food the Ladakhis take with them on a journey into the mountains is a small bag of tsampa, a brick of tea, some butter, a little salt and sometimes some dried cheese. The tsampa and cheese can then be mixed with the salt butter tea to the consistency of porridge, or into a stiff dough. This is then rolled into balls and eaten either immediately, or saved for later in the day. It takes very little time or fuel to boil a pan of water and if a storm or lack of wood make it impossible to light a fire, the tsampa can be eaten straight out of the bag with a little water. As with all good trekking food, it's versatile and simple.

The Western palate takes a little time to get used to the nutty taste of tsampa along with salty tea. A more palatable alternative is to mix tsampa with dehydrated soup or sweet tea. Although it's highly nutritious, you do need to eat a fair amount before you feel full, so experiment a little before you commit yourself. Tsampa is rarely sold in general stores and finding it can sometimes be hard. Try asking the owner of your guest-house or ask shopkeepers if you can buy some of their personal supply.

How to pack it
Plastic bags are the best things to pack your food directly into but they are
hard to obtain in Leh and of poor quality requiring much double and triple
packing to guard against splits. To save time on the trail and to make sure
that you don't run out of food halfway through your trek, divide all your food
into the right portions for each meal. If you are taking bread with you wrap
it in some plain material to keep it fresh. It may be hard to keep it dry if it
rains, but wrapping it in plastic is a sure way to make it go mouldy.

The food takes a battering when on the ponies so it is best to pack the
breakable/squashable items either in wooden packing cases or in a tin trunk.
Several jute sacks are ideal for the rest of your food. To close up the sacks,
simply roll over the top and sew it loosely with wool and a thick needle. This
can easily be undone at the end of the day and sewn up again each morning.

Buying food on the trail
Occasionally you will come across a village with a shop or a seasonal tea
tent but as you can never guarantee that they will be open or have anything
in stock, they are only useful for non-essentials like biscuits and chocolate.

CAMPING

In the main trekking areas there is almost no real wilderness as most land is
subject to village or communal rights. In effect you are walking and camping in someone's backyard and should therefore behave appropriately. You
are generally free to pitch your tent on any open ground, but if you want to
camp in a village you should ask permission, unless there's an obvious
camp-site. Also be prepared to pay a nominal fee if the villagers ask for one.
In popular trekking areas villagers will often walk a considerable distance to
collect this fee before you leave in the morning. The typical rate of Rs20 per
tent represents a considerable income for very little effort.

This is a perfectly fair deal, especially if you have pack animals which
are grazing on their pastures. However, there is a common misconception

❑ **Apricots**
The Ladakhis' use of apricots exemplifies their tradition of wasting nothing. The
fruit is eaten fresh, or dried for the winter; the sweet kernels are eaten and
enjoyed for their almond-like flavour.

Bitter kernels are ground for oil, which is then used for cooking, in lamps for
lighting, or for putting on the skin and hair. The cake that remains after extract-
ing the oil is used as animal fodder.

Dried apricots are even used for cleaning tarnished metals, while the apricot
wood from pruned trees is a fine hard wood that is used for making tools and
musical instruments.

❏ **Small change**
Rs100 notes are next to useless in the hills as people rarely have change. Stock up on lots of Rs2, Rs5 and Rs10 notes in Leh so that you can pay for camping charges and any food that may be for sale on the trail. As always, make sure that none of them is damaged as you won't be able to get rid of them.

among pony-men and guides that you pay this fee in lieu of the villagers clearing up your litter. This is not the case; they have no satisfactory way of disposing of metals and plastics and if this attitude prevails the villages will begin to look like rubbish tips. Please carry all your litter out with you and dispose of it properly in Leh.

If you are using pack animals the choice of camping spots will be determined by where the best fodder can be found. It can occasionally lead to an early halt if your pony-man isn't sure of the availability of fodder or water further on.

PREPARING YOURSELF

Leh stands at an altitude of about 3500m/11,500ft. Most visitors will have flown in from altitudes barely above sea level. It is vital, therefore, to acclimatise to at least the altitude of Leh before you set off on your trek. Failure to do so will lessen your enjoyment and could, in extreme cases, be fatal.

It takes a minimum of three days to begin feeling at ease with the thinner air and about a week before you start feeling like doing anything energetic. The longer you spend acclimatising the more you'll enjoy the trek without constantly wondering why you left home in the first place.

Day walks around Leh

For your first few days in Leh you can kid yourself that consuming huge quantities of banana and honey pancakes is all part of your rigorous acclimatisation programme. However the time may come when you feel like taking a bit of exercise and fortunately this seems to help speed up the acclimatisation process.

There are plenty of interesting places to walk to around Leh and the first on people's list is usually the short climb to the Palace and then on up to Leh and Tsemo gompas. There are wonderful views of the town from here and you can plan slightly longer jaunts from this vantage point. For instance, you could walk out through Chanspa, up the 554 steps to the Shanti Stupa and then return via Sankar Gompa all within a couple of hours. More demanding is a lovely short day walk from Leh to the village of Sabu (p221, Map 31). This little-used route takes you over two low and easy passes which cross the hills to the north-east of Leh.

PART 7: TRAIL GUIDE AND MAPS

Using this guide

Above all do not lose your desire to walk. Every day I walk myself into a state of well-being and walk away from every illness. I have walked myself into my best thoughts and know of no thought so burdensome that one cannot walk away from it. **The Buddha**

The treks in this trail guide have not been divided up into rigid daily stages since people walk at different speeds. Possible camping places (or guest-houses where available) have been indicated so that you can make your own decision on how far you want to walk each day. Walking times for both directions are given on the maps to enable you to plan your own itinerary; and there are also suggested itineraries on p270 based on the distances usually covered by organised trekking groups. For an overview of each of the treks see pp23-43 and for the **trekking routes map** (see pp24-5).

These trail guides are designed to be used alongside large-scale sheet maps of the area.

ROUTE DESCRIPTIONS
The route descriptions can be followed in either direction. There are advantages, however, in walking some routes in a particular direction. Any information solely relevant to trekkers walking the route in the opposite direction to that described is marked by '▲'.

To make route descriptions clearer, a compass point is given in brackets after the direction, 'left (S)', or occasionally the other way round, 'south (L)'. Geographical terminology has been used when a trail follows a river or stream: the 'left' bank or side means the 'left' bank as you face downstream. To clarify this, the compass point is also included.

ROUTE MAPS
Walking times
In steep mountainous areas, approximate walking times are far more useful than distances in miles or kilometres. These walking times are given along the side of each map and the arrow shows the direction to which the time refers. Black triangles point to the villages between which the times apply. Note that the **time given refers only to time spent walking**, so you will need to add 20-30% to allow for rest stops. When planning the day's trekking, count on five to seven hours actual walking. Allow yourself a few extra days for resting, side trips and for acclimatisation.

Up or down?

The trail is shown as a dotted line. An arrow across the trail indicates a moderate slope; two arrows show that it is steep; a single dotted arrow shows that it is gentle. Note that the arrow points towards the higher part of the trail.

If, for example, you were walking from A (at 3800m) to B (at 4000m) and the trail between the two was short and steep, it would be shown thus: A - - - > > - - - B. A dotted arrow signifies a gentler slope: A - - -:> - - - B.

Altitudes

Altitudes are given in metres on the maps and in metres/feet in the text. They are based on my measurements with an altimeter and where possible have been verified or correlated with other reliable sources. As they are rough measurements they have been rounded to the nearest 10 metres/feet except where a height is officially recognised as being correct (for example, by the Indian Mountaineering Foundation). Their prime purpose is to allow trekkers to work out a safe acclimatisation schedule for themselves (see pp272-5 for further information).

Place names

As there is no standard way to transliterate Ladakhi names into English, most place names have accumulated several weird and wonderful spellings. The most commonly used spelling has been chosen for the maps and the text; other familiar spellings are also mentioned in the text so that cross-references are possible with other maps, books and guides.

Camping and sustenance

Possible places to camp are marked with a tent symbol. These are flat areas of ground where it is possible to pitch at least two lightweight tents. Unless otherwise specified, they are always by a water source. Some villages on popular treks have official camp-sites; but these are rare.

Reliable sources of water are shown by a 'W' in a circle. Tea shops and tea tents are also shown but they are seasonal and won't necessarily be open, or even there.

Changes

The Ladakhi landscape is constantly and rapidly changing all the time. Each year sees bridges swept away, paths destroyed by landslides and streams changing their course. Follow maps and directions as far as is practicable and use your common sense when navigating.

❑ **Walking times on trail maps**
Note that on all the trail maps in this book the times shown alongside each map refer only to time spent actually walking. Add 20-30% to allow for rest stops.

Markha Valley trek

(6-10 DAYS)

GETTING TO THE START

There are buses from Leh to Spituk (7km) every 30 minutes, or for Stok (14km) at 7.30am, 2pm and 4.30pm. Alternatively you could get a taxi for the short journey; Rs165 to Spituk bridge or Rs285 to Stok. Bring all your supplies from Leh as you won't find much in these villages.

STOK TO RUMBAK (alternative start)

For information on this alternative start to the Markha Valley trek see 'Stok to Spituk via the Stok La' p193.

SPITUK TO JINGCHAN
[MAPS 1-2, pp177-8]
Spituk/Pitok/Spitok (3200m/10,500ft)

Spituk is the site of the first Gelukpa gompa in Ladakh which is well worth a visit if you have the time, particularly for its commanding views over the Indus Valley.

Pass through the village and carry on along the bumpy road to the bridge across the Indus. There are some flat pastures here where it is possible to *camp* and this area is often used by the pony-men as they await their next group of trekkers.

Leaving Spituk An early start to this stage is important as it can get very hot

crossing the plain between here and the Jingchan Gorge. Take plenty of water as it may be over three hours before you can refill.

Cross the bridge, follow the jeep track south for 300m and then west (R) to a small village with two impressive houses. You leave all vegetation behind as you begin crossing a flat and desolate plain at the foot of the Stok mountains. You may witness the impressive skill of Indian Airlines pilots guiding their planes between the mountains as they come down to land at Leh airport; it's reassuring to have your feet firmly on the ground. This may not be your idea of a Himalayan wilderness experience with the busy Leh-Srinagar road on the north bank of the Indus but you will soon be leaving all signs of the 20th century far behind.

After about $1^{1}/_{2}$ km across this plain the path splits. The jeep track stays on the higher ground while a pony track cuts a more direct route across the plain. The latter is slightly shorter but crosses a number of small, dry ravines which the jeep track avoids.

Hemis National Park The path swings to the south-west following the Indus into a narrower valley. You soon reach a sign on a rock welcoming you to the national park. Just beyond is a chorten and prayer flags; from here you get impressive views down the Indus Gorge. This stretch of river is popular for rafting and it's exciting to watch the rafts shoot the rapids below from the safety of dry land. There

❏ Route map key

Trail _ – ‒	Cairn ∴	Chorten(s) ⌂	Cliff ⌐⌐⌐⌐⌐
Building ▢	Gorge	Jeep track ⹀ ⹀ ⹀	Mani wall(s) • ▬
Field ⅙ ⅙ ⅙	Trees ♧	Prayer flags ⌵	Prayer wheels ⊡
Pass ──✕	Dam ⌒	Camp-site △	Landslide 〰〰

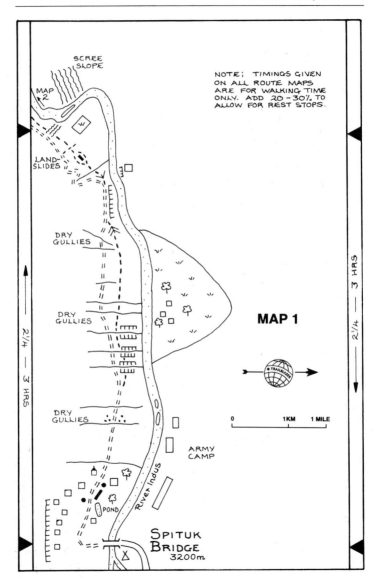

SCREE SLOPE

MAP 2

NOTE: TIMINGS GIVEN ON ALL ROUTE MAPS ARE FOR WALKING TIME ONLY. ADD 20-30% TO ALLOW FOR REST STOPS.

LANDSLIDES

DRY GULLIES

DRY GULLIES

MAP 1

DRY GULLIES

3 HRS

2¼

2¼ — 3 HRS

2¼ — 3 HRS

ARMY CAMP

River Indus

0   1KM   1 MILE

TRAILBLAZER

POND

SPITUK BRIDGE 3200m

is a choice of two trails from here. It does not matter which you take at this stage, but when you reach a mani wall, move onto the lower trail as they don't meet up again.

Jingchan Gorge (Zinchan/Zinchen/Jingchen) The route gets exciting from here as you leave the Indus behind and head into the mountains along the pretty, willow-lined Jingchan Gorge. Follow the stream bed as best you can, sometimes scrambling up the valley side and occasionally fording the stream if necessary.

Jingchan (3380m/11,090ft) There are two *camp-sites* here, one just before the village and the more secluded one just after. These can get filthy in the main trekking season and trekkers are totally responsible for this. A toilet has been built, so please use it. Do not bury, burn or leave any rubbish – pack it all out with you and dispose of it properly in Leh. It is unacceptable for trekkers to vandalise a beautiful area where people live and work. Please tread lightly on your trek and

encourage everyone else to do likewise.

If you're planning to go up to the Ganda La base camp next day it would be wiser to push on to Rumbak. It's at a much better height for acclimatising as it's 300m higher than Leh (3500m/11,480ft) to which you should already be acclimatised. This is far more sensible than sleeping at Jingchan (3380m/11,090ft) which is 120m lower. However, you may need to be particularly persuasive to get your pony-man to go on to Rumbak the first day, as Jingchan is the usual stop.

JINGCHAN TO YURUTSE
[MAP 3, p180]

The route is straightforward as you are simply following the Jingchan Nala upstream. Leave the village on the higher path which avoids fording the stream. Down by the river is a small hut which is the official entry point to Hemis National Park. If anyone is in residence you will be asked to pay an entry fee (Rs20 per person per day within the national park, reduced to Rs1 if you are a student).

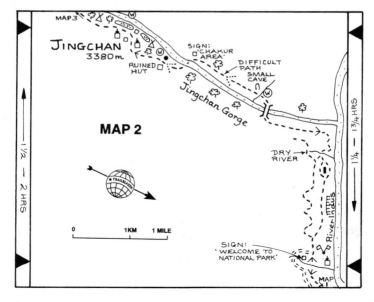

Please ask how this money is being spent. Does any of it go to the villagers or to clean up the filthy camp-sites?

The valley soon narrows and you pass between two rock buttresses beneath graffiti on the rock which reads 'PRESERVE WILDLIFE'. There is a choice of two paths. It's easier and drier to take the trail which rises away from the stream to the right (W). Horses usually take the trail which stays close to the stream but crosses it several times.

Do not get too excited by the sign that says you are in a 'SNOW LEOPARD AREA'. Although this is true, your chances of seeing one of these rare creatures are almost nil. You are far more likely to see small herds of *bharal* (blue sheep) clinging to the impossibly steep sides of the gorge, but they can be hard to spot as their colouring merges with the rock. After about 1½km you get to another sign that has an arrow pointing to 'GOLDEN EAGLE NEST'. You could be forgiven for wondering if you are on a nature trail! The nest is impossible to see but there are lovely views ahead to a spectacular jagged ridge.

The stream forces the path closer and closer to the right (W) side of the valley until you have no choice but to wade across. If you've put on stream crossing shoes, keep them on as there's another crossing in about 10 minutes. When the valley splits at a walled willow plantation, take the right fork (SW). The trail carries on up this narrow gorge for 2½km until the valley widens revealing the snow-topped peaks of the Stok mountains.

Rumbak (3800m/12,470ft)
Prayer flags on a wide pasture mark the junction with the trail leading east (L) to the main part of Rumbak village and to the Stok La (see p193 for a continuation of this route). You can see the pass to the right of the toothy skyline ridge. This pasture makes a good *camp-site* but there are other options a little further up the main valley. You should consider leaving Rumbak only if you are having no problems with the altitude as it's a further 500m up to the Ganda La base camp and 1000m up to the pass.

Continue walking upstream to a water mill and a bridge. If you have not inspected one of these mills yet, peer inside. Although this method of grinding barley is simple, the technology is ingenious and has remained unchanged for centuries. The mill is usually used for grinding roasted barley into tsampa.

Cross the bridge and continue upstream until the valley forks. Take the right (SW) fork and follow the path as it cuts up the right (N) side of the valley.

Yurutse/Urucha/Yuruche (4120m/13,520ft)
is little more than a large house. You can fill up with clear spring water from a pipe below the main building.

YURUTSE TO SHINGO [MAP 4, p181]
Just past the village the valley is split by a beautiful purple band of rock. Take the right branch, past a mani wall and cairn.

Ganda La Base Camp (4380m/14,370ft)
There are a number of places where you could camp in this valley, but the stream flows intermittently so it's worth going on to the top camp where there's a spring. Follow the stream up the obvious left (W) valley and not the smaller valley on the right going off to the north-west. The *camp* is 200m on after passing a blue and purple scree slope, before the valley divides again. There are wonderful views back to the Stok La. If you've come all the way up from Jingchan you may well be feeling the effects of the altitude as you are 1000m higher. If in doubt about your condition descend to Rumbak.

Climb the spur above the camp leaving dry stream beds on your left and right. You are aiming for the left (SW) valley but want to keep above and to the right of the small stream. A clear path soon appears which takes you west towards the Ganda La. Stok Kangri dominates the south-eastern skyline as you climb. You may see yak, brought up here so that the fodder close to the villages has a chance to grow during the short summer.

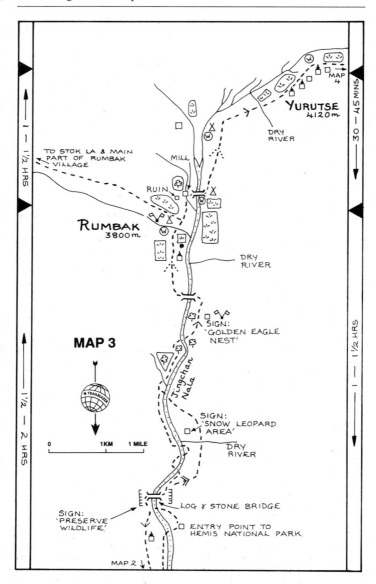

MAP 3

TO STOK LA & MAIN
PART OF RUMBAK
VILLAGE

MILL

RUIN

RUMBAK
3800m

DRY
RIVER

SIGN:
'GOLDEN EAGLE
NEST'

Jingchan Nala

SIGN:
'SNOW LEOPARD
AREA'

DRY
RIVER

0   1KM   1 MILE

SIGN:
'PRESERVE
WILDLIFE'

LOG & STONE BRIDGE

ENTRY POINT TO
HEMIS NATIONAL PARK

MAP 2

YURUTSE
4120m

MAP
4

DRY
RIVER

1 – 1½ HRS

30 – 45 MINS

1 – 1½ HRS

1½ – 2 HRS

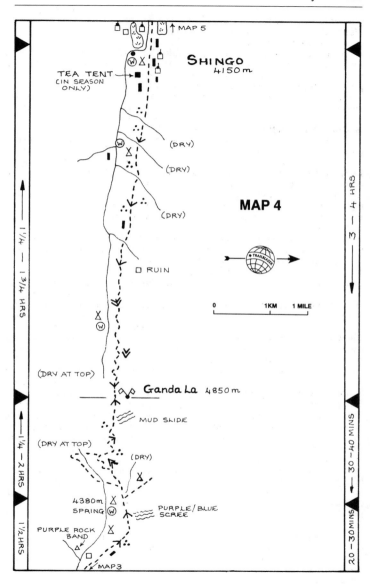

↑ MAP 5

SHINGO 4150 m

TEA TENT
(IN SEASON
ONLY)

(DRY)

(DRY)

MAP 4

(DRY)

◻ RUIN

0   1KM   1 MILE

(DRY AT TOP)

Ganda La 4850 m

MUD SLIDE

(DRY AT TOP)

(DRY)

4380m
SPRING

PURPLE/BLUE
SCREE

PURPLE ROCK
BAND

MAP3

1¼ — 1¾ HRS

1¼ — 2 HRS

½ HRS

3 — 4 HRS

30 — 40 MINS

20 — 30 MINS

Ganda/Kunda/Gandha La (4850m/ 15,910ft) From the pass you can see the Zanskar Range to the west, while there are views to the Stok Mountains and beyond to the east. If you want better views climb either of the ridges by the pass. The fields of Shingo can also be seen far down in the valley. This is where you are aiming for.

▲ **Opposite direction** Route finding is simple enough from here; you cannot go far wrong if you just head down hill.

Descent to Shingo Keep an eye out for marmots as you descend from the pass as they seem to thrive in these desolate, high-altitude spots. They are remarkably unconcerned about humans and will often just sit watching you pass. If you approach too close they give a shrill whistle of alarm and dive into their burrows.
The trail down to Shingo is straightforward and passes a number of possible *camp-sites*.

▲ **Opposite direction** The highest camp is an ideal base camp for the pass.

Shingo (4150m/13,620ft) Notice the solar panel on the roof of the main house. These are common in even quite remote villages and can provide power for simple needs.

SHINGO TO SKIU   [MAP 5, p183]
Shingri Nala
The next stage takes you through a spectacular gorge with beautifully coloured and eroded rocks. Follow the intertwining streams below the hamlet, crossing and recrossing downstream through the willow grove. There is no path; follow the hoof prints and horse manure. Eventually the trail becomes established on the left (S) bank. You continue down the gorge for 2¼-3 hours, crossing the stream on stepping stones several times. The bottom of the gorge is thick with willows and sea buckthorn, which provides convenient shade from the fierce sun. Water is never a problem as the stream is always close. About 1½km before the end of the gorge

the stream disappears underground leaving just a dry bed.

Skiu/Skyu/Skio   (3400m/11,160ft) As you enter the tiny village the towering rock-faces ahead of you are awe-inspiring. There is an attractive gompa on top of the cliff on the right (W). Turn east (L) upstream and the pretty *camp-site* is 400m ahead among the trees.

● **Day trip** From Skiu you can make a day trip downstream to the Zanskar Gorge, passing many apricot trees and the village of Kaya. The round trip takes four to five hours.

SKIU TO MARKHA
[MAPS 6-7, pp184-5]
The trail to Markha is not too strenuous, rising about 300m over 22km. Being at a relatively lower altitude it can get very hot in the sun.

Markha River Skiu sprawls along the right (N) bank of the Markha for about 1½km and then you start walking through thorny scrub. There are a few clearings here where it's possible to pitch one or two tents but the only source of water is from the silty river. After about 9km on the right bank cross a solid wooden bridge high above the water onto the left (S). The trail goes 100m or so through the scrub and then climbs away from the valley bottom to traverse a steep slope prone to landslides. Descend to a grassy patch which could make a good *camp*. The stream running through the grass is your best source of **water** for a while.

Chaluk/Chalak After passing this hamlet keep your eyes open as the path veers off to the right (SW) cutting through some crumbly cliffs and climbing steeply upwards. Cross the river again at **Tunespa** (Thinlespa), a village with very basic dwellings but well-kept fields. At the top of the rise out of the village you reach a collection of large chortens and mani walls. There are wonderful views back down the valley.

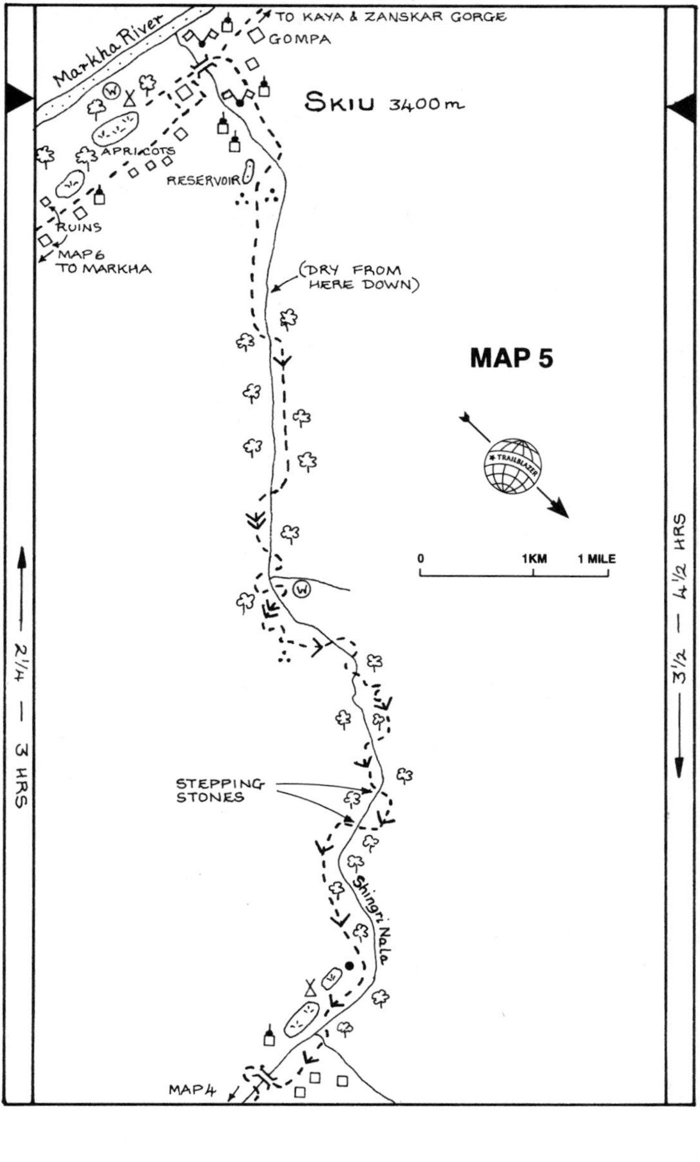
Markha River
TO KAYA & ZANSKAR GORGE
GOMPA
SKIU 3400m
APRICOTS
RESERVOIR
RUINS
MAP 6
TO MARKHA
(DRY FROM
HERE DOWN)
MAP 5
TRAILBLAZER
0
1KM
1 MILE
2¼ — 3 HRS
3½ — 4½ HRS
STEPPING
STONES
Shingri Nala
MAP 4

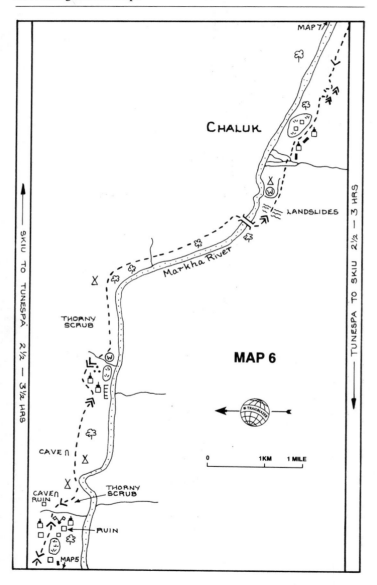

As you approach Markha you get the first glimpse of the snow-covered slopes of Kang Yaze/Nimaling (6400m/ 21,000ft). This magnificent mountain commands the view for the next two days. There is a wolf trap on the outskirts of the village which may have a carcass at the bottom as bait. The wolf runs up the ramp into the trap and because the sides are sloping slightly inwards it cannot escape. It is then stoned to death by the villagers. During the summer the wolves are not a problem, but as food supplies dwindle during winter they often come down to the villages in search of livestock.

Markha (3700m/12,140ft) Keep to the trail by the river and after about 500m you will have to ford it. The current can be quite strong so if possible cross with others. Carry on up the left (SW) bank to a level grassy spot among some trees. It's possible to *camp* here or beneath the main farmhouse 500m further on. This is a lovely camp-site but finding clear water is a problem and you will probably have to make do with silty water from the main river. Don't pollute the river with soap (see p161) as a channel from it takes water to the other houses.

Cross the river on the bridge by the camp-site and follow the path as it climbs up to the main part of Markha village. The remains of a fort lie up to the right. To visit the monastery take the path on the left. Otherwise carry on through the village and fields.

MARKHA TO TAHUNGSTE [MAP 8, p187]

The trail soon splits, the left (E) fork climbs and then traverses a steep cliff face while the right (S) fork heads down to the river. Unless the river is particularly high it's safer to take the right fork and ford it rather than risk the precipitous cliff path. This path is usable but it is badly eroded in parts; a careless step could be fatal.

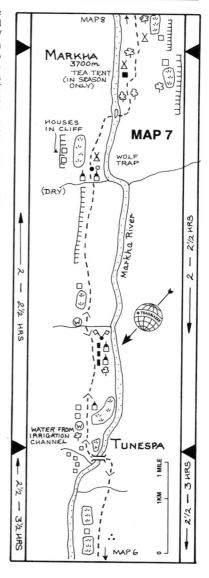

If you cross the river, carry on up the left bank, passing a valley on your right (SW). A large rock spire marks the entrance to this valley. This is the beginning of the Jumlam, an extremely demanding route into Zanskar (see p264). Progress on this side of the river is soon stopped by a rock wall and you are forced to ford the river again. Despite the double river crossing, this route is still safer than the cliff path unless the water is very high.

Umlung Gompa (Dinlung/Humlung/ Omlung/Omung). Feeling cool and refreshed after the river crossings you may have the energy to climb to the gompa high up on the left. After slogging to the top consider the poor monks who had to build the monastery and those here today who have to go down and up this path just to collect water. The views are not that spectacular but you get a great sense of height as you stand far above the valley bottom. The monastery is often closed during the summer as the monks have to go back to their villages to help with the harvest. Unfortunately, the only way to find out is to climb to the top!

Umlung As you approach the village keep the fields on your right-hand side. It's a wonderful level walk between here and Hankar with the towering peak of Kang Yaze standing over the valley.

Hankar/Hangkar/Hanker There's a good *camp-site* just beyond the fields. The trail then takes a sharp left turn and climbs steeply to a group of chortens and mani walls. Up on the right, the ruined outline of Hankar Gompa merges beautifully with the rocky ridge on which it sits.

The trail then crosses a stream and winds through fields before reaching a river.

Nimaling Chu Don't cross this. The trail divides here. If you crossed the river and followed the valley straight ahead you'd eventually end up in Pang on the Leh-Manali road (see 'Across Karnak', p210). Instead, you want to follow the trail to Nimaling which heads up the right (N) bank of the Nimaling Chu through a gateway formed by large rock buttresses.

A little further on there are some fascinating geological creations of large boulders balanced precariously on top of consolidated earth spikes. The trail drops to a bridge; cross and continue up the other bank.

Tahungste (4150m/13,620ft) In about 300m you reach the walled pastures of Tahungste/Chachutse/Tchatchutse /Thachungtse. This is a lovely valley to *camp* in; you can cool off from a long day's trek in the icy stream. A popular watering spot for bharal, it's a magnificent sight to see a herd slide and bound down the steep cliffs with incredible agility.

TAHUNGSTE TO CHUKIRMO [MAPS 9-10, pp189-190]
The trail continues to climb up above Tahungste and soon starts heading off to the south-east, away from the main valley. Note the beautifully eroded rock spikes that you can see down to the left (N). Follow a small stream until it starts veering around to the south. The trail then leaves it and zigzags back on itself as it gains height.

▲ **Opposite direction** It can be easy to miss the path down to the stream and

---

❑ **Walking times on trail maps**
Note that on all the trail maps in this book the times shown alongside each map refer only to time spent actually walking. Add 20-30% to allow for rest stops.

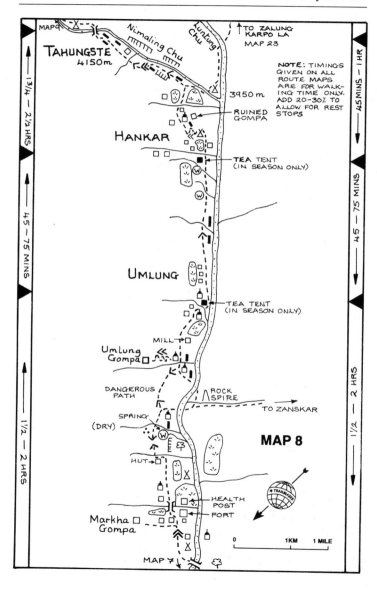

MAP 9

TO ZALUNG
KARPO LA
MAP 23

Nimaling Chu

Lunlung Chu

TAHUNGSTE
4150m

3950 m

NOTE: TIMINGS
GIVEN ON ALL
ROUTE MAPS
ARE FOR WALK-
ING TIME ONLY.
ADD 20-30% TO
ALLOW FOR REST
STOPS

RUINED
GOMPA

HANKAR

TEA TENT
(IN SEASON ONLY)

UMLUNG

TEA TENT
(IN SEASON ONLY)

MILL

Umlung
Gompa

DANGEROUS
PATH

ROCK
SPIRE

TO ZANSKAR

SPRING
(DRY)

MAP 8

HUT

HEALTH
POST

FORT

Markha
Gompa

0   1KM   1 MILE

MAP 7

1¾ – 2½ HRS

45 – 75 MINS

1½ – 2 HRS

45 MINS – 1 HR

45 – 75 MINS

1½ – 2 HRS

continue on a path straight ahead.

You pass several mani walls before reaching a small mountain tarn. There are wonderful views both of Kang Yaze, whose bulk gets reflected in the still waters of the lake, and also of the Markha Valley which you are now well above. There is a path from the lake to Kang Yaze *base camp*. This peak is a popular mountaineering objective and is usually climbed by way of the north-west ridge. While the climb to the lower secondary summit is not considered particularly difficult, reaching the main summit is far more demanding.

If you are going on to Nimaling, keep the mountain on your right all the time. The trail rises gently past lots of mani walls and then descends slowly to the high-altitude valley of Nimaling.

Nimaling (4720m/15,490ft) This large flat-bottomed valley has a semi-permanent population of villagers who come up from the Markha Valley to graze their livestock on the summer pastures. It is a beautiful and remote place to *camp* and one could easily spend a day or two relaxing or exploring the surrounding ridges and valleys. However, you should be warned that the weather can change rapidly at this altitude and you must come prepared for snow, even in summer.

● **Alternative route** It's possible to continue up the Nimaling Valley to cross two passes to the south-east which will bring you down onto the Leh-Manali road just north of Rumtse near the village of Lato.

Gongmaru/Kongmaru/Longmaru La (5100m/16,730ft) The pass lies on the east side of the valley opposite Kang Yaze.

There's usually a simple bridge across the Nimaling Chu which is replaced annually by the shepherds. However, it sometimes gets washed away by floods so if you can't find it you'll have to ford the icy stream. The trail climbs steeply from behind a small group of shepherds' huts. The gradient soon eases but the trail becomes a bit indistinct. Carry on eastwards. Soon a saddle in the ridge ahead comes into view; this is the **Gongmaru La**. If there isn't any snow you should be able to make out a path meandering up the slope. As you climb the last short but steep slope to the top there are good views over the Zanskar Range and of the vertical ice walls on the north face of Kang Yaze.

Descent Until Chogdo the descent is particularly difficult for pack animals and very tiring for humans! It starts by descending steeply from the pass for 300m and then more gently down to a stream. Just above a ruin there are some small, flat terraces with enough *camping* space for about five tents. There is a similar camping spot just after crossing the stream. It's a good idea to collect **water** here because the stream gets more and more discoloured the further down you go.

▲ **Opposite direction** The camping spot mentioned above would make a good base camp for the pass.

Route finding is easy from now on as you follow this tributary until it meets the Shang River and then you follow that downstream to the Indus. The trail follows the stream as best it can, sometimes in the stream bottom and sometimes clinging to the steep valley sides. It changes from season to season, so you'll

❑ **Recycled parachutes**
Parachutes must be the most widely recycled bits of Indian army surplus kit in Ladakh. Not only are they used as temporary restaurants but also as tents by pony-men and shepherds. If you're thinking that there is no way you would jump out of a plane with one of those, fear not, they were used only for cargo drops.

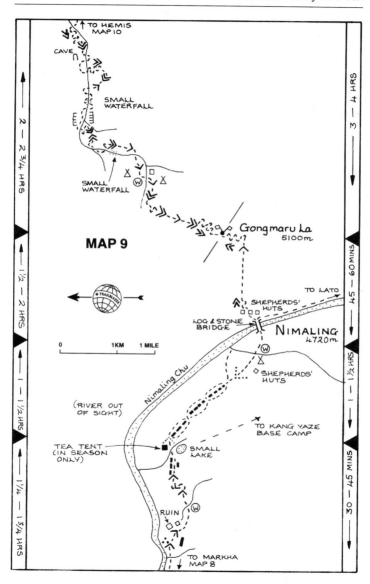

MAP 9

TO HEMIS
MAP 10

CAVE

SMALL
WATERFALL

SMALL
WATERFALL

Gongmaru La
5100m

TO LATO

SHEPHERDS'
HUTS

LOG & STONE
BRIDGE

NIMALING
4720m

SHEPHERDS'
HUTS

Nimaling Chu

(RIVER OUT
OF SIGHT)

TO KANG YAZE
BASE CAMP

TEA TENT
(IN SEASON
ONLY)

SMALL
LAKE

RUIN

TO MARKHA
MAP 8

0   1KM   1 MILE

* TRAILBLAZER

2 — 2¾ HRS

1½ — 2 HRS

1 — 1½ HRS

1¼ — 1¾ HRS

3 — 4 HRS

45 — 60 MINS

1 — 1½ HRS

30 — 45 MINS

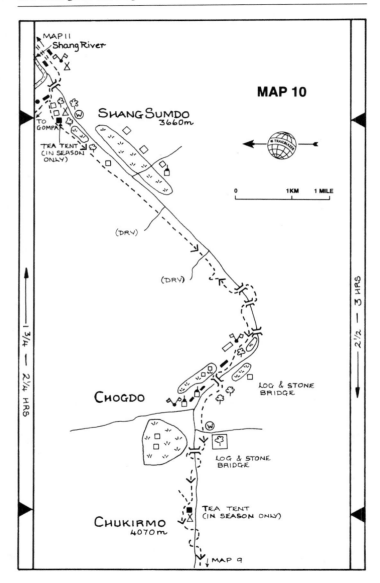

MAP 10

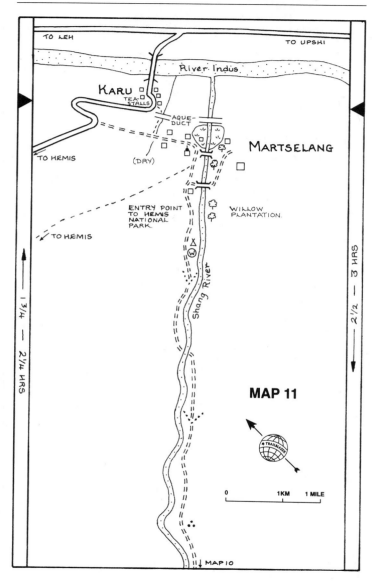

TO LEH

TO UPSHI

River Indus

KARU
TEA-STALLS

AQUE-DUCT

TO HEMIS

(DRY)

MARTSELANG

ENTRY POINT
TO HEMIS
NATIONAL
PARK.

WILLOW
PLANTATION.

TO HEMIS

Shang River

MAP 11

I 3/4 — 2 1/4 HRS

2 1/2 — 3 HRS

0   1KM   1 MILE

TRAILBLAZER

↓ MAP 10

have to use your initiative to find the best route. Frequent stream crossings are inevitable, but it's usually possible to keep your feet dry by jumping across at the narrower sections; the boulders are slippery so some kind of stick will make this much easier.

The trail first descends into a valley of pink rock which soon narrows into a mini canyon. Then it follows the stream as it tumbles over boulders and small waterfalls and enters a gorge.

CHUKIRMO TO KARU
[MAPS 10-11, pp190-1]
Chukirmo (4070m/13,350ft)

After 5km of hard going you reach several small terraces where it is possible to *camp*. There is also room down by the stream. It's not the most attractive of camping spots so it may be worth pressing on to the lovely village of Shang Sumdo, about two hours away.

Leave the 'hotel' by taking the path down to the river and not the one rising up a bank ahead of you. The best route among the pebbles and boulders can be hard to find, but it's usually marked by a series of small cairns. Walk in the stream bed until you are almost past the neat village of **Chogdo**, situated up on the north (L) side of the valley. Then cross onto the left (N) bank if you have not already done so. At last there is a good trail that rises out of the river bed up to the left (N); this takes you to Shang Sumdo. About 20 minutes later there's a short section along the river bed again but the rest is easy going.

Shang Sumdo (3660m/12,010ft)

The *camp-site* is beautifully situated in front of the farmhouses with irrigation channels flowing around the grassy site. The village gompa is up the Shang River valley to the north-west, some 20 minutes' walk away.

It's an easy 8km from here to the road at Karu which should take about two hours. There's a bus from Karu to Leh at about midday so there's no need to rush in the morning if you stayed at Shang Sumdo.

Leave Shang Sumdo by walking downstream to a bridge. Cross over onto the right (S) bank and follow the jeep track to **Martselang** (Marcheylang/ Merchelong).

▲ **Opposite direction** There is an entry point to the Hemis National Park here. If it is staffed you will be asked to pay an entry fee (Rs20 per person per day within the national park, reduced to Rs1 if you are a student). Please ask how this money is being spent. Does any of it go to the villagers or to clean up the filthy camp-sites?

If you want to visit **Hemis** (p146) follow the pony track that leaves the trail to the north-west (L) just as you enter Martselang. It's about an hour from here. Alternatively you could catch the midday bus as it passes through Karu on its way up to Hemis. There is usually only one bus a day so you may have to stay the night. There is a *camp-site* just by the monastery and there are several simple restaurants in the village.

As you enter Martselang the track swings round to the left (NW) away from the Shang River. In a few hundred metres you reach the dry stream bed over which an aqueduct passes. This aqueduct is part of a project planned to irrigate a wide area of the land on the left bank of the Indus. Follow the dry stream bed downhill to the road where you will find a small collection of *tea stalls*. This is **Karu** and is the best place to wait for the midday **bus**.

▲ **Opposite direction** Buses for Karu and Hemis leave Leh at 9.30am and 4pm daily and take about two hours. Taxis cost Rs750 to Karu and take an hour.

(**Opposite**) Mani walls and chortens along the trail add a spiritual element to walking through the village of Kuru in Zanskar (see p239).
(**Overleaf**) The spectacular gompa at Lamayuru (see p141) is perched above the village with the 'moonland' landscape beyond.

Stok to Spituk via the Stok La

(2-4 DAYS)

STOK TO STOK LA

Route information for the first section of this trail is provided in the description of Stok Kangri Ascent p266, Map 66.

Where the trails to Stok Kangri and Stok La divide continue following the trail up the left (N) bank of the tributary stream. After about 30 minutes the trail appears to veer right, up a side canyon – do not go this way. Instead, follow the trail which winds around some ruined herders' huts and then continues straight ahead. You reach more herders' huts ($1^1/_4$ hours to $1^3/_4$ hours above the ruined huts) where there is a possible site for *camping* (4500m/ 14,760ft), although water is inconveniently located back down a steep part of the trail.

From here to a false summit takes about one hour. The trail continues round a bend, descends then ascends to the real summit of the pass (4800m/15,750ft), a further 25 minutes.

STOK LA TO SPITUK

Descent from the pass to Rumbak takes about two hours and there are several good *camp-sites* on the way down.

Below Rumbak the trail joins the main trail to the Markha Valley along the Jingchan Nala. For continuation of the route either into the Markha Valley or to Spituk see p179 and Map 3.

Likir to Temisgam

(2-4 DAYS)

GETTING TO THE START

There's a daily privately operated bus from Leh to Likir (two hours), which leaves from the main bus stand at 4pm. As Likir lies just to the north of the main Leh to Srinagar highway, you can, of course, get any bus that travels along this route. You reach the village of Likir from the highway by following a side road signposted to Likir monastery. A bus to Leh from Likir leaves daily at 7am. A taxi will cost you Rs795.

LIKIR TO YANGTANG
[MAP 12, p195]
Likir/Lekir (3500m/11,480ft)

This small, spread-out village, situated on the banks of the Likir Tokpo, a tributary of the Indus, is a lovely place to come to after the hustle and bustle of Leh. You can pass the time idling around the gompa (see p140) or exploring further up the valley which eventually leads into Nubra over the Likir La (5350m/17,550ft).

● **Accommodation** The *Ghap Chow Garden Camp-site* (Rs50 per tent) is simple and adequate, but as it is often used by organised trekking groups it can sometimes get quite crowded. The alternative to camping is to stay at the guest-house here or at either the *Norboo Guest House* where the owner's nephew is a skilled Buddhist artist, or the *Lharjay Guest House*.

● **Other services** There is a basic **shop** here but don't rely on it for large supplies. You should bring everything you need from Leh. You can **hire ponies** or **donkeys** in the village, and also arrange a **guide**. You should allow a couple of days

---

(Opposite) Approaching the Zalung Karpo La from the north (see p213). A reliable and knowledgeable local guide is essential if you intend to trek along the more remote trails in Ladakh.

❏ **Food and accommodation**
In most of the villages along this route it is possible to stay in rudimentary guest-houses where, for a modest charge (usually about Rs100) the owners will provide you with somewhere to sleep and will expect you to eat with the family. This is an excellent way of gaining an insight into Ladakhi village life. Occasionally when you come to pay for your accommodation and food you may be told 'pay as you like'. This isn't as liberal as it sounds as some owners are disappointed with less than Rs200 per person. Many travellers consider this is expensive when you compare prices with other areas of Ladakh, so try to come to an agreement before you unroll your sleeping bag.

to sort out these arrangements, as it takes time for word to get around and to bring the animals down from the pastures.

Leaving Likir Take the jeep track west out of the village. Instead of following this all the way it is more interesting to take the small path which descends steeply to the Likir Tokpo just after a chorten. This runs parallel to the road up to the **Pobe La** (3550m/11,650ft), where you leave behind all greenery and enter an arid moonscape. From here you can either continue on the jeep track or, to avoid its twists and turns, take the small path below, rejoining it briefly before Sumdo.

Sumdo (3470m/11,390ft) The green fields and trees of Sumdo soon come into view. As you come parallel to the village, leave the jeep track again and take the path leading down to the river on the left (W). This path junction is clearly marked by prayer flags and a cairn. Cross the Saspol Tokpo on a wooden bridge and walk up through lush pasture beneath the village. This makes an ideal *camp-site* and the stream is a good place to fill up your water bottles. The trail heads uphill to a chorten and prayer flags, and then skirts around the left side of the village to begin the ascent of a dry, barren valley. It's a long climb (45-60 minutes) through desolate surroundings but eventually you rejoin the jeep track at the top of the **Charatse La** (3650m/11,980ft).

Yangtang/Yantang/Yangthang (3600m/11,810ft)
The track descends gradually to this prosperous-looking village (35 minutes). Follow a signposted path opposite the primary school down to the village *camp-site*, where there are wonderful southerly views over the village to the Zanskar Range beyond. There are at least two *guest-houses* in the village if you are looking for accommodation.

● **Side trip to Rizong Gompa (3400m/11,150ft)** Take any of the trails leading down the valley from Yangtang. Follow a good path along the Wuleh Tokpo for 1-1¼ hours. The gompa (see p141) lies up the first major side valley to join from the right (NNE), this junction is marked by a few small chortens and some prayer flags strung between the willow trees. It will take you about another half hour's walking up the gorge to reach the monastery.

Rather than retrace your steps to Yangtang you can follow a trail to Hemis-Shukpachu from Rizong. Go through the gompa complex and continue up the valley (N) from the gompa toilets and water tap. After about 10 minutes the trail splits by some water holes and a tree. The right-hand trail returns to Yangtang over a low pass. If going to Hemis-Shukpachu, take the left-hand trail and follow it along a stream bed for ½ to ¾ of an hour. The trail then swings round to the west. Climb

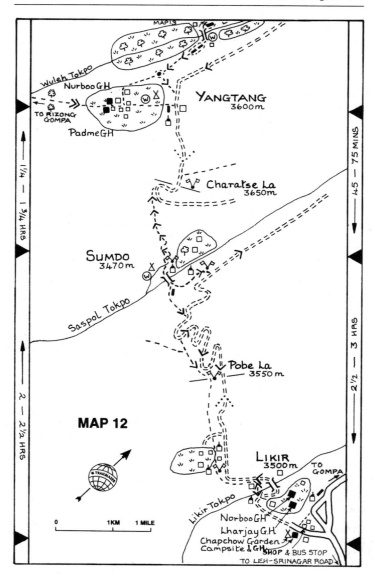

MAP13

Wuleh Tokpo

Nurboo GH

TO RIZONG
GOMPA

Padme GH

YANGTANG
3600m

Charatse La
3650m

SUMDO
3470m

Saspol Tokpo

Pobe La
3550m

MAP 12

0   1KM   1 MILE

LIKIR
3500m

TO
GOMPA

Likir Tokpo

Norboo GH
Lharjay G.H.
Chapchow Garden
Campsite & GH
SHOP & BUS STOP
TO LEH-SRINAGAR ROAD

1¼ — 1¾ HRS

2 — 2½ HRS

45 — 75 MINS

2½ — 3 HRS

steeply for 30-40 minutes before the trail eases near the top of the pass. From the pass descend steeply for about an hour until you reach a bridge across a stream. Cross this and head uphill past the school to the village of Hemis-Shukpachu.

YANGTANG TO HEMIS-SHUK-PACHU   [MAP 13, p197]

From the camp-site at Yangtang go back up to the jeep track, turn left (N) and after 50m take a path leading down to the left (W). The route descends to the tree-lined Wuleh Tokpo, crosses it on a bridge and then, between stone walls, climbs the other side of the valley. You soon leave all signs of the village behind as you begin to ascend. As it climbs, the route keeps cutting across the corners of the jeep track to which you are running parallel.

Sarmanchan/Sermanchan La (3750m/12,300ft)

There are views down to the beautiful village of Hemis-Shukpachu from the pass. Again, don't be tempted to take the jeep track to the village as it's much longer than the good path directly ahead. The trail enters the village through the fields, drops steeply down to cross the Akheur Tokpo and emerges above the gompa overlooking beautiful pastures (2-2½ hours from Yangtang).

Hemis-Shukpachu (3600m/11,810ft)

Also written as Hemis-Skurbuchan, Hemis-Shukpachan, Hemis Schuk-pachen, Hemis Skur-buchan and Himis Shukpa, this is a tranquil village with a small gompa, green pastures and bubbling brook. It's an easy place to relax for a few idle hours in the mid-day heat, or even to stay the night. Pitch your tent at one of the *camp-sites* or stay in a *guest-house*. There are also two reasonably stocked *shops* here. Three *buses* a week connect Hemis with Leh.

HEMIS-SHUKPACHU TO TEMISGAM [MAP 13-14, pp197-8]

To pick up the trail again, cross the pastures in a north-west direction skirting the left (SW) side of the fields. Just after passing some chortens the trail divides. Take the right (N) fork that passes the mature cedar trees (on the right) that give the village its name, (cedar is *shukpa*). The trail rises gently over arid ground until you reach a small **pass** (3710m/12,170ft).

The path drops steeply away in front of you and you look across the valley at the pink- and mauve-coloured mountains ahead; the trail can just be made out as it zigzags up the steep mountainside in the distance. Head right from the pass and drop down to the stream bed where you can pick up a path heading off to the right (N), rather than the one that goes straight down the valley (W). Traverse the slope to the base of a short but steep climb.

Lago/Meptek La (3750m/12,300ft)

The path winds up the precipitous mountainside to this pass. Walk a little way along the ridge on your left (SW) for magnificent views across to the south side of the Indus Valley. The trail descends steadily along a dry stream bed to the village of Ang (two to three hours from Hemis-Shukpachu).

▲ **Opposite direction** Approaching this pass from Ang, keep to the path on the south-west side of the valley as you near the top of the climb.

Ang (3400m/11,160ft)

The villages get more prosperous and fertile the further west you travel along this route. Ang is a fine example, with its beautiful fields and trees. There is a *guest-house* and **shop** here and a good *camp-site* on the banks of the wonderfully named, Dang-dong Tokpo.

The trail crosses the river on a bridge by the camp-site and then turns downstream along the right (N) bank. Follow this down the valley where it soon becomes a more substantial jeep track which takes you all the way to the large, spread-out village of Temisgam.

Temisgam (3200m/10,500ft)

Also written as Timisgam, Themisgang,

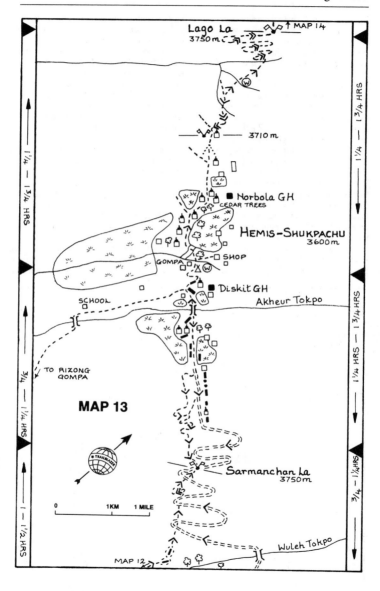

Lago La
3750m

↑ MAP 14

3710 m

Norbola GH
CEDAR TREES

HEMIS-SHUKPACHU
3600m

SHOP

GOMPA

Diskit GH

Akheur Tokpo

SCHOOL

TO RIZONG GOMPA

MAP 13

TRAILBLAZER

0   1KM   1 MILE

Sarmanchan La
3750m

MAP 12

Wuleh Tokpo

1 3/4 HRS — 1 1/4

1 3/4 HRS — 1 1/4 HRS

1 1/4 HRS — 1 3/4 HRS

3/4 — 1 1/4 HRS

1 — 1 1/2 HRS

3/4 — 1 1/4HRS

Tingmosgang, Tamesgan and Temesgam, this is the largest, most prosperous village on this trek. Set amongst fertile fields and spreading orchards there are some fine examples of large, whitewashed Ladakhi homes. As a result of the division of Ladakh in the 14th-15th centuries, the lower kingdom was controlled from Basgo and Temisgam. Little remains of its glorious past; the castle is in ruins but on the hill behind the village there are still two temples which you can visit.

In 1684 the village of Temisgam was the scene of the signing of a far reaching treaty between Ladakh and Tibet. It established a border between the two nations (across Pangong Lake) after the Ladakh-Tibet war and it guaranteed that only Ladakhis could buy the valuable pashmina wool (used in the manufacture of cashmere shawls) from western Tibet.

● **Services** There are a couple of *guesthouses* here and a *camp-site* near the bus stand. You should also be able to make arrangements for **guides** and **ponies** if you are starting your trek from here. As always you will need to allow two days or so to sort this out. There are two small **shops** and a regular **bus** service to Leh, leaving every morning at about 9.30am. If you are going west, or if you miss the bus, you can walk down the road for an hour to Nurla, on the Leh-Srinagar highway, where you shouldn't have to wait long for a passing bus or truck.

▲ **Opposite direction** Buses from Leh to Temisgam leave Leh at 1pm every day. Taxis cost Rs1375.

● **Trek extension** You can make this trek one stage longer by continuing west to **Khalsi** (Khalse/Khaltse) from Temisgam (3½-4½ hours). Instead of turning left (S) down the road to Nurla, turn right (N) up the valley to Tea (Tia). From here you cross the Bongbong La and descend via a small pass to the highway.

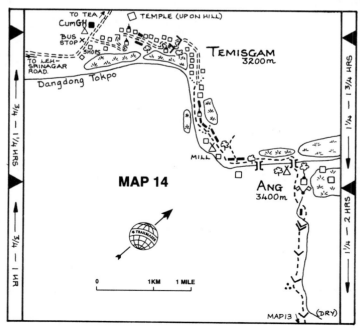

To reach Khalsi from here, try to hitch a ride to save yourself an uninteresting walk of over an hour west along the road.

Lamayuru to Alchi

(4-6 DAYS)

GETTING TO THE START
Lamayuru is 124km west of Leh on the Leh-Srinagar highway. It's a six-hour journey on any of the buses going to Kargil (see p142) or Srinagar. A taxi costs Rs1952.

LAMAYURU (3450m/11,320ft) [MAP 15]
When you arrive by road you may wonder why everyone says it's such a wonderful place. You are greeted by a collection of run-down tea stalls, reminiscent of roadside halts all over India. The main village and gompa (see p141) lie out of sight at the bottom of the valley but when you see them you'll want to linger here.

● **Accommodation** Lamayuru is an important stop on the tourist circuit and also the starting and finishing point for a number of treks. Because of this, there are a surprising number of places to stay. There are two *camp-sites*: the first is a soulless place on a bare piece of ground by the roadside shops. It has absolutely nothing to recommend it, especially when you compare it with the alternative below the village. This peaceful place to camp is in a mature willow grove by a stream. The most popular of the guest-houses (Rs100 upwards) is

the *Monastery Hotel and Restaurant* which is within the gompa walls and run by the monks. If you can't get a place here, there are other options: the simple *Tashi Guest House* behind the post office; the *Shangrila Hotel* on the west side of the village; and the larger *Dragon Hotel* down towards the stream. If all else fails there is the purpose-built *Dekong Labrong Restaurant* below the highway. **Food** is available at all these and also at the tea stalls by the road; choice is limited.

● **Shops** There is a shop in the main part of the village; you will need to ask a local where it is, as it has no sign and is usually closed. The shops by the road are better stocked and it should be possible to scrape together enough supplies for your trek, including basics such as kerosene and rice. This is handy if you haven't come from Leh, but prices are higher and you may have to adapt your diet to the limited selection. Lamayuru also boasts a **post office**.

● **Guides and pack animals** Compared with most Ladakhi villages finding guides or pony-men in Lamayuru is relatively easy. This is because the village is at the end of the Across Zanskar trek from Darcha or Padum and, consequently,

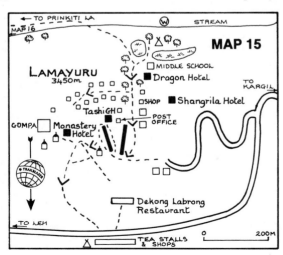

pony-men having just finished that trek will be looking for employment at this end. Obviously they prefer trekkers who are going into Zanskar so that they get a paid trip home but they are usually happy to undertake other treks as well. If you are travelling relatively light, there are some local young men with donkeys who are usually more than willing to accompany you on your trek. The advantage with them is that they know the area better than those from Zanskar and Lahaul and are marginally cheaper. You'll find them by asking around in the village.

LAMAYURU TO WANLA
[MAP 16, p201]
Leaving Lamayuru
Walk down to the stream and follow its bed east (L). After 15 minutes take a path that cuts uphill to some chortens and prayer flags. The trail goes over arid land in a southerly direction following a stream bed (often dry) until it splits. Walk up the bottom of the small gully on the left until that also splits, this time in three directions. Again take the left fork which winds steeply up to the Prinkiti La.

Prinkiti La (3700m/12,140ft) The climb to this pretty notch in the ridge is easy. From the top you look over the complicated terrain of the Zanskar Mountains to snow-clad rock spires and the Konzke La in the east, over which the route passes. Descend steeply into the narrow gully which you follow for over an hour until it brings you to the Shillakong (Shilakang/ Shelakhong) Valley.

Shilla/Sheela Cross the bridge and continue downstream on the right (S) bank, past a possible *camp-site*, as far as Wanla (¹/₂ hour).

Wanla/Wanlah (3200m/10,500ft)
This pretty village, with its 11th century gompa high up on a crag, makes a pleasant place to stop. The gompa was built during the time of Rinchen Zangpo, the man credited with the revival of Buddhism in this area because of his many translations of Sanskrit texts.

The *Shangrila Hotel* offers food but not accommodation as does the hotel across the bridge in the main part of the village; the **shop** next door has most supplies. The *camp-site* is conveniently situated opposite on the banks of the Yapola River. There is a spring with good **water** just after crossing the bridge up the slope to the left by an old chorten.

▲ **Opposite direction** There is a **bus** to and from Leh one day a week if you do not wish to trek on to Lamayuru. Ask locally for the day and time of departure.

WANLA TO HINJU
[MAPS 17-18, p202-3]
Head upstream on the right (NE) bank of the Yapola along the jeep track which is totally devoid of shade. The muddy river is your only water source for over two hours. Just before a group of houses, you pass a jumble of huge boulders in a field, which must have fallen from the ridge on your left – a sobering thought.

Phanjila/Phenjilla/Fangila (3300m/ 10,830ft)
The *Spangthan Hotel and Shop* has very little to offer apart from a glass of chai. The trail to Alchi turns north-east up the Ripchar Valley. The main trail crosses the Ripchar River continuing to Hanupata and Padum. If you are trekking to Padum on the Across Zanskar trek see p260 for the continuation.

▲ **Opposite direction** There is a **bus** to and from Leh via Wanla one day a week if you do not wish to trek on to Lamayuru. Ask locally for the day and time of departure.

After the main group of houses the trail climbs a bank and traverses a high, steep, unstable slope for 2¹/₂km (don't take the level path which leads to the fields). This section could be dangerous in rain. There are a few places to *camp* in the meadows below you, by the stream.

The trail drops down to the river and passes a small *camp-site* in a willow

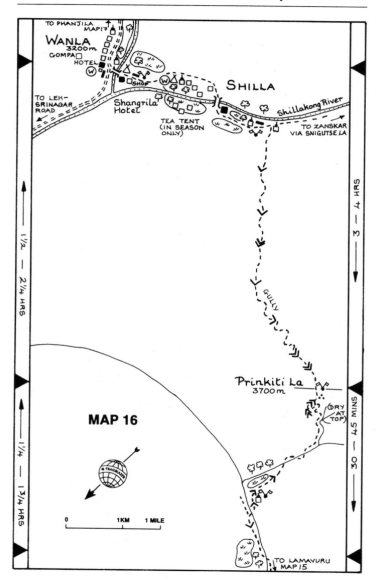

MAP 16

TO PHANJILA
MAP17
WANLA
3200m
GOMPA
HOTEL
TO LEH-
SRINAGAR
ROAD
Shangrila
Hotel
SHOP
TEA TENT
(IN SEASON
ONLY)
SHILLA
Shillakong River
TO ZANSKAR
VIA SNIGUTSE LA
GULLY
Prinkiti La
3700m
DRY
AT
TOP
TO LAMAYURU
MAP 15

3 — 4 HRS
30 — 45 MINS

1½ — 2¼ HRS
1¼ — 1¾ HRS

0   1KM   1 MILE

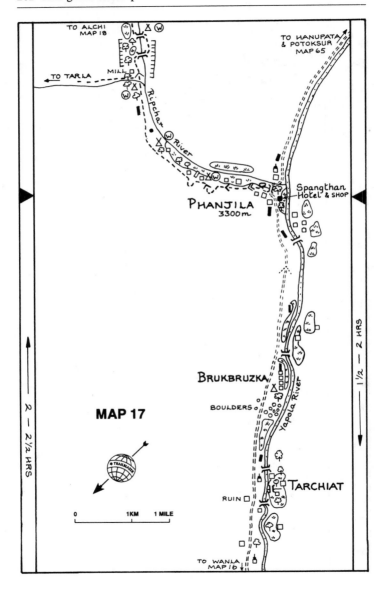

TO ALCHI
MAP 18

TO TARLA

MILL

TO HANUPATA
& POTOKSUR
MAP 65

Ripchar

River

Spangthan
Hotel & SHOP

PHANJILA
3300m

2 — 2½ HRS

1½ — 2 HRS

BRUKBRUZKA

Yapola River

BOULDERS

MAP 17

TREKMAPS

0   1KM   1 MILE

TARCHIAT

RUIN

TO WANLA
MAP 16

grove, before crossing a side stream
and entering a mini-gorge.

● **Alternative route** Another way to
Alchi is to turn north up this side
stream which takes you via Urshi, over
the difficult Tar La (5200m/17,060ft),
down through the villages of Tar, Mang
Gyu, Gira and Lardo (three days).

It's about 1-1¹/₂ hours to Hinju from the
turn off to Urshi. The Ripchar Valley gets
more and more beautiful the higher up
you walk, with its thick growth of willows and dramatic views back to rock
pinnacles on the sky line. Don't mistake
the couple of houses you pass after about
1¹/₂km for Hinju – the main village is
marked by prayer flags across the path.

Hinju (3750m/12,300ft) There are
pastures just before and after the village where you can *camp*.

HINJU TO SUMDAH-CHENMO
[MAPS 18-20, pp203-5]
The trail continues up the valley,
crossing several side streams and
passing a few *camp-sites*. Follow the
main stream all the time. The gradient
increases as you approach the head of
the valley where the trail leaves the
stream, climbing steeply up to the left.

**Konzke/Chot/Konke/Choke/
Konze La (4900m/16,080ft)** It's a
strenuous climb to the top of this pass,
but you're rewarded with views all the
way back to the Prinkiti La. The initially steep descent to the valley becomes
more gentle towards Sumdah-Chenmo
(2¹/₂-3 hours). There are good *camping*
places in this valley before the village;
you won't find more until five to six
hours after it. During the summer
months shepherds from Hinju cross the
Konzke La so that they can graze their
livestock in this valley. The trail passes
some of their huts and enclosures
where they make butter, curd and
cheese. You may see the cheese spread

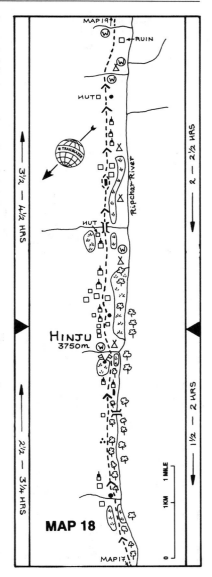

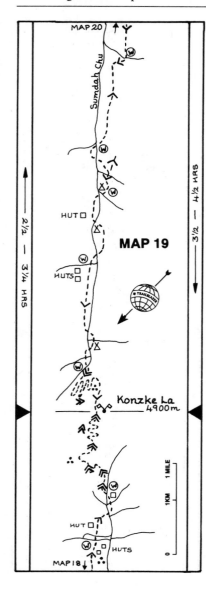

out on the ground to dry. It is dried into small white nuggets which will then keep for years; very little is eaten fresh.

Sumdah-Chenmo/Sumda (3900m/ 12,800ft) The name literally means 'great Sumdah'. This isolated village shows few signs of change and the villagers are still largely self-sufficient. There are two resident monks at the small gompa here, which comes under the jurisdiction of Hemis. Remember to take your shoes off if you go inside and to leave a small donation. As you leave the village there is a ruined gompa far below. This is probably of a similar age to the one at Alchi, but the villagers have resisted any attempts to restore it believing it would bring bad fortune on the whole community.

● **Route to Chiling (see p209)** Two routes that lead to Chiling split off from the Alchi trail just after Sumdah-Chenmo. This link can be used to join the trail from Lamayuru with the Markha Valley, opening up several possibilities for longer treks.

SUMDAH-CHENMO TO SUMDAH-CHOON [MAP 20-21, pp205-7] Stay up high on the shoulder out of Sumdah-Chenmo and after about one to 1½ hours descend to the river.

Sumdah Chu The trail follows the river as it curves around to the east. After 1km you cross it on a simple log bridge and continue on the right (S) bank. This whole section is difficult and prone to change so keep an eye out for any alterations to the route. In another kilometre you cross back over to the left (N) bank, this time high above the river on an impressive bridge that spans the narrow gorge. Ford the river 1km further on; if you're wearing stream-crossing shoes keep them on as there is another crossing very soon.

The best way now is to scramble up

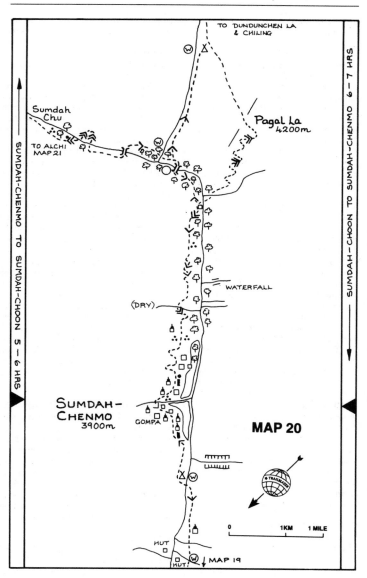

TO DUNDUNCHEN LA
& CHILING

Sumdah
Chu

Pagal La
4200m

TO ALCHI
MAP 21

WATERFALL

(DRY)

SUMDAH-
CHENMO
3900m

GOMPA

MAP 20

SUMDAH-CHENMO TO SUMDAH-CHOON 5 – 6 HRS

SUMDAH-CHOON TO SUMDAH-CHENMO 6 – 7 HRS

★ TRAILBLAZER

0   1KM   1 MILE

HUT

HUT   ↓ MAP 19

the steep scree slope in front of you, cross over a shoulder and scramble back down to the river. This is far too precipitous for pack animals which will have to wade down the stream instead. Cross back to the left bank for the last time. The path is a little hard to follow as it picks its way through the vegetation of willow, rose and sea buckthorn.

The river rushes through a gorge and the way ahead is on a trail that has been ingeniously built onto a sheer rock face. This is not a place to linger. After passing some boulders balanced precariously on top of earth spires, the path turns northeast and crosses a small tributary. Leave the main trail (which goes to the Zanskar River and on to Nimu) and follow the willow-lined tributary upstream to the village of Sumdah-Choon.

Sumdah-Choon (3850m/12,630ft)
The inhabitants of this whole area are skilled metal workers and you can sometimes hear the banging of a hammer against metal as you pass the house of a craftsman. *Choon* means small so this is the little relation of Sumdah-Chenmo. The two Sumdahs have in fact linked themselves together as an administrative group along with Chiling.

There is an impressive gompa standing on the hillside above the village, whose design and paintings are very similar to the temple at Alchi. Like Alchi it was constructed at the time of Richen Zangpo, which makes it one of the oldest in Ladakh. If there are no monks in residence, find the gompa caretaker in the village. Remember to remove your shoes before entering the temple and to put a small donation in the box provided.

There are no flat pastures for camping near the village but it is possible to *camp* on the flat roofs of the stables behind the lower houses.

SUMDAH-CHOON TO ALCHI
[MAPS 21-22, pp207-8]
The trail to the Stakspi La
Ascend a valley to the north-east of the village along the side of a small tributary.

Opposite some huts there is a small uneven flat area which is sometimes used as a base *camp* for the pass. Just above this the stream stops flowing, so you will need to fill up with enough **water** for at least four hours.

The going gets harder as you ascend a series of giant steps formed in a past glacial age. There is not much of a path, but a dry stream bed soon materialises giving you something to follow in the right direction.

As you approach the head of the valley you are faced with a choice of routes to the pass. There is no path so route finding is critical. Both the routes to the top are demanding and involve ascending steep, loose scree. You can either choose the more direct line and ascend to the left of the crags in front of you, or go up to the right of the crags until you reach a rock band; traverse left below this, cross over a shoulder ridge and rejoin the other route as it reaches the top of the climb. As you trudge wearily up the scree wishing for the top, you can keep your mind busy searching for quartz crystals which litter this side of the mountain. The final section to the pass is over rocky ground with the way indicated by a series of cairns. The panoramic views that unfold as you climb and the lack of any properly established path over the scree give this route a real mountaineering feel.

Stakspi La (4950m/16,240ft)
The whole of the Likir to Temisgam trek can be seen laid out beneath you to the north. Likir monastery is just about visible and the closer village in the foreground, of which you can only see half, is Saspol (Saspul, Saspool). Descend steeply through the rocky terrain in a northerly direction from the pass. After going down a central spur between two streams cross the stream on the left (W) to reach a shepherd's hut.

▲ **Opposite direction** The roof of this hut is the only bit of flat ground around and is occasionally used as a place to *camp* before crossing the pass. If you do

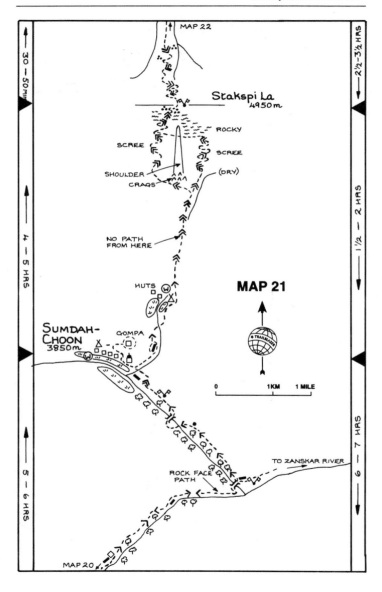

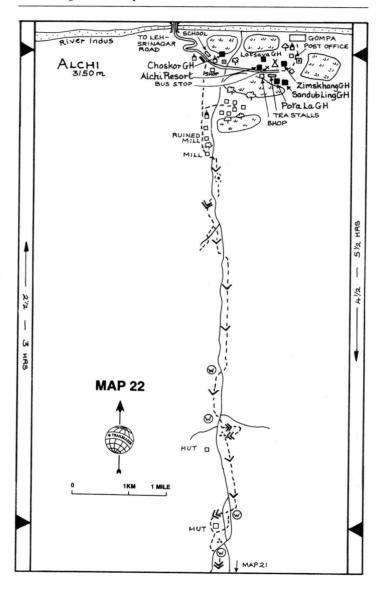

River Indus

TO LEH-
SRINAGAR
ROAD

SCHOOL

GOMPA
POST OFFICE

ALCHI
3150 m

Choskor GH
Alchi Resort
BUS STOP

Loesaya GH

ZimskhangGH
SandubLing GH

Pora La GH

TEA STALLS

SHOP

RUINED
MILL

MILL

2½ — 3 HRS

4½ — 5½ HRS

MAP 22

0   1KM   1 MILE

HUT

HUT

MAP 21

camp be sure to check that any inhabitants who might be here do not mind. You can see the pass from here; it's the flattened 'U' in the ridge due south. Seeing it from here makes navigating up to it much easier. The trail goes up just to the right of the pass, through the crags and then traverses below it as it nears the top.

From the hut the trail follows the valley all the way down to Alchi (2½-3 hours). In half an hour the trail becomes established in a barren and rocky valley devoid of shade. **Water** is no problem at first as you are constantly by the stream but after 3km a side stream enters the main stream and discolours the water making it undrinkable from here on.

Alchi (3150m/10,340ft) When you reach this large prosperous village carry on down the trail to the road. Turn right (E) to the village and gompa, or left (W) for the main highway and a lift back to Leh.

Most people come to Alchi to see the unique iconography of its famous low-lying gompa (see p140). With plenty of accommodation available and its proximity to Likir, Saspol and Rizong, it also makes an ideal base for a few days of sightseeing.

● **Accommodation** Places to stay (Rs100 upwards) are mainly centred around the gompa complex. The *Zimskhang Guest House* is popular with its open air restaurant and also has a *camp-site* (Rs30) in the garden. Behind the tea stalls by the bus stand are the *Pota La Restaurant and Guest House* and the *Sandub Ling Guest House*, while opposite them is the *Lotsava Guest House* and the *Alchi Resort*. If you want to be further away from other tourists *Choskor Guest House and Camping* along the road towards the river should be suitably isolated.

● **Guides and pack animals** Because most trekkers finish at Alchi there are often guides with animals who are only too happy to be paid for a return trip to Lamayuru.

● **Shops** The tea stalls sell basic supplies and there are also two small shops, but it could be hard to find enough provisions for a trek here. There is a **post office** on the path to the gompa and also plenty of souvenir sellers.

● **Buses** Buses to Leh (three hours) leave at 7am from the bus stand in the village. You can also get a bus west from here, to Lamayuru and Kargil (see **warning** p79). If you miss the appropriate bus you should be able to pick up a truck or bus on the Leh-Srinagar highway which is only a 45-minute walk from the village.

▲ **Opposite direction** Buses leave Leh at 4pm daily for Alchi or you could get a taxi, Rs935.

Sumdah-Chenmo to the Markha Valley

LINK ROUTE VIA CHILING – 2-3 DAYS

SUMDAH-CHENMO TO CHILING [MAP 20, p205]

Route to Dundunchen/ Dungdungchan /Dundochonila La
● **Option 1** Stay up high on the shoulder out of Sumdah-Chenmo and after about 1-1½ hours drop down to the river. A tributary joins the Sumdah Chu from the south, just before it curves round to the east. Ford the Sumdah Chu upstream of the tributary by the building in the river bed. Then cross the tributary. Climb the ridge in an east-south-east direction following the zigzag path to a minor pass, the **Pagal La** (4200m/13,780ft) (1½ hours). There are amazing views from the top. Traverse a steep slope to pastures where you can *camp* (30 minutes). From the camp-site it's 1½ hours' steep climb to the Dundunchen La.

● **Option 2** Stay up high on the shoulder out of Sumdah-Chenmo and after about 1-1½ hours descend to the river. The trail follows the Sumdah Chu as it curves around to the east. After 1km it crosses the river on a simple log bridge. The main trail to Alchi continues down the valley; the way to the Dundunchen La is up the slope ahead, following a small tributary to pastures where you can *camp* (as above). From the camp-site it's 1½ hours' steep climb to the Dundunchen La.

Dundunchen La (4700m/15,420ft)
There are fantastic views from this pass. Traverse for 30 minutes and then descend into the valley (S). Follow the path and stream down the valley to Chiling (3½ hours).

Chiling (3250m/10,660ft)
This village is famous for producing some of the best metalwork in Ladakh. It is believed that the people may be descended from Nepalese craftsmen who came to Ladakh in the 17th century to help construct the statue of Buddha at Shey. You'd be foolish not to find space in your pack for the beautiful cups and spoons made here; prices are much lower than in Leh. There's a good *camp-site* where the valley that you descended joins the Zanskar River. The only water available is rather silty, so filtering it would be wise. There's also a *shop* in the village which should be well supplied as there is a road up the Zanskar from Nimu. You should at least be able to find basic supplies such as rice, tea, dal and vegetables, which could be useful if you're planning an extended trip up the Markha Valley.

CHILING TO SKIU
Before you leave Chiling you need to ask for the man who operates the cable-car across the Zanskar. The cable-car is supposed to be free, as the man gets paid by the government, but tourists won't get across without giving a small tip. You obviously can't take pack animals across the river so this is as far as they can go with you. You can sometimes find a willing pony-man in one of the villages on the other side but don't rely on it. Some very well-organised groups arrange for ponies from Leh to meet them on the other side of the river.

Follow the easy trail past the village of Kaya to **Skiu** (3½ hours, see p183, Map 5). An alternative to going into the Markha Valley is to follow the Zanskar downstream to the beautiful oasis of Chok-sti and then on to Nimu. Here you'll be able to pick up a bus or truck going in either direction along the Leh-Srinagar road.

Across Karnak

(8-10 DAYS)

GETTING TO THE START
Buses for Karu leave Leh at 9.30am and 4pm daily bound for Hemis. Taxis cost Rs750.

▲ **Opposite direction** There is a daily bus from Karu to Leh at about midday.

KARU TO CONFLUENCE OF NIMALING & MARKHA RIVERS
[MAPS 11, 10, 9, 8: pp192-186]
For the first three or so days of this trek you follow the last few days of the Markha Valley trek (pp176-192). The altitude gain on the first stage is rapid; you must be very well acclimatised or you'll have to take the climb up the Gongmaru La very slowly (three to four days).

● **Alternative route** I've been reliably informed that there is another trail which takes you from Nimaling over a pass and down to the Luntung Chu, half way along its length. This would avoid having to go to the confluence of the Nimaling and Markha rivers and would undoubtedly take you through some impressive scenery.

CONFLUENCE TO THE ZALUNG KARPO LA
[MAPS 23-24, pp211-2]
Up the Luntung/Langtang Chu
Upstream of this confluence, the river previously known as the Markha becomes the Luntung Chu. Ford the Nimaling Chu to the flat grassy area

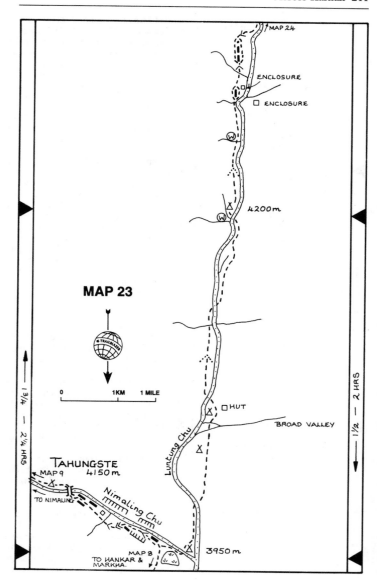

MAP 24

ENCLOSURE

ENCLOSURE

4200m

MAP 23

★ TRAILMAKER

0   1KM   1 MILE

HUT

BROAD VALLEY

Luntung Chu

1½ — 2 HRS

1¾ — 2¼ HRS

TAHUNGSTE
4150m

MAP 9

TO NIMALING

Nimaling Chu

3950m

MAP 8
TO HANKAR &
MARKHA.

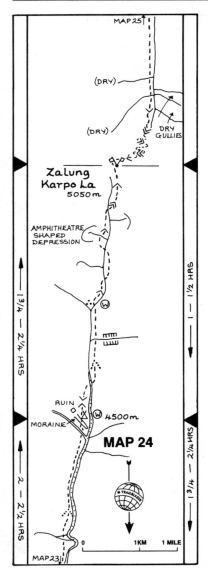

between the two rivers; this is a possible *camp* (3950m/12,960ft). It's a good feeling to be turning off the popular Markha Valley route and to be going up this less frequented, inviting valley. The trail stays close to the river, crossing it several times when necessary.

After 1¾ to 2¼ hours you reach a pleasant *camp* (4200m/13,780ft) below the west face of Kang Yaze (6400m/21,000ft) by a stream that flows from the same mountain.

Mani walls Continue up the valley crossing a few side streams as you go. When you get to some mani walls there are good views looking back towards the steep west face of Kang Yaze and a small mountain further down the valley, that has exposed stratified rock like the inside of a Swiss roll. The mani walls up remote valleys like this are maintained by passing monks. Monks going on this route would most likely be heading for the gompa at Dat.

Moraine wall Further up the valley you cross a main stream and climb up and over a wall of moraine immediately ahead of you. There are flats for *camping* either on top of the moraine, by a ruined hut, or down on the other side.

The main valley begins to narrow and the stream becomes smaller and easier to cross, which you have to do several times to pick out the best route. Pass a tributary on the right (W), which squeezes through a narrow opening in the rocks. Soon after this, the stream splits in a perfect 'Y'. Take the right branch that heads south-west. There are lovely views to snow fields up the left branch.

False summit The gradient increases slightly as you climb through stony, barren ground. It looks as though the pass is only just ahead but this is a false summit. Carry on walking easily through this rolling scenery to the pass proper.

ZALUNG KARPO LA TO SORRA
[MAPS 24-25]
Zalung Karpo La (5050m/ 16,570ft) Jagged rock pinnacles, typical of the Zanskar Range, lie to the north, while the Kang Yaze massif fills the skyline behind you. Head west from the pass and descend the steep zigzag trail to the south-west.

Sorra (Kurma) Chu The trail follows the stream all the way down this remote valley. At first the stream bed is dry but as you progress it fills with water, swelling in size when a tributary joins from the north-east. There is a pleasant *camp* (4300m/14,110ft) by this confluence and several others further down on the left bank. Continue to the village of Sorra, fording the stream twice.

Sorra/Kurna Kur (4080m/13,390ft) This collection of simple buildings and small fields of inter-cropped barley and peas is often deserted in the summer months when the inhabitants take their livestock to higher pastures.

SORRA TO DAT
[MAPS 26-27, pp214-5]
Sorra Gorge Follow the river into a dramatic and beautiful canyon. One can only guess at the magnitude of the river that once formed this magical place. Today only a small clear stream runs along the bottom. The mature willows that carpet the floor of the gorge are highly prized by the locals as so little of this region is wooded. The people of this valley make the most of this natural bounty by selling the wood in Leh and you may pass donkey caravans undertaking the long journey to the capital.

When the canyon splits, ford the Sorra Chu onto the left (S) bank, go over a rise with a ruin on top, then ford the Khurna River and follow this new valley upstream all the way to Dat. The Khurna eventually flows into the Zanskar River

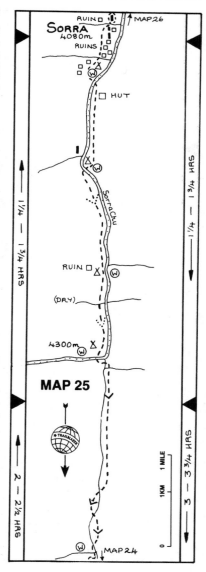

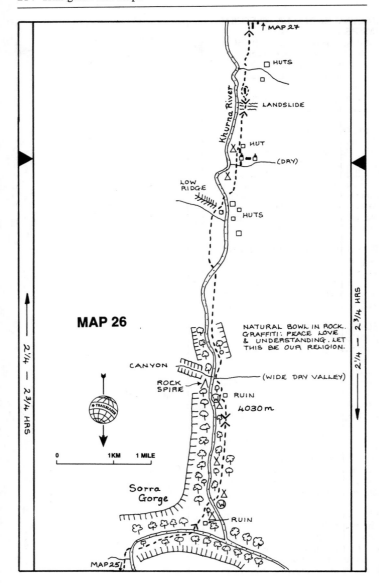

↑ MAP 27

HUTS

Khurna River

LANDSLIDE

HUT

(DRY)

LOW
RIDGE

HUTS

MAP 26

NATURAL BOWL IN ROCK.
GRAFFITI: PEACE LOVE
& UNDERSTANDING. LET
THIS BE OUR RELIGION.

CANYON

(WIDE DRY VALLEY)

ROCK
SPIRE

RUIN

4030 m

TRAILBLAZER

0   1KM   1 MILE

Sorra
Gorge

RUIN

MAP 25

2¼ — 2¾ HRS

2¼ — 2¾ HRS

about 10km south of Chiling, but you are following it in the other direction.

There are several *camp-sites* (4030m/13,220ft) in this part of the gorge and spending a night here would be a wonderful experience although it can get very cold, the floor of the gorge seeing little sun during the day.

Eventually the route emerges from the canyon into a broad valley. Keep following the Khurna River through flat pastures – you may need to ford it a couple of times. The valley narrows and then widens again, and tall cliffs tower above you on the left (E). Just before Dat, the trail goes up and over two small rises, both decorated with lots of mani walls, a definite sign that a monastery is nearby.

Dat and Datgo/Khurna (4250m/13,940ft)

These two villages are unlike any in other areas of Ladakh. They are the winter quarters of semi-nomadic herders who leave in summer with their live-stock for high-altitude grazing grounds. Each simple low shelter is set in a small stone enclosure; there are no cultivated fields and the poor, shabby buildings reflect a harsh lifestyle. Even the gompa looks neglected. If there are no monks to let you in, you can see into the temple by climbing the steps to the roof and peer-ing down through the open ceiling.

There are plenty of places to *camp* on the wide flood plain beneath the villages, although the best is prob-ably by the spring just beyond Datgo (its name literally means 'upper Dat').

DAT TO THE YAR LA [MAPS 27-28, pp215-7]

There is **no water** on this section of the trail until the base of the Yar La, over three hours away, so take plenty from Dat. The grandeur of the landscape with its sweeping plains and vast val-leys marks the transition between the Zanskar Mountains and Rupshu.

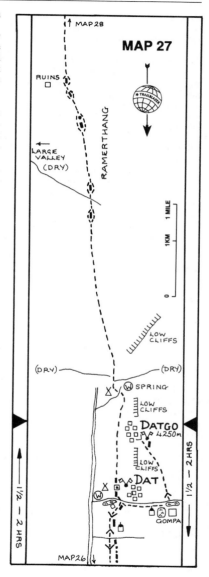

Ramerthang The trail heads south-south-east across a vast flat-bottomed valley known locally as Ramerthang. The path sticks to the left (E) side of this plain and is marked at intervals by mani walls. The trail is easy to follow across the parched earth and the walking is very gentle. This valley is inhabited by herds of *kiang*, or Tibetan wild ass, but this shy and fast animal is very hard to spot if you haven't the keen eyes of a local.

As you approach the end of the main valley the trail swings east (L) into a side valley and follows a dry stream bed. Here you can see some inviting caves high up on the left (N). The valley soon divides. Don't take the valley to the north-east; carry on following the main dry stream bed (east-south-east) to the base of the Yar La. Here you will find a spring and a small and stony *camp* just large enough for a couple of small tents.

Yar La (4850m/15,910ft) It's a short and easy climb to the top where you'll find a large chorten brightly decorated with prayer flags. It's incongruous in this underpopulated area and one wonders who would have built such a monument here. The rolling scenery of Rupshu lies ahead of you, while to the north-north-west you can see all the way back to the Zalung Karpo La.

YAR LA TO POGMAR
[MAPS 28-30, pp217-9]
Descend easily down a sandy spur to the confluence of two streams beds. Follow the stream down for 1km until a wide green valley appears on the left. This makes an ideal *camp-site* (4580m/15,030ft). Inexplicably a jeep track is being built up the side of this valley, creating an ugly, damaging scar. It starts and finishes abruptly; its worth to the tiny semi-nomadic population is not apparent.

Lungmoche Carry on downstream to the abandoned village of Lungmoche. Instead of taking the prominent trail down the left (NE) bank of the stream (which

leads to the Leh-Manali road as it crosses the More Plains), cross over to a chorten and two mani walls on the right (SW) bank. The trail is ill-defined but continues along the right (SW) side of the valley.

▲ Opposite direction The chorten on top of the Yar La is visible from here and gives you something to aim for.

After passing two mani walls the trail gradually climbs the arid valley side to some prayer flags that mark the top of the rise.

Desert The next stage takes you across an intimidating desert landscape for about an hour. The trail goes in a southerly direction but can be very indistinct. From the flags, go down into the small valley ahead and follow this down until it starts to bend to the south-east and another valley enters from the right (SW). Climb the slope ahead and cross two small ravines. Pass a small cairn and then descend steeply down a small gorge flanked by low cliffs. At the bottom there is a mani wall from which you'll see some white chortens ahead. Walk towards them along the dry stream bed.

Sangtha (4300m/14,110ft) Many of the inhabitants of this small place are Tibetan semi-nomadic herders and so the village is likely to be deserted in the summer. It is situated on the banks of the Zara River and it's amazing to see so much water flowing through this parched land.

Wade across to the other side of the river and pass between the ten white-washed chortens and mani walls. Follow a dry stream bed to the south-east, across more desert. The trail climbs gradually to the green pastures below the village of Pogmar.

● Alternative route A harder finish to this trek than the trail via the Pogmar La is to head south from Sangtha along the Zara River before branching off to cross the Morang La (5100m/16,730ft). The route descends to the Tsarap River which

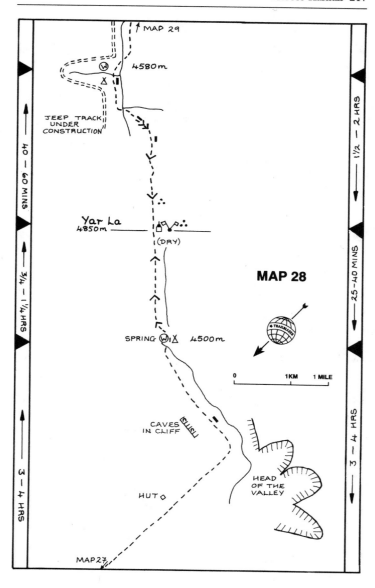

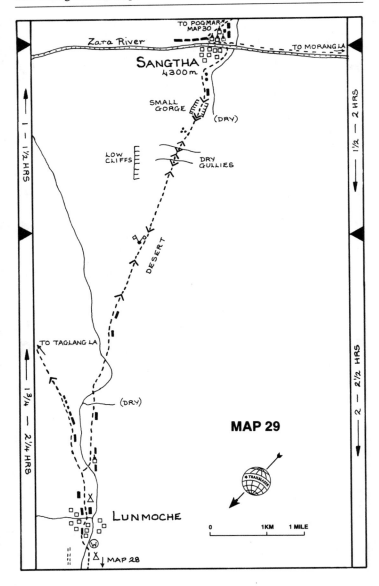

MAP 29

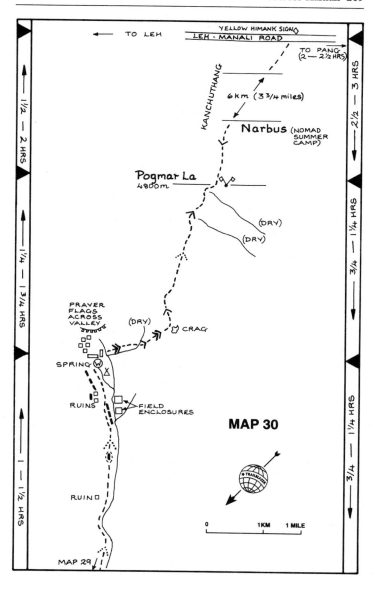

TO LEH

YELLOW HIMANK SIGN ◇
LEH - MANALI ROAD

TO PANG
(2 — 2½ HRS)

KANCHUTHANG

6 km (3¾ miles)

Narbus (NOMAD SUMMER CAMP)

Pogmar La
4800m

(DRY)
(DRY)

PRAYER FLAGS ACROSS VALLEY

(DRY)

♡ CRAG

SPRING ⓦ

RUINS

FIELD ENCLOSURES

MAP 30

RUIN ▯

MAP 29

0   1KM   1 MILE

1½ — 2 HRS

1¼ — 1¾ HRS

1 — 1½ HRS

3 HRS

2½ —

1¼ HRS

3¾ —

3¾ — 1¼ HRS

you follow upstream until reaching the Leh-Manali road. This alternative takes about four days from Sangtha.

Pogmar (4500m/14,770ft) The inhabitants of this village are Tibetan refugees. This is reflected in the design of the houses, which are very different from the Ladakhi buildings seen in other villages. Not only are they more solidly built but much thought has gone into combating the cold – a constant winter enemy at this high altitude. The buildings are joined together in an 'L' shape, all facing into a central courtyard to provide shelter against the icy winds that blow up the valley. There are no windows on the down-valley side for the same reason.

Despite the harsh conditions in Rupshu, some of the semi-nomadic people are relatively prosperous. Pogmar is a good example: there are 12 households here and between them they own over 300 yaks, along with horses, sheep and goats. Their lifestyle has, however, hardly changed in centuries, still revolving around the annual migration to the summer pastures, where a black yak-hair tent becomes the family home for a few months.

The pastures beneath the village make a lovely *camp-site* before crossing the Pogmar La. The main stream is usually dry but the small spring that irrigates the pasture will provide ample water for cooking and drinking. There are wonderful views over the desert to the mountains beyond.

POGMAR TO PANG
[MAP 30, p219]

Just above the camp-site there is a gully off to the right (S). The trail to the Pogmar La follows this up the steep hillside to a crag on top of the ridge. The trail heads south-east along the ridge and then more southerly as it gently contours round the head of the valley to the pass (1½ hours).

Pogmar La (4800m/15,750ft) Below the pass, stretching south to distant mountains on the horizon, is the wide plain of Kanchuthang. This is one of the summer grazing grounds for the people of Pogmar. They usually come here in the second half of the summer and construct a tented village at the bottom of the pass, which they call Narbus.

Halfway across the plain is the Leh-Manali road, only visible if vehicles are travelling along it throwing up a cloud of dust in their wake. The trail descends to Narbus and then crosses the plain in a south-south-east direction, basically straight down the valley. There is no path but the walking is easy over hard desert and scrub until you hit the Leh-Manali road (1½ to two hours from the pass).

▲ **Opposite direction** If you are starting the trek here leave the road by a large yellow Himank sign, 'JULE, NAMASKAR...', and head north-north-west across the plain to the low pass that can be seen on the skyline. That's the Pogmar La.

Pang (4450m/14,600ft) It's not essential to go to Pang which is a two to 2½ hour slog along the road from here. You could try flagging down a passing bus or truck. Pang lies at the bottom of a spectacular gorge through which the road descends in a series of hairpin bends. You can by-pass these if you're walking by taking the steep path down to the left.

Pang itself is a grim depot for the army and road builders. There is a collection of *tea tents* over the bridge, about 1km further on where you can stay the night and get some hot food. You could *camp* down by the river, but this is not an inviting proposition after the solitude you have been used to.

If you are planning to trek into Rupshu from here or are trekking across to Karnak starting from here, you could get basic **supplies** from the tea tents. Noodles, rice, dal, chocolate, biscuits and kerosene are all available during the main tourist season.

● **Buses** There are a number of different buses throughout the day going to Leh, Keylong and Manali. Most of these will stop at Pang to give the driver and passengers a break. It's impossible to give accurate times for when the buses will pass through. As a rough guide, buses to Leh should arrive in the morning, which could mean anything from 9am to 1pm, while those going to Keylong and Manali should arrive from about 11am onwards. If you are fed up with waiting for a bus you could try hitching on a truck. Expect to pay the same as the bus fare and establish the rate before you set off.

Leh to Nubra

(4-6 DAYS)

GETTING TO THE START
You can either walk from Leh to Sabu (three hours) or catch a bus. There are J&KSRTC buses from Leh at 8am, 2pm and 4.30pm (20 minutes). Sabu is a very spread-out village, so if you want to avoid

a long walk make sure you get on the bus to the top of the village (ask for Sabu Phu). Sabu Phu is also a convenient place to meet your pony-man. If you want to get back to Leh you can get on any of these buses as they all return directly. A taxi to Sabu will cost you about Rs150.

LEH TO SABU   [MAP 31]
One of the advantages of this trek is that you can walk directly from Leh. This three-hour hike to the pretty and prosperous village of Sabu also makes a good day walk. Head east out of Leh above the polo ground towards a small triangular-shaped mountain. The first part of the route is not pleasant as it passes an area used for dumping rubbish. The route ahead is visible as it angles up the slope to a small pass. Go down the other side into a quiet, arid valley and then walk southeast to the next pass, which entails a steep but short climb. There is a collection of cairns at the top and good views to the tall poplar trees of Sabu village. Descend the

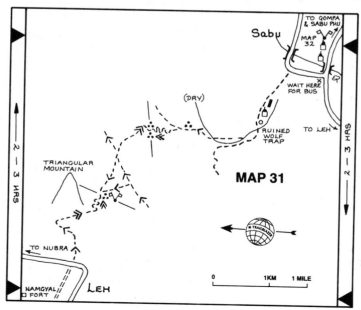

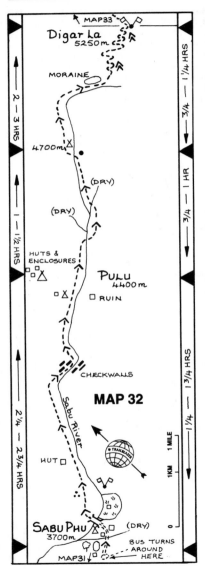

steep winding path, through crags to the valley floor.

Follow the dry stream bed down to the outskirts of Sabu which is marked by an old wolf trap, a chorten and a mani wall. When you reach a road, turn right and follow it to a junction by a bridge. This is the best place to wait for a bus heading in either direction. To walk, turn left over the bridge and follow the road up to the gompa (2km) and Sabu Phu (5km).

SABU PHU TO THE DIGAR LA [MAP 32]

Sabu Phu (3700m/12,140ft) The bus turns around where the road ends. Follow the track uphill, past a few houses and fields (possible *camping*). Cross the bridge over the clear, tumbling Sabu River and follow this upstream on the right (W) bank. You walk up through green pastures between high boulder-filled moraines, climbing steadily for about two hours until you arrive at a simple hut on your left and a ruin on the right.

Pulu Digar (4400m/14,440ft)

There's a small flat area here where you could pitch two tents, but a better alternative for *camping* is to head up the steep slope on the left (NW) which takes you up to the main cluster of shepherds' summer shelters (often empty).

The path becomes hard to follow from here on, so just continue along the main stream. When it forks, after about 1km, take the left fork. Keep an eye on the **water** in the stream as it sometimes vanishes underground. Before it does, make sure you fill up as there may be no water higher up.

Digar La Base Camp (4700m/ 15,420ft) After walking for 1-1½ hours up from Pulu Digar there is another possible *camp* on the right (NW) bank of the stream. This is about

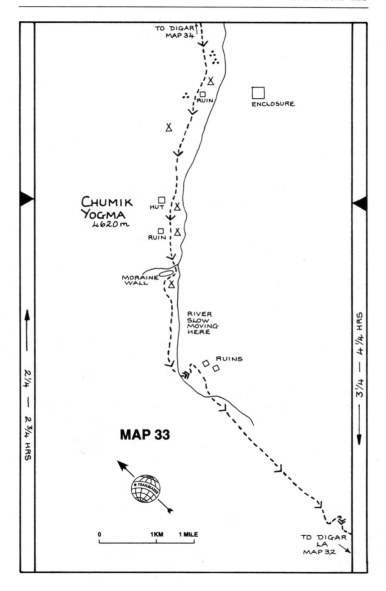

TO DIGAR
MAP 34

ENCLOSURE

RUIN

CHUMIK
YOGMA
4620 m

HUT

RUIN

MORAINE
WALL

RIVER
SLOW
MOVING
HERE

RUINS

MAP 33

★ TRAILBLAZER

0   1KM   1 MILE

2¼ — 2¾ HRS

3¼ — 4¼ HRS

TO DIGAR
LA
MAP 32

as close as you can camp to the Digar La and makes a convenient base camp. There are wonderful views over the Stok mountains with Stok Kangri dominating the scene.

Continue up from here until the ground levels off. You are faced with a wall of mountains ahead of you and the easiest way over them appears to be to the north-west. Unfortunately the pass lies to the east.

Digar La (5250m/17,230ft) You should be able to make out the path as it zigzags up the steep and tiring slope to a string of prayer flags at the top. Follow the stream to the east, skirt a large moraine and begin climbing. As you struggle up the stiff climb to the pass, you'll be glad to know that William Moorcroft found it equally tiring in the early 1820s: 'Being on a steep ascent, it was also very fatiguing, and the difficulty of breathing was more troublesome and painful than I had before experienced: this extended to the animals, particularly the horses; but the yaks were not wholly exempt, and we were obliged to halt repeatedly to give the cattle relief.' (*Travels in the Himalayan Provinces of Hindustan and the Panjab*).

The views from the pass are excellent. The mountains you can see to the north are the Saser Range of the eastern Karakoram, which contain Ladakh's highest peak, Saser Kangri (7670m/25,165ft) is the most easterly of the great Karakoram mountains. There has been very little mountaineering activity in this area because of military restrictions and many peaks have not yet been climbed. If you're expecting a glimpse of K2, you'll be disappointed. Unfortunately it lies too far to the north-west to be visible. However, behind you to the south are stunning views of the Zanskar Range.

DIGAR LA TO CHUMIK YOGMA [MAP 33, p223]

Head north from the pass descending into the valley. You soon pick up a small stream which flows all the way to Digar. After descending a short, steep slope below some ruins, cross onto the left (W) bank as it gets wet and difficult if you stay on the right. The route crosses a beautiful small plateau where the stream loses most of its energy forming long, deep, slow-moving pools. The going is quite hard as the ground is hummocky and wet but it soon eases at the far end of the plateau where it's flat enough to *camp*. Though there are more camping places further down the valley, they get fewer the closer to Digar you get.

Chumik Yogma (4620m/15160ft) The path skirts the right side of a small wall of moraine that blocks the end of the plateau and then descends gradually through boulder-filled pastures. These are the summer grazing grounds for the livestock of Digar and you'll find a couple of shepherds' huts here.

The path begins to move away from the river and becomes harder to follow. Fill up with **water** if you are running short. As you make your way down the widening valley, head gradually towards the left (N) side where you will eventually pick up a more definite trail.

CHUMIK YOGMA TO THE SHYOK VALLEY [MAP 34-35, pp226-7]

Digar (3900m/12,800ft) As you near Digar the path drops steeply to a collection of chortens and prayer flags. The aridity of the Nubra landscape becomes starkly apparent as you see it contrasting with the vibrant fertility of the village fields in front of you. The stream disappears into a deep gorge on your right (SE) and flows far

---

(Opposite) Zanskar is enclosed by giant mountains. **Top**: Entering from the east, trekkers cross the 5000m Shingo La (see p235) after snowfall in August. **Bottom**: Crossing from the west over the 4400m Pensi La (see p144) provides fantastic views of the Great Himalaya and the Drung-Drang Glacier.

below the village. Across on the other side of the valley is a collection of houses whose inhabitants seem to be fighting a losing battle against erosion as the river takes away more of their fields every year.

Places to *camp* are very limited here but this is your last chance until you are down in the Shyok Valley. Cross the village's irrigation channel and follow the stony, walled path between the fields to the main cluster of houses. Wind through the village passing a rock covered in Buddhist graffiti and an interesting temple built onto a huge boulder.

As you leave the village you are starting a particularly desolate section of the route. Make sure you have plenty of **water** as you won't find any for at least two hours. The scenery gets increasingly barren with hardly any vegetation in sight. The trail starts heading in a north-westerly direction and rises to a mani wall. Its positioning is perfect with sweeping views of the Shyok flood-plain which stretches into the distance. If you look behind you can see the lush fields of villages up the Lazun Lungpa. This remote valley leads via the Chang La to Sakti and can therefore be used as an alternative route into or out of Nubra.

Plateau Drop down to an amazing plateau that sits above the Shyok Valley. You want to head across it in a north-westerly direction, and the 3km trudge can be painfully slow as there are few landmarks by which to mark your progress. The plateau suddenly ends with a precipitous drop to the valley floor, 300m below.

You can now see the route ahead which follows the left side of this vast valley.

▲ **Opposite direction** From the plateau you will see that there are two possible ways ahead. Either the one men-

tioned above or, a 'short cut' heading steeply up to a pass on the right (SW) side of the plateau. The former is the easier option as the ascent is far more gradual.

Zigzag steeply down from the plateau and then go up a short rise to the top of a sand dune. The descent down the long north face of this dune is great fun as the sand allows you almost to ski as you slip and slide to the bottom. An ascent of this would be extremely hard work, akin to walking on a treadmill!

ALONG THE SHYOK VALLEY TO RONG   [MAPS 35-36, pp227-8]

Shyok Valley (3300m/10,830ft) There is a small stream on your left (W) and the ground is flat enough for *camping*. There isn't any grazing, which could be a problem if you are using pack animals. Collect **water** if the stream is flowing, it gets dirtier further on and the next source of good, clean water is 2^1/$_2$ hours away.

You need to exercise a certain amount of caution when relying on these desert streams as they do not necessarily flow all year round. If you do run out, the main Shyok River is never far away, but the water needs filtering being heavily laden with silt.

Desert Cross the desert in a northerly direction, heading towards the rocky spur which juts out into the valley. There is no path as such and you may need to cross the stream a few times to seek out the best route.

▲ **Opposite direction** You will be able to see the path winding up to the plateau 3km ahead. Aim for the bottom of this path.

Cliff path As you pass the spur, keep an eye out for a trail which climbs up through the cliff on your left (W). There's

---

(Opposite): The dramatic Zanskar Gorge viewed from the Parfi La (see p253) is impassable in summer but becomes Zanskar's lifeline to the outside world in the depths of winter (see p40).

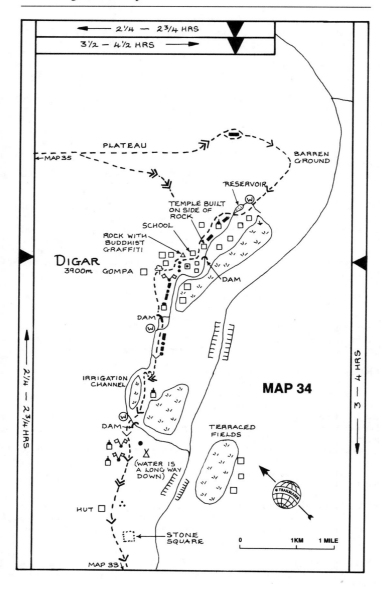

2¼ — 2¾ HRS

3½ — 4½ HRS

PLATEAU

MAP 35

BARREN GROUND

RESERVOIR

TEMPLE BUILT ON SIDE OF ROCK

SCHOOL

ROCK WITH BUDDHIST GRAFFITI

DIGAR
3900m GOMPA

DAM

DAM

IRRIGATION CHANNEL

MAP 34

DAM

(WATER IS A LONG WAY DOWN)

TERRACED FIELDS

TRAILBLAZER

HUT

STONE SQUARE

MAP 33

2¼ — 2¾ HRS

3 — 4 HRS

0   1KM   1 MILE

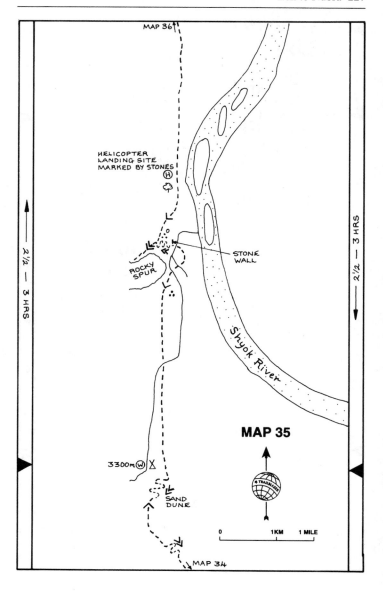

MAP 36

HELICOPTER
LANDING SITE
MARKED BY STONES Ⓗ

STONE
WALL

ROCKY
SPUR

2½ — 3 HRS

2½ — 3 HRS

Shyok River

MAP 35

● TRAILBLAZER

3300m Ⓦ X

SAND
DUNE

0   1KM   1 MILE

MAP 34

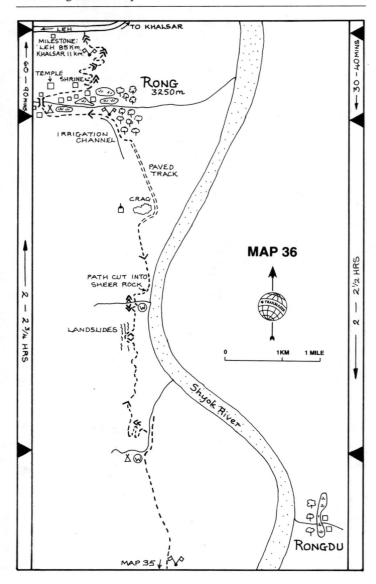

❑ The Silk Route

Nubra was on a major branch of the Silk Route between Leh and Yarkand until the trading was stopped in 1949. There were two main routes. In winter the traders followed the huge loop of the frozen Shyok River, while in summer they were able to take the short cut over the Saser La (5330m/17,490ft), north-east of Panamik. Although not the highest of the five passes, it was the most feared. Its treacherous glaciers were responsible for the loss of many lives and some recent expeditions have reported the huge number of animal bones that litter this section of the trail.

A typical year would see 300 caravans making the month-long journey to Yarkand, each caravan consisting of up to 200 camels, donkeys and horses. The traders were spurred on by the enormous profits that could be made on the silk and carpets from Yarkand or the spices, cotton, hashish and opium that were transported north from India. The only remnant of this past age is a distinctive herd of the two-humped Bactrian camel, which still roams in the Nubra Valley.

a stone wall marking its start. This path is steep and difficult in parts, especially for animals, but it saves you several deep crossings of the Shyok River. From the top of the climb, by a cairn and small shelter, there are good views both up and down the valley. You can see the multiple braiding of the Shyok and can appreciate how complicated it would be to find a route along the valley floor. The path gradually descends and you continue along the stony alluvial bed, sticking to the west (L) side of the valley.

Valley floor Again there is no path to follow and the next 5½km are hard and monotonous along the stone and sand of the flat valley floor. If you stay on the west (L) side of the wide valley and are not tempted up onto the valley sides, you won't go far wrong. The monotony is alleviated briefly by a prayer flag and cairn, around which are scattered hundreds of tiny piles of stones. It's a fascinating sight and you have to tread carefully in order not to knock any of them over. They are presumably placed there by passing travellers but one wonders if they are washed away each year by the flooding river. Across on the other side of

the valley is the village of Rongdu, whose fields are irrigated by a tumbling mountain stream.

Soon you come to a small stream where it's possible to *camp* if there's enough water. Again, there is little fodder for animals. Follow the stream down for a few hundred metres and then take the large and obvious track which winds up the steep valley side. The gradient soon eases and you walk along an easy path, high above the river. There are a few areas where landslides have swept the path away and you have to scramble around the obstacles.

You soon reach a section where the road engineers' craft is expertly displayed: they have carved a route across a sheer rock-face while the river flows directly below. Keep an eye on the loose rock above as, judging by the debris underneath, large chunks appear to fall onto the track at random.

The trail descends to the valley floor and skirts the right side of a small rocky outcrop. From here the track turns into an extraordinary paved track across the desert which suddenly begins, and just as suddenly finishes, about a kilometre further on. It is reminiscent of a Roman road, being dead straight and made of large stones. When you see an irrigation channel running parallel to the track, on the far left (W) of the valley, cross over to it. This leads past a large wood to a river. Follow this upstream to the village of Rong.

Rong (3250m/10,660ft) Just before the bridge there's a beautiful *camp-site*. This peaceful village is a wonderful place to stay and rest among the mature poplar and willow trees. Cross the stream and follow the trail that goes above the main part of the village. The trail then climbs steeply above the last house, giving stunning views of the village and of the Shyok Valley. It's a stiff climb, but it's also your last. You eventually reach the main road at the top.

Leh to Nubra road Turn left for the Khardung La and Leh, or right for Khalsar and the rest of Nubra. As long as you arrive at the road quite early in the day you should easily get a lift on a truck in either direction.

Buses to Leh pass by very early in the morning, at about 6am.

▲ **Opposite direction** See p151 for buses from Leh. If you are starting the trek from here keep your eyes peeled for the '85km' marker post ('LEH 85KM, KHALSAR 11KM'). This is a few hundred metres uphill from the beginning of the trail, and is where you should get off. Alternatively, you could walk from Khalsar following the beginning of the new road to Agham (see below).

● **Alternative route** On my last visit to Nubra I noticed a road was under construction between Khalsar and Agham, the village below Digar, along the south side of the Shyok River. If the early stages of this have been completed it will provide a more convenient but less interesting finish to this trek.

Across Zanskar

(15-21 DAYS)

GETTING TO THE START
See p100-3 for details of getting from Manali or Keylong to Darcha and p199 if starting the trek from Lamayuru.

Alternative routes into Zanskar via the Phirtse La and the Sarichan La
The most popular way into Zanskar via the Shingo La is described below. There are also two other routes which eventually link up with the main trail along the Kargyak River. Both begin further north on the Leh-Manali road, across the Baralacha La, near Sarchu. The routes begin by following the Lingti Chu west to the pastures and herders' shelters at Chumik Marpo. Here the routes divide. The most popular trail crosses the Phirtse La (5450m/17,880ft) and descends to Table (see Map 43). The other little used trail crosses the Sarichan La to the south-west of the Phirtse La and descends to Kargyak. These alternatives take four days from the Leh-Manali road to the Kargyak River.

DARCHA TO ZANGSKAR SUMDO [MAPS 37-39, pp231-4]

Darcha (3400m/11,150ft) Darcha is a tiny village largely made up of a collection of *dhabas* where it is possible to get a warm meal and a space to unroll your sleeping bag (Rs50). You can also sleep in some basic *tents* for a fee which gets more outrageous the higher the demand (Rs150-200 per person including a meal). It's cheaper to find a space for your own tent.

If you are a small group there will be little difficulty, in the main season, in finding a **pony-man** and pack animals here within a day or two. If you are out-

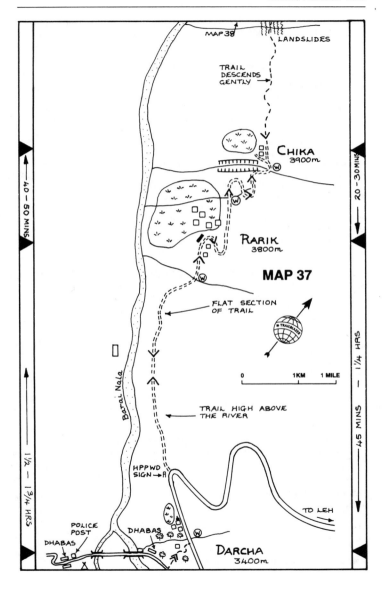

MAP 38

LANDSLIDES

TRAIL
DESCENDS
GENTLY

40 – 50 MINS

CHIKA
3900m

20 – 30 MINS

RARIK
3800m

MAP 37

FLAT SECTION
OF TRAIL

TRAILBLAZER

0   1KM   1 MILE

1¼ HRS

Barai Nala

TRAIL HIGH ABOVE
THE RIVER

45 MINS

HPPWD
SIGN → A

TO LEH

1½ – 1¾ HRS

POLICE
POST

DHABAS

DHABAS

DARCHA
3400m

side the main season it may be easier to recruit the help of a trekking agency in Keylong. Keylong is also the best place to buy last minute supplies to supplement those brought from Manali or Leh.

Acclimatisation Coming straight from Manali you won't be used to the altitude and so it is vital that you take the first section of this trek to the Shingo La very slowly. A sensible rate of acclimatisation would be to spend two nights at Darcha, one at Palamo, two nights at Zangskar Sumdo and then one night at either Ramjak or Chumik Nakpo before crossing the Shingo La. If you feel any symptoms of AMS do not go higher. Remember, **if you are in any doubt as to the seriousness of yours, or another person's AMS symptoms, descend**. See p272 for more information on AMS.

Leaving Darcha Head towards Leh along the road over the bridges and past the dhabas to a well-worn short cut on the left which rises steeply to the next bend in the road. Continue along the tarmac to the following bend where you leave the main road on a jeep track continuing straight ahead.

Rarik and Chika The trail rises gently past the small village of Rarik and the last hamlet of Chika where the jeep track ends, becoming a well-used trail. Continue along this gentle path up the true left bank of the Barai Nala which flows far below you.

You reach a deep chasm through which the foaming river forces a course. There's a small shrine and some prayer flags here. Muster up courage to cross the small bridge high above the whirling water.

Palamo (3900m/12,790ft) You remain on the right bank (SW) of the Barai Nala until Zangskar Sumdo. This area above the bridge is called Palamo and there are several good *camping* places in the vicinity.

Beyond Palamo are several other *camp-sites* and water is never a problem

as you cross several small streams. The rough trail over boulders gains height very slowly with some short but steep ups and downs as it crosses glacial debris. Shortly before Zangskar Sumdo is a river crossing which can be difficult if there has been a lot of rain or snow-melt. If this is the case, wait until the level falls and refer to p279 for further information on river crossing techniques. In good conditions it's simple to hop from boulder to boulder.

Zangskar Sumdo/Zanskarsamdu/ Jankar Samdo (4000m/13,120ft) This wide flat valley is a popular *camping* ground for most trekkers before the long grind up to the Shingo La begins in earnest. If you feel you need more time to acclimatise, spend a few days here exploring further up the beautiful valley or climbing the ridges for excellent views.

ZANGSKAR SUMDO TO SHINGO LA [MAPS 39-40, pp234-5] Cross the Barai Nala on the suspension bridge which has replaced the old pulley system, previously the only dry way across the river. The trail now follows the small side *nala* all the way to the pass. Climb strenuously to the top of the hillside and then carefully follow the narrow path above the precipitous drop to the stream. The trail eases and the danger passes allowing you to take in the fantastic views all around. There are several small spaces for *camping* along here.

Ramjak (4100m/13,450ft) The next possible *camp-site* is marked by a few ruins and a mani wall. Climb over an area of landslide and continue gently along the stream. For the next few hours the trail is generally easy with the occasional traverse across steep slopes with long drops below. There are many possibilities for camping and also a few roofless shelters which the local herders convert into temporary dwellings with the aid of a tarpaulin.

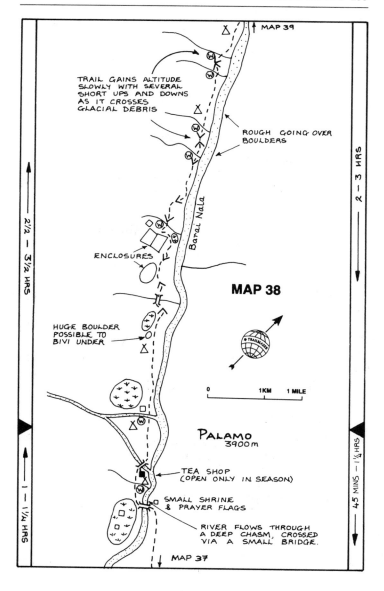

↑ MAP 39

TRAIL GAINS ALTITUDE
SLOWLY WITH SEVERAL
SHORT UPS AND DOWNS
AS IT CROSSES
GLACIAL DEBRIS

ROUGH GOING OVER
BOULDERS

2 – 3 HRS

Baral Nala

ENCLOSURES

MAP 38

2½ – 3½ HRS

HUGE BOULDER
POSSIBLE TO
BIVI UNDER

TRAILMARK

0   1 KM   1 MILE

PALAMO
3900 m

TEA SHOP
(OPEN ONLY IN SEASON)

SMALL SHRINE
& PRAYER FLAGS

RIVER FLOWS THROUGH
A DEEP CHASM, CROSSED
VIA A SMALL BRIDGE.

1 – 1¼ HRS

45 MINS – 1½ HRS

MAP 37

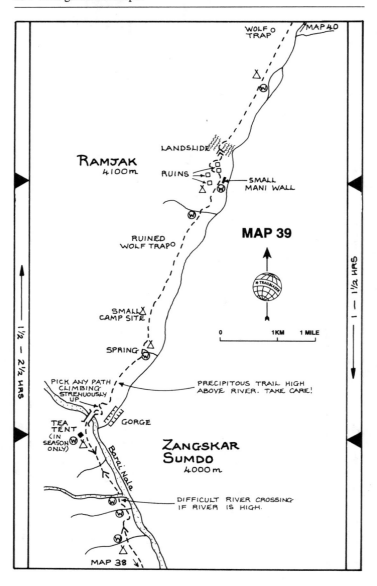

WOLF O TRAP

MAP 40

RAMJAK
4100m

LANDSLIDE

RUINS

SMALL
MANI WALL

MAP 39

RUINED
WOLF TRAP O

* TRAILMASTER

0   1KM   1 MILE

SMALL
CAMP SITE

SPRING

PICK ANY PATH
CLIMBING
STRENUOUSLY
UP

PRECIPITOUS TRAIL HIGH
ABOVE RIVER. TAKE CARE!

TEA
TENT
(IN
SEASON
ONLY)

GORGE

ZANGSKAR
SUMDO
4000m

Barai Nala

DIFFICULT RIVER CROSSING
IF RIVER IS HIGH.

MAP 38

1½ — 2½ HRS

1 — 1½ HRS

Chumik Nakpo (4400m/14,430ft)

Two to three hours above Ramjak is the last possible *camp* before the pass. The trail now begins to climb steeply through bleak landscape over glacial debris. Soon a small glacier comes into view on the right (E); this is the source of the stream you have been following. The trail stays on the west side of the valley climbing across steep scree slopes.

After one final steep, breathless climb you will be relieved to see the trail ease, to cross a new-born stream and meander around the east side of a small lake to the pass.

Shingo/Shinkun/Shinkul La
(5000m/16,400ft) Crossing the Shingo La in either direction in poor visibility or when a recent fall of snow has obscured the path is unwise without a guide who knows the route. The route is not at all obvious in such conditions and as much of the terrain is glacial, it would be easy to stray onto a glacier or over an ice cliff.

In good conditions the trail should be fairly easy to follow and you will be rewarded with wonderful views of several 6000m peaks.

SHINGO LA TO KARGYAK
[MAPS 40-43, pp235-8]
The trail down the north side of the pass heads east at first to avoid an ice cliff and then skirts round the west side of another small glacier; gradually working its way over to the west side of the valley and then beginning a steep descent to a permanent snow field and the junction with another valley.

▲ **Opposite direction** Where the valley divides, branch up the south trending valley across the permanent snow field and steeply up the west side of the new valley.

Lakang (4700m/15,420ft)
The trail descends high above a stream on the right (S) bank. You soon reach

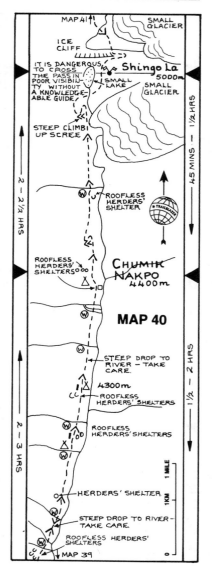

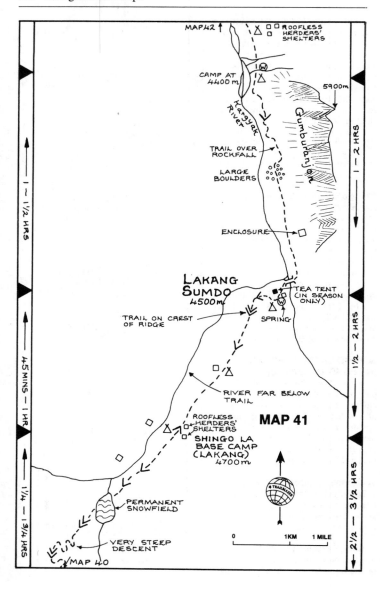

MAP 42 ↑

□ □ ROOFLESS
□ HERDERS'
SHELTERS

CAMP AT
4400 m

5900m

Kargyak River

Gumburanjon

TRAIL OVER
ROCKFALL

LARGE
BOULDERS

ENCLOSURE

LAKANG
SUMDO
4500m

TEA TENT
(IN SEASON
ONLY)

TRAIL ON CREST
OF RIDGE

SPRING

RIVER FAR BELOW
TRAIL

ROOFLESS
HERDERS'
SHELTERS

MAP 41

SHINGO LA
BASE CAMP
(LAKANG)
4700 m

PERMANENT
SNOWFIELD

VERY STEEP
DESCENT

MAP 40

● TRAILBLAZER

0   1KM   1 MILE

1 ~ 1½ HRS

45 MINS — 1 HR

¼ — 1¾ HRS

1 — 2 HRS

½ — 2 HRS

2½ — 3½ HRS

an obvious **camp-site** where there are a few herders' shelters. If you are crossing the pass in the other direction, this makes an excellent base camp. If continuing into Zanskar a nicer and lower camp awaits you at Lakang Sumdo.

Lakang Sumdo/Lakong (4500m/14,760ft)

The trail drops steeply down a ridge to this **camp** in the beautiful upper Kargyak Valley. There are wonderful views all around: to the north the bare jagged mountains typical of Zanskar, while to the south lie the snow mountains of the Great Himalaya.

From here the trail crosses the Kargyak River, barely more than a stream in these upper reaches, and follows the right (E) bank under the huge vertical west face of **Gumburanjon**. This 5900m (19,350ft) shark's fin of a mountain is best viewed from the north where its full profile can be fully admired. It has been climbed several times, usually by the challenging north ridge.

As you carry on north down the valley you will pass the summer grazing camp or *doksa* belonging to Kargyak village. The grazing in these high-altitude pastures is better than around the villages so most of the village's cattle, horses, sheep and goats are moved up here during the summer to be tended by a few of the young villagers. You may be offered some delicious cheese and curd to buy; an opportunity not to be missed.

The walking is gentle and easy all the way to Kargyak, enlivened by the sighting of countless marmots who stand on their hind legs and whistle when alarmed. Glance behind you every so often to capture the changing light on Gumburanjon's precipitous walls.

Kargyak (4200m/13,780ft)

This is the first and highest village in this valley. It is a small and beautiful place of about 120 people with a tiny gompa on the hillside above. The best **camping** is beyond the village down by the river.

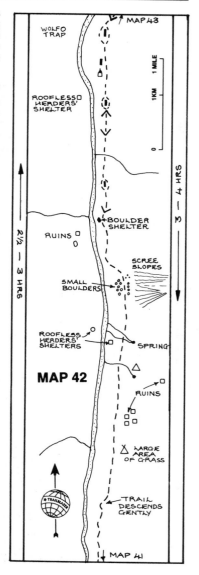

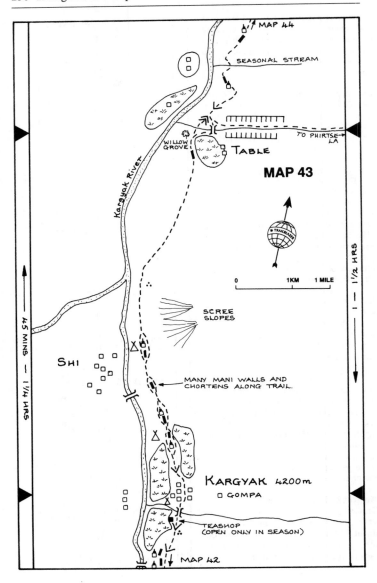

MAP 44

SEASONAL STREAM

TO PHIRTSE LA

WILLOW GROVE

TABLE

MAP 43

TRAILBLAZER

0   1KM   1 MILE

Kargyak River

SCREE SLOPES

SHI

MANY MANI WALLS AND CHORTENS ALONG TRAIL.

KARGYAK 4200m

GOMPA

TEASHOP (OPEN ONLY IN SEASON)

MAP 42

45 MINS — 1¼ HRS

1 — 1½ HRS

KARGYAK TO PURNE
[MAPS 43-45, pp238-41]

As you leave Kargyak you pass many
chortens and mani walls. The tiny
hamlet of **Table** is the next habitation.
The trail to the Phirtse La heads east
up a gorge from here.

Tangzen (Tanze) is heralded by a
large group of mani walls. There is a
small gompa on the hillside behind the
village. The trail descends to the river
and then crosses onto the left (SW)
bank. Traverse some steep scree slopes,
which would be dangerous during or
after rain. The trail leaves the river and
climbs to a willow plantation, before
descending between the fields of the
pretty village of **Kuru** (Karu).

Testa/Teta (4100m/13,450ft) You
soon reach this larger village where
there are plenty of places for *camping*,
with water available from the irrigation
channels. Meandering through these
villages provides an excellent opportunity to observe Zanskari village life up
close and to appreciate how much work
has to be achieved in the short summer.

As you leave the village, walking
between fields, you pass a prayer wheel
and a beautifully ornate row of chortens. The valley soon narrows and the
trail descends to a suspension bridge of
dubious strength. Do not cross but continue along the left (SW) bank following the river through a tiny gorge. The
trail rises to the village of **Yal** (4050m/
13,280ft) where it is possible to *camp*.
If there are only a few of you, you may
prefer to camp in this friendly village
rather than in Purne which can become
busy in the peak season.

After Yal the trail splits. If you
want to visit the magnificent gompa at
Phuktal descend the steep trail and
cross the bridge into Purne.

Purne (3950m/12,960ft) Purne is a
collection of houses owned by two families who do very well off the passing
trekkers because almost everybody

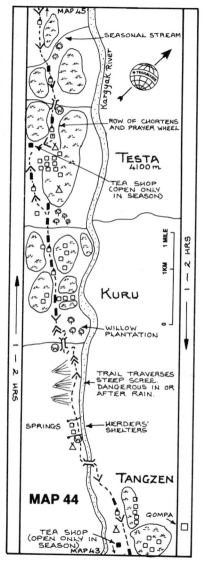

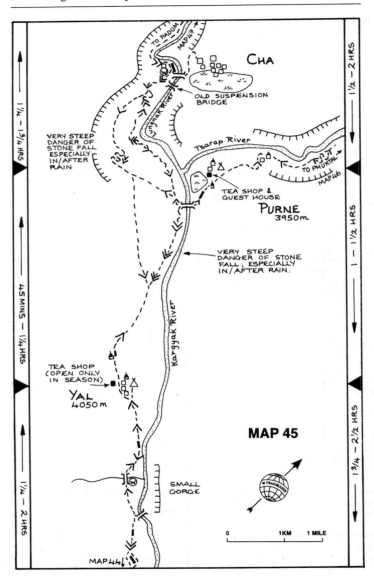

stops at the *camp-site* for at least one night. If you are sick of spending nights under canvas there is also a small **guesthouse**. The two very well-stocked **shops** could provide you with almost everything you would need for a trek. The owners make the round trip to Manali at the beginning of the season to buy enough stock to sell through July, August and September.

● Side trip to Phuktal/Phugtal Gompa (MAP 46)

Phuktal Gompa is the reason for Purne's popularity and rightly so: it is the most spectacularly situated gompa in Ladakh. To reach the monastery follow the trail up the left bank of the Tsarap River for between 1½ and 2½ hours as it winds through a red rock gorge. The trail is not hard but be aware of landslides in the rain. When you reach a bridge cross over onto the right bank. After a stiff climb you round a corner and see the gompa for the first time, clinging to the sheer cliffs below a large cave. The ochre temple is deep within the cavern while the white monks' cells sprawl below.

This Gelukpa monastery is built around a sacred spring which flows all year, even in the depths of winter when other springs freeze. Nobody is quite sure who founded it, but it's most likely that it was the prolific Rinchen Zangpo, also known as the 'Great Translator'. However, there's also a legend that a lama called Chansen Cherap Zampo decided that it was a suitable place for a gompa after finding three Indian holy men living in the cave. They complained that it was far too small to house lots of monks. Undaunted, the lama miraculously increased the cave to its current size.

There is nowhere to camp near the gompa, but it is often possible for men to stay overnight in the monastery for a small charge. If you walk 20 minutes north of the gompa (go through the gompa complex, not down to the river) there are wonderful views ahead. This is the start of a difficult route by way of Shade and Thongde to Padum (see p264).

PURNE TO PADUM
[MAP 45: p240, MAPS 47-51: pp242-6]
Cross back onto the left bank of the Kargyak River which, after joining the Tsarap at the confluence below, becomes the Lungnak River. Stay on the lower trail to avoid a steep climb.

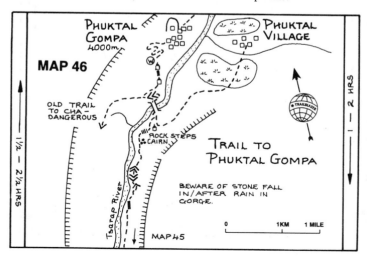

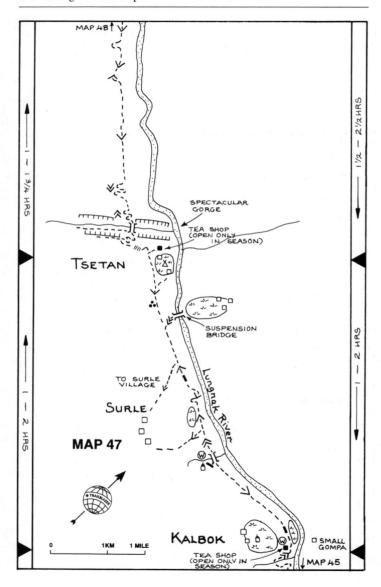

MAP 48

SPECTACULAR
GORGE

TEA SHOP
(OPEN ONLY
IN SEASON)

TSETAN

SUSPENSION
BRIDGE

TO SURLE
VILLAGE

SURLE

MAP 47

Lungnak River

1 ~ 1¾ HRS

1 ~ 2 HRS

1½ ~ 2½ HRS

1 ~ 2 HRS

● TRAILBLAZER

0   1KM   1 MILE

KALBOK

TEA SHOP
(OPEN ONLY IN
SEASON)

SMALL
GOMPA

MAP 45

The river enters the Lungnak Gorge which you will be walking through for at least a day. Several small sections of trail are destroyed by landslide each year: a testament to how unstable the sides of the gorge can become in heavy rain. Be on the alert for rockfall and take the utmost care where the trail has been washed away.

After about three km the trail climbs to the hamlet of **Kalbok** and then passes below the village of **Surle**. Beyond **Tsetan** you cross a spectacular tributary gorge on a precarious bridge of boulders wedged into a narrowing of the gorge walls over the stream.

The next *camp-site* in the Lungnak Gorge is at **Pepul** (3800m/12,460ft), a flat, dusty piece of ground where the trail descends to the river.

Continue along the roller-coaster trail past a fort in the cliff on the opposite bank near the village of **Dorzong**. **Ichar** is equally impressive with its houses perched on top of a crag and there are wonderful views west to snow-capped mountains.

A constriction in the gorge a little further on creates a series of foaming rapids. The trail cannot follow and is forced up a steep, long incline to detour behind a crag and out over the lip of the gorge which has enclosed you for so long.

The landscape has changed markedly to a dry, desert stretch. Follow the path away from the river and down to a bridge across a fast flowing glacial stream. Just before the bridge is a *camp* with a small stream of clear water.

Reru The main trail to Padum bypasses Reru to the west and just beyond joins the jeep road which is slowly but steadily being extended up the valley. It is planned to take this all the way to Kargyak and one has to wonder whether this is in the best interests of the villagers. Communications need to be improved for these very isolated villages, particularly in winter, but perhaps an upgraded pack-animal trail

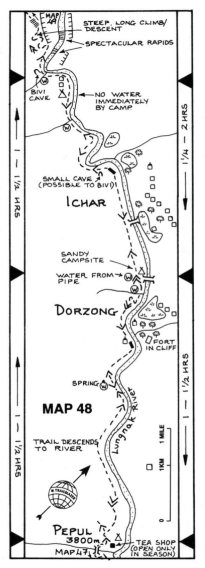

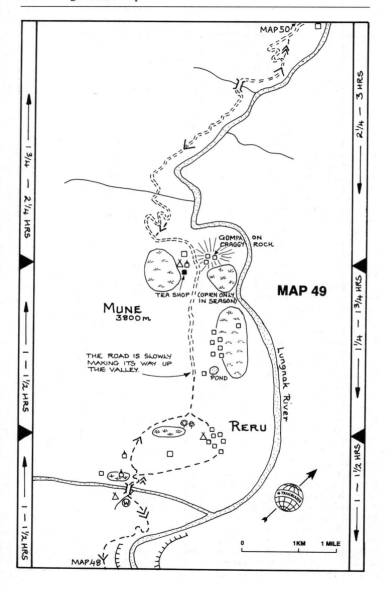

MAP 50

1¾ – 2¼ HRS

2¼ – 3 HRS

GOMPA ON ROCK

TEA SHOP (OPEN ONLY IN SEASON)

MAP 49

MUNE
3800m

THE ROAD IS SLOWLY MAKING ITS WAY UP THE VALLEY.

POND

Lungnak River

RERU

1 – 1½ HRS

1 – 1½ HRS

1¼ – 1¾ HRS

1¼ – 1½ HRS

TRAILBLAZER

0   1KM   1 MILE

MAP 48

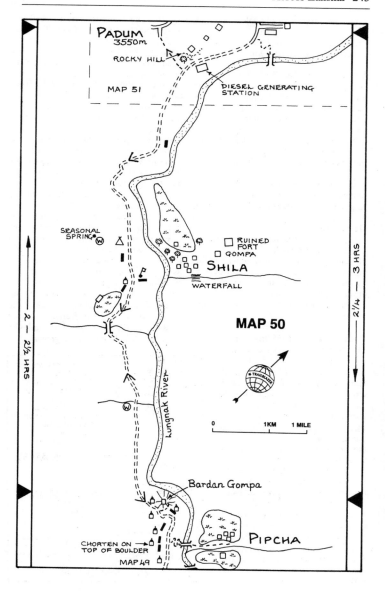

would be a more sustainable option, as well as being less costly. The way to Padum follows the road which makes for rather dull and dusty walking.

Mune (3800m/12,460ft) Mune Gelukpa Gompa is spectacularly situated on a crag on a bend in the river and the friendly monks will lift your spirits. This peaceful village makes a lovely overnight stop. There is *camping* by the stupas close to the gompa and a lodge is under construction by the monks to raise money for this rather neglected but beautiful building.

Four or so kilometres beyond Mune is an impressive monastery belonging to the Kagyupa sect at **Bardan**. This has been built on a tall plug of rock which rises high above the Lungnak River. The best views of the gompa are from the west.

The rocky hillock of Padum with its glistening tin-roofed government buildings can be seen from some way off. Beyond are the sharp stratified rock walls of the Zanskar Mountains.

Follow the jeep track all the way into Padum.

Padum/Padam (3550m/11,640ft)
The 'capital' of Zanskar is little more than a large village. It has a sizeable minority Muslim population, mainly Baltis from the Kargil area, who have settled here since the mid-17th century. The settlement itself has little charm but it is situated in the beautiful central Zans-kar plain, surrounded by stunning mountains with several interesting villages nearby (see p144-5).

The traditional heart of the village is below the gompa where two large chortens stand above old buildings. Padum has known much change since the road over the Pensi La was completed in 1980; the steady shift from a traditional and largely self-contained culture to one increasingly linked to the global economic system is much in evidence here and perhaps heralds the changes prepar-

ing to sweep across the rest of Zanskar.
● **Accommodation and food** There are several places where it is possible to *camp*, the site before the forestry plantation being the most convenient. If you are looking for more comfort, places to stay are strung along the Kargil road. *Hotel Chorala*, named after the 5650m mountain above Karsha, is the closest to the main village and in a good position for catching the early morning bus to Kargil. The other options, *Hotel Haptal View*, *Hotel Tourist Camp*, and the excellent value *J&K Tourism Tourist Complex*, are further out of the village, past the mosque, near the road junction to Pipiting.

Restaurants are scarce in Padum and the cuisine basic but anything will be a welcome break from a monotonous trekking diet. The hotels can usually provide food and the *Lhasa Restaurant* and *Hotel Chang Thang* are also worth a try.
● **Guides and pack animals** These are usually available in Padum or the surrounding villages. Start by making enquiries at the hotels, restaurants and shops; if they can't help go to one of the larger villages such as Karsha, Sani or Thongde to ask there. You should allow a couple of days to make arrangements.

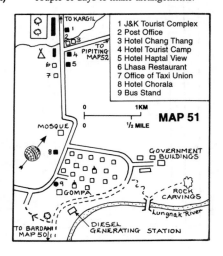

1 J&K Tourist Complex
2 Post Office
3 Hotel Chang Thang
4 Hotel Tourist Camp
5 Hotel Haptal View
6 Lhasa Restaurant
7 Office of Taxi Union
8 Hotel Chorala
9 Bus Stand

TO KARGIL

TO PIPITING MAP52

0   1KM
0   ½ MILE

MAP 51

MOSQUE

GOVERNMENT BUILDINGS

GOMPA

ROCK CARVINGS

Lungnak River

TO BARDAN MAP 50

DIESEL GENERATING STATION

● **Shops** There are plenty of general stores where you can buy simple supplies for trekking such as noodles, rice, dal, tinned tuna/mackerel, soup, biscuits, etc. Vegetables can sometimes be hard to find and there is no supply of petrol for your stove, although kerosene is readily available. For those trekkers who just can't wait until they reach Kargil, Leh, Manali or Delhi, there are several obligatory Kashmiri souvenir sellers, only too willing to increase the weight of your rucksack whilst helping to lighten your wallet.

● **Information** If you need help with anything in Padum a visit to the super-efficient **tourist officer** at the Tourist Complex will soon put you right. If you have an **emergency** he can arrange helicopter evacuation. There is a radio and helipad here.

● **Communications** There is a small **post office** in town and there are rumours that an **STD/ISD telephone office** will appear soon.

● **Transport** Buses to **Kargil** (see warning p79) depart every other day (Rs200) at about 5-6am. The bus from Kargil arrives in the evening, the driver then has a day to recover from the exhausting journey, before departing for Kargil the morning after. You should try to buy tickets in advance from the conductor to ensure a seat – the 13-14 hour journey is not pleasurable if you are forced to stand. For buses from **Kargil to Padum** see p142.

Taxis are available to Kargil costing Rs7000 one way, plus Rs1100 if you want to take a more leisurely two days over the journey. You can also visit the sites of central Zanskar by taxi: prices range from Rs150 one way to Pipiting to Rs1500 one way to Zangla, plus an extra Rs300 for the return. Go to the office of the taxi union for more information.

PADUM TO PARFI LA
[MAPS 51-57, pp246-54]

● **Alternative trail to Sengi La via Zangla and Nerak** The main route to the Sengi La via Karsha and Lingshed along the west bank of the Zanskar River is described below. There is an alternative trail along the east bank of the Zanskar River via Zangla which doesn't meet up with the west bank trail until it crosses the

□ **Zanskar ban**
Having allegedly been neglected by the state government for some years the Zanskaris are calling for greater political autonomy and the construction of a road up the Zanskar Gorge. This would link Padum with Leh, thereby allowing continuous winter access to Zanskar for the first time. At present, road access is limited to four snow-free months of the year via Kargil and the Pensi La. There are also political ramifications if this ever happened as it might enable principally Buddhist Zanskar to become part of Buddhist Leh District as opposed to Muslim-governed Kargil District as at present. To attract the attention of the state government to these demands the Zanskaris instituted a ban on tourists entering the region for several weeks in the summer of 1995.

Unfortunately for the Zanskaris this didn't have the desired effect but it demonstrates that they felt they had little to lose by targeting tourists and trekkers. Not only would they receive more publicity but they were making the fundamental point that almost all of the benefits from tourism went to outsiders. All the Zanskaris receive is loss of grazing, pollution and disturbance. This highlights the key role trekkers play in making sure we don't destroy the very thing we have come to see. We must realise that our actions have wide-ranging consequences and it's time we took more individual responsibility for them.

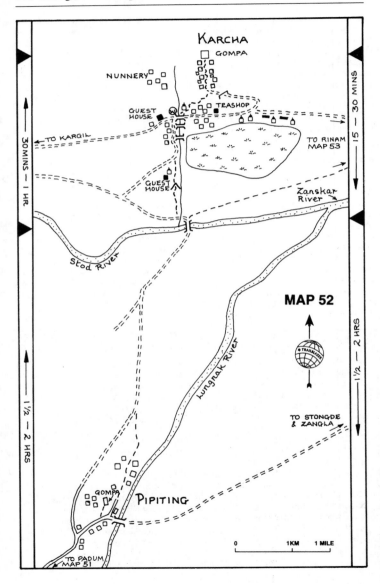

KARCHA

GOMPA

NUNNERY

GUEST HOUSE

TEASHOP

TO KARGIL

GUEST HOUSE

TO RINAM MAP 53

Zanskar River

Stod River

MAP 52

TRAILBLAZER

Lungnak River

TO STONGDE & ZANGLA

PIPITING

GOMPA

30 MINS — 1 HR

1½ — 2 HRS

15 — 30 MINS

1½ — 2 HRS

0   1KM   1 MILE

TO PADUM
MAP 51

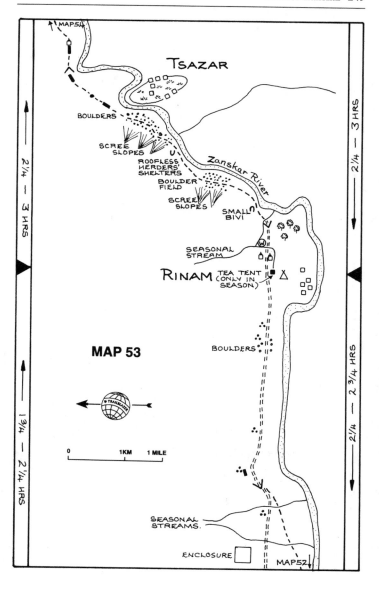

MAP 54

TSAZAR

BOULDERS

SCREE SLOPES

ROOFLESS HERDERS' SHELTERS

BOULDER FIELD

SCREE SLOPES

SMALL BIVI

Zanskar River

SEASONAL STREAM

RINAM TEA TENT (ONLY IN SEASON)

BOULDERS

MAP 53

TRAILBLAZER

0   1KM   1 MILE

SEASONAL STREAMS.

ENCLOSURE

MAP 52

2¼ — 3 HRS

2¼ — 3 HRS

2¼ — 2¾ HRS

1¾ — 2¼ HRS

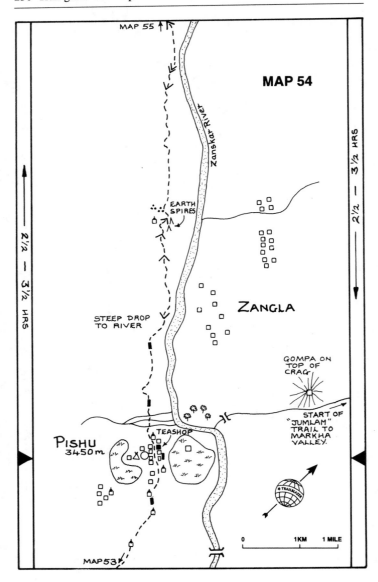

MAP 55 ↑

MAP 54

Zanskar River

EARTH SPIRES

2½ — 3½ HRS

2½ — 3½ HRS

STEEP DROP TO RIVER

ZANGLA

GOMPA ON TOP OF CRAG

START OF "JUMLAM" TRAIL TO MARKHA VALLEY.

PISHU 3450m

TEASHOP

TRAILBLAZER

0   1KM   1 MILE

MAP 53

Zanskar River between the Kiupa La and Sengi La. This route takes about the same time as the main route. However, it is harder with some difficult route-finding and parts of the trail are tricky for pack animals. Take a guide with you as there are few settlements along the way.

Follow the jeep road via Thongde to Zangla and then on to Honia. The trail then crosses the Namtse La (4450m/14,600ft) continuing along complicated and demanding terrain until you cross the Thakti La (4700m/15,420ft). From here descend to the village of Nerak (Nyerok) below which you can cross the Zanskar River. Ascend the other side of the gorge via Yulchung to either the Sengi La or Kiupa La.

Karsha Simple but monotonous walking along a road takes the trekker across the Padum plain, past Pipiting to Karsha. The climb from the bridge across the Stod River to this beautiful Gelukpa gompa whose whitewashed buildings sprawl down the hillside, is well worth the effort, particularly for the views to the Great Himalaya range which you are unable to appreciate from Padum. This is the largest monastery in Zanskar with about 140 resident monks and there's also a nunnery on the hill to the west of the main monastery. There are a couple of *guest-houses* in the village and space for *camping*.

To the east of Karsha, the Stod and Lungnak rivers meet to form the Zanskar River which you follow for the next couple of days. A jeep road goes to **Rinam** and along the way there are good views south to Thongde and the Thongde La behind; this can be crossed to follow a difficult route to Phuktal.

The jeep road comes to an abrupt end, but as elsewhere in Ladakh there are probably plans to push it as far up the valley as possible. Continue along a

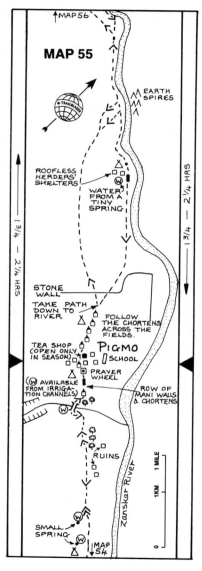

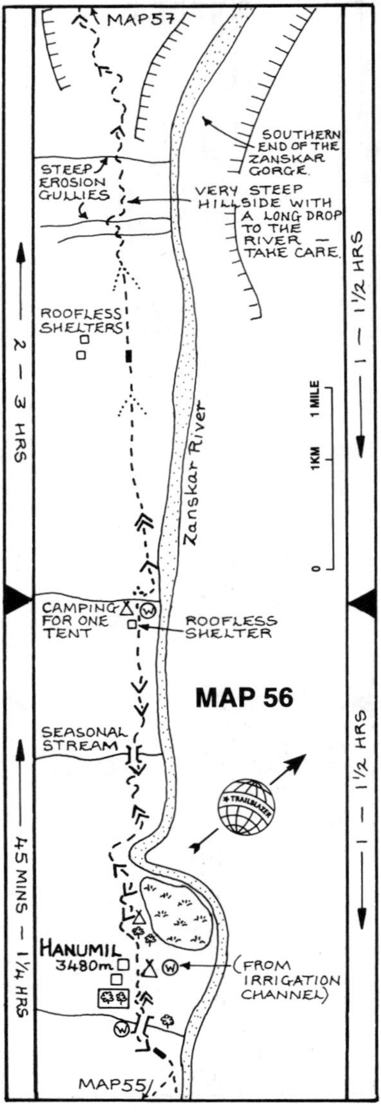

MAP 57

SOUTHERN END OF THE ZANSKAR GORGE

STEEP EROSION GULLIES

VERY STEEP HILLSIDE WITH A LONG DROP TO THE RIVER — TAKE CARE

ROOFLESS SHELTERS

2 — 3 HRS

1½ HRS

1 MILE

1KM

Zanskar River

0

CAMPING FOR ONE TENT

ROOFLESS SHELTER

MAP 56

SEASONAL STREAM

1½ HRS

45 MINS — 1¼ HRS

HANUMIL 3480m

(FROM IRRIGATION CHANNEL)

MAP 55

sandy trail as it threads its way between boulders under huge scree slopes on the left (N) bank of the Zanskar River. The day-time temperatures are noticeably higher on this stage of the trek because of the lower altitude and this coupled with the sandy trail can make the walking tiring. Soon after passing **Tsazar** on the opposite bank the path climbs onto a plateau which you cross to the village of Pishu.

Pishu (3450m/11,310ft) The *camping* here is dusty and there is little water. Be prepared to queue at the standpipe with the rest of the village in the morning and evening. If you want to visit **Zangla Gompa**, visible on the opposite side of the river, you will find a bridge quite a long way upstream from here. Cross here also if you want to return to Padum through the villages of Zangla and Thongde – a convenient circuit of central Zanskar.

The trail beyond Pishu is easy over gently undulating land, essentially following the river downstream. Having crossed a small stream you climb up the opposite bank to an elaborate gateway chorten on the crest. This is the entrance to **Pigmo** (Pidmo/ Pidmu). Follow the row of chortens out of the village and take the trail descending to the river. There is a higher alternative trail which is used when the water level floods the lower route. The trail stays close to the river until you approach **Hanumil** (Hanuma). Cross a tributary stream and climb to the two houses which make up this pretty settlement. There is *camping* (3480m/ 11,410ft) in front of the houses or 200m further on in a secluded copse.

Drop back down to the river and follow it until you reach a substantial stream flowing from the south-west. There is a shepherd's roofless shelter here and *camping* space for one tent. Cross the stream and follow the trail as it rises up onto a small plateau. The plateau is soon replaced by a very steep hillside which the trail traverses; this slope is scarred by gullies caused by rock and water erosion. The trail is often precarious and the long drop to the Zanskar River below will prompt you to take care.

Zanskar Gorge This is the beginning of the Zanskar Gorge where the river cuts an impressive path east and then north through the mountains. In summer whitewater rafters and kayakers are the only people who can continue through this magnificent chasm. Those on foot are forced against the grain of the land, up and over the chaotic ridges of the Zanskar Range. For two months in winter the river below becomes the improbable 'Chadur' trade route to Nimu in the Indus Valley, when temperatures dip so low that the Zanskaris can venture on foot along its frozen surface.

The climb to the Parfi La soon begins in earnest as you ascend the switchback trail through a line of low crags. Soon the views to the north open up to reveal the difficult landscape through which the Zanskar River flows. You can appreciate the inherent difficulties of constructing a road along the side of this gorge which, if ever realised, would allow winter access to Zanskar and would connect the region to Buddhist central Ladakh. This has been a long-term political aim for the majority of Buddhists in Zanskar who object to being governed from Kargil, which is largely Muslim.

Parfi La (3900m/12,790ft) The small pass is reached without difficulty; a sentiment not shared by those who have made the stiff ascent in the other direction. This is the first of the eight passes you cross on your way to Lamayuru.

PARFI LA TO LINGSHED
[MAPS 57-60, pp254-7]
The descent is very steep and tiring. About halfway down there is a roofless shelter, a tiny spring and *camping* space for about two small tents. Unless you are benighted, you will soon reach better camping, whether walking towards Padum or Lamayuru. There are several *camp-sites* by the side of the **Oma Chu** in the valley below you.

One of the possible routes to Dibling and Rangdum (see p265) follows the Oma Chu south-west from the bridge. If continuing towards Lamayuru, begin the long sandy ascent up the northern side of the valley. Eventually the trail levels off, traversing a steep hillside and then descending gently to the *camp* (3770m/ 12,370ft) and shepherds' huts at **Snertse** (Nyetse). The last time I camped at Snertse was at the end of the trekking season and there was a disgusting amount of discarded litter around the huts, along with turds and lavatory paper down by the stream. Both are inexcusable, although the latter is understandable and illustrates the problem of where to 'go' in a narrow gorge with tempting privacy in the trees by the river. Please don't succumb to temptation. Enjoy a walk and find somewhere else to squat a long way from people's drinking water supply.

Leave by going down to the stream or by climbing over a small ridge behind the herders' shelters. The path follows the stream up the gorge, through willow trees at first and then through increasingly barren scenery. The only difficulty in the steady climb is when you reach a permanent snow bridge. As this changes from season to season the way ahead may involve a short section of scrambling to avoid any difficulties. The gradient lessens as this beautiful arid valley opens out.

A small herders' hut (4230m/ 13,870ft) provides the only shelter between Snertse and the Hanuma La. There is space here for one or two tents but the ground is stony and uneven; not the best *camp*. The trail is flat for almost a kilometre, then starts to rise towards the pass, taking the northerly valley where the valleys divide. Fill up your water bottles before the valley divides as the stream coming from the pass is often dry.

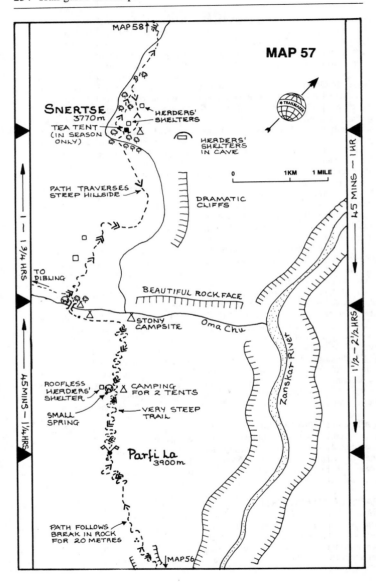

MAP 58

MAP 57

TRAILBLAZER

SNERTSE
3770m

HERDERS'
SHELTERS

TEA TENT
(IN SEASON
ONLY)

HERDERS'
SHELTERS
IN CAVE

0   1KM   1 MILE

PATH TRAVERSES
STEEP HILLSIDE

DRAMATIC
CLIFFS

TO
DIBLING

BEAUTIFUL ROCK FACE

Oma Chu

STONY
CAMPSITE

Zanskar River

ROOFLESS
HERDERS'
SHELTER

CAMPING
FOR 2 TENTS

SMALL
SPRING

VERY STEEP
TRAIL

Parfi La
3900m

PATH FOLLOWS
BREAK IN ROCK
FOR 20 METRES

MAP 56

45 MINS – 1 HR

1½ – 2½ HRS

1 – 1¾ HRS

45 MINS – 1¼ HRS

Hanuma/Hamalun/Haluma La (4700m/15,410ft)

The Hanuma La is easily reached and provides wonderful views on to Lingshed and the convoluted terrain that lies ahead. The white gompa buildings are just visible at the bottom of the stratified mountain wall to the north.

Descend the steep zigzag trail to a stream at the valley floor. There is space for *camping* at its confluence with another stream. There are two routes over the ridge that lies between you and Lingshed: either carry on up the valley to cross the ridge higher up, or climb the steep and obvious trail to the south-east. The latter trail crosses a small pass and then traverses the eastern side of the ridge to join the alternative path. The trail then contours around to the north to avoid the ups and downs of this undulating terrain. Just before descending to a bridge you pass the trail which heads north-west via Dibling to Rangdum (see p265).

From a chorten and prayer flags on a crest descend through fields to Lingshed.

LINGSHED TO POTOKSUR [MAPS 60-63, pp257-61]
Lingshed/Lingshot/Lingshet (3900m/12,790ft) The best *camping* is on the other side of the valley, just beyond the gompa where you will also find a small *guest-house*. The Gelukpa gompa is said to have been founded by Rinchen Zangpo on a rock from which an auspicious flame was seen burning. The trail continues easily over the **Margun** (Murgum/Nietukse/Netuke) **La** (4370m/14,330ft) and down to the small village of **Skyumpata** (4060m/13,320ft). Soon after, cross a stream below the village of **Gongma** and begin the hard climb to the **Kiupa** (Khupte/Khyupa) **La** (4430m/14,530ft).

▲ **Opposite direction** After crossing the stream, stick to the higher path where the trail splits, unless you want to visit Skyumpata.

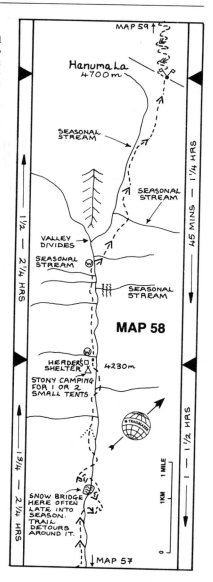

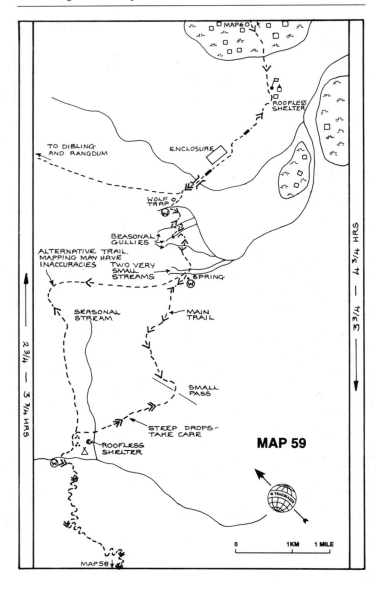

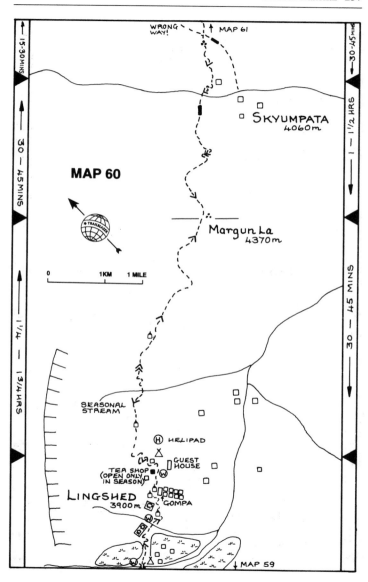

MAP 60

15-30 MINS

30 - 45 MINS

1¼ - 1¾ HRS

30-45 MINS — 1-1½ HRS

30 — 45 MINS

WRONG WAY!

↑ MAP 61

SKYUMPATA
4060m

Margun La
4370m

TRAILBLAZER

0   1KM   1 MILE

SEASONAL
STREAM

Ⓗ HELIPAD

GUEST
HOUSE

TEA SHOP
(OPEN ONLY
IN SEASON)

LINGSHED
3900m

GOMPA

↓ MAP 59

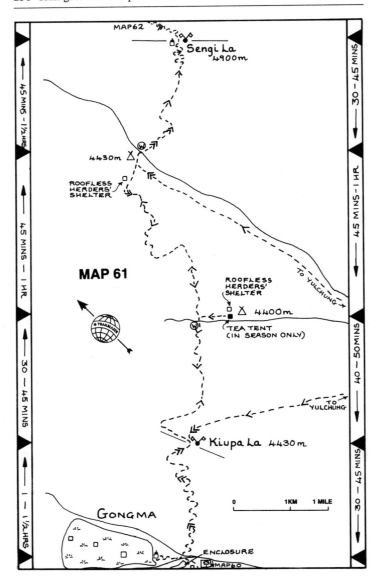

MAP62

△⌂ Sengi La 4900m

45 MINS – 1½ HRS
45 MINS – 1 HR
30 – 45 MINS
1 – 1½ HRS

30 – 45 MINS
45 MINS – 1 HR
40 – 50 MINS
30 – 45 MINS

4430m △

ROOFLESS
HERDERS'
SHELTER

MAP 61

S TRAILBLAZER

ROOFLESS
HERDERS'
SHELTER

□ △ 4400m

TEA TENT
(IN SEASON ONLY)

TO YULCHUNG

TO
YULCHUNG

Kiupa La 4430m

0   1KM   1 MILE

GONGMA

ENCLOSURE
MAP60

From the top of the **Kiupa La** don't continue down the steep trail straight ahead which leads to the collection of houses called Yulchung. Instead, follow the more obvious trail which stays at a level height, contouring round to the north-west. You soon reach a large *camp-site* (4400m/14,430ft) below the trail which is often used as a base camp for the Sengi La. There is another *camp* (4430m/14,530ft) directly below the pass which you will reach in about 45 minutes.

● **Alternative route** There is an alternative trail to Padum via the east bank of the Zanskar River which branches off the main route at the southern base of the Sengi La. See p247 for further details.

Sengi La (4900m/16,070ft) The ascent to the highest pass on the route is never very steep and the views from the summit are spectacular. To the south you can see Nerak (Nyerok) and the start of the alternative trail to Padum along the east bank of the Zanskar River; to the north-west is a beautiful peak resplendent with hanging glaciers. This, the 'Lion Pass', also appears on maps as Sengge, Singi, Senge, Singay, Singila and Singe.

Descend the short steep slope from the pass and on down the broad valley. At some stage you need to cross over onto the left (SW) bank to pick up a trail which climbs away from the stream and makes its undulating way to the small **Bumiktse** (Bramiktse) **La** (4400m/14,430ft).

Potoksur(Photoksar/Photosar/ Photaksar/Photaskar) 4130m/ 13,550ft Having crossed the pass, descend to the valley bottom and cross the bridge to climb easily to the pretty village of Potoksur. The houses are perched together above a stream in such a jumble that it is easy to get lost in the maze of narrow alleyways. The best

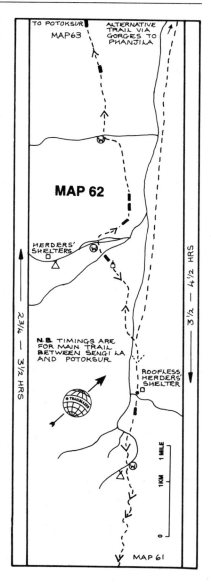

camping is by the bridge before the village. There are also some unofficial *guest-houses* in the village.

● **Alternative route to Phanjila via the Yapola Gorge** There is an interesting alternative trail to Phanjila which follows the gorges of the Yapola River below Potoksur. This used to be a hard route only possible when river levels were low, but an improved trail and several bridges have made the journey simpler and accessible at most times of the year. The trail is very narrow in places and the locals may not be willing to take heavily-loaded pack animals along it.

To follow this alternative trail after crossing the Sengi La, continue down the right (NE) bank of the stream, rather than veering north-west towards the Bumiktse La. This trail can also be joined from Potoksur (see Map 63). The journey through the gorges is relatively straightforward and takes about a day, although you may want to savour the silence and majesty of these special places by spending a night in a cave sandwiched between the rock walls. Eventually you join up with the trail from Hanupata near the village of Sumdo (see Map 65).

POTOKSUR TO PHANJILA
[MAPS 63-65: pp261-3, MAP 17: p202]
Sirsir La (4800m/15,740ft)
The trail climbs to a large chorten and then rises gradually to the Sirsir La, first along the south-west side of the valley and then crossing to the north-east. There is a final steep climb to the summit. From the pass you can see back to the Sengi La and ahead to rock spires near the Snigutse La.

● **Alternative trail to Lamayuru via Snigutse La** It is possible to cross the Snigutse La and descend the beautiful gorge of the Shillakong River to Shilla, which is close to Lamayuru. This route involves many river crossings and is only possible from August to October.

If continuing along the main trail to Hanupata descend in a northerly direction

from the pass. When you reach a bridge cross onto the left (W) bank of the Spang Nala and carry on down the valley. Before the settlement of **Amat**, there is a large uneven *camp-site* often used by groups. If you are a small independent party there are two small spaces to *camp* by the river before reaching Hanupata.

Hanupata (3830m/12,560ft)
You enter this attractive village along a willow-lined path passing a chorten, prayer flags and shrine underneath two huge sacred cedar trees. The first house you reach proclaims itself to be a *guest-house* and *restaurant,* but it is usually possible to stay in other houses in the village as well. There is a small gompa on the hill behind the village.

Take the lower path out of the village and continue down the valley. Willow trees line the river and the valley begins to narrow into a gorge. Make the most of any opportunity to fill up your water bottles as the trail is often high above the river until Phanjila.

The gorge is spectacular and makes interesting walking. There are several caves if you wish to bivi and one area by a mani wall and chorten where you could *camp*. As there is no grazing in the gorge this is only a possibility for backpackers. After about three kilometres of walking through it, another valley enters from the south.

Cross onto the right (SE) bank at the second bridge and soon after back onto the left over an interesting natural bridge. The next kilometre or so can be difficult for the pack animals with several steep, narrow sections; just hope you don't meet another trekking party coming in the opposite direction.

The gorge comes to an abrupt end. Cross via the bridge onto the right bank and follow the jeep road to **Phanjila**.

Turn to p202 and Maps 17, 16, and 15 for the continuation of this trek to **Wanla** and **Lamayuru**, or if starting this trek from Lamayuru.

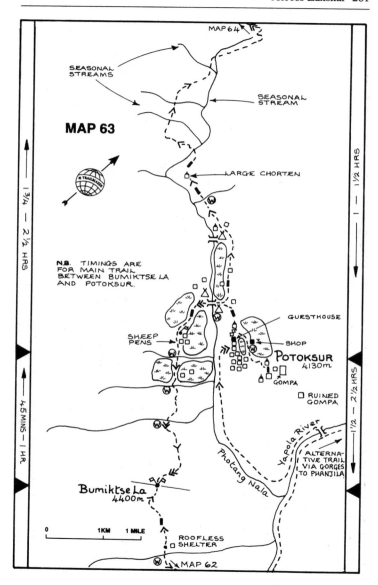

MAP 64

SEASONAL
STREAMS

SEASONAL
STREAM

MAP 63

+ TRAILBLAZER

LARGE CHORTEN

N.B. TIMINGS ARE
FOR MAIN TRAIL
BETWEEN BUMIKTSE LA
AND POTOKSUR.

GUESTHOUSE

SHEEP
PENS

SHOP

POTOKSUR
4130m

GOMPA

☐ RUINED
GOMPA

Yapola River

Photang Nala

ALTERNA-
TIVE TRAIL
VIA GORGES
TO PHANJILA

Bumiktse La
4400m

0   1KM   1 MILE

ROOFLESS
☐ SHELTER

MAP 62

1 3/4 — 2 1/2 HRS

45 MINS — 1 HR.

1 — 1 1/2 HRS

1 1/2 — 2 1/2 HRS

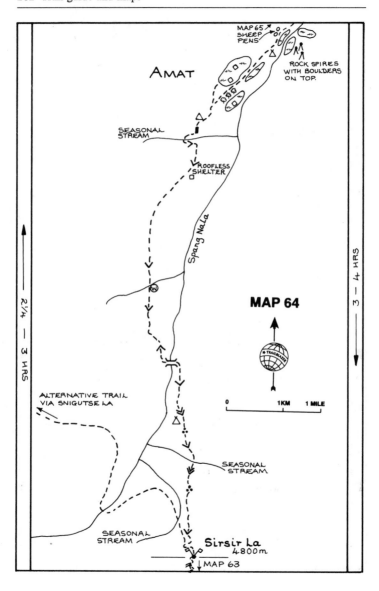

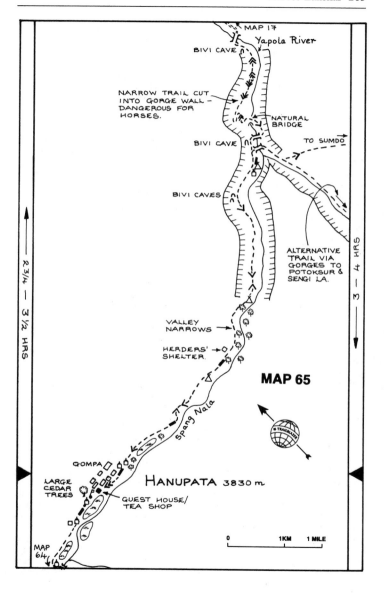

MAP 17

Yapola River

BIVI CAVE

NARROW TRAIL CUT
INTO GORGE WALL -
DANGEROUS FOR
HORSES.

NATURAL
BRIDGE

BIVI CAVE

TO SUMDO

BIVI CAVES

ALTERNATIVE
TRAIL VIA
GORGES TO
POTOKSUR &
SENGI LA.

2 3/4 — 3 1/2 HRS

3 — 4 HRS

VALLEY
NARROWS

HERDERS'
SHELTER.

MAP 65

Spang Nala

GOMPA

HANUPATA 3830 m

LARGE
CEDAR
TREES

GUEST HOUSE/
TEA SHOP

0   1KM   1 MILE

MAP
64

Wild treks in Zanskar

As explained in Route Options (p39) these routes are a serious undertaking and require the knowledge of a local guide. The following descriptions are purely for planning; they are not detailed enough for navigation.

ZANGLA TO THE MARKHA VALLEY VIA THE JUMLAM

From Zangla head east to Zangla Sumdo and then north over the Charchar La (5000m/16,410ft). Water is hard to come by on the southerly climb to the pass. Descend through an extremely narrow gorge; there is no camping for about four hours this side of the pass, but from then on you pass sites every two hours or so.

By the time you reach Tilut Sumdo (three days) at the confluence with the Khurna River, you will already have made around 50 river crossings. This difficult terrain continues until you reach the Markha River. You can either gain access to the Markha Valley by going over the Ruberung La (5000m/16,410ft) and then down the Char Cham Chu to Markha (see p185-6), or you can carry on over the Zalung Karpo La (5050m/16,570ft – see p212) and descend the Luntung Chu to Hankar (both take two to three days). You are now on a well-trodden route and can go north-west to Spituk and Stok (four to five days) or east to Hemis (three to four days).

THONGDE TO PHUKTAL TO PADUM (5-6 DAYS)

From Padum go north-east to Thongde and head south-east over the Thongde La (5150m/16,900ft). The trail descends the Shingri Chu, following the gorges and crossing the river many times. There is then a difficult section of trail across steep slopes before crossing to Shade, a small village up a side valley to the north (two to three days). (There's a rarely trav-

elled route leading north from here that goes to Kharnak). Return to the main valley, continue south-east past the tiny gompa of Tantak and then swing south to the Tsarap River having crossed onto the right (W) bank. There is now a new trail to Phuktal Gompa which makes this section much easier than it was in the past. From Phuktal follow the main route back to Padum (see p24).

PHUKTAL TO LEH-MANALI ROAD VIA TSARAP RIVER (5-6 DAYS)

The trail begins at the gompa at Phuktal. Go through the gompa complex and follow the improved trail to the confluence of the Shade (Shadi) and Tsarap rivers (four to five hours). Shade River can be crossed by a suspension bridge over a narrow gorge. Between here and the village of Murshun is the cliff-face path which will either delight or terrify you. It runs along the right (N) bank several hundred feet above the Tsarap River, making use of natural breaks in the cliff and occasionally crossing steep scree and boulders. The way is not always obvious so be prepared to retrace your steps if you find yourself at a dead end. Some sections are very steep, unstable and dangerous – take extreme care. Camping in the gorge is possible at one or two sites but it's possible to walk from the junction with the Shade River to Murshun in one long day. (For those who don't like the sound of the cliff path, there is an easier alternative further north, starting near Tantak and joining the Tsarap just east of Yurshun. This is frequently used by locals and although it crosses two passes, it is possible to walk in a day.)

Just before Murshun, cross the suspension bridge on to the other (S) bank to reach the village. Beyond the next village of Yurshun you cross back to the right (N) bank of the Tsarap and continue along this to the Leh-Manali road which you will reach in two to three days. The trail is easier from here with the valley opening out more. You pass another small village, Sutak (Satak), and the trail north over the Morang La to Sangtha, before reaching the road at the southern base of the Lachulung La.

ZANSKAR'S SOUTHERN PASSES
The Kang La to Lahaul is the only southern pass which doesn't cross into Jammu and Kashmir and is therefore safe from militant activity. This is approached by a trail heading south from Bardan Gompa up the Temasa Nala. Follow this for most of its length, before heading south-east up the Kang La Glacier to the pass itself (5500m/18,000ft). Descent on the southern side is down the long Miyar Glacier and the beautiful Miyar Nala to the small town of Udaipur, in Lahaul.

At the head of the Temasa Nala is another pass, the Poat La. This is a difficult pass occasionally used to cross into the upper Dharlang Valley in the Kishtwar region of Jammu. Crossing into the same valley is the Umasi La south of Ating village and the Hagshu La south of Abran. The former was a popular trekking route into Zanskar before the militant activity escalated in Kishtwar. Further west still is the Chilung La, south-west of the Pensi La. Other passes over the Great Himalaya exist in this region but they offer no advantages over the others, remaining the preserve of dedicated mountaineers.

PADUM TO RANGDUM VIA DIBLING (8-10 DAYS)
Leading off the main trail between Padum and Lamayuru, between Lingshed and the Parfi La, is a choice of trails heading west to the village of Dibling. These can provide an interesting and remote way to Rangdum or Kanji.

The hardest and least used of these trails is the one following the Oma Chu west from the north base of the Parfi La. The Oma Chu can also be joined higher up by heading west from Lingshed and crossing the Barmi La to Lingshed Sumdo. The two trails converge here and head north-west to Dibling. The latter part of this route involves many stream crossings and shouldn't be attempted until September.

A less trying route to Dibling crosses the Kesi La, west of Lingshed. From Dibling it's another two days west to the foot of the Puzdong La (5000m/16,400ft). Having crossed the pass you now follow the Kanji Nala downstream, choosing whether to head north over the Kanji La to Kanji and Lamayuru (see below), or continuing down the river to Rangdum (two days from camp at the eastern base of Puzdong La).

Rangdum to Heniskot, Lamayuru or Khalsi

(4-7 DAYS)

The route from Rangdum (mid-way on the road from Kargil to Padum, see p144) to Kanji initially follows the Kanji Nala north-east from Rangdum. The route you take will depend on the height of the river. If it is high you will have to traverse the left (S) bank. There is a good camp (five to seven hours) under a maroon-coloured hill, just before the tributary gorge from the north joins the Kanji Nala.

Follow this narrow northerly veering gorge for about two hours before slogging up the south-facing screes to the Kanji La (5200m/17,060ft). The river crossings at the start of the gorge will be very difficult during June and July when the river is high.

From the pass there is a steep descent down along the left (W) side of a permanent snow field and then across a ridge before dropping down to the broad valley of the Kong Nala. This is the next available *camp-site* (seven to eight hours from previous camp).

Descend beside the river towards Kanji. After about one hour you reach a huge bowl formed by the junction of three valleys. Continue straight ahead. (If you are coming in the opposite direction take the most westerly and narrowest of these three valleys).

As you descend further the scenery gets even more impressive with soaring rock walls and colourful mountains. Three to four hours' walking from the previous camp brings you to Kanji.

It's a further four hours from Kanji to the main highway just to the west of the Fatu La. The new trail descends along the left (W) side of an amazing gorge which horses may find difficult to negotiate. The alternative is to follow the difficult old trail along the river bed. After the gorge, always take the right-hand path to reach the road. Here there is a small shop and a place to stay near the village of Heniskot, while Lamayuru (see p141) is an hour's bus or truck ride to the east.

Alternative routes

If you want to continue your trek on to Lamayuru or Khalsi from Kanji, cross the Yogma La (4700m/15,420ft) and camp by the Shillakong River (five to six hours). You can follow this downstream, through more beautiful gorges until it joins the trail between Lamayuru and Wanla. This route involves a lot of river crossings and is best walked in August, September and October when water levels are low. Alternatively, carry on east over the Snigutse La (5050m/16,570ft) and then pick up the Lamayuru to Padum trail (see Map 64, p262) to Hanupata (eight to nine hours). It's another long day to Lamayuru or Khalsi from here. Take someone from Kanji to accompany you on these other routes if you are unsure of the way.

Stok Kangri ascent

(4 DAYS MINIMUM)

This elegant 6153m mountain is an ideal peak for amateur Himalayan mountaineers. Competent trekkers with experience using crampons and an ice axe should find the ascent of Stok Kangri a challenging but attainable goal – **given good conditions**.

GETTING TO THE START

Stok is easy to get to from Leh. There are buses at 7.30am, 2pm and 4.30pm which return at 8am and 3.15pm. You want to go all the way to the top of the village if the bus is going that far. A taxi will cost you Rs285.

STOK TO THE BASE CAMPS [MAPS 66-67, pp267-8]

Follow the trail up the true left (NW) bank of the river from the bridge at the top of Stok village. You soon come to a checkpoint for Hemis National Park where you may be asked to pay an entry fee (Rs20 per person per day within the park, reduced to Rs1 if you are a student). Carry on upriver, first across a meadow and then through a gorge.

A tributary valley and stream joins the gorge from the west. The trail climbs up into this valley and divides. There is a good *camp-site* just beyond the junction. The trail following the left (N) bank of the stream up the side valley leads to the Stok La (for continuation of this trek see p193). The trail to Stok Kangri crosses the stream and climbs a short slope to a small pass.

Drop down from the pass to rejoin the river you were following earlier, then continue to ascend gently. You soon cross another tributary stream from the west and a little further on there is a good *camp-site* by a group of herders' huts at the start of another valley. Between 20 and 30 minutes upstream is another collection of herders' huts and more *camping*. For acclimatisation it makes sense to camp at one of these.

Above this last group of huts the valley divides. You can see Stok Kangri up the first valley from the west and this would seem the most logical route to the mountain. However, the terrain makes walking difficult and many people choose to continue south-west up the main valley before ascending the next valley from the west which is easier. Both valleys have suitable flat areas which can be used as a *base camp* (BC) for your climb. I have numbered these BC1 and BC2 on Map 67.

To reach *advanced base camp* (ABC) from BC1 climb west up the obvious steep path to a small pass at the top of the ridge. Traverse south-west along the side of the ridge before a short climb to ABC, where spaces for about four tents have been cleared among the boulders.

From BC2, scramble over the terminal moraine heading south-east to the ridge. There is a faint path and several cairns marking the route, but they are easy to miss. Traverse the side of the ridge to ABC.

It is quite possible to climb the mountain from either BC1 or BC2 but a start from ABC offers several advantages: sleeping that little bit higher can aid acclimatisation and is a good test to see if you are well enough acclimatised to head for the summit; the distance to the summit is obviously shorter allowing you to make the most of early morning snow conditions without getting up ridiculously early; negotiating the trail from BC1 in daylight is a cinch; and, finally, ABC is a beautiful place to camp, surrounded by majestic high mountain scenery with wonderful views over the Indus Valley. One word of caution; you need to be very well acclimatised to contemplate

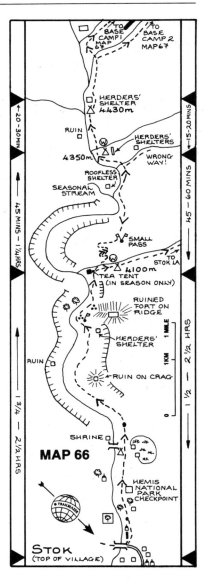

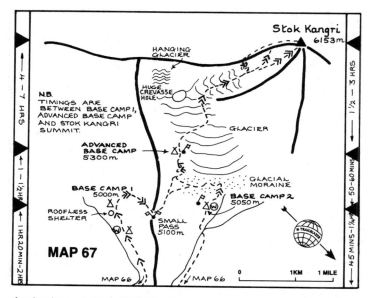

Stok Kangri
6153m

HANGING GLACIER

N.B.
TIMINGS ARE BETWEEN BASE CAMP I, ADVANCED BASE CAMP AND STOK KANGRI SUMMIT.

HUGE CREVASSE HOLE

GLACIER

ADVANCED BASE CAMP 5300m

GLACIAL MORAINE

BASE CAMP I 5000m

BASE CAMP 2 5050m

ROOFLESS SHELTER

SMALL PASS 5100m

MAP 67

★ TRAILBLAZER

0   1KM   1 MILE

MAP 66   MAP 66

4 – 7 HRS
1 – 1½ HR
1 HR 20 MIN – 2 HRS

1½ – 3 HRS
50 – 60 MINS
45 MINS – 1½ HR

sleeping here, at 5300m/17,280ft. On the other hand, climbing from BC1 over the ridge, or the even harder trail from BC2 over the moraine, is not easy in the dark and confusion of an alpine start.

ADVANCED BASE CAMP
TO SUMMIT [MAP 67]
An early start is essential to make the most of the early morning snow conditions. Ideally you should be walking by 5am at the very latest. How long it takes to climb to the summit depends on your fitness, acclimatisation, mountaineering experience and conditions. Expect anything from four to seven hours just to reach the summit and 1½ to three hours for the return down to ABC.

From ABC descend to the glacier. If you are in any doubt of the safest way

across the glacier avoiding crevasses, either take a guide or follow a guided party. Make your way up the west side of the glacier and then ascend its steep western arm.

The east face of Stok Kangri gets gradually steeper as you ascend. There are several possible ways to reach the summit which depend on your level of mountaineering competence. The easiest is to gain the south-east ridge early on by climbing a moderate snow slope and then follow the ridge along airy arêtes and sections of loose rock to the summit (6153m/20,188ft). An alternative is to scramble over steep, loose rock and gain the ridge further along. The hardest is to continue directly up the east face. Reverse any of these routes for the descent.

APPENDIX A: INDIAN EMBASSIES

Australia: Canberra
3-5 Moonah Pl, Yarralumla
Canberra, ACT 2600
(☎ 06-273 3999)

Australia: Melbourne
15 Munro St
Coburg, Vic 3058
(☎ 03-9384 0141)

Australia: Perth
49 Bennett St
East Perth, WA 6004
(☎ 09-9221 1485)

Australia: Sydney
25 Bligh St
Level 27
Sydney, NSW 2000
(☎ 02-223 9500)

Belgium
217 Chaussée de Vleurgat
1050 Brussels
(☎ 02-640 9802)

Canada
10 Springfield Rd
Ottawa, K1M 1C9
(☎ 613-744 3751)

Denmark
Vangehusvej 15
2100 Copenhagen
(☎ 045-3118 2888)

Finland
Satamakatu, 2A8
Helsinki-00160
(☎ 608927)

France
15 Rue Alfred Dehodenoq
75016 Paris
(☎ 01-40 50 70 70)

Germany
Adenauerallee 262-264
53113 Bonn 1
(☎ 0228-54050)

Ireland
6 Leeson Park
Dublin – 6
(☎ 01-497 0483)

Israel
4 Kaufman St,
Sharbat House
Tel Aviv 68012
(☎ 03-510 1431)

Italy
Via XX Settembre 5
00187 Rome
(☎ 06-488 4642)

Netherlands
Buitenrustweg 2
2517 KD, The Hague
(☎ 070-346 9771)

New Zealand
180 Molesworth St
Wellington
(☎ 04-473 6390)

Norway
Niels Juelsgaten 30
0244 Oslo 2
(☎ 022 443194)

Spain
Av Pio XII 30-32
28016 Madrid
(☎ 91-345 0406)

Sweden
Adolf Fredriks Kyrkogata 12
11183 Stockholm
(☎ 08-10 7008)

Switzerland
Effingerstrasse 45
3008 Berne
(☎ 031-382 3111)

UK: London
India House, Aldwych
London WC2B 4NA
(☎ 0171-836 8484)

UK: Birmingham
20 Augusta St
Birmingham B18 6JL
(☎ 0121-212 2782)

USA: New York
3 East 64th St
New York NY10021-7097
(☎ 212-774 0600)

USA: San Francisco
540 Arguello Blvd
San Francisco, CA 94118
(☎ 415-688 0662)

USA: Washington
2107 Massachusetts Ave NW
Washington DC 20008
(☎ 202-939 7000)

APPENDIX B: ITINERARIES

The preceding trail guide was deliberately written without specific daily stages in recognition that trekkers walk at very different paces and have varied objectives. A suggested itinerary for the most popular treks is, however, given below purely to help you plan your trip. Most of these are based on itineraries commonly used by trekking companies and would suit people who walk at a moderate pace. If you are a strong walker you could reduce them by a day or two but remember that none of these itineraries include rest days. Note that some of the daily stages climb higher than the recommended altitude gains for each day. To work out a safer rate of ascent read the advice on p273 and use the altitude figures in the trail guide.

Markha Valley Trek
Day: 01 Spituk to Jingchan
02 Ganda La base camp
03 Skiu
04 Markha
05 Tahungste
06 Nimaling
07 Shang Sumdo
08 Karu

Likir to Temisgam
Day: 01 Likir to Yangtang
02 Ang
03 Temisgam

Lamayuru to Alchi
Day: 01 Lamayuru to Wanla
02 Hinju
03 Camp before Sumdah-Chenmo
04 Sumdah Choon
05 Alchi

Across Karnak
Day: 01 Karu to Shang Sumdo
02 Gongmaru La base camp
03 Nimaling
04 Luntung Chu
05 Sorra Chu
06 Dat
07 Camp before Lungmoche
08 Pogmar
09 Pang

Leh to Nubra via the Digar La
Day: 01 Sabu Phu to Pulu Digar
02 Chumik Yogma
03 Shyok Valley
04 Rong
05 Khalsar or Leh by bus or truck

Across Zanskar (Lamayuru-Darcha)
Day: 01 Lamayuru to Wanla
02 Hanupata
03 Potoksur
04 Base of the Sengi La
05 Lingshed
06 Snertse
07 Hanumil
08 Pishu
09 Padum
10 Mune
11 Pepul
12 Purne
13 Purne to Phuktal to Purne
14 Tangzen
15 Kargyak
16 Lakang
17 Chumik Nakpo
18 Zangskar Sumdo
19 Darcha

Across Zanskar (Darcha-Lamayuru)
Day: 01 Darcha to Palamo
02 Zangskar Sumdo
03 Ramjak
04 Lakang Sumdo
05 Kargyak
06 Purne
07 Purne to Phuktal to Purne
08 Pepul
09 Mune
10 Padum
11 Pishu
12 Hanumil
13 Snertse
14 Lingshed
15 Base of Sengi La
16 Potoksur
17 Hanupata
18 Wanla
19 Lamayuru

'Travel broadens the mind and loosens the bowels' goes the old adage. Judging from the fact that the latter subject features prominently in conversations whenever travellers get together you might think that stomach problems are altogether unavoidable. This is not true. Similarly, it is easy for trekkers to get the hazards of the mountains out of all proportion. Although infectious diseases are much more common in India than in the West and there are inherent dangers of travelling in high and remote mountains, if you follow a few simple guidelines for reducing the risks you should have a trouble-free trip.

YOUR RESPONSIBILITY

It is impossible in this section to give more than basic advice on the most common and easily preventable health problems. On the majority of treks in Ladakh you are likely to be at least two or three days away from any rescue/medical facilities (see below) and should therefore be able to deal with situations that are beyond the scope of basic first aid only designed to assist or treat a casualty until a doctor arrives. In the mountains the doctor won't arrive! A rudimentary understanding of basic medical care, the ability to deal with injuries resulting from impact (falls and falling objects are one of the most common hazards in the mountain environment), knowing when and how to perform CPR (cardio-pulmonary resuscitation) and how to recognise and respond to altitude illness should be part of every mountain traveller's repertoire.

Many trekkers get by with little or none of this knowledge but if you want to minimise the risks take along a handbook written for medical amateurs in wilderness situations (see p53) and consider booking yourself onto a short first-aid course designed for people going to remote areas (in the UK contact the **British Mountaineering Council**, ☎ 0161-445 4747, 177-179 Burton Rd, West Didsbury, Manchester M20 2BB).

EATING AND DRINKING

Good health can be maintained by taking care over what you eat and drink:
● Food can be considered safe if it has been freshly cooked, boiled or is piping hot.
● Local dishes are generally safer than attempts at Western cuisine because the cooks know how they should be prepared.
● Only eat raw fruit or vegetables if you peel them yourself; don't eat salads.
● Avoid ice and ice cream.
● Avoid anything that flies have been on.
● Don't drink tap water. Purified water, bottled mineral water (check that the seal has not been tampered with), carbonated bottled drinks and hot drinks are usually safe.
● Chang is not usually safe to drink as untreated water is used in its preparation. Illegally distilled *arak* sometimes contains poisonous wood alcohol – stay clear.
● If you can't avoid eating or drinking something that you suspect to be unsafe, have less of it: the chances of getting sick are proportional to the amount you ingest.
● Keep your hands clean!

WATER PURIFICATION

There are a number of waterborne parasites, bacteria and viruses that can cause illness in the unwary traveller. No water in India should be assumed safe to drink or even to clean your teeth, until it has been purified. This rule is just as important while trekking as it is in towns. Sparkling mountain streams could have been polluted further upstream by human or animal faeces. The first step before purifying is to collect water from the cleanest available source. Most guest-houses have filtered water available for the asking, which is cleaner than tap water (but not safe to drink); when trekking try to use spring water or water from the cleanest stream (the fastest current in a stream is best avoided as the water contains more sediment). If the only water available is heavily silted make sure that you either filter it (using a Millbank bag or coffee filter paper) or allow the sediment to sink to the bottom of your container, then decant the clearer water from the top. This is necessary because fine sediment, 'rock flour', in glacial meltwater can irritate the gut, thus causing diarrhoea.

Boiling
This is the most effective way to make water safe to drink but is not practical for all your water requirements as it is time-consuming and means carrying extra fuel for your stove. Water needs only to be brought to the boil (even at high altitude where water boils at a lower temperature), not continuously boiled, to ensure that it is safe.

Chemical purification
Iodine-based purification methods are reliable, cheap and convenient and are better than chlorine-based methods, because iodine is more effective against amoebic cysts, acts faster and is less pH-sensitive. Iodine is not thought to be harmful when used for purifying water but, to be on the safe side, it is recommended that you don't use it for more than about three months at a time. If you will be travelling for longer than this you could alternate between iodine and using a portable water filter.

The standard concentrations that you should use are given below. If the water is particularly cloudy or cold you should double the contact time, or double the normal concentration. If you dislike the taste of iodine in your water you could use half the normal concentration (which won't taste as strong) and double the contact time. The alternative is to add fruit juice powders to mask the taste, but as these can sometimes react with the iodine and stop it working, it should only be added after the iodine has had a long enough contact time. Iodine is available in various forms (none of which is available in Leh):

● **Tincture of iodine** This is the cheapest method and the most widely used by trekkers. It is usually sold as a 2% solution, but you must verify this to determine the concentration to use. Buy it in the West where such information is reliable and buy plenty. To dispense the correct amount you will need to buy a dropper as well. For a 2% solution use four or five drops per litre of clear water and leave for 20-30 minutes. Tincture of iodine must be kept in a glass bottle; wrap it in lots of plastic bags in case it breaks. The tincture will resist freezing.

● **Iodine tablets** There are a number of brands of tablets containing tetraglycine hydroperiodide (eg Potable Aqua). One tablet should be left for 10-15 minutes to purify one litre of water. Once the tablets are exposed to air the amount of iodine begins to decrease, so opened bottles should be used or discarded within a few months.

● **Iodine solution** Iodine crystals (eg Polar Pure) are dissolved into a solution in a tiny bottle, then the solution is added to your drinking water. A temperature indicator on the side of the jar helps you determine the correct dose.

Micro filtration devices (water filters)
These can be a convenient way to purify water; there are many makes on the market whose capacity and intended use varies widely. If the unit does not combine filtration with chemical treatment, you will need to add iodine or chlorine at some stage in the process in order to destroy any viruses. The main thing against them is that they are bulky, expensive and some are fragile.

ACUTE MOUNTAIN SICKNESS (AMS)
Travellers to Ladakh must be continuously on their guard against this sometimes fatal sickness. Anyone is potentially susceptible to its serious consequences above altitudes

of about 3000m or 10,000ft. The height at which individuals are affected varies enormously from person to person and with each time a person goes to altitude but is not related to their physical or mental strength. Its cause is not the altitude itself but rather a result of getting to that altitude too quickly. Atmospheric pressure decreases with height and it is that pressure that our bodies rely on to drive the oxygen from the air into our blood. For instance, at 5500m or 18,000ft (the same height of Everest base camp or the Khardung La) there is half the amount of pressure that there is at sea level; humans are perfectly capable of living at that height, and higher, as long as the body is given enough time to adapt. The body adapts in a number of ways including breathing more, producing more red blood cells and making the heart work faster (especially in the first few days of being at altitude). This process takes about two months to complete fully, but about 80% is finished after about 10 days. Therefore, by choosing the appropriate rate of ascent for your body, the illness is entirely preventable.

Prevention

● **Follow a safe rate of ascent** The safe rate of ascent for each person is different and varies every time that person goes to altitude. However, various rates have been recommended and act as useful guidelines:

The **standard recommendation** for ascent is that before reaching 3000m/10,000ft you should spend at least one night at an intermediate altitude of 1800-2400m/6000-8000ft (eg Manali 2050m/6700ft), and when above 3000m/10,000ft, sleep no higher than 300m/1000ft above the previous night's altitude. After every 1000m/3000ft gain above 3000m/10,000ft you should have a rest day and spend two nights at the same altitude. This regime should be followed whenever possible. It is practical for those trekking into Ladakh from Manali and for following while on your trek.

An **alternative for those travelling faster** to sleeping altitudes of between 3000m/10,000ft and 4200m/14,000ft (eg on a bus) would be to spend three or four days exercising gently at an intermediate altitude (1800-2400m/6000-8000ft) first. A similar two- or three-day stop at 3700-4000m/12,000-13,000ft would be sensible before going to between 4600m/15,000ft and 5500m/18,000ft.

The **third option** for those going rapidly to about 3500m/11,500ft without stopping (eg from Delhi to Leh by air) is to rest and do very little for three or four days after you have arrived. Then build up your daily activity slowly and follow the first example if you want to go any higher.

To help you work out your own rate of ascent, the altitudes of popular stopover points are as follows: **Delhi** 216m/710ft; **Manali** 2050m/6730ft; **Keylong** 3350m/10,990ft; **Darcha** 3400m/11,150ft; **Sarchu** 4250m/13,944ft; **Pang** 4450m/14,600ft; **Leh** 3500m/11,480ft; **Kargil** 2650m/8690ft; **Srinagar** 1730m/5680ft.

● **Sleep low, climb high** This mountaineers' maxim emphasises that it is the altitude you sleep at that is more important than how high you climb during the day. Therefore, you can climb as high as you feel comfortable, as long as you return at the end of the day to your previous night's sleeping altitude or no more than 300m/1000ft above it.

● **Drink lots of water** Avoid alcohol. (See 'dehydration' below).

● **Eat well** A good appetite at altitude suggests you are acclimatising well and by eating well you can promote good health. It is quite common to lose your appetite at altitude though this does not necessarily mean you are getting AMS. It can sometimes be a warning sign so be on your guard.

● **Avoid over-exertion** as this can lead to HAPE (see below). Pace yourself so that you don't have to keep stopping to rest.

● **Keep warm** This will lessen your chances of getting HAPE.

● **Look out for symptoms of AMS** If you feel ill you should assume that you have altitude sickness (unless you can prove otherwise) and take the necessary action.

● **Using Diamox** Acetazolamide (Diamox) can reduce some of the symptoms of AMS and help to promote acclimatisation. Its benefits must be weighed against the possible side effects which include tingling sensations, altered taste and increased urination. It must not be taken by those allergic to sulfas, or those with liver or kidney diseases. You may consider taking it if you have to ascend rapidly to altitude by road or air, or if you have suffered from AMS on previous occasions. The usual dose is 250mg every 12 hours, starting one or two days before ascent and continuing for two or three days after arrival. However, it has been shown that taking 125mg instead of 250mg is just as effective and causes fewer side effects. You may find it preferable to wait until you arrive at altitude before making a decision (based on how you feel) as to whether to take the drug or not. This has little effect on its performance.

MILD AMS – NEVER GO HIGHER!

Any of the following symptoms can indicate mild AMS: **headache** (which gets better after taking a mild painkiller eg aspirin or paracetamol), **nausea, loss of appetite, difficulty in sleeping** (never take sleeping pills at altitude), **dizziness**, or generally **feeling unwell**.

If you suffer from any of these symptoms assume it is because of AMS. While these are not serious in themselves, they provide vital warnings of a possible progression to serious AMS. If the symptoms do not go away you must remain at the same altitude for a day or so, until you feel better. If they get worse, you should descend to the last altitude where you felt well. When the symptoms disappear you can begin ascending again.

Diamox can be helpful with some of these symptoms: 125mg taken at bedtime can help sleep, or take 125mg every 12 hours until you feel better (see side effects and warnings above). No drug should ever be a substitute for descent.

SERIOUS AMS – DESCEND IMMEDIATELY!

This is life-threatening and death can follow rapidly. There are two types of serious AMS: high-altitude pulmonary edema (HAPE) which is a build up of fluid in the lungs; and high-altitude cerebral edema (HACE), which is a swelling of the brain. They can occur together or on their own.

Symptoms to look out for include: **headache** which does not disappear after administering medicine; **ataxia** (loss of co-ordination and balance) – test for this by drawing a straight line on the ground and getting the subject to walk along it heel to toe and compare this with someone who has no symptoms (ataxia is often followed by a coma); **altered mental state** characterised by the subject not speaking, thinking or acting clearly or normally; severe **fatigue**; **nausea**; frequent **vomiting**; **shortness of breath** after very little activity; **rapid breathing** at rest (more than 20 breaths per minute); **rapid pulse** at rest (above 110 beats per minute); **cough** which can be dry or producing sputum; **blueness** of the lips and the beds of the fingernails; and occasionally **fever**.

Any of these symptoms, either together or on their own, can indicate the onset of serious AMS. They can sometimes be hard to detect in yourself so warn your companions at the first sign that things are not well and keep a careful watch on everybody else.

Descend immediately if serious AMS is likely, even in the middle of the night. A descent of 300-1000m/1000-3000ft can sometimes see improvements, but the lower you go the better. Do not wait for the subject to make this decision for themselves;

make it for them even if it's against their will. Similarly, if you are with a group you may have to go against the wishes of the leader who might not want to disrupt their schedule. If you have made the decision early enough the subject should be able to walk down (always accompanied), but it may be necessary to carry them or put them on a pack animal.

Diamox may help reduce the symptoms of severe AMS (250mg every 12 hours), but **descent must always be the priority** as it is the only sure way of saving someone's life.

Other effects of altitude

● **High-altitude systemic edema** This is a swelling of the feet, hands and face which affects about 20% of high-altitude travellers. Women are more susceptible than men, but it is not a serious condition and will clear up when you reach lower altitude.

● **HAFE** High-altitude flatulence/fart emission. This genuine syndrome is more annoying for your tent companion than you!

● **Birth control pills** Taking oral contraceptives could theoretically increase the risk of blood clots at altitude but there is no evidence to suggest that this is the case. The consequences of coming off the pill may involve more risk.

● **Acclimatisation wears off as quickly as it is gained** Therefore most of the benefits disappear after one or two weeks at sea level.

DIARRHOEA

Diarrhoea is a common problem in India and many travellers suffer from mild forms of it. It is often accompanied by nausea, vomiting, fever and chills. It is usually passed on in contaminated water and food and is mainly caused by bacteria, viruses, parasites (giardia or amoeba), or by toxins in food you've just eaten. The best way to prevent it is to follow the guidelines under 'eating and drinking' and 'water purification' above.

Initial treatment

If you are unfortunate enough to get a bout of diarrhoea you should rest assured that it is rarely life-threatening and urgent treatment is not necessary. The diarrhoea will often clear up on its own within a few days, so the best course of action to begin with is just to wait and see what happens. Drink plenty of water to offset the dehydrating effect of the illness and if possible add an oral rehydration salt solution (available from most pharmacists in India). Soft drinks that have been allowed to go flat, weak tea and soups are also useful. Eat plain food if you are hungry (avoid greasy or spicy food and most raw fruits apart from ripe bananas) and be as active as you like – if you feel your body needs a rest give it one. Taking drugs which are designed to block you up, such as Imodium or Lomotil, can prolong the illness by not allowing your body to get rid of the infection. However, situations occasionally arise when their use is preferable to intense embarrassment (on a long bus journey) or discomfort (stuck in a tent with a blizzard howling outside).

Stool test

If the diarrhoea doesn't get any better after a few days and particularly if it is severe (10 stools or more a day); contains blood, mucus or pus; or is accompanied by a fever or chills, you should get a stool test to determine what the cause of the illness is. These are available in most towns in India and are cheap and usually reliable – film canisters make excellent containers for your sample. It must get to the laboratory within two hours.

Self treatment

When trekking you will be a long way from any such facility and will have to rely on treating yourself. Self-diagnosis is not as easy as some books suggest which is why you should get a stool test if at all possible. The best way to go about self treatment is to work through the most likely causes and deal with each in turn. This isn't as hit and miss as it sounds as two drugs can cure most frequently-encountered causes of diarrhoea.

● **Onset of diarrhoea** Do not take antibiotics at the first sign of diarrhoea because the illness will often clear up on its own in a few days. Antibiotics tend to be indiscriminate about which bacteria they kill, so a course of them will often kill off many harmless bacteria which naturally live in your gut and keep you healthy. The absence of these friendly bacteria can increase the risk of further illness later. If the cause of your diarrhoea is food poisoning or a virus (both common), antibiotics will have no effect on them anyway and the only cure is to wait until your body has got rid of the offending agent – five or six hours in the case of food poisoning or up to a week or so if it's a virus. Just drink lots and keep your strength up by eating if you are hungry.

● **No improvement after three or four days** If there has been no improvement in three or four days and particularly if the diarrhoea is severe (10 stools or more a day); contains blood, mucus or pus; or is accompanied by a fever or chills, then you should begin more active treatment. A **bacteria** of some sort is the most likely cause of the illness and ciprofloxacin is very effective against these; the dose is 500mg twice a day for three days. Take this two hours after eating, if possible. Do not take with anti-inflammatory drugs (ibuprofen or aspirin) as fits may occur.

● **Still no improvement after three more days** If there is still no improvement after three days of taking this drug the cause is likely to be either a parasite or a virus. As there is no treatment for a virus (apart from making sure you don't become dehydrated) you should begin treatment for a parasite infection. The two likely culprits are giardia and amoeba which can both be treated with metronidazole. However, different doses are required for each parasite so some kind of diagnosis is necessary.

Giardia is far more common and the onset of the illness begins one or two weeks after ingesting the parasite. It is characterised by foul-smelling sulfurous burps and wind, and three or four soft (rather than liquid) stools a day which don't have any blood, mucus or pus in them. Take two grams of metronidazole daily in one dose for three days. You must not drink alcohol while using this drug and for at least 24 hours after you finish the course.

Amoebic dysentery is rare among trekkers and usually starts slowly with just a mild diarrhoea that sometimes comes and goes in cycles. As it gets more serious so does the diarrhoea, with liquid stools often containing blood and mucus. The person will often tire easily, feel aches and pains in their body and may have a slight fever. Treatment is 800mg of metronidazole three times a day (every eight hours) for five days. As this is a large dose it is advisable to get a stool test and seek medical opinion if at all possible before commencing the treatment. You must not drink alcohol while using this drug and for at least 24 hours after you finish the course. Metronidazole does not always eradicate the parasite and further treatment may be deemed necessary after a medical examination. Complications can arise if this parasite is allowed to spread to the liver or lungs, so if you suspect you had any contact with amoeba while on your trip, you should have a proper examination when you return home.

OTHER HEALTH PROBLEMS
Bedbugs, scabies and lice
These can be a nuisance to travellers but rarely carry diseases. Bedbugs and scabies can be avoided by using your own sleeping bag rather than a borrowed blanket, or by using a clean sleeping-bag liner in a rented bag. Frequent airing of your sleeping bag in the sun will also reduce your chances of being irritated by these night-time com-

panions. Lice are spread by direct human contact. Head lice can be kept away by frequently combing your hair and can be killed (along with scabies) by using an insecticide lotion (available in India).

Blisters
Care of your feet will stop blisters developing in the first place. If you feel any 'hot spot' on your feet while you are walking, stop immediately and apply adhesive tape, moleskin or Second Skin to the area. If you catch it too late and a blister has developed you can either surround it with moleskin or the like, so that it is protected, or if it is too painful, clean the skin and burst the blister with a needle (hold the needle in a flame for a few seconds to sterilise it). Apply Second Skin or any other non-adhesive dressing and hold that in place with adhesive tape.

Gynaecological problems
The menstrual cycle can be upset by travel and exercise so periods may become irregular or even stop altogether. This is not a cause for concern.

If you are susceptible to urinary tract/vaginal infections you should bring a course of treatment in case it recurs.

Sore throat and cough
The dry air in Ladakh can sometimes cause a sore throat and a dry cough. Sucking boiled sweets is the best way to relieve this irritation. If the cough is persistent and produces green and yellow sputum the cause could be bronchitis. If you are a long way from medical help a broad spectrum antibiotic (such as amoxycillin, 500mg every six hours for five days) should probably be given to prevent a possible progression to pneumonia (indicated by a high fever along with obvious sickness). If pneumonia is suspected immediate descent to lower altitude is essential, along with medical help.

ENVIRONMENTAL HAZARDS
Dehydration
It is extremely easy to become dehydrated while trekking in Ladakh and it is vital that you replace the lost fluid to maintain good health and to avoid heat illnesses. Much of this is lost through perspiration owing to the heat and the high level of physical exertion but another significant factor is the loss of fluid while breathing. Not only does your body have to moisten the extremely dry air that you inhale but because of the altitude and the exercise you also tend to be breathing with increased rapidity. Up to four litres a day can be lost through the lungs alone. Unfortunately, thirst is not a particularly reliable indicator of your need for water and it is better to judge your condition by the frequency and colour of your urine. Frequent passing of clear or pale yellow urine is a good sign. If it becomes darker and is passed less often you must drink more. Drinking at least four litres a day is a good rule of thumb, the bulk of which should be made up from water, fruit juice, soft drinks or soup, but not coffee, tea or hot chocolate which contain diuretic agents. If you become dehydrated adding a sachet of oral rehydration salts (available in India and Ladakh, often called electrolyte solution) to a litre of water can be very helpful.

Water is not abundant in the mountains of Ladakh and every opportunity to fill up your water bottle should be taken.

Heat exhaustion
A long trek in the heat of the day coupled with not enough to drink can cause nausea, headache, dizziness, vomiting and even fainting. It is important that this is not allowed to progress to heat stroke. The individual should lie down in the shade and drink lots of water, preferably with oral rehydration salts added.

Heat stroke

This is a very serious condition which can progress to being life-threatening very quickly. The body temperature will rise dramatically and is sometimes accompanied by a lack of sweat in proportion to the amount of exercise that has been performed. The person's mental state will also be altered (this will be the most obvious sign to others), walking will be difficult because of poor co-ordination, and fits and unconsciousness are common. The body temperature must be cooled rapidly either by immersing the victim in water, or by covering in wetted clothing and then fanning the body. Rehydration is also important.

Hypothermia

This condition, also known as exposure, results when the body can't generate enough heat to maintain its normal temperature and the body-core temperature begins to drop. It is caused by not wearing suitable clothing for wet, cold and windy conditions and by not eating high-energy foods regularly enough. Other important causal factors include exhaustion, dehydration, high altitude and low morale.

It is important to recognise it early on and take appropriate action. As it is almost impossible to recognise hypothermia in yourself all members of a group should keep an eye on each other. Early warning signs are feeling cold and tired, with involuntary shivering. This is soon followed by strange behaviour, poor co-ordination, slurring of speech and problems with vision. If these signs are left unattended the individual will stop shivering and unconsciousness, coma and death will follow quickly.

Treatment of the early stages is simply a matter of finding shelter and then rewarming with a hot drink and some food. If the hypothermia is more serious a tent will have to be pitched and the victim warmed as quickly and thoroughly as possible. Often the best way to do this is with bare skin contact – another person getting into a sleeping bag with the victim.

Frostbite

High-altitude trekkers frequently come across conditions where frostnip (the early stages of frostbite) and even frostbite could occur. By wearing warm gloves, hats, socks and boots most people easily avoid these hazards. With frostnip your extremities (feet, hands and face) become cold and painful and then lose their feeling and go white. You must heat them up by putting them on a warm part of your (or anyone else's) body – armpits, groins and mouths are all good heat sources.

Frostbite occurs when the cells actually freeze and this can lead to permanent damage. The skin will look similar to frostnip but will feel frozen and blisters may form. Rewarming (in hot water at 40°C) should not be attempted until there is no chance that refreezing could occur, as this will cause even more damage.

Snow blindness

This is not a serious medical condition but it can be very painful, frightening and potentially dangerous if you temporarily lose your sight. It is caused by over-exposure to UV light and can even occur when there isn't any snow on the ground because of the high concentrations of UV light at altitude. It feels like having sand in your eyes and it can cause temporary blindness. It is treated by resting your eyes in the dark. The obvious way of avoiding it is to wear good quality sunglasses with 100% UV protection. Emergency protection 'goggles' can be made by cutting thin slits or pinholes in card shaped like glasses.

Landslides

As much of the ground in Ladakh is steep and dry with little vegetation to stabilise it, landslides are fairly common. They are most likely to occur during and after heavy rain when travel through narrow, steep-sided valleys would be very unwise. However, they can occur at any time so one should always be on the lookout in areas that are potentially dangerous. Quick reactions and a fast pair of legs are your best allies.

River crossings

There are few treks in Ladakh which don't involve a river crossing or two. While there is always some element of risk, you can make the crossing as safe as possible by following the simple guidelines below.

If the river looks dangerously high wait until the water level drops. Most streams in Ladakh are fed by melting snow and glaciers and will be at their lowest first thing in the morning. The water level is at its highest in the spring and early summer. However, if the water level has obviously been affected by a recent downpour of rain, the level should drop within a few hours of the rain stopping.

It's tempting to cross at the narrowest place, but this is usually where the stream is strongest and deepest. Cross where it's wide and shallow. Don't cross the river barefoot as it will be very hard to keep a secure footing on the sharp and uneven river bed. If you are trekking with pack animals it's worth bringing along a pair of running shoes or sports sandals to prevent your walking boots getting soaked. Otherwise, take your socks off but keep your boots on. Your rucksack will provide quite a lot of buoyancy, especially if the contents are in sealed polythene bags, so keep it on as you cross; have the waist strap undone and be ready to slip it off one shoulder should you miss your footing.

When crossing always face upstream so that the flow does not buckle your knees, keep your feet wide apart and shuffle slowly across. A rope provides the most security, particularly if you use the continuous loop method by tying both ends together. The person crossing ties the rope around their chest, another person stands on the bank upstream feeding the rope out, while a third member stands downstream, ready to pull the crossing member into the bank should they take a swim. However, not everyone carries a rope. A stick placed upstream can also give much needed support to an individual or a whole group.

There are various methods for groups of people to get across using each other for stability. Two or more people can link arms together and cross in a line parallel to the direction of flow. Or alternatively, all face upstream, one behind the other, holding on to the waist of the person in front, then moving across sideways together. It helps if the first person uses a stick for support. Another method, if there are three of you, is to form a huddle by holding on to the shoulder strap of each other's rucksacks. Make sure you all face upstream. If you have ponies, it's sometimes possible to ride them across. Finally, if you do fall in, hang on to your rucksack, float feet first downstream and slowly work your way over to one side. Do not fight the current.

RESCUE

Medical and rescue facilities are few and far between in Ladakh and it is best to assume that you will have to get yourself out of any difficult situation you get into. As pack animals are commonly used in the mountains these are your most reliable form of evacuation. On many treks there will also be villagers and other trekkers who can lend a hand, but some areas are very remote and you may not see anyone else for days – yet another reason to take pack animals rather than a backpack.

There are basic health posts in some of the main villages, but for serious incidents you will need to be evacuated to Leh. If land travel is impossible, Indian Air Force helicopters can be summoned from principal villages and towns along the Indus Valley or from Padum; they are co-ordinated by J&K Tourism. The helicopter won't leave the ground until payment has been guaranteed which is why it is so important that you take out medical insurance which includes evacuation costs, and leave at your embassy in Delhi details of people who can be contacted and who will be prepared to foot the bill. The service doesn't come cheaply either, costing in the region of Rs25,000 (£400/US$600) per flying hour. As an example, evacuation from anywhere in Zanskar will take at least five hours. Flying conditions in the region are extremely hazardous and in bad weather you may have to wait several days before the pilot is prepared to fly. Never request a helicopter unless the situation is life-threatening.

AFTER YOUR TREK

If you have been ill while in India it is important that you get a medical check-up when you return home and let your doctor know where you have been and what you have been doing. Some people advise check-ups even if you haven't been ill as some diseases can lie dormant for a considerable time. If you become ill within a year of returning home, you should remind your doctor that you have been in India, as this may help diagnosis. Malaria, for instance, can often be misdiagnosed as flu.

If you have been taking anti-malarials it is important to carry on taking them for at least four weeks after leaving the malarial area.

APPENDIX D: FLORA AND FAUNA

Ladakh's flora and fauna are more similar to those of Tibet than to the main Himalaya and are a product of the dry climate, cold winters and short growing season. An outline of what you can expect to see is given here; for more detailed information you will need to consult some of the books listed on p53.

FLORA

The main plants in the temperate and subalpine zones are willow and poplar trees which grow wherever there is water, which is usually along man-made irrigation channels. Walnut and apricot trees are found at lower altitude. Conifers can also occasionally be found.

In the alpine zone you may find bushes of wild roses and sea buckthorn and sometimes junipers which are usually clinging to steep cliffs, out of reach of the woodcutter's knife. Alpine meadows with wild flowers are rare in this arid landscape and this zone is characterised by scrub and low shrubs. However, even when crossing high passes the trekker will notice plants that have adapted to the harsh environment by growing hairy leaves which capture any moisture in the air. Where there aren't any other signs of life you can still find the occasional lichen clinging to the rocks.

MAMMALS

Ladakh is home to several rare and endangered species of mammal as well as having some of the richest diversity of sheep and goats. Trekkers outside the busiest tourist season or on less frequented trails are likely to see at least one or two different species. The most commonly encountered is the **marmot**. This member of the squirrel family lives in deep burrows on mountain sides and will allow you to get quite close before giving a whistle of alarm and disappearing underground. Occasionally you'll come across **martens**, **weasels**, **hares** and **pikas** (a relative of the hare, but with round ears and no tail) and see **foxes** (*Vulpes vulpes*) along the trails in summer. **Wolves** (*Canis* *lupus*), common and widespread throughout the mountains, rarely appear until winter when they descend to the villages to prey on the villagers' livestock. They have occasionally worried trekkers' ponies in parts of the Chang Tang during the summer months.

Among the various wild sheep and goats, **bharal** (*Pseudois nayaur*), or blue sheep, are the most numerous and are commonly seen. These horned, grey-brown sheep-like animals have characteristics of both sheep and goats. They prefer rugged, steep terrain and large herds are often encountered in the Hemis National Park on the Markha Valley trek where they help maintain the healthy snow leopard population that preys on them.

Siberian ibex (*Capra ibex sibirica*) live in the west of Ladakh and are the second most common hoofed mammal here but this wild goat's preference for steep and high ground means that they are rarely spotted by trekkers. The **Ladakh urial** (*Ovis orientalis vignei*) is a rare wild sheep found in and around the Indus Valley but this proximity to a large population of humans means that it is constantly under threat from hunters. Another rare sheep is the **argali** (*Ovis ammon hodgsoni*) which can be found at higher altitude and has huge curled horns.

Herds of **Tibetan wild ass** (*Equus hemionus kiang*), or kiang, are not as common a sighting as they once were, but trekkers in the Rupshu and Chang Tang areas are still likely to see groups of this beautiful horse-like ass. Other animals of the grasslands and steppes of the Chang Tang are the **Tibetan gazelle** and the rare **Tibetan antelope**.

Every trekker hopes to stumble across the legendary and endangered **snow leopard** (*Panthera uncia*) but the chances of doing so are extremely small. This solitary high-altitude cat is found in Zanskar and in the Hemis National Park (where there is a population of 50-75). It's about the size of a large dog and has a grey coat with black spots; sightings are very rare because of its depleted numbers and ability to blend into the landscape. There are a few **lynx** (*Felis lynx*) in Ladakh's wilder areas and also **Pallas's cats** (*Felis manul*) which are about the size of a domestic cat. **Brown bear** (*Ursos arctos*) are found in very small numbers in northern Zanskar and the Suru Valley.

BIRDS

A large variety of both resident and migratory birds are found in Ladakh and some 240 different species have been recorded. Most visitors will see **magpies, sparrows** and **crows** which are all common around villages. Other common birds include various species of **lark, twite, finches** and **snow pigeon**.

In the mountains you are likely to see the **chukor partridge** and the occasional **kestrel**, while soaring high on the thermals are huge scavenging **lammergeyer** (bearded vulture) with a 2.5m-wingspan, and also **Himalayan griffin vultures, buzzards** and the occasional **golden eagle**.

Of the migratory birds, the **black-necked crane** is one of the rarest, its numbers have been reduced to just a handful of breeding pairs in the Chang Tang lakes. The **barheaded goose** also makes the incredible journey over the Himalaya each spring to breed on these high-altitude lakes having spent the winter in the wetlands of the Ganges floodplain. The **great crested grebe** also breeds here. Another visitor is the **hoopoe**, which is easy to spot with its long curved beak, and pink and black crest. This bird's arrival traditionally heralds the beginning of summer.

APPENDIX E: LADAKHI WORDS AND PHRASES

It is well worth making the effort to learn even a few words of Ladakhi as this will affect positively the attitude of the local people towards you and you will be made to feel all the more welcome. By being able to communicate with local people, you will not only be able to learn more about their culture, but will be able to give them a first-hand account of the realities of life in the West and how it differs from the stereotyped image portrayed in the cinema and on TV.

The few words and phrases below will serve only as a very basic introduction to the language but will give you something to practise before you reach Ladakh. It was compiled from the excellent phrasebook, '*Getting started in Ladakhi*' by Rebecca Norman (with kind permission from the publishers, Melong Publications). Try to get hold of a copy so that you can learn more. It's widely available in Leh, or you can write to the publishers (Melong Publications, c/o SECMOL Compound, PO Box 4, Leh, Ladakh, 194101, India).

The pronunciation is based on English, except that Ladakhi makes a difference between aspirated (*t'*, *p'*, *ch'*, *k'*, and *ts'*) and unaspirated, or soft (*t*, *p*, *ch*, *k*, and *ts*) consonants, whereas English makes no difference. English speakers usually aspirate, which means there is a little puff of air after the sound. For example, the 'p' in 'positive' is aspirated, but unaspirated in 'opposite'.

Capital *T*, *D*, and *S* are pronounced with the tip of the tongue curled back into the palate as if to say *r*, so they have a faint hint of an *r* sound in them.

Ju-le
This is the first word that most foreigners learn and is used as a general greeting: hello, goodbye, good morning, good night, please, thank you, etc.

General words
Are you well?	*k'amzang?*
I'm well	*k'amzang*
I don't understand	*hamago*
I understand	*hago*
Yes, please	*o, ju-le*
No, thank you	*man, ju-le*
That's enough (thanks)	*Dik-le*
Ladakh is very nice, beautiful	*ladak ma-ldemo duk*

Family
mother	*ama (ama-le*)*
father	*aba (aba-le*)*
grandfather	*me-me (me-me-le*)*
grandmother	*abi (abi-le*)*
older brother	*ach-o*
older sister	*ach-e*
younger brother	*no*
younger sister	*no-mo*
uncle/aunt	*azhang/ane*

Terms of address
It is considered polite to call people *ama-le* or *acho-le* etc. Choose the appropriate term to reflect the difference between your age and theirs.

* Always add -*le* to names or sentences to show respect

Questions and answers

What's your name?	*nyerang-i minga chi in-le*?*
My name is ...	*nge minga ... in-le**
Where are you from?	*nyerang ka-ne in-le*?*
I'm from America	*nga america-ne in-le**
What is it? (gesturing to something)	*chi in-le*?*
How much is it?	*tsam in-le*?*

Food and drink

Please give me Ladakhi food	*ladaksi k'arji sal-le**
Is there water?	*ch'u du-a -le?*
(Yes) there is water	*ch'u duk*
(No) there isn't (water)	*mi-duk*
I don't eat meat	*nga sha za-met*
tea (common: your own tea)	*cha*
tea (honorific: anyone else's tea)	*solja*
butter tea	*gur-gur cha*
fresh barley wine/'beer'	*ch'ang*
water	*ch'u*
boiled water (always served hot)	*ch'u skol*
meat	*sha*
milk	*oma*
yoghurt	*zho*
rice	*das*
roasted barley flour	*tsampa/ngamp'e*
noodle soup	*t'ukpa*
pasta dishes	*skyu/ch'u-tagi*
common apricot	*chuli*
dried apricot with edible nut inside	*p'a-ting*

Animals

male yak	*yak*
female yak	*dimo*
cow	*balang*
bull	*langto*
cross between yak and cattle	*dzo/dzomo*
donkey	*bungbu*
horse	*sta*

Time

hour, time	*ch'uts'ot*
day	*zhak*
morning	*ngatok*
evening	*p'itok*
night	*ts'an*
yesterday	*dang*
today	*dering*
tomorrow	*tho-re*

* Always add *-le* to names or sentences to show respect

Trekking

What is the name of this village?	*i-yul-i minga chi inok?*
How far to the next village?	*yul stingma tsam-zhig thakring yot?*
How far to ...?	*...-a tsam-zhig takring yot?*
Where is the path to ...?	*... lam karu yot?*
Where does this path go?	*i-lam karu ch'anok?*
Is there a shop there?	*deru hati yoda?*
left	*yoma*
right	*yospa*
straight	*k'aTang*
uphill	*gyen*
downhill	*thur*

Numbers

In the market in Leh more people use the Hindi numbers than Ladakhi.

	Hindi/Urdu	Ladakhi
1	*ek*	*chig*
2	*do*	*nyis*
3	*tin*	*sum*
4	*char*	*zhi*
5	*panch*	*nga*
6	*chhe*	*Tuk*
7	*sat*	*dun*
8	*at*	*gyet*
9	*nau*	*gu*
10	*das*	*chu*
11	*gyara*	*chuk-chig*
12	*bara*	*chuk-nyis*
13	*teran*	*chup-sum*
14	*choudan*	*chup-zhi*
15	*pandara*	*cho-nga*
16	*sola*	*chu-ruk*
17	*satra*	*chup-dun*
18	*atra*	*chop-gyet*
19	*unis*	*chur-gu*
20	*bis*	*nyi-shu*
25	*pachis*	*nyi-shu-tsa-nga*
30	*tis*	*sum-chu*
40	*chalis*	*zhip-chu*
50	*pachas*	*ngap-chu*
60	*saatt*	*Tuk-chu*
70	*sattar*	*dun-chu*
80	*assi*	*gyet-chu*
90	*naebe*	*gup-chu*
100	*sau*	*gya*
200	*doso*	*nyip-gya*
1000	*hazar*	*stong chig*
10,000	*das hazar*	*Thi chig*
100,000	*lakh*	*bum chig*
1,000,000	*das lakh*	*saya*
10,000,000	*crore*	

APPENDIX F: GLOSSARY

arak	distilled spirit
bivi (bivouac)	to spend the night in the open
bivi bag	simple and lightweight overnight shelter
bodhisattva	an enlightened being who has renounced nirvana
cairn	pile of stones to mark a path
chai	tea
chang	barley or rice beer
chapati	flat Indian bread
chorten	Ladakhi/Tibetan word for stupa
chumik	spring
crampons	spikes which fix to boots for walking on snow and ice
dal	lentils
dhaba	small, basic restaurant
doksa	herder's hut
dzo	cross between a yak and a cow
ghat	steps on a river bank
gompa	Tibetan Buddhist monastery
gongma	upper
gur-gur cha	butter tea
kangri	snow mountain, or glacier
kongka	ridge
kushok	head of a gompa
la	pass
lakh	100,000
lama	Buddhist personal teacher, also used to mean a monk
mani stone	stones engraved with mantras; piled up to form a *mani wall*
mantra	Buddhist incantation
momo	Tibetan stuffed dumpling
moraine	debris carried down and deposited by a glacier
nala	stream
ngamphe	Ladakhi word for tsampa
nirvana	the Buddhist aim to be free from the cycle of rebirth
pashmina	fine soft wool used for cashmere shawls
perak	turquoise-studded head-dress
phu	high pasture
ri	mountain
Rinpoche	high lama
sham/stot	Lower/Upper Ladakh
stupa	hemispherical Buddhist monument
sumdo	confluence
tar-chok	prayer flag
tarn	small mountain lake
thanka	Tibetan Buddhist religious painting on cloth
tokpo	stream
tsampa	roasted barley flour
tsemo	summit, or peak
tso	lake
yogma	lower
yul	village
yura	irrigation channel

INDEX